Moncreiff

MORE BY THIS AUTHOR

Imperial Control of Colonial Legislation 1813-65

Ruggles' Regiment: The 122nd New York Volunteers in the American Civil War

Imperial Appeal: The Debate on the Appellate Jurisdiction of the Judicial Committee of the Privy Council

The Life and Times of Dundee (with C.A. Whatley & A.M. Smith)

The Fall of the Tay Bridge

Moncreiff

The life and career of James Wellwood Moncreiff 1811-1895 1st Baron Moncreiff of Tullibole

David Swinfen

Shakenoak Press

Copyright © David Swinfen 2015

Shakenoak Press
ISBN 978-0-9932372-2-5

David Swinfen has asserted his moral right under the Copyright, Designs and Patents Act, 1988, to be identified as the author of this work.

All Rights reserved. No part of this publication may be reproduced, copied, stored in a retrieval system, or transmitted, in any form or by any means, without the prior written consent of the copyright holder, nor be otherwise circulated in any form of binding or cover other thanthat in which it is published and without a similar conditionbeing imposed on the subsequent purchaser.

Cover design by JD Smith www.jdsmith-design.co.uk

For

Ann

Lord Moncreiff
Photo courtesy of the Faculty of Advocates

CONTENTS

Acknowledgements ix
Foreword by Lord Wheatley PC xi

I The Young Moncreiff

Chapter 1 Childhood and Family 1
Chapter 2 Student Days 15

II The Young Lawyer

Chapter 3 The Making of an Advocate 31
Chapter 4 Chalmers, Church Extension, and the Moderatorship 43
Chapter 5 The Road to Auchterarder 60
Chapter 6 Church *versus* Courts 75
Chapter 7 The Trial of the Chartists 91

III Lord Advocate

Chapter 8 The 'Minister for Scotland' 117
Chapter 9 Nationalism v. Assimilation 143
Chapter 10 Reforming Scotland's Education 163
Chapter 11 Madeleine Smith 188
Chapter 12 The Yelverton Affair 201

IV Lord Moncreiff

Chapter 13 On the Bench… 215
Chapter 14 …And Off It 235

Note on the *Reminiscences* 243
List of Cases 244
Notes 246
Select Bibliography 276
Index 284
The Author 297

Acknowledgements

All historians rely heavily on libraries and archives for their material, and I am no exception. I am truly grateful for the help and guidance I have received from the staff in the University libraries of Dundee and St Andrews; in the libraries of New College, Edinburgh, and University College, London; the National Library and National Archives of Scotland; and the British Library and National Archives in London. I should also like to thank the Duke of Buccleugh for permission to consult the Buccleugh Papers in Register House.

I have also received a great deal of practical advice and moral support from many friends and colleagues. I should like to thank in particular Gordon Cameron, Barbara Crawford, Mary Evans, Owen Dudley Edwards, Donald Elliot, Christine Findlay, Ross Macdonald, William Thomas, Norman Thomson, Christopher Whatley, John Wheatley, and of course my wife Ann, whose own dedication to writing is a constant inspiration.

I owe special debts of gratitude to members of the Moncreiff family. The present Lord and Lady Moncreiff welcomed me most kindly to Tullibole Castle, and gave me free access to the Tullibole collection of documents and pictures. The biography would certainly not even have been begun, and perhaps never finished, without the help and support of Vivienne White, herself a direct descendant of the first Baron Moncreiff. It was Vivienne who first introduced me to the Moncreiff memoirs, and thus to the remarkable character who was James Wellwood Moncreiff.

David Swinfen
Broughty Ferry
November, 2015

Foreword

Until 1707 Parliament House in Edinburgh was the home of the Scottish Parliament. Thereafter, and until the present day, it has accommodated both the senior Scottish civil courts, and the Faculty of Advocates. At the north end of Parliament Hall, where the Parliament sat, and where for generations lawyers have walked up and down discussing their cases and much else, there are hung full life-sized portraits of John Inglis and James Wellwood Moncreiff, unquestionably the two giants of the Scottish legal world of the nineteenth century.

The Scottish bar has always been a fruitful source of recruitment into Scottish public life, a tradition which continues to this day. In recent times, the leaders of both the United Kingdom Labour and Liberal Democrat parties started their careers as advocates in Edinburgh. But few, if any, of the multitude of Scottish political lawyers over the years can lay claim to such a distinguished and influential public and political career as James Moncrieff, as this book clearly and ably shows. As a member of an eminent family, as someone of obvious ability from an early stage in his public life, and as an excellent public speaker, his opinions carried considerable weight. His contribution and legal analysis of the issues and events which led to the Disruption of 1843 were highly significant. As Lord Advocate in the 1850s and 1860s, a position which at that time included not just the role of overseeing criminal prosecutions as now, but in addition most of the duties and responsibilities that were later given to the office of Secretary of State for Scotland, he was much engaged in all of the important issues of the day. During his periods in office he showed great skill and determination in pursuing an impressive variety of legal reforms. His passionate interest in education paved the way for many important changes. His time as Lord Justice Clerk was one of significant development in the law of Scotland.

All of this, in very general terms, might be understood by any young counsel coming to the Scottish bar a hundred years or so later, as I did. Lord Moncreiff's judgements are occasionally cited in current cases, although perhaps not so often as those of his boyhood friend John Inglis. More significantly, perhaps, even from just a reading of reported legal cases and general legal history from that time, the realisation emerges that the period covered by James Moncreiff's public and legal life was one of very great importance for Scotland. This book fully confirms that feeling, comprehensively covering all of the events and issues of his time, in which Moncreiff played the fullest of roles. Professor Swinfen's description of Moncreiff's enormous energy and range of interests, in the context of the great issues of his day, offers a fascinating and satisfying account of a remarkable man, who becomes a very real and recognisable figure in these pages. The causes and consequences of the Disruption, the government of Scotland in the mid-nineteenth century, the legal practice of a busy and successful lawyer of that age, and much else, are all illuminated by this study of an extraordinary and useful life devoted to public service. And, as all good histories should, this study of James Wellwood Moncreiff discloses fascinating comparisons with the issues that concern his country today.

John Wheatley

I

The Young Moncreiff

Chapter 1
Childhood and Family

When James Wellwood Moncreiff was a very small boy, just old enough to attend divine service, he was taken one Sunday by the family servants to an unfamiliar church. As he recalled many years later in his *Reminiscences*, at first his behaviour had been exemplary, until after a time, 'a mania seized me. I broke out, at the top of my infantile voice, with one of the Watts hymns which I had been taught, and ended by jumping on the back of a man who sat beside me.' Needless to say, he was smartly marched out of church in disgrace, 'amid a sea of disapproving looks'. Yet looking back on the incident from the perspective of old age, he could still 'recollect vividly the glow of secret, though unprincipled satisfaction which the perpetration of this outrage created in my mind. I was very glad I had done it and was not impressed as I ought to have been by the feelings of the popular assembly'.[1]

The full length portrait now hanging in the Faculty of Advocates in Edinburgh of Lord Moncreiff, First Baron Moncreiff of Tullibole, Member of Parliament, Lord Advocate, Lord Rector of Edinburgh University and latterly Lord Justice Clerk, tends to reflect a somewhat humourless image of one of the great Scotsmen of the nineteenth century. Yet how refreshing it is to discover Lord Moncreiff, recently retired from one of the highest judicial offices of the country, remembering with undisguised pleasure, and without the slightest regret, this youthful misdemeanour.

James Wellwood Moncreiff was an able man, an intelligent and educated man, politically astute, loyal to his friends, and a hard and conscientious worker. As a boy, despite his own claims to laziness, he seems in fact to have been almost the embodiment of the Puritan ethic, winning prizes at school and university; something of an athlete; being admitted to the Scottish Bar at a young age, occupying important positions in the law, politics, government, and the bench. But he was also a humane and likeable man. He had a wide circle of friends across the country, and he was welcomed wherever he went. His life was one of effective public service, most particularly in the fields of law reform and the reform of education, but he was also a family man, proud of his children's achievements, and anxious for their futures.

Moncreiff was born in Edinburgh on the 29th of January, 1811, the second son and third child of Sir James Wellwood Moncreiff and his wife Ann Edinburgh at that time was the undoubted capital of Scotland, leading the country in wealth, culture, and political power. To be a member of the legal fraternity was to be a member of the city's political and social elite. As Moncreiff himself noted much later, Edinburgh in the early years of the century was, especially 'during its busy winter months, while the University was in session and its Courts of Law in their fullest activity, the resort of men of position from many quarters; and this gave to its social circles, and the men of intellect and education who had influence over them, a certain national character which has hardly been maintained since.'[2] These were very much the social circles in which the Moncreiffs, themselves men of intellect, education, and position, naturally moved.

Since the mid-eighteenth century, the city had increased rapidly in both the number of its citizens, and in physical extent. In 1755, the population stood at 57,220, in 1801 this had risen to 82,560, and thirty years later had almost doubled to 162,403.[3] In 1766 James Craig had won the competition to design the New Town, laying out George Street, Princes Street, and Queen Street. If some of the great names of the Scottish Enlightenment had passed on, others, like Sir Walter Scott, were still active, and a new generation of writers and intellectuals was coming to the fore – often including lawyers and politicians, Henry Brougham, Francis Jeffrey, and Henry Cockburn among them. Both on account of its intellectual and its architectural excellence, Edinburgh was proud to be known as the Athens of the North. While Scottish politics had been for a long time dominated by the Tory party, this was about to change, and over the next few decades the Whigs were to take their place on the national political scene.

The Moncreiffs were a family on the Whig side of the political divide, and with strong connections to both the law and the church. Moncreiff's father was an Edinburgh advocate, sometime Dean of the Faculty of Advocates, and a judge of the Court of Session in Edinburgh, while his grandfather, the redoubtable Sir Harry, was a pillar of the Church of Scotland until his death in 1827, when Moncreiff was fifteen. [Sir Harry was generally known as Sir Harry Moncreiff Wellwood.] Moncreiff's elder brother, Henry, became a minister of the Church of Scotland, while he himself was to have a notable career in the law, in politics, as a Member of Parliament and Lord Advocate for Scotland, and on the Scottish Bench. He retired as Lord Justice Clerk in 1888, at the age of 77, and died in 1895.[4]

Moncreiff was born at 13, Northumberland Street – described by him many years later as by that time 'a rather dingy street' in the New Town. The house had been built by his father, James Wellwood Moncreiff senior, who had chosen the location for the magnificent view it commanded to the north, across open fields as far as the shores of the

Firth of Forth. Even before Moncreiff died, the intervening land had been largely built over, but thinking back to his youth he remembered it as 'a bright sunny spot', then 'quite open and finely wooded'. 'I can recollect running from the gate of the garden plot across a wide extent of sward, called the Bellevue Park, down to the entrance of Inverlieth House. King Street was only just commenced, and the opposite side of Northumberland Street remained unbuilt for some time afterwards.'[5]

In his *Reminiscences*, Moncreiff writes affectionately of the various members of his immediate family. His mother Ann, daughter of a naval captain and granddaughter of the famous Principal William Robertson of Edinburgh University, married Moncreiff's father in 1808, and they had a large family.[6] Her son described her as 'a very admirable person, and one of great cultivation and refinement', being very well read, and an accomplished musician. She evidently set the tone for the rest of the family, since 'evil speaking and detraction were unknown in the circle, whatever we may have learned or practiced afterwards.' Interestingly, Moncreiff expresses particular gratitude to his mother for her efforts to prevent her children from acquiring a broad Scottish accent, occasioning her much labour and wearisome iteration. Evidently stung by some criticism for holding this point of view, Moncreiff spends a page or two in its defence. 'I know,' he writes, 'that my good friend Professor Blackie thinks it very unpatriotic to speak with an English pronunciation or accent. It should be a Scotch accent, not an English one. Attic Greek, but with never anything but a Doric accent.' This attitude Moncreiff denounced as 'the essence of provincialism in its most preposterous form..... Does my worthy contemporary see anything derogatory in sending his daughter to France to acquire a true Parisian accent – or ought to be content with the French of Bowe........ If we speak French, let us speak it as the French speak it; and so of English. Professor Blackie can no more speak the Scotch of George Heriot's time than I can.[7]

In championing the use of English and English pronunciation, Moncreiff was to an extent reflecting the views and usage of the professional urban middle classes of his day. Writing in the late 1980s, Alexander Murdoch and Richard Sher pointed out that 'by the mid eighteenth century, English had become the medium of a polite, urbane Scottish culture in the universities of Edinburgh, Glasgow and Aberdeen. It flourished particularly among the professional classes of lawyers, clergymen, physicians, and professors. Above all, it provided the linguistic and cultural foundation for the set of men known as the "literati".[8] In the 1760s, attempts were made to arrange for systematic tuition in English, and in 1761 the Select Society hired Thomas Sheridan, the father of the playwright, to give courses for gentlemen in St. Paul's

Chapel. The courses lasted for four weeks and cost a guinea a head. A similar course for ladies lasted only two weeks, 'perhaps assuming,' commented Douglas Young, 'they were quicker on the uptake.'[9]

Darting down a side alley in this way is a characteristic of the *Reminiscences*, and is what gives them much of their charm. Likewise the little incident where Moncreiff on a visit to Bruges found himself separated from the rest of his party, and tried to make himself understood by a local Flemish woman. His attempts to find his way out of a church in German, English and French made no impression. Only when he shouted at her in broad Edinburgh: 'Whem wantin' the wey oot!' was he at last clearly understood.[10]

Moncreiff's mother was clearly an important influence in his childhood, which seems to have been remarkably happy, at least for the first eight years. Then in 1819, tragedy struck. Moncreiff's older sister Nancy died at the tender age of nine, with a devastating effect on her older brother Henry, and of course on her mother, on whom, we are told, 'the blow fell with intense and lasting severity. Of course time, as it went over our heads, softened it, but her gaiety of spirit never returned.'[11]

We learn little more of Moncreiff's mother from the *Reminiscences*, though quite a lot more of her own family, the Robertsons. She had been one of four sisters, daughters of George Robertson, a captain in the Royal Navy. He had married an American, the daughter of a Mr Lewis of New York, one of the signatories of the Declaration of Independence. Lewis was vehemently opposed to the match between his daughter and this obscure and relatively poor seaman, so Robertson took the bold step of eloping with his bride and carried her off in his ship – 'an improvement on young Lochinvar'. Unfortunately the captain died young, leaving his widow, disinherited by her unbending father, to bring up her four children in Scotland.

Although she herself also died prematurely, her children prospered. The only son, Thomas Campbell, joined the East India Company and rose to be Governor of the North West Province. Each of the three daughters married successful husbands. The eldest, Elisabeth, 'a very handsome woman', married her relative Captain Thomas Robertson, also in the service of East India Company – 'a service at that time lucrative and sought after'. The second, Marianne, married the Reverend John Bird Sumner, later Archbishop of Canterbury, and the third also married a clergyman, who rose to become the Bishop of Calcutta.

At the time of Moncreiff's birth, his father James would have been in his mid thirties. ('James' and 'Henry' were common first names in the Moncreiff family, leading to some potential for confusion). The second son of the Reverend Sir Harry Moncreiff, eighth baronet of Tullibole, and his wife Susan, this James was a staunch Presbyterian and a prominent Edinburgh lawyer. Educated in Edinburgh, Glasgow University, and Balliol College Oxford, Sir James, as he became on the death of his father Sir Harry in 1827, was called to the Scottish Bar in January 1799, and over the next few years built up a substantial legal practice. Being of the Whig persuasion in politics, he was effectively debarred from appointment to office until the creation of the so-called Ministry of All the Talents by Lord Grenville in 1806 gave the Scots Whigs their first opportunities for preferment for twenty years.

In February, 1807, James Moncreiff was appointed Sheriff of Clackmannan and Kinross.[12] Lord Cockburn, in his *Life of Lord Jeffrey*, offers a somewhat mixed encomium of Moncreiff senior, whom he describes as while being 'grounded in the knowledge necessary for the profession of a liberal lawyer,' he was not a well read man. He lacked his own father's dignified manner, and his outward appearance was rather insignificant, 'but his countenance was marked by a pair of firm, compressed lips, denoting great vigour and resolution…Always simple, direct, and practical, he had little need of imagination; and one so engrossed by severe occupation and grave thought could not be expected to give too much to general society by lively conversation. With his private friends he was always cheerful and innocently happy'. He added to these somewhat negative qualities 'great powers of reasoning, unconquerable energy, and the habitual and conscientious practice of all the respectable and the amiable virtues. Everything was a matter of duty with him, and he gave his whole soul to it.'[13]

The most dramatic expression of that sense of duty came in 1828, two years after he had been elected Dean of the Faculty of Advocates. Following the accepted principle that no criminal, however poor, should be undefended at his trial, Moncreiff senior undertook to defend the notorious 'resurrectionist' William Burke in his trial for murder. The case will be considered in detail in a later chapter.[14]

This of course was only one of many cases in Sir James' thirty year career at the Scottish Bar. At one point his son recalls that, during the family's regular summer retreat to Eldin House, such were the demands of his 'enormous practice', that his father continued to ride the six miles into Edinburgh each morning, and return in the evening for dinner. Elected Dean of the Faculty in 1826, in the following year he was offered a place on the Bench, which he declined – at least in part because of his continued interest and active involvement in Whig politics. As early as 1795, aged only nineteen, he had attracted some notoriety at a meeting to protest against the war with France by holding up a tallow candle to allow the face of the then Dean of the Faculty, Henry Erskine, to be publicly revealed. In meetings of the General Assembly, he had spoken on behalf of the popular party, and had stood unsuccessfully for the office of Procurator of the Church of Scotland in 1805, his rejection for the post being attributable to his character as a staunch Whig. In 1850, when our James Moncreiff was appointed to be Solicitor-General for Scotland, Cockburn, himself a prominent Whig, commented that when father James was turned down for the Procuratorship, one of the reasons given was the he was 'a bird of a foul nest' – meaning that he was a son of the Whig Sir Harry. 'This one's nest is still fouler, for to the filth of the grandfather is added the steady abomination of Lord Moncreiff the father.'[15]

It is important, however, not to exaggerate the role of politics as a factor in professional advancement in the early nineteenth century, or perhaps more accurately we should say that its importance as a factor noticeably diminished as the century wore on. If his Whig allegiance really was the cause of Moncreiff's father being refused the Procuratorship in 1805, it was clearly no bar to his elevation to the Bench in 1829. Cockburn, as usual, had some perceptive comments to make on the subject. 'I have mentioned,' he wrote, 'that Whig opinions were dangerous accompaniments for success in life, especially to the young, whose fresh minds, however, presented the soil most favourable for their growth. The fate of the junior Whig lawyers, therefore, was looked to, for encouragement or for despair, by all those, but chiefly by the young, who were cherishing liberal principles.' These young Whig lawyers, 'were not only suppressed as much as they could be by the opposite party, but were for some years not very cordially received even by the seniors on their own side. They had now however got their feet fairly in the green sward. Their talents had worked them up into obviously coming power in their profession.'[16]

For Cockburn, the rise to prominence of a group of young liberal minded lawyers, in which our Moncreiff was to be numbered, was of a significance which went far beyond the boundaries of the legal profession. 'The rising or sinking of a few professional lawyers, as such, is seldom of much public importance. But these lawyers represented a *class*; and this class consisted of all the younger men in Scotland to whom the prevailing intolerance was distasteful, but who were hourly warned that submission to it was essential for worldly success. The disenthralment of those who had liberated themselves from it in Edinburgh was like liberty proclaimed for all slaves.'

The effects of this change were felt not only in 'the more numerous and daring' towns and cities, but 'there was scarcely a considerable village, which did not contain someone who breathed more freely from what he had heard of the success of those in the metropolis, who had been in a similar state of depression with himself. There was an elevation of the whole liberal surface.' It seemed to some observers that 'the whole cause of independence in Scotland hung upon the characters and exertions of about half a dozen young men in the Parliament House.'[17] The James Wellwood Moncreiffs, father and son, were at the heart of this liberal and liberating process.

For many years, then, Moncreiff's father took a leading part in the agitation for reform in Scotland. In December 1820 he presided at a Pantheon meeting at which resolutions were passed in support of a petition to the Crown for the dismissal of Lord Liverpool's Tory ministry. Again, in 1828, he presided at a public meeting in support of the repeal of the Test and Corporation Acts, and in the following year made 'a very vigorous and remarkable speech' on the Catholic Disabilities, supported by such luminaries as Thomas Chalmers, Cockburn and Francis Jeffrey.

In 1829 Sir James was finally persuaded to accept a place on the Bench. He did so with some reluctance, and subsequent heart searchings, but according to his son he had seen a colleague fall out of practice, and feared the same fate. 'It was', so Moncreiff recorded in his *Reminiscences*, 'done very reluctantly. It seemed to take much of the spring and elasticity of spirit from him. There is no life so depressing as that of a briefless barrister, but there is no avocation in which success has such a charm. There is no romance or adventure in the position of a Lord Ordinary in the Outer House in Edinburgh, not even that of differing from your colleagues, for you have none: and altho' my father made as great a reputation on the bench as he did at the bar, I think he cast some lingering looks behind.'[18]

Ten years before his elevation to the Scottish bench, Moncreiff's father took an important step which had a significant effect on the lives of his family – he rented 'a charming little property on the Esk', about six miles from Edinburgh, called Eldin House. Included in the property were a couple of acres of grassland, an attractive garden, and a small wood. 'It consisted of a very good house, about two acres in grass, a pretty garden and gardener's house, and a ridge of wood, overlooking the village of Lasswade, with the Pentlands in the distance. In short, it was a spot to enchant a boy's fancy, and much was loved and much we learned among the branches of the trees, and the breezes, and the flowers of this charming retreat.'[19]

Moncreiff being Moncreiff, he noted the educational benefits of the experience. Under the tuition of the gardener, Peter Crichton, he learned a good deal of the practical aspects of gardening, 'to dig, trench, mow, rake, at which I worked as hard as a hired labourer, save that I got no wages, and gained only toil, health and enjoyment'. In this he was in close communion with his younger brother William, with whom

Moncreiff 'accomplished most of my employment and all my mischief……….With gardening, carpentering, seat building, and sundry avocations incident thereto, a happier life could hardly be fancied for two healthy lads, full of enthusiasm in their exploits, out in all weathers and utterly indifferent as to the moisture in the clouds or their garments.' The last 'great constructive work' performed by the two brothers was to create a garden from a piece of waste ground, prepare the soil and stock it with gooseberry and rose bushes, and then build a substantial summer house. The summer house did not survive the years.[20]

Eldin House had at one time belonged to a Mr. John Clerk, the author of a controversial book on naval tactics, and a notable artist and engraver. Moncreiff recalled how, in 1826, Clerk's son, Lord Eldin, visited Eldin House while the Moncreiffs were in residence, looking for some etched copper plates which had been the work of his father. Moncreiff ran them to earth in one of the turrets, and they were later published in a folio volume by the Bannatyne Club.[21]

Cockburn described Clerk as 'a striking gentleman with his grizzly hair, vigorous features and Scotch speech', whose claim to have been the originator of the tactic of breaking the enemy's line in naval warfare had been disputed on grounds which were at least plausible. But in Cockburn's view, 'my conviction of the honesty of Clerk is so complete, that I am certain he would have disdained to claim a discovery he had not made'. In any case, Clerk had other claims to distinction, and was, we are told, 'looked up to with deference by all the philosophers of his day, who were in the habit of constantly receiving hints and views from him which they deemed of great value.'[22]

His son, also a John Clerk, became 'one of the greatest lawyers and jurists of Scotland', appointed to the bench in 1825, with the title of Lord Eldin. Elizabeth Grant of Rothiemurchus, the 'Highland Lady', had some harsh things to say about Lord Eldin, to whom she had taken a strong dislike. 'The immorality of his private life,' she wrote, 'was very discreditable; he was cynical too, severe, very, when offended, though of a kindly nature in the main.' A man of undoubted talent, 'his reputation certainly was enhanced by his eccentricities and by his personal appearance, which was truly hideous. He was very lame, one leg being many inches shorter that the other, and his countenance, harsh and heavy when composed, became demoniack when illumined by the mocking smile that sometimes relaxed it. I always thought him the personification of the devil on two sticks, a living actual Mephistopheles.'[23]

On Sundays, while at Eldin, the Moncreiff family went to church at Lasswade – a walk of about a mile down to the river Esk, and back up the hill to the Church. Sunday, Moncreiff recalled, 'was always hot at Eldin, sunny and glittering. Looking down from the bridge, the woods of

Roslin and Hawthornden lay up the stream, and those of Melville and Dalkeith below. My recollection of the toil up the remaining hill, and of the huge ash tree half way up, probably gives that sultry tinge to my memory.'[24]

The services at Eldin Church unfortunately did not live up to its idyllic setting. 'The worthy pastor of that parish was of the driest and dustiest school. Not a spark could be struck out of him.' Reminiscing about Eldin Church prompted Moncreiff to comment on the general subject of church architecture. 'I am not an aesthete,' he declared, 'in Church building.' In his opinion, a church 'should be constructed for the comfort and convenience of the congregation... and that there is neither sanctity nor profanity in the form of the building. There may, no doubt, be good taste or bad taste in the design, beauty or hideousness: but the half-informed cant now prevalent, among persons who do not even understand their silly role, has more bad taste, and ignorance of true art, than our own forefathers' heritors had when they constructed the barns of the last century.'[25] The church at Lasswade, however, 'was not without some pretensions to the effective.'[26] The Moncreiffs sat in the Eldin seat – in effect a largish room big enough to have accommodated a party of a dozen or more at dinner.

For a full ten years, from 1819 to 1829, the Moncreiff family took full advantage of summers at Eldin House. In the autumn of 1829 there was a change of scene, as the family spent the season at Burntisland, on the east coast of Fife, described by Moncreiff as 'a bright little seaport, quite unconscious of railways, and very conscious of the curing of herrings.' Almost nothing of any interest took place in the sleepy little town, which happened to be a Royal Burgh, possessed of both a Provost and a Baillie. The election of a new Provost was shortly to take place, and for want of any other excitement, 'the town was all agog about the new Provost: who it would be.' 'At last the day came. The Provost was wont to head the procession, and the Baillie followed him. Imagine our disgust, when we found the Baillie had become the Provost and the Provost had become the Baillie, and that not even a change of countenance, which might perhaps have been changed with advantage, was to occur.'[27] Let us not read too much into this incident as throwing any light on the subsequent development of Moncreiff's political convictions.

1829 also saw their departure from Eldin House to the family's country property – the castle of Tullibole, in the Crook of Devon, still today the seat of the present Lord Moncreiff. Tullibole had been inherited along with the baronetcy by Moncreiff's father James on the death of his father, Sir Harry, two years previously. Although an ancient construction – the original keep dates from the twelfth century – it had not been in the possession of the Moncreiff family for more than three generations. Since the late sixteenth century it had been owned by the Halliday family, but their fortunes gradually dwindled, and it was then put up for sale in 1738. Our Moncreiff's great-grandfather, Sir William Moncreiff, married a daughter of Wellwood of Garvoch, who purchased both the Castle and the Mains of Tullibole, and entailed it on Sir William's eldest son, Moncreiff's grandfather, Sir Harry Moncreiff. On the latter's death in 1827 it passed down to Moncreiff's father, Sir James.

In his *Reminiscences*, Moncreiff provides an extensive description of the castle and its surroundings. At the time of writing, Moncreiff noted that the original three storied keep with outside staircase still stood much as it had always done, and to it the first Halliday proprietor had added a wing with an escutcheon over the doorway with the initials of J.H. and H.O. – for John Halliday and his wife Helen Oliphant, and dated 1608. The castle was surrounded by trees – some of them dating from when the Hallidays took possession, and many of a more modern planting. 'The rage for planting, ' Moncreiff noted, 'inspired by Samuel Johnson's taunt that he could not find a tree in Scotland on which to hang himself, reached this somewhat secluded region last century, and most of the timber in the plantations is from 120 to 150 years old.' Secluded the region indeed was – at least until the coming of the railway in the mid-nineteenth century. For a time, tradition would have it, Tullibole served as a staging post for the kings of Scotland on their progress between Stirling and Falkland, and 'there is a well accredited ghost of one of the Royal attendants, who was vanquished by a Tullibole man in a drinking bout.' But the kings ceased to call, and the Halliday fortunes came to be eaten up by the demands of Cromwell's troops for billeting and supplies – followed by the no less ruinous exactions of the restored monarchy. Finally the last Halliday 'went down ignobly before the lance of one of his own feuars' – in a court case which, although won by the Hallidays, proved a Pyhrric victory, and led finally to the sale of the property.[28]

Summer holidays spent at Eldin House were very happy occasions in Moncreiff's young life, and help to cement good relations between himself and his father, who had a significant formative influence on the values, political tendencies, and religious principles of his second son. This influence was exerted by the example he set, by the provision of a loving family life and a stimulating environment, and by, as we shall see, an educational experience which affected Moncreiff for the rest of his life. 'At home', the son wrote of him in later years, 'he was all that a father could or should be -: always serene, taking an interest in all our pursuits, and listening to all our hopes, woes, and enthusiasms'. In the spring of 1830 Moncreiff had the opportunity to get to know his father even better, when they travelled the North Circuit together. This being before the age of railways, they rode in a carriage and four – 'a pomp and panoply very gorgeous to behold' – and took the opportunity to call on friends on their country estates. One of these was Sir Thomas Dick Lauder, owner of Relugas, on the banks of the Findhorn in Morayshire – an area devastated in the previous year by unusually severe floods. 'I shall never forget the aspect of the country we passed through,' Moncreiff later recalled. 'It seemed as if it had been graveled with shingle. Roads, fields, woods, all presented the same appearance. We saw the bridge at Fochabers, of which only one arch was left standing. Two men had been on it when it fell, one of whom was drowned and the other miraculously escaped.' In another incident, a young girl was saved from being swept away only by climbing up through the chimney of her cottage, - 'she took to the lumm' as her mother said. She was rescued by a neighbour who clambered up on to the roof. 'Along the rivers, the Spey, the Nairn, the Findhorn, the Dee, the desolation was awful. At Relugas, the residence of Sir Thomas Lauder, he looked out one morning on a river bank of old timber; on the next morning, a mile of it was gone – the soil shaven down to the rock.'[29]

Their host, the egregious Sir Thomas Dick Lauder, was a man of many and varied talents. A prolific writer, the author of such now largely forgotten works as *Enochdhu* and *The Wolf of Badenoch*, he also published his own substantial history of the 1829 floods. His *Account of the Great Floods of August 1829 in the Province of Morayshire and adjoining Districts,* contained a wealth of detail, and was published in the very next year, 1830. According to Lauder, one of the worst aspects of the disaster was that in recent years very substantial amounts of money had been expended on capital improvements to the region, and these had now largely been destroyed. 'Magnificent bridges,' he wrote, 'were built on the Spey at Fochabers, the Findhorn near Forfar, the Nairn, and other large rivers. The grand iron bridge of Craigellachie of 150 feet span was projected and executed; and innumerable bridges of lesser importance were constructed.' Turnpike acts were obtained from Parliament, so that the 'ancient parochial roads, hitherto little better that tortuous indications of a primitive track…were now superseded by well-lined and well constructed highways…a daily post was established which, by the gradual improvement of circumstances, ultimately reached Forres in little more than 24 hours from Edinburgh.'[30]

The floods, however, had done huge damage to these improvements, which had formed 'a part of the vast arterial system of national communication – the district and parochial branches giving life and energy to every estate and farm, many of them created by proprietors at immense cost, and, in many instances by incurring deep pecuniary engagements' in addition to 'the very extensive and dear purchased private improvements, executed both by landlords and tenantry.' These had 'all been more or less ruined, wherever they lay within the reach of the direful ravages of these floods.'[31]

Lauder was not only a novelist and a chronicler of the Morayshire floods, he also had some talent as an artist and a musician, and above all perhaps, knew how to enjoy himself and provide enjoyment for others. Elizabeth Grant, the 'Highland Lady', described him as a very accomplished man. 'His taste was excellent....He drew well, sketched very accurately from nature, was clever at puzzles, *bout rimés*, etc. – the very man for a country neighbourhood.'[32]

Relugas, the country house owned by Lauder, also received warm praise from the same quarter. According to the Highland Lady, Relugas had been a 'common, small Scotch house, but an Italian front had been thrown before the old building, an Italian tower had been raised above the offices, and with neatly kept grounds it was about the prettiest place that ever was lived in'. Sadly, the old house was destroyed by fire later in the century. But what really seems to have impressed Elizabeth, more even than the attractions of the house and its situation, was 'the heartiest merriest welcome within. Mr and Mrs Lauder [this was before Lauder inherited a baronetcy] were little more than children themselves, in manner at least; really young in years and gifted with almost bewildering animal spirits, they did keep up a racket at Relugas. It was one eternal carnival. Up late, a plentiful Scotch breakfast, out all day, a dinner of many courses, mumming all evening, and a supper at the end to please the old lady.'[33]

As a further illustration of the life at Relugas, Elizabeth told the story of a military man who, on being posted to India, called on the Lauders to say goodbye. 'It was in the evening, and instead of finding a quiet party at tea, he got into a crowd of Popes, Cardinals, jugglers, gypsies, minstrels, flower girls, etc., the usual amusements of the family.' After spending some twenty years in the east, the Colonel returned to Morayshire, and once again paid a courtesy call on the Lauders. 'He felt as in a dream, or as if his military service had been a dream – there were all the crowd of mountebanks again.' Among them was to be found Sir Thomas himself, almost unchanged. He 'wore as full a turban, made as much noise, and was just as thin as the Tom Lauder of twenty years before, and his good lady, equally travestied and a little stouter, did not look a day older with her grown up daughters around her.[34]

It is hardly surprising to learn, therefore, that when the Moncreiffs arrived at Relugas in 1830, the travellers were received most warmly. As they approached the property they heard the sounds of music, and Sir Thomas was discovered in his shirt sleeves, playing a Highland reel on the violin, while two young men in full Highland dress danced the Hoolachan. The men turned out to be neighbours of the Lauders, known by the name of Allan Hay, but were widely believed in the district to be of royal descent, apparently bearing a marked resemblance to the Stuarts – a name which they later took as their own. The truth of the matter was never revealed. Not long after, Moncreiff and the two brothers were members of a party who took a boat out on Lochindoch – a wild inland lake about fifteen miles from Relugas. A sudden storm blew up. 'The waves were high, and our boatman from fright or whisky or both was incapable of rowing, and lay in the bottom of the boat.' Only the strong arms of the two mysterious brothers saved the party from drowning.[35]

This expedition to Morayshire with his father evidently made a lasting impression on the young Moncreiff. There was one other member of the family who likewise contributed to Moncreiff's education in the larger sense – his formidable grandfather, the eighth baronet, the Reverend Sir Harry Moncreiff, described by J.C. Watt as 'a splendid type of the old self-reliant Scottish gentleman'.[36] 'He was a majestic old man, this grandfather of mine,' wrote Moncreiff. 'Vigorous, practical, entirely fearless, and at home in all classes of society, his individual influence was probably as great as that of any man in Scotland, but gifted with unusual force of character.' 'Nobody', commented a contemporary, 'can look upon the Baronet without perceiving that nature meant him to be a ruler, not a subject' – an assessment with which Moncreiff fully agreed. Yet to his grandchildren he was always kind and loving, laying on for their enjoyment Twelfth Night parties, visits to exhibitions, and on one occasion a breakfast party for a famous ventriloquist, Alexandre. One member of that party was the prominent churchman, Dr Thomas Chalmers. 'After going thro' various performances, the ventriloquist made a nice speech, apparently out of Chalmers' stomach. The imaginative Dr said it was "a most remarkable experience".'[37]

Sir Harry himself came of a long line of clergymen – for six generations the eldest sons of Moncreiffs were ministers of the kirk[38] – including his father Sir William, whose former parish of Blackford was kept open for the son for when he should come of age. At the age of 25 the parish of St Cuthbert's in Edinburgh was bestowed on him, and he soon became the acknowledged leader of the Evangelical party in the Church. He was frequently consulted by leading Scottish Whigs of the day, and amongst his grandfather's papers Moncreiff came across the draft of a Bill for the repeal of the Catholic Disabilities sent to him for his advice by Lord Lauderdale, with whom he had had a voluminous correspondence.[39] Amongst Sir Harry's disciples were Andrew Thomson, and the aforementioned Dr Thomas Chalmers, who later became his successors as leaders of the Evangelical wing of the Church.

Their future and that of the Moncreiffs were to march closely together in the 1830s and 1840s, as events moved inexorably towards the great Disruption of the Church in 1843.

Henry Cockburn, for one, recalled with relish Sir Harry's Sunday suppers:

> This most admirable, and somewhat old-fashioned, gentleman was one of those who always dined between sermons, probably without touching wine. He then walked back – look at him – from his small house in the east end of Queen Street to his church, with his bands, his little cocked hat, his tall cane, and his cardinal air; preached, if it was his turn, a sensible practical sermon; walked home in the same style; took tea about five; spent some hours in his study; at nine had family worship, at which he was delighted to see the friends of any of his sons; after which the whole party sat down to roasted hens, the goblets of wine, and his powerful talk. Here was a mode of alluring young men into the paths of pious pleasantness. Those days are now passed, but the figure, and the voice, the thoughts, and the kind and cheerful manliness, of Sir Harry, as disclosed at those Sunday evenings, will be remembered with gratitude by some of the best intellects in Scotland.[40]

As we have noted, Sir Harry died in August, 1827. During the last two years of his life he and his grandson had grown to be particularly close companions. 'He talked to me', Moncreiff recalled, 'with the utmost freedom, and all was noble, large minded, and instructive.' Not long before Sir Harry's death, Moncreiff walked with him to a meeting of the General Assembly, and waited for him in the gallery until he came out. 'He rose, but stood till all the rest had left: then slowly looked around the old building – the scene of his questions from youth to old age, leaning on his ivory headed cane, as if after leave taking, turned and departed. The old man knew he was not to see it again. He never did.'[41]

During his childhood and youth, James Moncreiff enjoyed a particularly secure and supportive family life. His parents and grandfather supplied influential role models; the summer retreats at Eldin House provided opportunities for adventure as well as instruction; his parents' friends and colleagues offered intellectual stimulus and food for thought. And already a pattern was emerging which would help to guide him in his future career – a pattern consisting of three dominant threads – the law, Whig politics, and the evangelical wing of the Church of Scotland.

Chapter 2
Student Days

Most commentators on Moncreiff's early education have insisted that he greatly valued the years spent at Edinburgh High School, and indeed in his public statements Moncreiff has given colour to this view. 'Throughout his life,' wrote Omond, 'it is almost a commonplace to say that he evinced abiding loyalty and affection for his school, regularly attending the dinners of the Mackay class until age compelled him to desist from those agreeable reunions.'[1] 'In retrospect', W.H Bain has written, 'Moncreiff had few doubts about the value of his schooling.'[2] 'The High School of Edinburgh was *the* school in Scotland,' Moncreiff himself wrote in the *Edinburgh Review* in 1872,[3] 'and at the cost of a few pounds a year the sons of peers and those of peasants were trained together. There Scott, and Brougham, and Horner, and Jeffrey received the elements of their instruction, and had the means of carrying scholarship to some degree of critical eminence.'

Lord Brougham, of an earlier generation to Moncreiff, had also commented on the practice of educating boys of all classes. 'Such a school', he wrote, 'is altogether invaluable in a free state. It is because men of the highest and lowest rank of society send their children to be educated together.' One of his fellow scholars, he recalled, was now in the House of Lords, while others had been the sons of 'menial servants', or of shopkeepers in the Cowgate. 'There they were, sitting side by side, giving and taking places from each other, without the slightest impression on the part of my noble friends of any superiority on the part of the other boys to them.' That was his reason for preferring the Old High School of Edinburgh to other, more patrician, schools, however well regulated or conducted.[4]

Yet in the privacy of his *Reminiscences*, Moncreiff was more critical. He had been sent to the High School in 1819 at the age of eight. He could already read quite well, thanks to his mother, and had 'already devoured the Parent's Assistant, Learning at Home, and Sanford and Merton,'[5] and had 'some scanty beginnings of Latin.' Perhaps because he was relatively advanced for his age, he was at least a year younger than his contemporaries, and while he had no particular difficulty with the lessons themselves, he found that the difference of a year affected his relationship with his classmates. Indeed, 'the constant association with boys older than myself, gave me a chronic sense of inferiority, which did not disappear during my six years of school life, and put a morbid strain on my spirits.'[6]

The school buildings Moncreiff found gloomy and depressing. 'There was,' he asserted, 'nothing aesthetic in this seminary of Scottish learning. It was not even old,[7] and was as dull and grey as the false taste of the 18th century could make it. Not a blade of grass had we for our games; two dingy graveled courts in front and behind formed our only playground. So much so, that play itself became out of fashion for the 4th and 5th years, and was looked on as a frivolity only fit for children.' The precincts of Infirmary Street 'always appear to me in memory as a region where the sun never shone. Such an epitome of six years of very early life, from the days in Oct 1819 when my brother Henry took me by the hand – a grasp ever ready for me – and plunged me shivering into these murky and very cold waters of life, until that on which, liberated from the long-room fetters, I began to breathe again in 1825.'[8]

Class sizes were very large – Mr. Carson's first year class, which Moncreiff entered in 1819, numbered 178, and the second year class over 200. The total school population, he calculated, must have been between 600 and 1000. Unlike Henry Cockburn, another notable Edinburgh lawyer who enrolled in the School in October 1787, he does not appear to have seen the class size as an obstacle to learning – but rather an indication of the high esteem the School enjoyed amongst the parents of Scottish children. Nor did he share Cockburn's criticism of the teaching staff, whom he reckoned 'on the whole were able men, and when we were turned out at the end of our decennial grind it was our own fault if we did not carry some substantial fruit along with us.'[9]

For his part, Moncreiff was perhaps fortunate that he had not been born a generation earlier. If he had shivered in apprehension on entering the school for the first time, then Henry Cockburn, aware of the reputation of the School for its severity and riotousness, confessed that on his first day 'I approached its walls with trembling, and felt dizzy when I sat down amidst above 100 faces.' His fears were soon realized. 'The person to whose uncontrolled discipline I was now subjected, though a good man and an intense student, and filled, rather in the memory than in the head, with knowledge, was as bad a schoolmaster as it is possible to fancy. Unacquainted with the nature of youth, ignorant of the character of even his own boys, and with not a conception of the art or the duty of alluring them, he had nothing for it but to drive them; and this he did with constant and indiscriminate harshness.' 'The effects of this', he went on, 'were very hurtful to all his pupils.' Out of the four years of his attendance at the High School Cockburn reckoned that 'there were probably not ten days in which I was not flogged, at least once'. This despite the fact that 'I never entered the class, nor left it, without feeling perfectly qualified, both in ability and preparation, for its whole business; which being confined to Latin alone, and in necessarily short tasks, since every one of the boys had to rhyme over the very same words, in the very same way, was no great feat.' The worst aspect of the experience was the sheer boredom 'of sitting six hours a day staring idly at a page, without motion and without thought, and trembling at the approach of the merciless giant. I never got a single prize, and once sat *boobie* at the annual public examination. The beauty of no Roman word, or thought or action, ever occurred to me; nor did I ever fancy that Latin was of any use except to torture small boys.'[10]

Cockburn's account was by no means untypical, and John Murray's *History of the Royal High School* contains several other contemporary accounts of the physical abuse meted out to pupils as a matter of course by members of the teaching staff such as Alexander Christison and Luke Fraser. This is curious in light of the fact that the Rector in these days was the famous Dr Alexander Adam, of whom his former pupils spoke with unalloyed praise and gratitude. Adam had no need to resort to the tawse, but seems to have exercised little restraining influence on certain members of his staff, who evidently enjoyed, if that is the right word (and perhaps it is), complete autonomy in the matter of corporal punishment.[11]

Adam retired one year before Moncreiff was born, to be succeeded by James Pillans, subsequently Professor of Humanity at Edinburgh College, and under whom Moncreiff was to sit during his first three years as a student there. The election of Pillans to the Rectorship had been warmly welcomed by Cockburn, who described him as the 'earliest and best of our reformed practical teachers,…who had been of incalculable use throughout the whole modern progress of Scotch education.'[12] The rector for most of Moncreiff's time at the High School was Dr. Aglionby-Ross Carson. By now, approaches to teaching practice had so far improved that we get no hint in either his public or private comments on the School of the brutality described by Cockburn and his fellows. Despite its dingy appearance, two aspects of the School particularly appealed to him – its republican character, and its teaching of Latin.

The point Moncreiff had made publicly in 1872, he restated in his *Reminiscences*; 'Peer's sons, and those of peasants, were jumbled together. There was no distinction recognised, excepting that the sons of gentry paid a little more if they chose.' (At this time, Moncreiff's father was paying one guinea per subject for his son's education.) 'In point of culture, I do not think the higher bred boys lost anything, while the lower certainly gained by the association. In point of conduct, I rather think the lower boys had the best of it. I had some dear old chums, who hailed from some very impossible places, and whom I never afterwards encountered, but who professed much originality, good feeling, and sometimes poetic sentiment.' While this last sentence verges on the patronising, Moncreiff's final comment here, in the light of his later interest in educational reform, is possibly significant. 'Probably,' he suggested, 'society has advanced too fast and too far to admit of the system being continued, but it had its advantages, and was manly, self reliant, and rigorous.'[13]

Classics teaching at the School had also obviously advanced a good deal since Cockburn's day. Moncreiff commended the teaching of Greek, which avoided the pedantry 'which makes light of the meaning of the author and considers scansion and quantity of articles and particles the only test of scholarship.' Likewise, 'we were not taught the idiotic doctrine that to compose Latin verses is a stroke of genius beyond Latin prose. We were well grounded in Syntax and Prosody, and above all to sympathise with the true meaning of the authors which we read – the true end and aim of all study of foreign languages'.[14] For his part, when he left the school in 1825, he knew his 'Horace and Cicero very well; critically as well as philologically; could write Latin prose with fair syntax and idiom, and should have been fairly abreast with Latin verse also, had I not hated Gradus ad Parnassum.'[15]

Not that this proficiency was entirely the achievement of the High School. Moncreiff had had a succession of private tutors, of whom he selected for special mention one William Harkness, a divinity student and later minister of Fala in West Lothian, to whom Moncreiff generously ascribed most of his success in later life. Harkness was clearly a born teacher. 'He was not only a finished scholar, but he had imagination and enthusiasm, and the art of exciting the first and arousing the second.' From Harkness 'I first learned to appreciate the spirit within the words I had been wont to treat as lifeless matter: the music of cadences – the loftiness of thoughts that breathed, sounds that burned, admiration for the noble, the patriotic, and the beautiful. As far as I learned or felt them, I owed it to him.'[16] Perhaps it would be fair to comment that the quality of these last few sentences themselves bears testimony to the teaching skill of this Mr. Harkness.

In an essay composed in 1870, Moncreiff expressed his belief in the classics as the pillars of his education. 'The liberalizing and enlarging effect of thorough education, in producing intellectual breadth; a thorough training in the classics, and a competent knowledge of modern languages, are the keys to jurisprudence.'[17] It was one of his few regrets, expressed in the same essay, that he had not been taught German – the lack of which he regarded as a serious disadvantage for a modern Scottish lawyer

Overall then, Moncreiff appeared to have learned a good deal at the High School, and done well. He ended up as Dux of the school, and showed considerable athletic prowess. In his *Reminiscences*, he supplied a succinct verdict on his time there: 'Farewell, old High School. I loved you not, and never knew how much I had been indebted to you until I left you.'[18]

But schooldays are not just about lessons. Just as important for Moncreiff were the lifelong friendships which were forged at the School. 'Of these' he wrote, 'I place John Inglis, the Lord Justice General, at the head. We entered school together – I fancy on the same day, and after the lapse of 70 years together, we were still [together] until last October, when I broke the record, as the slang phrase is, and threw up my place on the bench.' Inglis' 'unbroken success,' Moncreiff commented, 'in all he ever attempted, of itself indicated powers of no ordinary kind.' Other friends were Sir Douglas MacLagan, John Ord Mackenzie of Dolphinton, and 'one who does not survive, but was nearest of all, Benjamin Robert Bell, Advocate and Sheriff of Moray, my brother-in-law to be.'[19]

In any case, there was much more to Moncreiff's boyhood, and even his education, than the High School and what he could learn there. He developed a number of outside interests, two of which he identified as politics and pugilism. He became as hooked on prize fighting as any modern teenager on football. The *Morning Chronicle* regularly contained full reports of bouts, and Moncreiff 'used to procure them, pore over them, think over them and dream of them as the romance of my life.' The great champion of those days was one John Winter Spring, whom Moncreiff regarded as 'the greatest hero of the time.' Moncreiff himself was taught to box by one of his father's servants, Alex McNab, who when in London with Moncreiff's father used to spar at the Fives Court with the great ones of the Fancy. This practice, however, did not preserve him on one occasion from being knocked down under the heels of the coach's horses by an irritated Yorkshire ostler at Ferrybridge, on the journey back from London.[20]

An interest in pugilism does not fit very well, perhaps, with the image of a respected judicial figure as Moncreiff later became. Politics is another matter, though what Moncreiff was referring to here was not so much the complexities of party manoeuvres, as to three particular events which took place in 1822, and evidently made a great impression upon him. These were the visit of King George IV to Edinburgh; the dinner given for Brougham and Denman to mark the 'acquittal' of the Queen; and the duel which led to the death of Sir Alex Boswell, the son of Dr Johnson's biographer, and who was, according to Moncreiff, a better man than his father.

The King's visit to Edinburgh, or 'the King's Jaunt' as John Prebble put it,[21] was stage managed by Sir Walter Scott in an attempt to create, or define, a Scottish identity – but a Scottish identity within a

British, or even an Imperial, context. For Scott, the best way to present this concept was within the cloak – or the plaid – of Jacobitism – which one historian has described as a 'politically defeated creed', but one which had served as the major vehicle for eighteenth century nationalism. 'The choice of pageantry, tartan, and tradition helped to underline the picturesque distinction between England and Scotland, and to reassure the British government that there was now nothing to fear from it.'[22] And this was at a time when such reassurance was timely. Only two years previously Scotland had witnessed an insurrection, when 60,000 workers in Glasgow had gone on strike, and a force of weavers bearing arms was forcibly dispersed by the Yeomanry – three of its leaders being executed outside Stirling Castle.

For the young Moncreiff, however, the visit of George IV, the first time a British monarch had set foot in Scotland's capital for two hundred years, was above all else an amazing spectacle, and his account of it, composed well over sixty years after the event, is fresh and detailed. Someone had arranged for him to witness the procession from a window of a house in Picardy Place, with a clear view of the Calton Hill and Leith Street along which the cavalcade had proceeded. 'I saw the First Gentleman of Europe,' he recalled, 'make his entry into Edinburgh....It was a sight to remember. The crowd was enormous. The Calton Hill was one mass of heads – not a blade of grass was visible: and the shouts and waving of hats as the Royal Carriage passed made the scene very striking. The King,' he observed, 'looked fagged, but interested. I could see the expression on his face, and he was plainly much gratified. But he was ill at ease, for the tidings of Lord Castelreagh's suicide had, if I remember right, just arrived. While, however, the populace were loyal and courteous, and were undeniably glad and proud of the visit of their sovereign, their demeanour was not effusive.'[23] Altogether a remarkable observation by a boy of eleven.

Another contemporary account, penned by Elizabeth Grant, was even more detailed and colourful. Both her mother and herself were unwell, and so they stayed at home with Elizabeth's Aunt Mary, but that did nothing to inhibit her account:

> This autumn King George IV, then, I think, only Regent, [This was incorrect – George IV became King in 1820] visited Scotland. The whole country went mad. Every body strained every point to get to Edinburgh to receive him. Sir Walter Scott and the town Council were overwhelming themselves with the preparations.....There were processions, a Review, a Levee, and a Ball.....A great mistake was made by the Stage Managers – one that offended all the Southron Scots; the King wore at the levee the highland dress. I daresay he thought the country all highland, expected no fertile plains, did not know the

difference between the Saxon and the Celt. However, all else went off well, this little slur on the Saxon was overlooked, and it gave occasion for a good laugh at one of lady Saltoun's witty speeches. Someone objecting to this dress, especially on so large a man, whose nudities were no longer attractive, "Nay," she said, "we should take it very kind of him, since his stay will be so short, the more we see of him the better." Sir William Curtis was kilted too, and standing near the King, many persons mistook them, amongst others John Hamilton Dundas, who kneeled to kiss the fat Alderman's hand, when, finding out his mistake, he called out, "Wrong, by Jove," and, rising, moved on undaunted to the larger presence.'

The King's visit provided Elizabeth's father, increasingly in financial difficulties, with a wholly unexpected and welcome return, although at the time the incident made his daughter 'very cross'. Apparently the King was partial to Scotch whisky, but would drink only pure Glenlivet, and there was none to be had. The Chamberlain, Lord Conyngham, searched everywhere for a supply, and the upshot was that Elizabeth's father sent word to her, as the family cellarer:

> to empty my pet bin, where there was whiskey long in wood, long in uncorked bottles, mild as milk, and the true contraband gout in it. Much as I grudged this treasure, it made our fortunes afterwards, shewing on what trifles great events sometimes depend. The whiskey, and the fifty brace of ptarmigan all shot by one man in one day, went up to Holyrood House, and were graciously received and made much of, and a reminder of this attention at a proper moment by the gentlemanly Chamberlain, ensured to my father the Indian Judgeship.[24]

The Brougham dinner, we are told, was arranged as a celebration for Brougham's role in the acquittal of the Queen. Queen Caroline had not in fact been charged with any criminal act, as the use of the word 'acquittal' might suggest. Her many indiscretions, however, had provided the ammunition the King was looking for to gain a divorce. The cabinet introduced a bill to dissolve the marriage, and this was followed by a public enquiry into her behaviour which lasted from mid August to early November. The Lords then passed the bill by a small majority, and the cabinet, persuaded that it had little chance in the Commons, decided to drop it. The queen accepted a pension of £50,000 a year and a house. The matter was concluded.

Brougham's part in all this was problematical. Three years earlier, in 1819, as her adviser, he had proposed that Caroline (not yet Queen) should be paid off with an annual allowance of £50,000, on condition that she renounced her claim to the title, and never came back to England. After the death of George III, and the accession of Caroline's husband, the Prince Regent, to the throne as George IV, the matter became more pressing, and an offer on similar lines was made by the then Prime Minister, Lord Liverpool. Brougham hesitated, at one time hinting that if he were appointed a King's Counsel, he would persuade the Queen to accept. In the end he advised her against acceptance, and in June, 1821, she returned to England, to face the enquiry and the possibility of divorce. As we have seen, the issue was eventually settled much along the lines suggested by Brougham in the first place.[25] In Scotland, or at least amongst Brougham's friends, this outcome was seen as a triumph for Brougham – hence the dinner – at which both Moncreiff's father, and his grandfather, Sir Harry, were present.

The third event of 1822 proved to be much more dramatic – this was the notorious and fatal duel between Sir Alex Boswell, and James Stuart of Dunearn. The origins of the tragedy were political. For some time the Tory party in Scotland had been carrying out a scurrilous campaign of personal vilification against their Whig opponents. By the time of the duel, this campaign had lost much of its force – to some extent it had backfired, and in any case the Whigs were gaining in strength and political support, either despite or because of it. The last shot fired in this campaign was a song, written by Boswell, a Tory, lampooning James Stuart, a Whig, and accusing him of cowardice. Stuart challenged him, and Boswell fell at the first shot. They met near Auchtertool, in Fife, on the 22nd March, 1822. According to Cockburn, Stuart, 'an awkward lumbering rider, had never fired a pistol but once or twice from the back of a horse in a troop of yeomanry. He stopped at this beautiful hillside near Aberdour, and arranged some papers and subscribed a deed of settlement. Boswell, who was an expert shot, told his second, Mr. Douglas, that he meant to fire in the air. He fell himself, however, at the first fire.'

Stuart was tried on 10th June, later that year. He seemed to have the sympathy of all those concerned – even some of his political opponents appeared as character witnesses, and he was duly acquitted. As for Boswell, Cockburn described him as 'able and literary, and when in the humour of being quiet, he was agreeable and kind. But in general he was boisterous and overbearing, and addicted to coarse personal ridicule.' Cockburn was particularly critical of 'the fact of a person of his rank writing anonymous libels, for a blackguard newspaper, against an acquaintance, in a disguised hand.' He also noted the curious circumstance that Boswell, during his brief time as a Member of Parliament, was instrumental in the repeal of the existing Scottish statutes against dueling.[26]

There were no more libels after that. Moncreiff could recollect, from the distance of more than seventy years, 'the clearing of the social atmosphere in Edinburgh, by this tragical termination of these ignoble and detestable practices.'[27]

Moncreiff left the High School in October, 1825, and enrolled in Edinburgh University (or Edinburgh College as he called it) at the age of fourteen. Here he found himself, to his great astonishment, treated as a man in College classes, and addressed as 'Mr. James Moncreiff'. Looking back on this event from the perspective of retirement, Moncreiff was characteristically self-deprecating about his own feelings on the occasion, and declared that 'in my inmost soul I felt as great a child as I had done in October 1819'. He had, however, 'stuffed my brain with a great quantity of miscellaneous furniture: aided thereto by a very rapid and tenacious memory,....and the main object to which I devoted it during my school days was to pretend the knowledge of the tasks of the day without learning them, in which I flatter myself I was to some extent successful. But I had thus acquired a kind of second hand assortment of notions, the true meaning of which I scarcely understood, but which, afterwards, I often contrived to utilize.'[28]

Moncreiff began his College life by entering the Humanity class of Professor Pillans, whom he described as 'a great scholar: a man of cultivated tastes, and with instinctive sympathies with the feelings and aspirations of young men.' Pillans had been a tutor at Eton and Rector of the High School, but now at the College he was faced with the almost intractable problem of a very large class (over 100 students) too many of whom had not yet mastered the rudiments of Latin. Moncreiff confessed that after three years at the College, he himself knew no more Latin than when he first began there. He blamed the situation on the low salaries of university teachers: 'Until the Professors are better endowed, and are less dependent on their fees, this result must ensue.'[29]

However, Moncreiff acknowledged that he learned a good deal from Pillans which stood him in good stead in later life. He had above all 'the rare and inestimable gift of making pupils think, and giving a "local habitation and a name" to the abstractions with which he dealt.' Yet according to his own account, Moncreiff was 'supremely idle' during all those years, to the extent that his success in the competition for the Gold Medal given each year by the Writers of the Signet, was not altogether popular. Pillans himself, to Moncreiff's lasting chagrin, concluded the long Latin oration, when awarding him the medal, with the words 'Et apage incuriam, quae corrumpit mores'. ('And away with carelessness, which corrupts morals').[30]

The activity which seems to have absorbed a good deal of Moncreiff's time and energies at the College had to do with the founding and maintenance of the Classical Society. The object of the Society was 'to encourage a higher Classical life', by means of reading essays and debating relevant subjects. To begin with the proceedings were to be conducted in Latin, but one session, incomprehensible to both speaker (Moncreiff) and audience, was enough to convince the members that it would be better to revert to the vernacular. The Society had 'a brilliant future', and flourished for several more years as a debating society. It was also the milieu in which Moncreiff made many friends, many of whom went on to highly successful careers, and several of whom remained his friends for many years into the future.

It so happened that in 1824, the year before Moncreiff entered the College, a new school was established in Edinburgh – the Edinburgh Academy – 'intended', according to Moncreiff, 'to attract boys from the upper classes, and to innovate on the somewhat grim traditions of the High School'. Moncreiff himself was not transferred to the new establishment, but William and his other younger brothers were enrolled there. Then in 1827 and 1828 a number of students from the Academy came on to the College, with whom Moncreiff established an immediate rapport. Amongst this cohort were included Archibald Campbell Swinton, George Macgill, John Thomson Gordon, later Sheriff of Edinburgh, Younger of Pilrig, and William Aytoun, afterwards Professor of Rhetoric, and author of the *Lays of the Cavaliers*. A contemporary, Archibald Tait, became Archbishop of Canterbury, and although a student at Glasgow College, during the summer he joined the others in the Classical Society.

According to Moncreiff, the Academy contingent had an electrifying effect on the Classical, and 'a very merry, witty, clever and gentlemanlike band they were. Not to be despised, by any means, when one of them rose in the Classical to wither up his enemy. That they spoke better than the House of Commons, I will not say, because that would be impertinent to the House, but that there are not six men in the House who speak better than they could, I make bold to assert.' It was from his association with these young men that Moncreiff was made aware of what had been lacking in the High School – 'there was no fun. All was so distressingly in earnest. My new associates did not see things thro' the same grey mist: and the amount of amusement and light they have injected into my life I can never be sufficiently grateful for. I found with them a combination of the intellectual with the lively which I had previously sighed for in vain. That my own solemnity, the reflection of Infirmary Street, was sometimes the subject of their mirth, did not in any degree diminish either their enjoyment of it or my own.'[31]

The Classical Society at the time was only one of several such societies, such as the Juridical and the Scots Law, which were described by Omond as 'purely professional'. Then there was the Forensic, a debating club popular amongst budding lawyers, which Moncreiff might have been expected to join but for the fact, as noted by a college magazine of the period, 'no Radical ever ventured to show his face there; scarcely a Whig is tolerated within these walls. All, or nearly all, are Tories – sleek, quiet, comfortable, but withal talented, Tories. Their debates therefore want the spirit which a systematic opposition produces, and the members are generally safe at home, and in bed, by the time they of the Speculative are in the height of discussion.'[32]

The Moncreiffs were of course committed Whigs. So it was the famous Speculative Society, not the Forensic, to which the young Moncreiff was elected on 16th March, 1830, following in the footsteps of his father and grandfather. The Speculative was not a political club as such – its activities focused on the reading of essays, and its debates were confined, we are told, to 'academic exercise and speculation',[33] but if the Forensic contained almost no Whigs, the Speculative, despite the fact that Sir Walter Scott had been secretary in the early 1790s, contained almost no Tories. Indeed, as one contemporary commented:

> Many are the battles which we have to fight, not with the Tories, for they are a race almost extinct in the Speculative,[34] but with the Radicals, who have here mustered their clans, and under the banner of a leader of no ordinary powers of eloquence, right obstinately do they advance to the combat, and though weekly foiled in their attempts to prove the injustice of a Church Establishment, and the evils consequent upon the existence of a standing army, weekly do they return to the conflict, and show, by the pertinacity of their opinions, that though defeated, they can argue still.[35]

As Moncreiff was to find in later life, conflict within the Whig ranks in Scotland between Liberals and Radicals was to be more or less constant, and to have a profound effect on his own political fortunes.

To Moncreiff, the 'old historic Speculative, to which my father and grandfather belonged, where Playfair and Dugald Stewart practiced their weapons, where Brougham and Horner, and Jeffrey served their debating apprenticeship,[36] and Walter Scott acted as Secretary – this was classic ground, and appealed vividly to all those inspirations and aspirations I had so long silently cherished.' Amongst the members of the 'Spec' he was to find an entirely new circle of friends, with many of whom he was to remain on intimate terms in the years to come.[37] 'Those days of the Speculative', he declared from the viewpoint of retirement, 'were the happiest of my life. They were full of interest and excitement, and brought so little care along with them. Those winter meetings when, fired by our patriotic zeal, we kept more than the midnight taper burning until 2 in the morning, had the sensation of real solid utility....We never stopped or cared to think of the mimicry and emptiness of the whole affair, tho' it was not half such an imposture as the House of Commons nowadays.' Moncreiff had evidently kept some of the records of the Speculative, and was amused to discover that the meetings seldom attracted an audience of more than a dozen. At one of the better attended sessions he had tried to persuade a meeting of twenty-two of the desirability of creating more peers, in order to pass the Reform Bill of 1832. He lost by 12-10. Of course in real life the Bill was passed, and 'the Constitution saved. The day may come', he mused, 'when my remedy will appear too Conservative.'[38]

Moncreiff soon became acknowledged as the best speaker in the Speculative – 'the Don of the Spec', and amongst the most prolific writer of the essays, the reading of which began each meeting. These appear to have been mostly on issues of contemporary politics – such as 'The Political Power of the People', 'Mr. Pitt's Financial Measures', and the like. Then in 1831 the first issue of the *University Magazine* appeared, edited anonymously by Moncreiff, whose role was uncovered by another new student publication known as *The Nimmo, or Alma's Tawse*. 'Who the editor was,' noted *The Nimmo*, 'was for some time a sort of mystery, but murder will out – 'twas wee Jamie, – Demosthenes parvulus – the future Dean – the Don of the Spec – the most precocious bantam that ever taught his grandmother to suck eggs.'[39]

Moncreiff spent three years studying under Professor Pillans before moving on to the feet of Professor John Wilson, Professor of Moral Philosophy, and also a prolific contributor to *Blackwood's Magazine*, writing under the name of Christopher North.[40] Moncreiff had been the medalist in Wilson's class in 1828, but apparently the Professor, living up to the image of absent mindedness, forgot to present it. The medal was discovered amongst his papers over sixty years later, and finally presented to Moncreiff by Wilson's granddaughter.[41] According to Moncreiff, 'My remembrance of the two sessions I spent with him is that of a long procession through a garden of flowers.' It is satisfying to note that one of his first actions on becoming Lord Advocate in 1851 was to persuade Lord John Russell to grant the ailing Wilson an annual pension of £300.[42]

Wilson/North is portrayed in the *Reminiscences* as something of a disappointed individual – brought up in the expectation of succeeding to great wealth, he 'saw the fabric suddenly melted away', and he was forced to rely upon his own resources. In later life he was inclined to envy the material success of his contemporaries, believing them to be in no way superior to himself in talents or deserts. He is reported to have complained to his friend Peter Robertson, who had been appointed to the bench, 'And there you are, Peter, clothed in purple and fine linen, and faring sumptuously every day, while I am nothing but a wretched dominie.' In Moncreiff's view, Wilson had not been intended by Nature to be a philosopher or a metaphysician, but that fact did little to diminish the impact of his teaching, since 'the most interesting as well as the most congenial part of Wilson's Professorial course was the literary rather than the philosophic aspect of it. He set his students in a blaze for belles lettres. Fired himself with a true poetic instinct, he created in his audience the sense of beauty in works of imagination and sent them to study with zeal and appreciation the authors to whom he referred. I learned more in this direction from him than I did of Aristotle or Descartes or Spinoza: or at least I liked it much better.'[43]

Moncreiff's experience of formal education at school and college had lasted for some thirteen years. He had endured the grim, humourless grind of the High School, and enjoyed the relative freedom and intellectual stimulation of Edinburgh College, with its inspirational professors, the comradeship of his new friends, and the invaluable experience (especially for a budding lawyer) of the Classical and Speculative Societies. Placed in context, he had had the benefit of an education designed for the sons of the professional Edinburgh elite. While he had approved of the High School practice of educating the sons of the aristocracy and the lower classes without distinction, it is significant that he seldom met with the latter again on equal terms in later life. His natural allies were the bright young men from the Academy, an avowedly upper class establishment, with their combination of intellectual endeavour and fun. The experience he gained, the friendships he made, were exactly what was required by a young Scot with an eye on future professional and political advancement.

Moncreiff left the University in 1832, well prepared for life in the political maelstrom which accompanied the new move for reform epitomised by the Reform Bill of the same year. As he later commented of this period: 'The sleepers started to their feet: the drowsy hum was changed to sharp challenge and disputation; received axioms were questioned; ancient doubts were revived; and when I left college in 1832, the war of principles and words raged more fiercely than ever, and the new dominion was laying, in energy, impetuosity, and power, the firm foundations of its sway.'[44] For 1832 was the very year in which Parliament passed the great Reform Act, which he, like many others, recognised as a watershed in British politics.

'The Reform Bill', he later recorded, 'transformed the face of the community, socially as well as politically. Place and power had changed sides. I feel still something of the exultant throb which filled my frame when I thought that altho' they had waited long, the steadfast asserters of popular rights, the men who in the *Edinburgh Review* had braved the persons of power, and defied the scorn of its underlings, were, after long years, to be rewarded.' Moncreiff's own response to the Reform Act at the time had been to deliver what was probably his first public political speech – not to the electors of Edinburgh nor in the House of Commons, but from an upper window in Tullibole Castle to a more or less captive audience of tenants and feuars of the estate.[45] It was to be the first of a great many.

II

The Young Lawyer

Chapter 3
The Making of an Advocate

In 1833, one year after leaving University, Moncreiff sat his final Bar examinations and was formally inducted into the Faculty of Advocates – thus embarking on a career in the law which was to continue for the next fifty-five years. Over that period he was to be a practitioner, a reformer, and ultimately a judicial interpreter of the law, and it is worth considering at the outset what it was which drew him so firmly and apparently unwaveringly to this profession in particular.

One obvious answer would be the influence, or at least the example, of his father. We have seen in a previous chapter that the Moncreiffs were a close knit family, and there is no doubt that father and son thought along similar lines when it came to matters to do with the Scottish church, politics, and reform. James senior was both successful and respected by his professional peers, and just as certainly by his son. Wilson Bain has made the point that the younger Moncreiff would very probably have attended some of his father's cases,[1] and though we know now that he was not actually in court during the most famous of them – the trial of William Burke, the 'resurrectionist', in 1829 – this is a mere detail, since he was well aware of the case, and comments on it his *Reminiscences*.[2]

Why parental example and influence may not be taken as the whole answer to the question is demonstrated by the fact that Henry, James' elder brother, chose a different path, and went into the Church. Indeed both brothers had had close personal relations with their famous grandfather, Sir Harry, minister of St Cuthbert's, and both were serious when it came to matters of religion and church government in Scotland. Yet there is no indication that James felt drawn at any time to follow his brother's example. His lodestone was the law – but not law in the abstract – not the theoretician's law, but the law in practice. At one point in the course of his *Reminiscences* he confessed openly to finding the study of Scots law distasteful[3], but if that really was the case, he overcame it, and became a highly successful advocate, acting in several of the century's most high profile and important cases, both civil and criminal. As Lord Justice Clerk, though sometimes compared unfavourably with his great contemporary and friend, John Inglis, his judgments were regarded as sound, and, on occasion, seminal.[4]

For Moncreiff's approach to the law, as to politics, and perhaps even to religion, was essentially practical and pragmatic. It is not difficult to believe that a major part of the attraction of a legal career was that in Edinburgh at that time – as in other places and at other times – a career in the law was the quickest and most direct route to a career in politics. Politics, it is clear, was his real love. And yet as we shall see, the triumvirate of religion, politics and the law are not easily separable in Moncreiff's case, and he was fortunate from time to time to be able to take on cases, as in the Disruption cases, where his own religious and political sympathies lay with those of his client.

We cannot know at precisely what point Moncreiff decided to pursue a legal career, and indeed there may not have been such a defining moment. His family and educational background, his growing interest in reform, both political and educational, inevitably drew him in that direction. His role in helping to found the Classical Society at Edinburgh College suggests that he was already conscious of the attractions of public debate, and the occurrence of the Burke case in 1828, with his father as defending counsel, certainly made a lasting impression.

The prosecution of William Burke, and his common law wife Helen Macdougal, for what were known as 'the West Port murders', for a time absorbed the attention of the public. Burke's accomplice in his crimes, William Hare, turned King's evidence, and so escaped prosecution. 'The hero of this "Cause Célèbre"', Moncreiff wrote later, 'who has added a new word to our language, was a man whose employment was to provide the surgeons with human objects of the dissecting room. It at last appeared that when he could not find them dead, he murdered them while living: and probably no more ghastly tragedy ever was revealed than that disclosure in the trial which ensued.[5]

To be strictly accurate, Burke, though often referred to as a 'resurrectionist', was not in fact a body snatcher – simply a murderer. And the Helen Macdougal referred to was not formally his wife – but a prostitute with whom he lived in Tanner's Close in the West Port, and for whom as we shall see he had a good deal of genuine affection. Both Burke and Hare were Irish immigrants from Ulster, who had come to Edinburgh to look for work on the New Union Canal in 1818. It was in Edinburgh that Burke met up with Macdougal. Hare likewise worked on the canal, and married one Margaret Laird, who ran a lodging house in the West Port. In 1827 Burke and Macdougal also moved to the West Port area and Burke and Hare became friends. According to the later testimony of William Hare, the first body they sold was that of a tenant of the house who died of natural causes, an old army pensioner who owed Hare £4.00. Having filled the man's coffin with bark, they brought the body to Edinburgh University to look for a purchaser, and found Dr Robert Knox, an anatomist in need of cadavers to demonstrate dissecting techniques to his students. Under the law in force at the time, only the bodies of executed criminals could be legitimately used for this purpose, and the supply of two or three corpses a year proved wholly inadequate – a situation which naturally encouraged criminals to raid recent graves for bodies.

Burke and Hare preferred a more direct method of increasing the supply. Their first cadaver brought them £7 10s, and they continued to build on their success by murdering, usually by suffocation or strangulation, a further sixteen victims. It was the death of the last of these – a Mary Ann Docherty – which led to their arrest, and Burke's trial. Docherty had been lured into the lodging house by Burke, but he had to wait before killing her for two other lodgers, James and Ann Gray, to leave the house. When they returned, Ann Gray's suspicions were aroused by Burke's refusal to let her approach a bed on which she had left her stockings, and the next day, when the Grays investigated, they found the body of Mary Docherty under the bed. They went to fetch the police, refusing the bribe of £10 a week offered them by Macdougal. Hare was offered immunity from prosecution if he would testify against Burke, with the result that only Burke and Macdougal were put on trial. No proceedings were taken against Dr Knox.

Moncreiff's father, then Dean of the Faculty of Advocates, and who has been described by Omond as the best lawyer in Scotland[6], and more recently by Owen Dudley Edwards as being at the height of his powers,[7] appeared for Burke, and Henry Cockburn for Macdougal. How a criminal like Burke was able to engage such eminent counsel is explained in the *Reminiscences*. It was normal practice in Scottish courts of the day for all prisoners to be defended by counsel, and if they were unable to engage them, then an advocate would be assigned by the Court, as in the modern system of legal aid. 'Public feeling and indignation ran very high against these miscreants, and on the day before that assigned for the trial three gentlemen of position at the bar called on my father, who was then the Dean of the Faculty of Advocates, to represent to him their fear that the prisoners would not have a fair trial, and to request him as head of their body to undertake the defence'. So it was arranged that Sir James Moncreiff should appear for Burke, and Cockburn for Macdougal.[8] Edwards, on the other hand, claims that the two eminent lawyers also had a political motive for coming to the defence of Burke and Macdougal – 'with a view to discredit a Tory administration they detested, and against which they had a long-standing and active enmity.[9]

It must have been, for Sir James, both a difficult and a distasteful task. There was almost no time to prepare a defence, and in addition to that, he came in for a good deal of public criticism for undertaking it at all. His son did not attend the actual trial, but acting as a guide to his uncle, Campbell Robertson, on leave from India, mingled with the crowd outside the court. There they were obliged to hear 'the most extreme expression of reproach used, in regard to the counsel for the prisoners, altho' they were among the most popular residents in the city. It was thought wicked and immoral to defend such monsters.'[10]

By all accounts, Sir James' speech was a remarkable achievement, and according to his son, 'has always been admired as a model of – a triumph of logic.....I know of no speech of modern times to compare to it, except Garrow's speech in the case of Patch, tried for the murder of Mr Bligh, about the beginning of the century.'[11] Counsel for Burke made no attempt to defend the character of his client, but instead argued that on the evidence as it stood, the crimes could just as plausibly have been committed by Hare – 'that cold-blooded acknowledged villain', who had saved his own skin by giving evidence for the Crown.[12] If that evidence were to be rejected, then the case against Burke was insufficiently conclusive to justify a conviction. But the jury would have none of it. Exhausted by a trial which lasted from the morning of one day, and through the night to the morning of the next, they took less than an hour to find Burke guilty.

Henry Cockburn, counsel for Macdougal, had an easier task, but Moncreiff commended him nevertheless for 'a brilliant effort, but of rhetoric more than of logic.'[13] It had been agreed in advance by the two defence counsel that Sir James would speak first, on being assured by Cockburn that the latter would say nothing to prejudice the case for Burke. The Dean should have remembered that he was dealing with a fellow lawyer. 'Gentlemen of the jury', Cockburn began, 'I appear solely for the woman. In what I have to say to you I shall assume, <u>altho' of course after what you have heard from the Dean I cannot admit</u>, that Burke committed this murder.'[14] The outcome was the conviction of Burke, and the acquittal of Helen Macdougal for lack of sufficient evidence.[15] Moncreiff was told later that after the verdict was announced, Burke turned to Macdougal and said to her, 'You are safe Nelly' – a remark Moncreiff described as 'a touch of nature not without pathos'.[16] The comment tells us at least as much about Moncreiff as it does about Burke, though Burke himself had insisted all along that Macdougal was innocent.[17] Cockburn recorded a very similar comment on Burke's part, on whose character he remarked, 'Except that he murdered, Burke was a sensible, and what might be called a respectable man; not at all ferocious in his general manner, sober, correct in all his other habits, and kind to his relations.'[18]

Dining with the Moncreiffs a day or two later, Cockburn could not refrain from reminding them of his success, and remarked 'I want to recommend to you, Lady Moncreiff, a most respectable person, of whom I know something, and who is anxious to get a situation. She would be invaluable in a nursery where there are many children,' 'Who is she?' 'Her name is Helen Macdougal – a relation of my wife.' Friendships have been destroyed for less, but not on this occasion.[19]

The Burke case is thus described by Moncreiff in his *Reminiscences* in some detail, and it clearly made a long lasting impression on him. Not perhaps until he himself became involved in the Madeleine Smith case some thirty years later did a trial in Scotland arouse such public interest and scandal. What effect it had, if any, on his decision to follow his father into the legal profession can be no more than speculation.

But it was in the same year as the Burke case that Moncreiff, aged eighteen 'took leave of the Arts classes and began to buckle on my petty armour for my coming profession of the law. Oh! How I hated it!' To a certain extent he felt at home with Civil Law, taught by 'my able and cultured friend Douglas Cheape,.....But oh! The pressure of that mass of what sounded on my ears as a barbaric and very stupid jargon, which was called Scots Law, or Conveyancing.'[20] (The modern student might have found the Civil Law course even more baffling – until the middle of the nineteenth century the lectures were delivered in Latin.)[21] Only later, did he come to know better. 'Indeed in spite of the honest and intense aversion with which she at first inspired me, I knew I should come to know her, and probably like her. Well, we have now known each other long enough to speak our mind. I not only like her, but I admire her. She is the Queen of sciences.' Nevertheless he obviously found ploughing his way through the legal jargon involved an uphill task. 'The day however did come, when I had to read Craig's De Feudis, and Stair's Institutes from end to end, as tho' they had been as the "Antiquary" or as "Ivanhoe", and the discipline was as irksome as my worst fears had anticipated.'[22]

In later years, long after the hard grind of mastering Scots Law was behind him, Moncreiff was to address professional audiences on what he considered to be the essential elements of the law curriculum. These included 'The law of nature and nations'; European municipal law, civil law, canon law, and the general principles of European jurisprudence, the constitutional law of Great Britain, including that of Scotland, 'while the next division was the Scottish municipal law, including real property, mercantile law, personal rights and obligations, and criminal law.'[23] None of this would be completely unfamiliar to a modern Scottish law student

But that was for the future. For the present, he had examinations to pass. In 1832 Moncreiff had satisfied the examiners in Civil Law, and a year later was faced with a severe test in Scots Law, never, as we have seen, his favourite subject. The examination took the form of rigorous questioning by the then Dean of the Faculty, John Hope, and the submission and defence of a thesis of one thousand words, written in Latin. Moncreiff's thesis was entitled 'De eo per quem factum erit quominus quis in judicio sistat.' [Commonly translated as 'One who prevents another appearing in court'.] This is in fact the title of a chapter from Justinian's *Digest,* and the normal practice in the nineteenth century and into the twentieth was for the Faculty to assign such a chapter title as the dissertation topic which formed part of the test for admission to the profession.[24] The author of the thesis was then required to engage in a defence of his argument, before his candidacy for admission to the profession was finally put to the vote of the Faculty.[25]

Moncreiff was of course successful. That hurdle surmounted, he was then introduced formally to the Lord President in the robing room, to don gown and wig, and embark on the profession which he was to follow without a break until retirement in 1888. In his Reminiscences, Moncreiff later described the event with characteristic self deprecation:

'It was', he wrote, 'a serious and agitating affair. A bench of ancient Advocates was appointed to try me, and other similar victims. The judgment hall was a subterranean vault, I believe the ancient torture chamber of the Scottish Privy Council, gruesomely lit by oil lamps. Stripped of its externals the ordeal was not severe. Slender as my juridical lore was, it was equal to the not unreasonable strain which was put on it.' But he was not to get off quite so lightly. '"One more question, Sir", said the Chairman (a certain Norman Hill, too genial and good-looking for his office). "Can you tell me the meaning of the phrase 'Causa data, causa non secuta'. I owned I was at a loss, when Minos said, "Never plead a cause, until you have got the fee," and with this grinned and dismissed me.' 'The report of the Tribunal was favourable. The other formalities were completed, and I stood forth to the world of Scots Law, as a duly qualified recipient of fees to any amount, which the wisdom or the folly of the learned might think fit.'[26]

Since Moncreiff's induction had taken place in March, at the end of the winter session 1832-3, he was obliged to wait until May before embarking on his new career in earnest. Like the central character of his 'novel', *A Visit to my Discontented Cousin',* who 'had actually received instructions from a real attorney on three occasions in two years and a half'.[27] 'Moncreiff', comments Wilson Bain, 'did not burst comet-like upon the forensic world'.[28] Perhaps the reluctance of attorneys to engage him had something to do with his Whig politics, or the disadvantage of having a judge as a father, or more likely his youth and inexperience. But in fact the opportunity to pursue his very first case came later that spring, as he accompanied his father on the Northern Circuit to Inverness, and was engaged to defend a Highland postal employee accused of theft. 'I remember,' he wrote many years later, 'the old dingy courthouse with its worn stone steps, …the utter bewilderment I had as an unfledged member of the bar was overmastered by a kind of senseless enthusiasm for the wild Highlander in the dock.'[29]

This was one Ewen Mackintoshen, a Post Office runner from Benbecula, who was 'unjustly accused of having converted to very private uses certain bank notes [five pounds] entrusted to him. He was the wildest looking creature I ever saw. A Celtic kyloe[30] – a nowt, as they are called, has much the same expression in its stare as his look to the jury had. If he was acting stolid unconsciousness he did it very well.' [It turned out later that as he spoke no English he had not understood a word of the proceedings] 'As for his counsel, the state of internal excitement which possessed him was intense – altho' he was able so far to subdue it as to present a reasonably sane exterior.' Moncreiff found in the accused 'the helpless lower animal look …..which appealed to my sympathies in a way which was no doubt ridiculous,' but 'perhaps the jury pitied him too, for they found the charge not proved.'

The effect of the verdict on Mackintoshen, who must have understood that much at least, was electric. 'He skipped out of the dock – executed a Highland fling in the stone passage outside – flung his plaid around him – dashed down the staircase, and was off like a shot to Benbecula.' Only much later did Moncreiff allow himself a few niggling doubts about the innocence of his first client.[31] At the time his personal satisfaction with his success was considerable, all the more so on account of the kind remarks on his performance by one of the two judges – Lord Medwyn – the other of course being Moncreiff's own father. Forty-three years later, in 1876, when Moncreiff himself first sat as a judge on the Northern Circuit, the Inverness Corporation conferred on him the freedom of the Burgh, referring to the fact that he had made his first speech there, and referring also to Lord Medwyn's words of praise.[32]

In 1833, Moncreiff's entry into the legal profession was marked by his induction into the Marrowbone Club, a club for rising young advocates, the object of which, he wrote later, was 'of course mutual improvement, but also to talk Whig politics, eat marrowbones, and Beef-Steaks, and to drink port in an obscure tavern on the Fleshmarket Close.' Its lowly surroundings, he explained, 'indicated its aristocratic and exclusive character.' A special Marrowbone Club spoon in solid silver, bearing the image of a marrowbone and inscribed with the Moncreiff family crest and the name of James Moncreiff, is still in the possession of the family. A peculiarity of the club was that no judge was allowed to remain a member, and if one of their number was so unfortunate as to be promoted to the bench, a note was inserted next to his name in the list of members: 'Out on the Bench.'[33]

The following year, 1834, Moncreiff married Isabella Bell, the daughter of Robert Bell, himself an advocate and Procurator of the Church of Scotland. They had first met some seventeen year earlier, when Moncreiff was no more than six or seven years old. It was one of those occasions which tend to stick in the memory, even if the eventual outcome had not been as happy as it undoubtedly was. The young Moncreiff had been invited to a children's party at the house of Robert Bell, an old friend of his father's. 'My mother', he recalled, 'had dressed me, as I thought, very fine: and had fastened my frill with a little hair brooch of her own, set in pearls. The family consisted of one son, a year older than myself, and one little girl, two years younger. As I was about to leave, I missed my brooch, and burst into tears about it – and the little girl came up to me to dry my eyes.' The brooch was found – and so, as time resolved, was something else. The brother became Moncreiff's closest friend, and the little girl became his wife. They were engaged in March 1834 and were married on the 12th September of the same year, Dr Chalmers performing the ceremony.[34]

The marriage was extremely happy, and lasted for forty seven years. 'I lost her,' Moncreiff wrote in his memoirs, 'on 19 Decr. 1881 – and thenceforth the blackness of darkness.'[35]

Before his marriage, Moncreiff had lived with his father at 47 Moray Place, but now the young couple moved in with Isabella's father, Robert Bell, at 20 St. Andrews Square. This arrangement had been at Bell's suggestion – he had lost his own wife three years previously, and his daughter was unwilling to leave him to look after himself. They all lived together in Bell's house for some eight years.[36] The arrangement also suited the Moncreiffs, since it was to take some time for James' legal practice to develop, but around 1840 he began to be more successful,[37] so that the family, including Bell, was able to move to 3 Moray Place, and later to 15 Great Stuart Street. Both addresses are still extant.[38] The family continued to grow, and by 1850, when Moncreiff was appointed Solicitor-General for Scotland, there were five sons and two daughters.[39] Three of the sons, Henry James, James William and Frederick Charles, followed their father into the legal profession. Henry James, who succeeded to the title of Lord Moncreiff of Tullibole on his father's death in 1895, became a Judge of the Court of Session in 1888. James William, became a prominent solicitor; and Frederick Charles, a Puisne Judge of the Supreme Courts of Mauritius and Ceylon. The youngest daughter, Marianne Eliza, married Lord Kinross, a Lord Advocate and Lord Justice General of the Court of Session.

This was in the future. Moncreiff continued to work conscientiously at his law practice, and in due course he was to be rewarded with engagement in some of the most notable – even notorious – legal cases in the mid-Victorian period. These began with the series of cases before the Court of Session between 1838 and 1843, which led more or less directly to the Disruption of the Church of Scotland, and the creation of the breakaway Free Church.

These cases, and some others, will be dealt with in subsequent chapters, so it will be sufficient at this stage merely to summarise. What we will call the Disruption Cases were sparked off by the acceptance by the General Assembly of the Church of Scotland in 1834 of a proposal by Moncreiff's father, (now a Court of Session judge with the title of Lord Moncreiff), of what became known as the 'Veto Law'.[40] This enactment was designed to limit the powers of lay patrons to appoint ministers to vacant parishes under their control, by requiring that if the proposed appointee failed to receive the support of a majority of heads of families in the parish who were members of the church, the appointment could not go ahead. Lord Moncreiff was almost certainly not himself opposed to 'lay patronage' as such, but wished to curb what he and others saw as abuses of the system. Over the next nine years, some 150 ministers were appointed to vacant parishes, and in only ten was there any difficulty caused by the application of the Veto Law.[41] But in four of these – the parishes of Auchterarder, Marnoch, Lethendy and Culsalmond – the patrons and their protégés took the issue to court, arguing that the Veto Law deprived them of their civil rights of patronage. Similar issues also arose in connection with the Chapels Act, adopted by the General Assembly in the same year as the Veto Act, and which sought to extend to presbyteries the power to create new parishes within the boundaries of existing ones. In every one of the thirteen cases[42] arising from the terms of these enactments taken to the Court of Session, the court ruled in favour of the patron. Increasingly the Evangelicals in the General Assembly – the majority party after 1834 – came to see the decisions of the Court as directly encroaching on the spiritual independence of the Church, until the whole affair blew up in 1843 as the Great Disruption. Around one third of all the ministers in the Church walked out of the Assembly with scarce a backward glance, and formed the Free Church of Scotland.[43]

These issues and events will be discussed in detail over the next three chapters. It is worth pointing our in advance, however, just what a 'family affair' these legal battles over the rights of lay patrons turned out to be. Lord Moncreiff, the father, had in a sense begun the whole process with his Veto Act, and continued to be involved in several of the court cases as a judge. Both of his elder sons, the Rev. Henry and James, were involved on the side of the presbyteries – the one through his writings, the other as junior counsel in a number of the cases. James' father-in-law, Robert Bell, Procurator of the Church of Scotland, also served as counsel in several cases, sometimes with James as his junior colleague.

There can be little doubt that in these cases, James Moncreiff not only represented the presbyteries against the claims of the patrons, but his sympathies lay with them also. All three Moncreiffs (though not Robert Bell) joined the Free Church after 1843. But it is never necessary for an advocate to identify with the position of his client. In the next high profile case in which Moncreiff was engaged for the defence – the trial of Chartist leader Henry Ranken on charges of conspiracy and sedition – it is certain that the former did not share the political beliefs of the latter, though he did find him attractive and impressive as an individual. It is also clear from the account of the trial that Moncreiff worked hard on behalf of his client, and while he failed to get the case against Ranken actually dismissed, he did succeed in persuading the Court of Justiciary to drop the charge of conspiracy, and to impose a minimal sentence of only four months imprisonment on the count of sedition.[44]

Many contemporary commentators praised Moncreiff for the way he conducted his cases – fair minded, courteous, dispassionate. Not for him the histrionics of more flamboyant advocates. 'He never allowed himself to be carried away by fervour of conviction or exuberance of language.'[45] This approach served him well in many cases, especially when acting for the defence. It may have been less of an asset when he was called upon to act as prosecutor. In his account of the Chartist trial of 1848, Henry Cockburn commented of James Moncreiff that 'He is as likely to reach the highest honours of his profession purely by deserving them, as anyone in it,' and described him as 'a good lawyer, a pleasing and forcible speaker, a most agreeable writer, judicious, honourable and friendly'.[46] In 1850, Moncreiff was appointed Solicitor-General for Scotland,[47] and in the following year was elected Member of Parliament for Leith Burghs, and appointed Lord Advocate. The role of the Lord Advocate in the mid-nineteenth century was multi-faceted - a combination of legal adviser on Scottish affairs to the government of the day, and, as the office of Secretary of State had been done away with in the eighteenth century, effectively 'Minister for Scotland', responsible only to the Secretary of State for the Home Department in London. It was a position Moncreiff held on three separate occasions – 1851-8, 1859-66, and 1868-9, and for much of that time (1858-69) was also Dean of the Faculty of Advocates. His heavy responsibilities as Lord Advocate undoubtedly got in the way of his active involvement in legal practice at home, but in 1857 he was called upon to prosecute in the most notorious criminal case of the century in Scotland – the trial of Madeleine Smith, charged with the murder of her lover, Emile L'Angelier. Famously, the case against the accused was found 'Not Proven', and she walked free. Doubts have continued to be expressed to this day as to the soundness of the verdict, and it could be argued that on that occasion Moncreiff's too delicate handling of the prosecution was a contributory factor in the outcome.[48]

The Disruption cases, the Chartist trial, and the Madeleine Smith case, were only a few – though certainly the most newsworthy – of the cases in which Moncreiff was engaged throughout his legal career. In very many of them he acted for the defenders against the pursuers, and seems to have been more comfortable in that role than when engaged in a prosecution on behalf of the Crown. But in the next high profile case he took on after Madeleine Smith – the unusual Yelverton case – he appeared as leading counsel on behalf of the pursuer – the unhappy but persistent Theresa Longworth. On that occasion it might be said that Moncreiff won the battle but lost the war.[49] The outcome of the hearing before the Court of Session was that Longworth was granted the declarator she sought to confirm the validity of her marriage to Major Yelverton,[50] only to lose the case later before the House of Lords.[51] Nevertheless, in the long run the case bore positive fruit in the form of the Marriage Act of 1870,[52] which at long last repealed the law which forbade the marriage in Ireland of Catholics with Protestants.

Nor should we overlook the fact that while building up an increasingly successful practice as an advocate, Moncreiff was also developing a parallel career as a writer – principally of review articles – and pursuing what was to be his lifelong interest in politics. The two of course were closely connected. In 1844, still in his early thirties, Moncreiff was invited to contribute to the first number of a new journal, the *North British Review*. His subject was close to his own heart – Francis Jeffrey's contributions to the *Edinburgh Review*[53] – since Jeffrey, like Henry Cockburn, and Andrew Rutherfurd, was both a professional colleague and a family friend of the Moncreiffs. 'A more congenial task', Moncreiff wrote later, 'could not have been allotted to me. I had always paid a neophyte's worship to the Edinburgh review, and to Jeffrey as its tutelary Divinity. I used to pore over the early numbers until I almost knew them by heart, and recognizing in Jeffrey not only a great Editor, and a great pleader, but a great political leader, I had always held him as sacrosanct, a glory apart. I little thought how great a harvest I was to reap from this simple act of willing worship.'[54]

Jeffrey indeed was greatly touched by the warmth of Moncreiff's article. One practical outcome of this relationship was that Moncreiff was invited to contribute more articles to the *North British* by the then editor, Professor Empson, who just happened to be Jeffrey's son-in-law. These included the review of the first two volumes of Macaulay's *History* in 1849, an article which was largely adulatory, and drew sincere thanks from its subject, and a commendation from Professor Empson.[55] By 1857, and his review of the third and fourth volumes of the *History*, we detect a more genuinely critical approach, in which the strengths of the historian are fairly commended, but his weaknesses in scholarship are not glossed over. The principal charge against Macaulay was that he failed to consult documentary materials which were potentially available to him, and that as a result his interpretation of specific events, most notably the massacre of Glencoe, was unsound. Thus while he was commended for making use of some of the wealth of family archives in English country houses, he was criticised for overlooking others, such as 'the remarkable collection' of papers at Littlecote House, Wiltshire, the seat of the Popham family, where William of Orange had slept after the Conference of Hungerford. More serious was Macaulay's account of the lead up to the Glencoe massacre, in which he sought to minimise the responsibility of King William, and put much of the blame for the tragedy on the shoulders of the Marquis of Breadalbane. In his review, Moncreiff accepted Macaulay's account of the roles of Breadalbane, Argyll, and Dalrymple, but could not accept the proposition that the King himself had been ignorant of their plans, and had signed the order to 'extirpate that set of thieves', the MacDonalds, without reading it. Documents had existed, and their existence had been known to Macaulay but not used by him, demonstrating that William had been kept regularly informed of the progress of the plans to subjugate the men of the Highlands. Moncreiff likewise had access to the collection, and included several of the relevant letters in his review.[56] While Moncreiff himself published no major historical works, in his reviews, speeches and addresses he displayed both a considerable body of historical knowledge, and a sure grasp of historical method.[57]

In fact Moncreiff had made Macaulay's acquaintance long before this, when after the latter's first election to Parliament in 1839 Moncreiff and one or two Whig friends had joined the Anti-Corn Law League. This action did not go down well with those 'of the more advanced party [i.e. the Radicals] who looked upon free corn as ground especially protected, and to be strictly preserved from Whig trespassers.'[58] Specifically, it brought down on Moncreiff's head a hostile speech from the Radical leader, Duncan McLaren – the first, but by no means the last occasion of a clash between the two on political issues.

Chapter 4
Chalmers, Church Extension, and the Moderatorship

In May, 1843, the Church of Scotland was torn apart by a cataclysm. After a decade of increasingly bitter wrangling – the so-called Ten Years' Conflict – 451 ministers of the Established Church, rising eventually to 474,[1] signed a Deed of Demission, whereby they renounced their churches and manses, and formed the Free Church of Scotland. A key figure in this development was Dr Thomas Chalmers, leader of the Evangelicals in the General Assembly, whose relations with the Moncreiff family were sometimes cordial and supportive, as over the issue of lay patronage, but on occasion were fraught and abrasive. In particular they fell out over Chalmers' management of the church extension scheme, designed to build many new churches to cater for the growing working class in Scotland's towns and cities. This conflict came to a head over the election of the Moderator of the General Assembly in 1837.

Ostensibly, the principal issue at stake leading to the Disruption was the 'right of patronage' – that is the power of a rich patron, typically a powerful landowner, to install a minister in a parish, regardless of the wishes of the congregation. But there was a much larger issue of principle involved here. Many in the Church believed that this alleged right, and the apparent support given to it by government and the courts, infringed the spiritual independence of the Church, and was in any case illegal, under the terms of the *Claim of Right* of 1689, ratified by the 1707 Act of Union. In 1834 the Assembly passed the Veto Act, proposed by Lord Moncreiff, declaring that a minister could not be 'intruded' into a parish against the wishes of a majority of the congregation, but this was followed by a series of court cases with outcomes incompatible with the convictions of the ascendant Evangelical Party in the Assembly. By the early 1840s the stage was set for the final walkout – the Great Disruption of 1843 – described by one modern commentator as 'the most important event in the history of Scotland in the nineteenth century.'[2] And indeed there is a strong argument for seeing the significance of the Disruption as extending well beyond the boundaries of the national church. As Stewart Brown expressed it in the early nineteen-nineties, 'The Disruption was not only the breakup of the national religious establishment, it was also a disruption in Scottish identity, a radical break from its Reformation and Covenanting past, and a turning away from the vision of a unified godly commonwealth. The

Disruption undermined the Presbyterian nationalism that had shaped early modern Scotland, with its ideal of the democratic intellect preserved in parish schools, kirk sessions and presbyteries.'[3] And as some would argue, by destroying the national bulwark of the Established Church, the Disruption weakened the ability of the Scottish nation to withstand the siren call of Anglicisation.

It is difficult for us, in the more secular age of the twenty-first century, to empathise with the many ministers and like-minded individuals who contemplated abandoning the certainties of life in the Church of Scotland for the unknowns of life outside it – all over an issue of deeply held principle. To leave the Church meant leaving the comfort and relative security of their homes, their churches, their stipends, and their status, yet they did so, according to Moncreiff 'in confidence of prevailing, risking all worldly possessions, but with the applause not only of Scotland but of Europe. Such was their answer to the Strathbogie Interdict.'[4] Some forty years after the Disruption, the Rev. Dr. Thomas Brown, on the authority of the Committee of the Free Church of Scotland on the Records of Disruption Ministers, published an extensive volume called *The Annals of the Disruption*, which drew on interviews, letters and memoirs of those personally involved in the great events of 1843 and after.[5] Typical of many was a Mr. Taylor of Flisk: 'I write at the distance of six years from the Disruption, and every time I look back I am filled with thankfulness to God for the part He led me to act in that trying time. No regrets or longings even for the temporalities have ever disquieted my mind.' The only occasion, so he claimed, on which he felt 'somewhat overcome', was on the evening when he left his manse, when, 'having sent every person and thing away, I remained behind, and the empty house resounded to the departing tread, and I turned the key on the outer door, and my back upon the house and church, in which I had hoped to have spent years of usefulness and happiness.' These regrets soon passed, and 'gave place to brighter feelings when I considered the blessed results which God speedily brought out of the Disruption to this neighbourhood.'[6]

One wonders how genuinely typical this positive attitude was amongst the great majority of ministers, who now had no manses to house them and their families, and no church into which to welcome their congregations. Amongst the many disadvantages and frustrations of the post-1843 experience was the reluctance of many landowners to provide new sites for Free Church churches – an issue which James Moncreiff spoke about publicly and forcibly.[7] But often it was the lay members of Free Church congregations who also suffered for the support they offered to their ministers. One correspondent wrote of a 'reign of terror' in his parish.[8] There were threats to exclude Free Churchmen from burial in parish churchyards. Brown cites one case where female 'collectors' – presumably women who collected funds for the Church – who were employed in a cotton factory, were told that if they continued to act in that capacity they would be thrown out of work. In another parish the minister reported that: 'About fifty servants and day-labourers, several of them with weak families and destitute of means, have been dismissed and thrown out of employment, and everything done against them to render their adherence bitter.'[9]

But there were many who refused to give in to pressure and intimidation. There was an owner of a tenement, who was warned that if he joined the Free Church, he was likely to lose his property to pay legal expenses. 'The plain working man was somewhat disconcerted by this appeal to his fears, and forthwith repeated the matter to his wife, who had a firmer faith. She encouraged her husband, and said, "Never mind Peter, just say to the gentleman, better lose our house than lose our souls."'[10] Only through time were passions allowed to cool, sites found for new churches, stipends paid, and even a new Free Church College founded – New College in Edinburgh – a mere three years after the Disruption.

Three generations of Moncreiffs were deeply involved in this controversy, broadly on the side of the Evangelical party in the General Assembly, led until his death in 1827 by the Rev. Sir Harry Moncreiff. His son, Lord Moncreiff senior, was the proposer of the controversial Veto Act of 1834, and as a member of the Scottish judiciary, several times sat in judgment on cases brought before the Court of Session relating to the powers of the Church courts. Sir Harry's grandson, the subject of this biography, wrote briefs for the presbyteries which refused to accept their patrons' nominees, and frequently spoke at public meetings on the issues.[11]. According to Moncreiff himself, he 'was engaged as counsel in some of the law suits which resulted from the decision in the Auchterarder case, and they were all decided adversely to the Church.'[12] In fact, Moncreiff is listed as counsel in seven of the thirteen cases before the Court of Session, spawned by the Veto Act. In addition, his father-in-law Robert Bell, the Procurator of the Church of Scotland, with whom he was very close, also acted as counsel in eight of the thirteen cases and in five of those both Bell and Moncreiff were engaged on the same side of the argument.

James Moncreiff was himself a member of the General Assembly in 1842 and 1843, and was appointed to an important Commission of the Assembly, formed in 1842, to try to resolve some of the outstanding issues before the crisis facing the Church became unavoidable.[13] Nor must we overlook the part played by his older brother, the Rev. (later Sir) Henry Moncreiff, a staunch supporter of his father's views on church affairs. In 1840, Henry published an extensive open letter to Lord Melbourne, urging the Government to intervene in the growing crisis over the judicial independence of the Church.[14] Henry not only joined the Free Church at the time of the Disruption, but also in later years published a number of books defending its position, including *A Vindication of the Free Church Claim of Right*, published in Edinburgh in 1877, and *The Free Church Principle: its Character and History,* in 1883. Then, as we have seen, there was a fourth member of the family – not a member by name, but by marriage – Robert Bell, James Moncreiff's father-in-law, who also became involved both personally and professionally in the developing controversies.

The origins of this dispute lay well back in Scotland's past – before even the union of the Crowns in 1603. Lay patronage had been a feature in Scotland since the creation of the parish system in the twelfth century. Abolished by the first Book of Discipline in 1560, and replaced by giving congregations the right to choose their own minister, it was revived after 1567, only to be denounced as a grievance in the Second Book of 1581. In 1690, following the Glorious Revolution and the re-establishment of Presbyterianism in the Church of Scotland, lay patronage in Scotland was abolished, and responsibility for the settlement of ministers placed jointly on the shoulders of kirk sessions and heritors. The Act of Union of 1707 assured Scots that Parliament would not meddle with the Scottish religious establishment. Nevertheless, in 1712 the right of lay patronage in Scotland was restored by the Bolingbroke ministry in the Church Patronage (Scotland) Act.[15] Under the terms of the Act, a patron, who might be a landowner, or in about one third of cases, the Crown itself, was entitled to present his nominee to be inducted as minister of the parish. Such a nominee would be either already an ordained minister, or a probationary. In the former case, the presbytery would admit him to the charge. If a probationary, then the presbytery would take him 'on trials', to satisfy itself as to his morals, education and doctrinal orthodoxy. [For those unfamiliar with the system of governance in the Church of Scotland at the time, and indeed since, presbyteries consisted of ministers and elders from parishes within a certain district. The presbytery had a general jurisdiction over the churches within its district, subject to the authority of the regional synod, and ultimately that of the General Assembly – the highest authority in the Established Church.] If he met these criteria, then he would be ordained and inducted. The presentation of a nominee was accompanied by what was known as a 'call' – a document signed by the male heads of families in the parish, to confirm that they were satisfied with him as their minister. This 'call' was regarded by many then and later as a mere formality, but in due course was to take on a much greater significance.

The Patronage Act was vigorously opposed by the General Assembly of the Church, which each year from 1712 to 1784 adopted a formal protest against it, but in practice the Church authorities remained powerless to bring about a change of heart on the part of a government largely indifferent to Scottish affairs. While opposition to lay patronage remained, by the early nineteenth century this opposition had become relatively quiescent. Within the Assembly itself, the principal division was between the 'Moderates', who enjoyed a majority until the early 1830s, and the 'Evangelicals'. The Moderates, according to one recent commentator, were 'ministers who were appointed under the system of patronage.. ...well educated, rather effective in debate with the rationalist critics of the day, good at composing elegant sermons, and of some social standing – but rather lacking in enthusiasm'.[16] The Evangelicals had their origins in the Popular party of the eighteenth century – orthodox Calvinists, they were committed to parish ministry, and as such supported the rights of parishioners in the selection of their own ministers, and naturally opposed lay patronage, which was seen as symbolic of the subordination of the Church to the landowning class. After 1733 lay patronage was the issue which saw thousands leave the Church of Scotland, and find a home in one of the protestant secession churches

Nevertheless, during the first quarter of the nineteenth century, divisions between the two factions had been on the wane for some time, due in large part to the enlightened leadership of the Evangelicals by James' grandfather, Sir Harry Moncreiff, a man who commanded almost universal respect in Church matters. According to Lord Cockburn, admittedly a family friend, Sir Harry, 'throughout his life...was the oracle of the whole Church in matters not factious, and the steady champion of the popular side. In comparison with him, every other Churchman who has appeared since I knew the world must withdraw. Nothing I could say would express one-half of my affectionate and reverential admiration of this great man'.[17] JG Lockhart, Walter Scott's son-in-law and biographer, was even more fulsome in his praise of Sir Harry. 'His air,' he wrote, 'is decidedly that of a man of birth and station...he holds himself with the true mien of a dignitary...and looks (under favour) very much like a Lord Bishop receiving the bows of his country curates at a visitation...Nobody can look on the Baronet without perceiving that nature intended him to be a ruler, not a subject...Had he come into Parliament, I have very little doubt his peculiar faculties would have made him as powerful a person there as he is here in the General

Assembly of the Kirk.'[18] Moncreiff's own love and admiration for his grandfather has been made abundantly clear in an earlier chapter.

In the early years of the nineteenth century, then, the question of lay patronage seemed no longer to be a serious issue. Sir Harry himself declared in 1818, with apparent equanimity, that he believed patronage to be now well established. In a work posthumously published in 1833, *A Brief Account of the Constitution of the Church of Scotland*, he wrote that 'the controversies relating to patronage are certainly now, in great measure, at an end…..It would be equally unwise and inexpedient to disturb the decision of more than half a century, and to agitate the country anew by controversies, which, by the influence of government on one side would always have the same termination.'[19] But that did not mean necessarily that Sir Harry would have opposed his son's attempt to restrict the power of patronage. According to Cockburn, in certain circumstances, Sir Harry would have 'resorted to some sort of popular restraint over patronage, the Church's power to introduce he would never have permitted to have questioned…..The spiritual independence of the Church he would have laid his head on the block rather than abandon,…and he would have deemed that independence at an end if the Court of Session could annul the Church's sentences of suspension or deposition.'[20] These are virtually the very principles which lay at the root of the Disruption.

We do not know exactly when Sir Harry's *Account* was written – obviously well before the date of publication. It contained a foreword by his son, Lord Moncreiff the elder, who, in pursuing the principle behind the Veto Act of the right of parishioners to enter their dissent to the appointment of a minister, was about to reopen these unlooked for controversies, and who may have hoped that Sir Harry's wise words from beyond the grave might have some influence over those who were about to plunge the established church into turmoil.

Be that as it may, by 1827 Sir Harry was dead, and the leadership of the Evangelicals passed into other hands – principally those of Dr Andrew Thomson,[21] and then, on his sudden and untimely death in 1831, Dr Thomas Chalmers[22] – both very different from Sir Harry in temper and opinions. Thomson and Chalmers were both powerful personalities – Thomson in particular being a notable orator, a supporter of social reform and popular education, as well as a passionate advocate for the abolition of slavery. Moreover, as became increasingly evident, the mood within the Evangelical party was also changing – less prepared to accept compromise, more dogmatic in matters of doctrine – and while, to some extent, this change of mood may be ascribed to the new leadership, it might be more accurate to say, with recent commentators, that 'probably it is an error to blame Thomson for the rising passion and uncompromising spirit with which ecclesiastical issues came to be judged; his passion was not so much a cause as a symptom of rising temperatures.'[23]

Why were these temperatures rising? One might point in the first instance to the great changes taking place in the Scottish economy, and the social and political ramifications of these changes. The development of the Industrial Revolution in Britain had been accelerating since the middle of the previous century. In Scotland this largely took the form of an expansion of the iron and steel industries, together with, of course, coal mining. These industries were highly labour intensive, and so called into being new communities, many of them as yet ill served by the Church. They also, and this was a not insignificant factor, led to an increase in the immigration of Roman Catholics amongst the workforce. In 1829 the Catholic Emancipation Act had removed many of the political disabilities under which they had suffered for centuries. Then again, at a national level, the demand was growing for an extension of the political franchise in favour of the emergent middle classes, and to provide for representation in Parliament of the great new cities, like Manchester. This demand was to culminate in the Great Reform Act of 1832 – forced through by the Whig administration of Earl Grey. It is almost certainly no coincidence that the general, though certainly not exclusive, tendency amongst the Evangelicals in the Assembly was also Whiggish. The Moncreiffs themselves were a very typical example, but there were important exceptions – Thomas Chalmers for one was a Tory.

Lord Cockburn, writing in 1838, saw a clear correlation between the rise of the more radical wing of the Evangelicals – whom he called the 'Wild Party' – and the issues of national politics of the day. 'From the beginning of Principal Robertson's reign till about four years ago, the Wild party was Whiggish, because the essence of the system introduced by him, and continued by his successors, was to repress the people, to uphold patronage even in its grossest abuses, and to discourage religious zeal.' In 1830, then, when the Whigs came to power, a natural alliance developed between them and this branch of the Church, and this in turn led to a situation where, from being a 'hopeless minority' in the Assembly, the Evangelicals now came to dominate it. This was due, according to Callum Brown, to increased evangelical representation in the new burgh councils, which were entitled to send commissioners to the Assembly, and so leading in 1834 to an Evangelical majority.[24] Amongst the consequences of this change were 'the veto law, the admission of the ministers of the chapels of ease and the suppression of the Moderate party, being the three objects which the Wild had most ardently desired. But the Whigs soon found they had raised a most impractical power. It was imbued with fanaticism.'[25]

'Chapels of ease', it should be explained, were churches in industrial towns created and paid for by private enterprise. Many in the Church were critical of these institutions, since they diverted church collections from the support of the poor, and could be misused as an excuse to avoid the services of an unpopular minister.[26]

If it were the case that, by the second decade of the century, the agitation against lay patronage had largely subsided, then one factor in its decline in importance was that many patrons in Scotland had begun to accept the necessity of paying some attention to the wishes of their parishioners in the matter of the choice of ministers. This trend is highly significant, since the issue which was to take centre stage in the debates within the Church over the next two decades was the larger question of an extension of popular rights within the Church itself. And as it turned out, the question of lay patronage as an issue in Church politics returned as the touchstone of the democratisation of church affairs.

The Church Extension debate

It would be a mistake to portray the Church at this time as concerned only with the single issue of lay patronage. Just like the rest of Scottish society in the early to mid nineteenth century, the Church was itself changing, and doing so largely in response to the same social and economic forces as those which affected society at large. The Church authorities were very well aware, for example, of the need to provide access to its communion for the growing proportion of the population without parishes or churches. The campaign to raise funds to build new churches – the 'Church Extension' policy – was vigorously promoted by Thomas Chalmers – a campaign which was in due course to bring him into conflict with the Moncreiffs. This conflict was to an extent over the policy itself, or perhaps more accurately over party politics, but it was manifested even more damagingly over the nominations for the Moderatorship of the General Assembly in 1836 and 1837.

The campaign to increase church accommodation through the construction of more churches in urban areas had both central and local origins. In 1828 a Committee of the Assembly was formed to lobby the government on the issue, but little was achieved until 1833, when Chalmers was added to the Committee, and then in the following year made its convener.[27] Early that same year, impatient of government inaction, the Glasgow Association for Promoting the Interests of the Church of Scotland embarked on a five year plan to build 20 new churches, each capable of seating one thousand people. Funding for the plan was to be raised from private subscriptions, each church to cost £2000, with a further £2000 to be invested, the proceeds to pay for part of the minister's stipend. With the costs subsidised from this source, it would be possible to keep the seat rents at a level affordable by the poorer families, encouraging them to attend. This focus on provision for poor working class families was a central feature of this and subsequent schemes, which would include provision for poor relief and educational programmes. Within two months of its inauguration, that is by March 1834, £6,800 of the projected £80,000 had been subscribed. A similar scheme in Aberdeen had been embarked on in February of that year. [28]

At its annual meeting in May, the General Assembly was impressed with the potential of such arrangements. Chalmers and his Church Accommodation Committee were instructed to build on their success by first of all gathering statistical evidence, which would both demonstrate the need for new churches and identify where they should be located, and devise plans for raising the necessary funds. Chalmers duly embarked on a two part strategy – encouraging the formation of more local church building societies and the setting up of a central Church Accommodation Committee Fund, designed both to pay the administrative costs of the Committee and contribute to the costs of local societies in the more deprived areas of the towns and cities. These practical arrangements were underpinned by a clear vision of the desired outcome – the creation of small integrated urban parishes, communities in which all classes would be represented, providing spiritual support for the poorest working families, as well as for the middle and upper classes. A key element in this plan was the establishment of variable seat rents, to ensure that the labouring class was not excluded from church attendance for lack of means.

In order to provide an example on which other schemes could be modelled, Chalmers planned to erect a new church in the Cowgate, one of the poorest areas of Edinburgh. He approached the Edinburgh Town Council, with a request that they support the plan by transferring a clergyman from another of the city's churches, and continuing to pay his salary – thus enabling the seat rents to be kept as low as possible. This request the Town Council, dominated as it was by dissenters, firmly declined, so Chalmers settled on a new location in the Water of Leith – conveniently outside the Council's jurisdiction. Here two-thirds of the seats would be made available to poor families at affordable rents, with the remaining one third set at the full Edinburgh rate for the wealthier classes. 'Thus constituting a Church occupied by such a gradation of wealth and rank as is exhibited in our agricultural parishes.'[29]

As an aside, it is worth remarking on the fact that this insistence on the creation of communities, based on the concept of a rural ideal, and including the representation of all classes, was remarkably similar to the contemporary concept of 'systematic colonisation', promoted by Edward

Gibbon Wakefield. A key feature of Wakefieldism was that of 'planned emigration', under which would-be emigrants were to be screened to ensure a viable mix of classes, occupations and sexes. One of the few places within the British Empire where an attempt was made to put Wakefield's ideas into practice was New Zealand, notably the provinces of Christchurch and Otago. The Christchurch scheme was supported by the Church of England, while Otago, of course, was a Free Church colony, initiated only a very few years after the Disruption.[30]

An essential requirement for the success of his plan, as Chalmers saw it, was the provision by Parliament of an endowment grant, which would contribute to the stipends of what were known as the new *quoad sacra* churches, thus enabling the seat rents to be kept low. *Quoad sacra* parishes in Scotland were used for ecclesiastical purposes only. It was not unusual for several *quoad sacra* parishes to exist within a single civil parish, each with its own parish church. Earlier attempts to persuade government to loosen their purse strings were, as we have seen, ineffective, but by 1834 Chalmers was confident that the time was ripe for a new approach. Armed with statistics collected by local church building societies, and able to demonstrate that Scots were now contributing to the church accommodation programme, Chalmers dispatched a delegation (he himself was not well enough to travel) to negotiate with the Whig government led by Lord Melbourne. The delegation came prepared with a detailed shopping list; an initial annual grant of £6,600 to endow 66 new churches, to rise to £50,000 over time to endow the 500 new churches he believed would eventually be needed.

There followed a long drawn out and ultimately fruitless negotiation, which resulted, not in an offer of actual cash, but in a promise that the government would attempt to introduce an endowment bill into the next session of Parliament. But as the leader of the delegation, Charles Fergusson, warned Chalmers, the reliance of the Whigs in Parliament on the support of the Dissenters, might make it difficult for them to keep their promise. As it turned out, the Whig administration fell in November 1834, to be replaced by a Tory government led by Sir Robert Peel, and while undoubtedly Peel was more genuinely supportive on the endowment question, he too was the leader of a minority government, with very limited room for manoeuvre. Chalmers' friend at court, as it were, was the young William Gladstone, not yet the great Liberal leader of the future, but a newly elected MP, and a protégé of Peel. He advised Chalmers to waste no time in putting forward his bill for the endowment, which he did in January 1835. Peel's response could not have been more welcome. 'I do assure you,' he wrote to Chalmers later that month, 'that the Church of Scotland has few more attached friends among its own immediate members than myself...Your proposals are therefore addressed to one favourably disposed to them, and who will take them into very early consideration.'[31] Sure enough, the King's Speech in February included an undertaking that the government would consider how best to meet the need for more church accommodation.

As we shall see, it was Chalmers' approach to a Tory government which did much to alienate the Moncreiffs, and James Moncreiff in particular. As the latter wrote in his *Reminiscences*:

> the Evangelical party were for a year or two infatuated enough to believe that it was to Tory politicians they were to look for aid in the spread of Evangelical opinions: and Chalmers allowed himself to be ensnared for the time by adulations from such parties in his campaign in favour of Church Establishments. At a dinner given to Sir Robert Peel in Glasgow in 1835 it was stated that there were not twenty ministers in the Established Church who agreed with the Whig party: and Chalmers' delusion in this direction had been so fostered by English applause and London audiences, that he thought himself justified to read a solemn lecture to Lord Moncreiff and others, who were older and better adherents of Evangelical truth than himself, on subordinating, as he verbosely expressed it, their ecclesiastical to their political opinions.

'Lord Moncreiff,' his son went on, 'did not condescend to take public notice of this attack which was as baseless as it was unmannerly.' He did however approach Chalmers privately to ask what lay behind it, to which the answer was that he, Lord Moncreiff, had refused to concur in the condemnation of the Irish Education scheme of the Whig Government; and that he had defended the Church Commissioners in Scotland on some trivial matters of procedure. 'I have the correspondence', his son wrote, 'but events so ridiculously answered Chalmers, that I prefer not to stir the embers of a forgotten dispute between such men.'

Moncreiff was evidently greatly incensed on behalf of his father, and indeed also on behalf of his father-in-law, Robert Bell, another victim of Chalmers' invective. His response was to take 'the liberty of firing off a pamphlet in reply, which was my first appearance in that line, and which relieved my feelings greatly.'[32] As he later commented, 'The meaning of all this extravagant excitement, and impatience with liberal allies, was simply that Chalmers had been led to hope that a conservative government would give the Church an additional endowment for the Church Extension scheme: to the great glory of the apostle thereof; and that therefore mere Whigs or liberals were of small account.' The only result, however, of what Moncreiff described as 'his foolish violence' was to leave the Church without political friends on either side of the party divide, 'and the Gauls were at our gates'. 'It is only just to say,' Moncreiff conceded, 'that even before the conflict had proceeded far, Chalmers had repented, in inward sackcloth and ashes, of the injustice he had done to his old comrades, and nothing but contempt was the lot of the few toad-eaters who had encouraged his aberration.'[33]

It is perhaps remarkable that Moncreiff could still write with such heartfelt passion after the passage of half a century. While he was evidently disgusted with Chalmers' willingness to put his faith in a Tory ministry, he was upset by Chalmers' personal attacks on close members of his own family. Naturally, Moncreiff would wish to defend his own father in such a situation, but as we shall see, he also wrote a robust defence of his father-in-law, Robert Bell, with whom he was particularly close. It was only natural that Moncreiff should defend Bell, even if it were not the case, as it was, that the two men were on the same side of the argument when the issue of lay patronage and the Veto Law came before the courts.

In point of fact, the whole question of Church endowment had become highly politicised in Scotland. A war of pamphlets broke out, in which Chalmers himself took part with gusto.[34] He found himself particularly at odds with the Whig dominated Edinburgh Town Council, one member of which, Adam Black, ridiculed Chalmers' vision of a commonwealth of small parish communities, which he compared to the Utopian schemes of Robert Owen, and denounced as being 'at utter variance with the constitution of our nature, and could only end in the mortification and distress of the unhappy schemer and his followers.'[35] The fall of Peel's Tory government in April, before it could deliver on the endowment bill, and the return of Melbourne, seemed to deliver fatal blows to the Church Accommodation scheme.

But there was good news to come from the Chalmers camp. At the meeting of the General Assembly in May 1835, Chalmers was able to present a glowing report of the achievements on the church accommodation front. The Church Accommodation Committee's general fund had raised over £15,000, and the local societies over £50,000.[36] Sixty-four new churches had been built, or were under construction. The report was received with huge enthusiasm, and resulted in the unanimous decision to combine together the Church Accommodation and Church Extension Committees into a single Church Extension Committee, under Chalmers' convenership and control. As Chalmers' biographer has put it, 'Chalmers thus became the head of the most powerful committee ever formed by the Church, including over 130 members, with authority over dozens of local societies throughout the country. He now assumed full authority not only over the church building campaign, but also over the negotiations with the Government.

The name of the combined committee, moreover, was important. The Church signified that it was not content simply to increase church accommodation, or 'stone and lime'; rather its purpose was to 'extend' Christian communal sentiment throughout the nation with an aggressive parochial ministry.[37]

There were further consequences for Chalmers himself. As Stewart Brown has pointed out, the creation of the new combined committee gave Chalmers personally tremendous power within the Church. He now controlled a vast network of local and regional societies, together with extensive financial resources. 'The Moderate party [within the Church] was in disarray – there were it seemed no rivals to Chalmers' ascendancy.[38]

While that was true in the sense that there was no single individual prepared to challenge Chalmers' position, that did not mean that his authority went unchallenged. For a start, there was the Whig government, unwilling or unable, in its continued dependence on the Dissenters, to agree to Chalmers' demand for an Endowment bill. Then there was Dr John Lee, a possible candidate for the Moderatorship of the General Assembly in 1836 and 1837, with very different views from those of Chalmers as to what reforms were needed to support the urban poor in Scotland; and finally there was the old guard of the Whig-Evangelicals, increasingly unhappy with Chalmers' leadership. In 1837 all these elements combined to produce a major, and very public, convulsion within the Church over the Moderatorship – with the Moncreiffs very much at its centre.

What connected all these protagonists was the decision of the Melbourne administration to set up a Royal Commission of Inquiry into Religious Instruction in Scotland, before coming to any decision on the Scottish endowment. To begin with Chalmers was in favour of the move, convinced as he was that the statistics collected by the local societies would prove conclusive to his argument in favour of the church building programme. He very soon came to change his mind. What particularly angered him was the membership of the Commission, which was almost entirely made up of Whigs, several of whom were known to be hostile to the Church. The chairman was the Earl of Minto, with whom Chalmers had crossed swords in the past. Then there was the belief, never wholly dispelled, that the Commission was either simply a delaying tactic, or worse, a device to justify the disestablishment of the Church. Assurances from Lord John Russell that the Commission had been set up in good faith, and that if it arrived at the conclusion that more church building was needed, the government would act on that conclusion, were only partly successful in defusing the situation. Chalmers and the Assembly grudgingly agreed to co-operate with the commission, and he himself gave evidence to it. But his position, as well as the credibility of his church accommodation scheme, were seriously jeopardised, as he saw it, by the part played by Dr John Lee – a Whig, and also a Moderate member of the Assembly.

In the months before war broke out over the Moderatorship, Chalmers worked hard to re-energise the Church Extension campaign. The Committee's report to the General Assembly in 1836 had been disappointing. Subscriptions to the general fund had fallen to a mere 10% of the previous year's figure, subscriptions to local societies had also declined, and the number of churches built in 1835-6 was down from 64 to 26. Chalmers' response to this situation was characteristic. The light touch of central control over the local societies was replaced with a new and firm discipline. Every synod, presbytery and parish was not just encouraged to raise money for new church building – they were required to do so. Agents were sent into the country to exhort their audiences to contribute. This certainly had the desired effect of increasing income, but it also had the effect of still further increasing Chalmers' power and status within the Church hierarchy.

As has been pointed out, by late 1836 Chalmers had created a highly effective propaganda organization, very much along the lines of the great propaganda machines of the future, such as the Anti-Corn Law League and the Chartist movement.[39] Not everyone, not even everyone in the Evangelical party, could view these developments with equanimity. The stage was being set for a showdown – primarily between Chalmers and the older generation of Evangelicals, men who had grown up under the influence of Sir Harry Moncreiff. Inevitably, this included the Moncreiffs themselves.

While the origins of the dispute, then, lay in differing opinions within the Evangelical party in the Assembly, the outward manifestation of it centred on the clash between Chalmers and Dr John Lee, the latter doubly suspect as both a Whig, and a member of the Moderate party. The immediate issue was the choice of candidates for the Moderatorship of the Assembly in 1835. Surprisingly, perhaps, Chalmers, himself Moderator in 1832, initially proposed Lee, but later withdrew his recommendation, and declared that Lee could not be trusted with the Moderatorship. His reason for this change of heart, Chalmers later explained, was due to the part Lee had played in the discussions in the special Commission of the General Assembly in September, 1835, over whether or not the Assembly should support the Whig government's plan for a Royal Commission of Inquiry to investigate the extent of 'religious destitution' in Scotland. As we have seen, to begin with Chalmers had favoured the scheme, but once he had changed his mind he successfully persuaded the Committee of the Assembly to oppose the proposal. Lee had been the one member of the Committee to refuse to fall into line, and had therefore, in Chalmers' opinion, given the Whig government encouragement to go ahead with the scheme. The differences between them on the question of Church Extension became more public as the Commission of Inquiry began its work of collecting evidence in February, 1836. Chalmers' strong personal preference was to promote an ambitious scheme of church building in the cities for the support of the urban poor. Lee was highly sceptical, arguing that the more practical approach was to increase church provision in the rural areas. Lee himself had been a minister amongst the urban poor for thirteen years, and on the basis of his personal experience he pointed out in evidence that workers in the towns were constantly on the move – the idea of creating parishes made no practical sense in an urban environment, when in any case a large proportion of the new labouring class was Roman Catholic. There were already enough churches in the towns and cities – what they really needed were more schools.[40]

There were other more fundamental differences which contributed to their mutual distrust. Chalmers' Church Extension scheme, with its encouragement to the laity to become involved in the campaign for church building, and thus in other aspects of church affairs, contradicted Lee's desire to promote the independence of the clerical profession. But for the present, Chalmers succeeded in thwarting moves to nominate Lee for the Moderatorship in 1836. By 1837, however, opposition within the Evangelical party itself to Chalmers' high handedness was growing – led essentially by the old guard of the party, including several members of the Moncreiff family. The battle between the two wings of the party would be fought out in the context of the Moderatorship election of 1837.

One of the leaders of this opposition was Robert Bell. In December 1836 a group with Bell as their spokesman issued a manifesto, demanding that the objections of Chalmers and his fellow former Moderators to Lee's nomination should be made public.[41] This sparked off an extraordinary exchange of published pamphlets, characterised by vicious personal attacks on opponents. In his response to the Bell manifesto, Chalmers first damned Lee with faint praise, then went on to declare that 'I am not blind to the dangers of his being Moderator at this time; or so long as the question of Church Extension remains unsettled', and attacked Lee in particular for his unilateral dissent from a resolution in the Assembly's Commission of 1835, criticising the Government for its lack of support for the Church Extension scheme. 'The man who could strike out from all his brethren in the ministry, might afterwards strike out from the general sense of the Church on the subject of Church Extension.'[42] Lee's supporters likewise incurred Chalmers' wrath 'as the declared and eager partisans of a Government that have been sorely embarrassed by this very question; and who in their anxiety for its indefinite postponement have more than once disappointed the Church of Scotland. *I have been made to understand that there are a few political lawyers of the Parliament House who are the most zealous and indefatigable supporters of his cause'.*[43] Of these political lawyers, Chalmers singled out Bell, for his role at a public meeting in Edinburgh 'on the question of the Irish Church, and in favour of the appropriation clause', and also Lord Moncreiff, for allegedly having sacrificed his Evangelical principles for the fellowship of his Whig friends. Then, addressing Bell directly, he went on: 'You will further recollect that, a few evenings thereafter, you did me the honour to call, when you informed me that Dr Lee,.....had come to you and stated that I was altogether wrong (about the relative stability or volatility of urban populations).' Chalmers had been made very angry, and in response warned Bell 'to be aware of Dr Lee's authority on this subject, who, however versant in the lore of church antiquities and the Church Law, was not to be trusted, either for his observation or his judgment, in those practical matters which entered into any question of Church economics.'[44]

Bell, seeing himself as 'the chief object of his attack', was goaded into no less vehement a response. He denied the various charges brought against him, including the complaint that he had been responsible for the withholding from Chalmers of the evidence before the Church Commission. He denied the claim that most of the Commissioners were supporters of the Government. Then he went for the jugular:

> Not contented with mixing up those whom he calls his *antagonists* with everything that is mean and base and contemptible, he tries to identify himself with all that is high, and honourable, and desirable in the cause he has so artfully introduced into this debate. He knows the deep interest which the cause of Church Extension has excited. Hence he himself and the Church Extension scheme are identified. Nay, opposition, as he calls it, must in some way be injurious to that object. Friendship to Dr Lee is enmity to him, and enmity to him must lead to the defeat of the scheme. Nay, he scarcely appears to consider even the scheme itself worth carrying, unless it is carried in exactly his own way. Any one who differs from him, even in the most trifling particular, must therefore at all hazards be destroyed.[45]

It would seem from these passages that Bell was more than able to defend himself. But as we have seen, James Moncreiff felt moved to enter the pamphlet war on Bell's behalf. He was almost certainly the author of *A Word More on the Moderatorship* published in 1837 under the name of 'A Bystander'.[46] It has to be said that the pamphlet was not aimed directly at Chalmers, but rather at one of his champions, the Rev. William Cunningham, but the object of the publication clearly was to defend Bell against Chalmers' accusations.[47]

Whether the author of the pamphlet or not, our Moncreiff himself was firmly in support of Lee, described by him as 'a man of great learning and undoubted orthodoxy', against Chalmers' nominee, an unknown rural clergyman called Gardiner, dismissed by Moncreiff as having 'never done anything sufficiently good or wicked to render him famous'. Chalmers, however, thought that Gardiner was 'thoroughly to be trusted on the question of Church Extension', and thought for no reason at all that Dr Lee was not'.[48] In the event, Chalmers carried the day. At the Assembly of 1837, Gardiner was elected to the Moderatorship by the overwhelming majority of 262 votes to Lee's 59.[49]

Chapter 5
The Road to *Auchterarder*

Eventually, as Moncreiff recorded in his *Reminiscences,* Chalmers seems to have repented, if only with 'inward sackcloth and ashes' of his injustice to 'his old comrades', amongst them prominent members of the Moncreiff family.[1] This was significant, since throughout the 1830s and into the early 1840s, Chalmers and the Moncreiffs were linked in what was to prove a much more divisive issue, with the resurgence of the lay patronage debate. In the early years of the century, as we have seen, this issue had largely faded from prominence. But in the early 1830s it returned to dominate debates in the General Assembly, and ultimately to lead directly to the Great Disruption of 1843.

Both Chalmers and the Moncreiffs were to play central roles in the decade of controversy. Put briefly, the issue was brought back into the limelight by Chalmers' motion before the General Assembly in 1833, to enable parishioners to express their dissent from the appointment of a minister by a patron. While the motion failed to win a majority on that occasion, a similar proposal put before the 1834 Assembly by Lord Moncreiff – the so-called 'Veto Act' – was passed. This Act empowered parishioners, who were heads of families and communicants, to veto the appointment of a minister who had been installed by a patron against their wishes, and marked the beginning of what has been styled the 'Ten Years' Conflict'. While the great majority of the presentations of ministers by lay patrons went ahead without causing any controversy, in four parishes in particular – Auchterarder, Lethendy, Marnoch and Culsalmond, the outcome was a series of some thirteen cases brought before the Court of Session, which raised serious questions about the respective jurisdictions of the civil court and the Church courts – questions which again and again were decided against the position of the Church. As we have seen, in several of those cases Moncreiff acted as junior counsel, and on occasion his father, Lord Moncreiff, was among the panel of judges.

As suit followed suit, the key issue was no longer whether congregations had the power to reject the nominees of lay patrons, but whether the General Assembly had the power to pass the 1834 Veto Act in the first place. Both sides understood that a fundamental constitutional issue was at stake. As Lord Rodger has recently put it:

> the battle which developed all those years ago between the courts and the majority party in the Church was in every sense a constitutional struggle, and was regarded as such at the time, even if the two sides saw the issue

differently. For the majority party in the Church, the Court of Session and the House of Lords were defying the constitution, as laid down in the Act of Union.....By contrast, the majority judges and the House of Lords thought that the Church was defying the authority of the law of the land.[2]

With regard to the central issue of the power of the Church to pass laws relating to ecclesiastical matters, it is interesting to note Lord Moncreiff's long history in defence of that principle. In the decade before the Veto Act rose to prominence, similar issues had been debated in connection with the holding of pluralities. Moncreiff, not yet a judge, but an advocate and a church elder, had made a speech on the subject which attracted the admiration of Dr Robert Candlish, the Principal of New College, and later to succeed Chalmers as the leader of the Free Church.[3] 'On the plurality question,' Candlish had written, 'the Lord Justice Clerk, or the Lord President (I forget just now which) made a very dogmatic and imposing speech against the legislative powers of the Church, and the fallacy of that argument was most ably and clearly answered by Moncreiff, in certainly the best speech I heard.'[4] In that speech, Moncreiff had firmly rejected the view that the Assembly had no power to deal with the abuse, or to pass any law on the subject, and that this could be done only by act of Parliament. 'Sir, the basis of that proposition is that the Established Church of Scotland has no existence, no power, but what it holds by Act of Parliament. Nobody certainly can doubt our Establishment....depends for its existence on the provisions of the system of government derived from the will of the people who have chosen it. But it is quite another thing to say, that all the powers of the Church established under such a government are derived solely from the express enactments of Acts of Parliament, in which certain things are committed to the Church, or that the measure of those powers is to be restrained within the limits of such express civil enactments.' The effect of this would be to declare that 'the Church Courts may indeed have certain powers as a part of the civil government; but that, as the judicatories of the ecclesiastical establishment properly considered, and independently of any special statutes, they have no power at all.'

The big question, of course was this – if the Church did indeed enjoy powers beyond those which had been granted by the civil authority, by the authority of Parliament, then from what alternative authority were those powers derived? This was an issue which was to trouble many minds in the following decade, and the answer to it was to lead directly to the secession from the established Church of more than one third of all its ministers. Moncreiff's answer to it was clear. He reminded his audience that the Revolution Act of 1690 had incorporated the Confession of Faith. 'Now,' he stated, 'the Articles in the Confession appear to me to be absolutely conclusive of this question as to a question of power.' Pointing out that the 31st Article declared that it was for 'the Synods and Councils to set down rules and orders for the worship of God', and their 'decrees and determinations, if consonant with the will of God, are to be received with reverence and submission, not only for their agreement with the Word, but also for the power whereby they are made, as being an ordinance of God, appointed thereto in his Word.' From this he concluded that 'There is the basis of the power of our Ecclesiastical Establishment. It rests not upon the force of Acts of Parliament, but in the nature of the Establishment itself, on the great principles on which our Reformers put it, acknowledging no other head than the Lord Jesus Christ, and no other warrant than the Bible itself.'[5] It would be unkind to point out that in relying on the Act of 1690, Moncreiff seemed to be accepting the validating authority of a statute for the Confession of Faith.

We in the west have become wary of those who would claim that their beliefs, and even more so their actions, have been directed and sanctioned by a higher power or a holy book. It is nevertheless vital to grasp the point that very many, perhaps most, perhaps all, of the protagonists within the Church in those days had no doubts upon the matter. Over the next few years, they were to witness the Court of Session ruling again and again that while the Church Courts did indeed enjoy certain powers over purely ecclesiastical matters, it was nevertheless for the civil courts, and not the General Assembly, to determine just where the line was to be drawn between the civil and ecclesiastical jurisdictions. No doubt in law the judges were right. But that is to miss at least part of the point. The ministers who left the established church in 1843 did so precisely because they believed what Moncreiff had spelled out for them – that where spiritual matters were concerned, they took their orders from the Lord Jesus Christ, and not from the Lord President or the Lord Justice Clerk.

The first serious test of the Veto Act came in the Auchterarder case of 1838, where the presbytery refused to induct the nominee of the patron, the Earl of Kinnoull. When the case was appealed to the Court of Session, by an 8-5 majority, the Court, in effect if not in actual words, declared the Veto Act to be *ultra vires*, and further went on to declare that the established Church was the creation of the state – and so challenging the view of many that the Church was independent of the state, at least in matters spiritual.[6]

The Auchterarder case was followed by the Marnoch case,[7] which produced the marvellously named 'Strathbogie Interdict' of 1839, when the General Assembly suspended seven ministers from Strathbogie, for proceeding with an induction against Assembly orders, only to have their suspension overturned by the Court of Session. The controversy finally came to a head in 1842, when the Evangelicals presented Parliament with *The Claim, Declaration and Protest anent the Encroachments of the Court of Session.*[8] The *Claim* was rejected, and this action led directly in the following year to the Disruption and the withdrawal of the dissenting ministers.

In his *Reminiscences*, Moncreiff spends several pages explaining the origins of the dispute to his potential readers, as well as the part played by himself and his father.[9] His account throws considerable light on the whole affair, at least from a position sympathetic for the most part with the Evangelicals and the so called 'Non-Intrusionists'.

'While the Church of Scotland,' he began, 'held the doctrine that the State was entitled to establish and endow the church – a principle to which all honest Free Churchmen have solemnly given their adherence – it also held that while in civil affairs the Civil power was supreme, the Church was supreme in matters spiritual. ...At the Reformation, lay patronage was abolished: and the privileges conferred on the Church of Scotland were expressly re-enacted by the Act of Union.' However, he noted, only a few years after the Act of 1707, 'the Jacobite ministry of Harley and Bolingbroke, in defiance of the Treaty of Union, restored lay patronage.'[10]

This act, he considered, was contrary to the law of Scotland as it has always been construed, that is that 'the ordination of the priesthood is a purely priestly function, which the Civil Magistrate has no power to enjoin.' He conceded that in England the law was different, 'but in Scotland ordination and the settlement of the pastor was always preceded by a call from the people.' As possibly something less than authoritative evidence for the long history of the practice, Moncreiff quoted from the account of Reuben Butler's ordination in *The Heart of Midlothian*:

> 'The Captain,' said David Deans, 'assures me that the call was unanimous on the part of the parishioners – a real harmonious call.' 'I believe,' said Duncan, 'it was as harmonious as could be expected when the half of the bodies were clavering Sassenach, and t'other skirling Gaelic, like sea maws and clack geese before a storm. And as to its being a unanimous call, I wad be glad to ken fat business the carles have to call onything, ony body, but what the Duke and myself likes.'[11]

In Moncreiff's own view the effect of the reintroduction of lay patronage – intentionally he was convinced – was to diminish the influence of the 'more earnest and congenial' of the clergy. Church discipline suffered, and the standard of learning of the clergy was lowered. The result was the secession of a number of evangelical ministers in 1732, taking their people with them. For a time, Church authorities in the Assembly remained indifferent, but, Moncreiff assured his readers, 'as the time of awakening commenced by Sir Harry Moncreiff and Andrew Thomson ripened, the General Assembly began to see that a crisis was at hand. The people had been leaving them in all directions, and as Reform in state policy proceeded, an attempt to stem the advancing tide was made in the Church.'[12]

In 1833 Chalmers proposed a motion in the Assembly, the object of which was to give reality to the principle of a call from the parishioners, not in the form of express consent, but of expressed dissent, so that if a majority of the heads of families opposed the presentation of a minister, it should not be proceeded with. According to Moncreiff, this was: 'a very mild restriction on a power solemnly abolished by Parliament, and restored in defiance of treaty obligations.' Chalmers' motion would have given to parishioners the power of veto over proposed appointments of ministers by patrons. Although his motion was defeated in the General Assembly of 1833, it was by a small majority only, being successfully passed, as we have seen, at the next Assembly, on the motion of Lord Moncreiff – our Moncreiff's father. Indeed it is clear from the correspondence between Lord Moncreiff and Chalmers in 1833 that the two men had been working closely together on the project for some time. On the 13th April, 1833 Lord Moncreiff wrote to Chalmers to ask him to meet with him, either 'today or Monday' to discuss a matter to do with the calling of ministers. Moncreiff was particularly anxious to 'learn what your views are as to the most prudent course to be taken in the Assembly on the particular measure to be proposed on the subject of the calling and admission of ministers.' The forthcoming meeting of the Assembly was 'looked to with great anxiety, and by no-one more than myself. It will be a very difficult thing to manage anyway.' A great deal would depend on 'our being prepared with a definite and workable scheme…I have some information as to the run of opinions through the Church – very favourable to moderate and reasonable measures from the West and some other quarters, very much otherwise from a part of the North.'[13]

Lord Moncreiff's resolution to the General Assembly in 1834, to be known as the Veto Act, described by Henry Cockburn as 'the popular Veto on patronage' meant that a minister would be debarred from a kirk if a majority of male heads of families, communicant members of the congregation, rejected him, whatever his patron wanted.'[14] Such a negative veto did not, and certainly was not intended to, amount to a move to abolish lay patronage, but simply to curb its abuses. Moncreiff senior, as his eldest son Henry recalled in later years, was opposed to popular election as a method for appointing ministers,[15] and in the year following the passage of the Veto Act, Moncreiff did his best to frustrate the attempt of 'a wild party'[16] to enforce the Act in all cases. It is probably fair to say that his support for the Act was an attempt to head off more radical demands for the complete abolition of lay patronage and the introduction of popular election of ministers.[17] Indeed Lord Moncreiff's attitude to lay patronage seems to have undergone some changes in the early eighteen-thirties. Son Henry recorded many years later that it appeared from a speech he made in 1832 that his father had not yet made up his mind about how best the church might proceed on the patronage issue. In the General Assembly of that year he did not speak decisively against proposals to have the law of patronage altered. And again 'from his evidence given to the House of Commons in March 1834 it may be inferred that his original prejudice was in favour of restoring the power of nomination to the heritors and elders on the footing of the Revolution settlement.'[18]

The best guide to Lord Moncreiff's thinking on the lay patronage issue lies in a series of letters he wrote to his old friend Henry Brougham between March and May, 1833. It should be remembered that only the previous year Parliament had passed the Great Reform Act, based on the principle of popular election of Members of Parliament, even if its application was still severely limited. Rumours now were abroad that the same principle might be applied to established churches, an eventuality which filled Moncreiff with fears for the future. 'Impressed by the rumours around me', he wrote to Brougham on the 3rd of March, 'I wish to say this, that if there be any intention of introducing the principle of popular election in the Govt. Churches – it is certainly a principle hitherto unknown to the Constitution in the past times; and that after it shall be so recognised, tho' it may succeed in particular cases if well managed, it is in itself full of much danger, and there will be no possibility of doing anything else in regard to the other patronages. It will be vain to speak of any measure by the General Assembly after this is done.' His great fear was that in so doing, the government would raise expectations which could not be realised, 'or being realised, may end in the ruin of the Church, and thro' it the disorganisation of all the valuable institutions of the Country.'[19]

Yet he was by no means opposed to some method of ensuring that 'every minister appointed should be acceptable to the people for whose benefit he is placed in the parish; and I do think that some measure is called for, for preventing the settlement of persons who are decidedly obnoxious to the whole people or the great body of them.' That was not at all the same thing, in his mind, as popular election of ministers.. 'Now, tho' I think the wishes of the people ought always to be consulted, I must say that with all my anxiety on that subject, and all my zeal for popular rights generally, I do very much dread the effect of popular election in any manner directly applied to the appointment....There is manifestly a mighty difference between a right of the people to object to an individual, whom they do not expect to be useful among them and the power of appointing or electing themselves.' He was personally convinced that 'if an effectual definement of the existing law as to the right of the people to object and to be heard could be arranged, the effect would be that the patrons would always take care to ascertain the probable sentiments of the people before committing themselves to a presentation.'[20] This turned out of course to be a tragic miscalculation. But in calling for a 'definement of the existing law', Lord Moncreiff was expressing the view, which he held to consistently throughout this affair, that in principle the Veto Act was essentially nothing new – but a restatement of old law. Writing to Brougham in May, 1833, he explained this in great detail – that the plan currently before the General Assembly derived directly from an Act of Assembly of 1649, entitled 'Direction of the appointment of Ministers'. Under this Act, where the majority of a Congregation dissented from the person nominated by the Kirk Session, the Presbytery was to proceed to a new election.[21]

Rodger draws our attention to a passage in Lord Moncreiff's judgment in the first Auchterarder case, where he speaks of 'the deep conviction I had formed of the extreme inexpediency and danger of the measure of abolition demanded of Parliament'.[22] What he was trying to do, in formulating what eventually became the Veto Act, was to find a middle way between the two extremes – total abolition of lay patronage on the one hand, and the substitution of popular election of ministers on the other – and at the same time to retain control in the hands of the Church of whatever process came to be adopted. Nevertheless, one criticism of the Act, and therefore of its promoter, was that by seeking to regulate the operation of lay patronage, it in effect gave implied recognition to the practice, and that 'Lord Moncreiff and the other authors of the Veto Act should therefore bear the blame for creating the conflict with the civil law which engulfed the Church.'[23] But as we have seen, it was never part of Lord Moncreiff's plan to do away with lay patronage, and his proposals for a solution to the problem had received a good deal of support from some very influential friends and colleagues, notably the then Lord Advocate, Francis Jeffrey, and the Solicitor General for Scotland, Henry Cockburn, who voted for the Chalmers' motion in the Assembly of 1833.[24] In March, 1834, a few weeks before the next meeting of the Assembly in May, Lord Moncreiff was summoned to London to give evidence on lay patronage to a House of Commons committee. In the capital he stayed with Lord Brougham, and together with Jeffrey they discussed the evidence he would present to the committee[25] – evidence which Jeffrey later described as 'most impressive and apostolic', and as having had a decisive effect on the committee.[26]

And so the stage was set for the next act. At the meeting of the General Assembly held in the Tron Church in Edinburgh on the 27th May, 1834, the Assembly passed an 'Act on the Calling of Ministers' – initially an interim act, but in the following year a fully fledged Act of the Church under the terms of the Barrier Act. While the Act set out in detail the procedures to be followed in the appointment and ordination of ministers, it was one regulation in particular which was to be at the centre of the ensuing constitutional conflict between the Church court and the Court of Session. This was the requirement that, after other formalities had been carried out, an opportunity must be given to the communicant heads of families in a parish to register their dissent. If a majority objected to a presentee, the presbytery was bound to reject him.[27]

Henry Cockburn shrewdly predicted that the Veto Act was likely to be challenged in the civil courts by both patrons and their protégés[28] as indeed it was, if only in a small number of cases. Out of 150 presentations to parishes between 1834 and 1839, only ten were vetoed, and only four of those – from the parishes of Marnoch, Auchterarder, Lethendy, and Culsalmond, found their way into the courts. (A fifth parish, the parish of Stewarton in the Presbytery of Irvine, was also the source of an action before the Court of Session, but it arose not from the Veto Act but from the Chapels Act of 1834. Nevertheless, the judgment in this case was to have a huge impact on the fortunes of the Evangelical party, which will be discussed later). These four between them, however, generated some twelve separate cases before the Court of Session, and in six of these, including at least one from each of the parishes involved, Moncreiff acted, with others, as counsel. Moncreiff's father-in-law, Robert Bell, Procurator to the Church, likewise served as counsel in six of the cases, in four of these alongside Moncreiff.[29]

Many commentators, especially in recent times, have discussed the Veto Act simply and solely in negative terms – in its role as precipitating the crisis within the Church. A notable exception is Stewart Brown, who has claimed that the Act worked effectively to ensure the peaceful settlement of ministers. Heads of families used their power of veto with restraint, and patrons themselves became more prepared to respond to popular opinion.[30] James Moncreiff also saw the Act in a positive light, and as having a most beneficial effect throughout the Church.

> 'For the next four years,' he noted, 'the Church of Scotland embraced a larger number of adherents in proportion to its population than any similar institution in Europe. All the schemes of the Church acquired additional vitality, and the people came back in great numbers to her communion.' Moreover, 'the rules which had been laid down for giving effect to the consent of the people worked smoothly.....The patrons were

quiescent, for they found that if they honestly looked out for men of the right stamp, the people were not likely to be unreasonable.'[31]

For some time after 1834, then, the combined efforts of Chalmers and Lord Moncreiff senior seemed to be having the desired effect of improving standards within the clergy, and thus increasing the size of the congregations. For his part, James Moncreiff junior was full of praise for the Veto Act and its beneficial consequences. 'A great benefit had been conferred on the Church and the community. It had been tried, tested, and had produced more than the anticipated advantages. No one was the worse. The Church was better manned. It was more popular and efficient than it had been for 100 years.' But evidently there was still what Moncreiff called 'a small knot of ecclesiastical pundits' who could not let well alone, one of the many ironies of the situation being that after the great schism had divided the Church and caused so many ministers to leave the Assembly for an unknown future, these same pundits now 'have renounced lay patronage, and broken up the camp of its defenders; a lasting and conclusive testimony to the merits and courage of their antagonists, in the Ten Years' Conflict. But it has come, like most reforms of wisdom in such quarters, just in time to be too late.'[32]

But this was for the future. In the meantime, in September 1834, the first of the 'Veto Act cases' began its tortuous course towards the Court of Session, and in the process highlighted the key constitutional issues which were to be revisited in subsequent cases. This was the Auchterarder case,[33] in which the patron, Lord Kinnoull, and Robert Young, his candidate for the ministry but rejected by the parishioners, brought an action against the presbytery, the eventual outcome of which was effectively, if not in so many words, to declare the Veto Act *ultra vires*.

The church and parish of Auchterarder had fallen vacant in August 1834, and on the 14th September, the patron, Lord Kinnoull had issued a presentation in favour of a Mr. Robert Young, of Seafield Cottage, Dundee, to fill the vacancy. On the 14th October, Lord Kinnoull's agent had laid all the appropriate documents in support of the presentation before the presbytery, and these were then ordered to be laid on the table until the next meeting, to be held on the 27th October. On this occasion the presbytery received an extract of Mr. Young's licence and a testimonial in his support from the presbytery of Dundee. A date was set for the moderation of a call to Mr. Young. On the 2nd December, they met again, and this time the call was signed by Lord Kinnoull's factor, a Mr. Lorimer, and signed by two heads of families, Michael Tod [sic] and Peter Clerk. The presbytery then proceeded 'in terms of the third regulation of the interim-act of the last Assembly anent calls, to give an opportunity to the male heads of families, whose names stand in the roll which has been inspected by the Presbytery, to give in special objections or dissents.' No special objections were lodged, so the session clerk, William Thomson, was instructed to produce the roll of male heads of families, and this was the point at which the process began to unravel. One Archibald Reid, Young's agent, now intervened to object to the presbytery either receiving or acting upon the said roll, 'inasmuch as the same was not made up either within the time, or in the manner prescribed by the Assembly'. When the presbytery dismissed Reid's objection, he lodged an appeal to the Synod of Perth and Stirling.

In the meantime, the congregation, in the form of the male heads of families, had spoken. After Young had preached in the church on two Sundays, out of the 330 parishioners entitled to vote, 287 recorded their dissent. Young duly appealed to the Synod, and from there to the General Assembly. On a motion proposed by Lord Moncreiff at the Assembly, his appeal was dismissed.[34]

And so the Auchterarder case at last came before the Court of Session itself. Two leading advocates with strong Moderate sympathies, Dean of the Faculty John Hope and Robert Whigham, raised an action on behalf of Kinnoull and Young. Opposing counsel, equally sympathetic to the Evangelical majority in the Assembly, were Solicitor General for Scotland, Andrew Rutherfurd, and James Moncreiff's father-in-law, Robert Bell. Although Moncreiff himself was not formally employed in this case, it seems reasonable to suppose that it was discussed between Bell and himself, and it was certainly the case that Moncreiff was engaged as counsel in the second Auchterarder case, *The Earl of Kinnoull v. Ferguson* in 1841, though Bell was not. Robert Whigham's speech filled 92 pages of the Auchterarder Report, and that of the Dean of the Faculty a further 192. More recently, Lord Rodger has summarised their arguments in a single paragraph:

'The argument for the pursuers,' he writes:

> was essentially simple. Taken in conjunction with the Act 1592 c.116, the Church Patronage (Scotland) Act 1711 provided that, if, after taking him on trials, the presbytery found that a presentee was indeed qualified to serve as a minister, then the presbytery was bound to induct him into the charge. It was therefore its statutory duty to take him on trial. In so far as the Veto Act cut across that statutory duty, it should simply be ignored. The Court of Session should accordingly declare that, by refusing to take trial of Mr. Young's qualifications, the presbytery had acted illegally and in violation of its statutory duty.[35]

For their part, counsel for the defenders were only too well aware of the implications for the authority of both courts – General Assembly and Court of Session – if the arguments of the pursuers were to prevail, and the latter were to order the presbytery to proceed with the induction of Mr Young. 'In one word,' Bell asked their Lordships, 'could the Court [of Session] charge us – an ecclesiastical court – to find the presentee qualified for the office, and consequently to induct him into it? Or failing of our doing so, could you do it yourselves?' 'Conflicts of jurisdiction,' he warned, 'are always unpleasant; and do the pursuers wish this supreme court to pronounce a judgment which it cannot enforce? Do they wish to create a collision between the civil and ecclesiastical judicatures....which without the uncertain aid of Parliament may never be cleared up?'[36]

But there were obvious practical problems in asserting the distinction between civil and ecclesiastical jurisdictions in the case of ordination and induction. Whigham, so Bell claimed, had conceded the point that 'the Church is supreme as to ordination....I only say at present that you can neither compel induction by the church courts on the one hand, nor prevent it on the other.'

Almost in the same breath, however, he himself conceded the power of the civil court 'to consider and judge of the proceedings of the church courts "ad hunc effectum" of determining who shall have right to the stipend'.[37] Part of the demand of the pursuers had been that Young should be declared to have the just and legal right to the stipend, manse and glebe, and all other related emoluments for the rest of his natural life. What would be the effect then if the Court found in his favour in terms of his pecuniary entitlement, but the Assembly refused to permit his ordination? There was clearly more at stake here than the fate of Mr Young. What if this situation were to be replicated in subsequent cases?

Bell's answer to this conundrum was to urge the Court not to go down that road, but to recognise and respect the separate but equal jurisdiction of the church, and the power of the General Assembly to make its own laws within its spiritual sphere. As he pointed out, 'from the very beginning of the reformation, the church had exercised the power ....of making and unmaking laws at its pleasure, in all matters whether of a spiritual or merely of an ecclesiastical nature,' while 'no civil court has ever ventured, or has ever been so much asked to exercise any controlling authority whatever', and he reminded the Court that 'Some of your Lordships who have been members of the General Assembly know this to be the case. You know that it is a power which has been exercised every year without complaint, and without objection, in every year of the existence of the church.'

Bell's plea for restraint on the part of the Court was reiterated in more sonorous tones by his leader Andrew Rutherfurd, Solicitor-General for Scotland. Referring to 'the majesty of the law', he declared that it 'shall then be best consulted when the different courts keep themselves in the exercise of their powers, within their proper jurisdiction, and do not commit encroachments on the peculiar provinces of each other. The constitution of this country has invested its courts not only with powers different in degree, but different in kind, *and each exclusive of the other.*' [My italics] Were these courts to come into conflict, 'not only would the majesty of the law be insulted and degraded in such a contest, but the law itself would be lost or destroyed.'[38]

And what of Lord Moncreiff himself, the author of the Veto Act, and now one of the eight judges sitting in judgment on the legitimacy of his own creation? His speech to his fellow judges began with an explanation of how he became involved in the giving of evidence before the House of Commons committee on lay patronage, and confirms the view, expressed by several contemporaries including his eldest son Henry, that he was moved to an extent by his 'deep conviction which I had formed, of the extreme inexpediency and dangers of the measure of abolition demanded of Parliament.' One of the questions raised at the time was whether the church courts had to power to enact a law such as the 1834 interim Act. Having now heard the arguments of counsel, and the opinions of several of his fellow judges, he found himself 'enabled and bound most conscientiously but firmly to declare,....that the church *had* the power to enact the law which is *said* to be the subject of this action, and that the action itself is both incompetent and groundless'.[39]

On the details, or indeed the wisdom, of the 1834 Act, he refused to be drawn. All he would say, somewhat disingenuously, was that 'the principle of it was simply to declare what those who framed it believed to be a fundamental law or principle of the church in the admission of ministers, and then to make a definite provision for the instruction of presbyteries.' Moreover, he was strongly of the opinion 'that the principle of the act has been much misapprehended, as if it were a very violent measure against the rights of patrons, whereas…it could easily be shown…that it was in fact a much milder form of giving definite effect to the call…'[40]

In any case, as far as he could see, the question of the legality of the 1834 Act was not before the court, and pointed out that in the summons, 'in which the character of the action, and the competency of its conclusions, must exclusively be found, there is no mention made of any act of Assembly.' Indeed there seemed to have been 'a studious avoidance of all allusion to the act of 1834, insomuch that, even in stating the proceedings of the presbytery, everything that could disclose the existence of such an act is carefully suppressed.' It seemed to have been felt, 'that it would have [been] too strong and too direct an exhibition of incompatibility, to ask this court to sit in judgment to *reduce* an act of the church, passed by one Assembly, confirmed by the presbyteries, and finally ratified by another General Assembly.'[41]

At the end of his address to the Court, Moncreiff came to four simple conclusions. First, 'that the summons…is incompetent in its form, nugatory as leading to no result against this presbytery, and *altogether involved in ecclesiastical matter alone, with which this court cannot deal'*. [My italics] Secondly, 'that the summons, defences, and record together, raise no question in competent form, relative to the act of Assembly 1834…'

Thirdly, 'that, so far as the question is before us, the presbytery were acting entirely within the powers vested in them by law in all that they have done – that they have done nothing which is not strictly ecclesiastical, and that, in so doing…they have acted in conformity to all the laws and principles of their own constitution.' And finally, he reiterated his belief that 'this Court has no jurisdiction to try *any* one of the questions attempted to be raised in this case.'[42]

It was a brave attempt. But in its final judgment the Court, by a majority of five to three, rejected Moncreiff's principal argument over jurisdiction, and dismissed the 'objections to the jurisdiction of the Court, and to the competency of the action as directed against the Presbytery.' Instead they found in favour of the Earl of Kinnoull and his presentee, the former having 'legally, validly, and effectually exercised his right, as patron of the church and parish of Auchterarder' in presenting Mr. Young. They accepted the argument of the pursuers, that the presbytery had acted illegally, and in violation of their duty, by refusing to take Mr. Young on trial, contrary to the provisions of the statute 10 Anne c. 12. And yes, it is true that they made no explicit mention of the Veto Act, at least in name. Yet it is impossible to conclude that their decision had no relevance to the status of that Act. Their principal criticism of the Presbytery was that they had refused to take Young on trial 'on the sole ground that a majority of male heads of families, communicants in the said parish, have dissented, without any reason assigned, to his admission as minister.' This was a direct reference to the appropriate regulation in the 1834 Act, with the clear implication being that that regulation, and the Act of which it was a component part, were themselves repugnant to the statute of 1712, which had restored the rights of lay patronage. It is also clear that from then on, it was accepted by the courts that the Auchterarder case had effectively declared the Veto Act to be illegal, and subsequent attempts to use its regulations as a defence were futile.

The story of the Auchterarder case does not quite end there. Two more hearings before the Court were to ensue, the first of these with James Moncreiff as junior counsel. Once again, the case had been brought by Lord Kinnoull and Robert Young – this time seeking to force the Presbytery to proceed with the taking of Young on trials.[43] For the Presbytery to continue to refuse to do so, the Court held, was a ground for damages, in respect of both the patron and the presentee. We have no record of Moncreiff's address to the Court, but part of what he had to say was referred to in the address by the Lord President, effectively dismissing the defence case. In this address, the difficult distinction between receiving and admitting a minister on the one hand – arguably conferring a civil right to the emoluments of the position, and ordination – arguably a purely ecclesiastical act, was simply ridden over roughshod. 'There is a strong argument in the papers', the Lord President noted, 'that there can be no civil obligation, because the induction of a minister implies ordination, which the civil courts have no power to order or enforce…..It is true we cannot order the Presbytery to ordain, but we can order them, in terms of the Act of Parliament, to receive and admit…. if, before you receive, it is necessary to ordain him, then you must ordain him.' Nor could he accept James Moncreiff's argument that the civil obligation on behalf of the patron was limited to the matter of the stipend alone, whereas 'the presentee must look to the spiritual office, he must not look to the stipend or endowment; that was an earthly motive, and entirely out of the question. I do not know how that matter stands, but I am afraid it is a bad argument in the mouth of the Established Church'.[44]

Indeed, from the point of view of the situation as it obtained before 1843, this *was* a bad argument. It was not practicable to detach from each other the two essential features of the admission of ministers to parishes – the spiritual and the earthly – the cure of souls and the financial support of ministers and church. But in a sense this is exactly what happened at the Disruption. The 451 ministers[45] who left their churches, glebes and stipends were indeed, in their own minds, putting their spiritual duty before earthly considerations. Whatever view one takes of the legal position, or their good sense, or their responsibilities to their families, by any measure that was a brave and principled decision.

Looking back at the Auchterarder case from the perspective of old age, James Moncreiff was highly critical of those pundits who had pressed for the action to be brought, describing 'this tardy challenge' as 'an act of wanton mischief'.

> The men who advised it did not believe that the operation of that Act was an evil. On the contrary, they thought, or at least came to think, that lay patronage was itself an evil, and ought to be abolished altogether. The legal question, no doubt, admitted of argument in both directions. The precise boundaries between civil and ecclesiastical jurisdiction had been a question in all Christian Churches. But in the interest of the public the remedy which had been applied had proved beneficial: the battle had

been fought and gained, and it would have been the patriotic and sensible course to have left it undisturbed.

Unfortunately, Moncreiff regretted, 'patriotism and good sense had no part in the headstrong councils of the Pundits. The wiser of the Moderate party saw only too clearly that success in this ill-advised appeal to the Courts of law would infallibly entail further complications. And the event has amply fulfilled their previsions.'[46]

Moncreiff deliberately did not go into an account of the hearing of the case in any detail, but confined himself to stating that ten of the judges of the Court of Session at that time were hostile to the Church, while five were in her favour. These five – Lords Glenlee, Moncreiff), Jeffrey, Fullerton and Cockburn – were in his opinion the 'flower of the judicial bench'. And so the case was lost, and an appeal to the House of Lords, an institution which was unfamiliar with the Scottish situation, and which regarded the Queen as head of the Church as well as the State, upheld the judgement of the Court of Session.[47] This appeal case also effectively destroyed the Veto Act, though once again without specifically mentioning it in the judgement. What it did do was state categorically that by rejecting Young 'on the sole ground that a majority of male heads of families had dissented without any reason assigned from his admission as minister, the presbytery had acted illegally and in violation of their duty, and contrary to the provisions of the statutes libelled, particularly 10 Anne c.12'.[48] No future attempt to justify the rejection of a minister on the basis of the Veto Act could possibly hope to succeed.

Chapter 6
Church *versus* Courts

The judgement in the Auchterarder case did not immediately lead to the Disruption – but the principles embodied in it informed the other court cases which followed. On the same day that the Assembly was in the course of discussing the outcome of the Auchterarder case, the Court of Session was considering the Lethendy case.[1] A Mr. Clark had been presented for appointment to the united parishes of Lethendy and Kinloch, only to have the Presbytery of Dunkeld reject him, under the terms of the Veto Act, on the familiar ground of an adverse vote by a majority of the male heads of families. Clark succeeded in obtaining an interdict from the Court of Session, however, preventing the Presbytery from appointing anyone else to the position. Despite this, the Crown proceeded to issue a new presentation in favour of Clark's rival, a Mr. Kessen, only for Clark to secure a second interdict. In June 1838 the matter was brought before the Commission of the General Assembly (such Commissions were regularly created with full powers to act on behalf of the Assembly between annual meetings) and the Presbytery was ordered to carry on with the ordination of Kessen. More interdicts were obtained; the Commission again ordered the Presbytery to ordain Kessen. They complied, but soon found themselves brought before the Court of Session for breach of the interdicts, in what Rodger has described as 'one of the great set pieces of the Disruption drama – ministers of the Church standing resolutely before the judges in their robes of office representing the State and the worldly power.'[2]

On this occasion, two members of the Moncreiff family were directly involved – Bell as counsel for the respondents, and Lord Moncreiff as one of the judges. The arguments they both employed were to deny that the complainant had the legal title to bring the case, and to deny that the Court of Session had jurisdiction. Clark's legal title was defective, they claimed, because his original 'presentation' to the parish had taken place while the incumbent, Mr Butter, was still alive. It had not been a presentation proper, but simply an 'arrangement'. The call to Mr Kessen was the valid one, and for that reason the Court of Session had no jurisdiction in this particular case. Lord Moncreiff even managed to appeal to the judgement in the Auchterarder case as support for his view. 'If, he argued, 'it was clear that the complainer had no title whatever, and consequently that the interdict demanded was an interdict against the induction of the lawful presentee, every finding in the case of Auchterarder, and every word of the argument employed in it go to show

75

that that there could be no jurisdiction to grant such an interdict.' If that was not the case, then the meaning of the judgement in the Auchterarder case 'must be, that the matter of the trial, ordination, and admission of ministers is not committed to the Church courts, as the statutes say it is, but belongs to the Court of Session, whenever a pretender may ask for their aid to resist the legal proceedings.' 'I am not prepared,' he went on, 'even after all that has passed in the Auchterarder case, to admit that this Court has jurisdiction to interdict a presbytery from exercising the ecclesiastical function of inducting a man into the spiritual office of pastor of a parish.'[3]

Lord Moncreiff then went on to explain to the Court the difficult position the Presbytery had found itself in – an explanation which may have had no bearing on the final judgement, but may very well have had a bearing on the Court's decision to let the ministers off with a warning, instead of sending them to prison. 'The Presbytery,' he explained, 'came to be surrounded by pressing and opposing duties. They had four times successively referred the matter for advice and direction to the superior Church courts, whom they were bound to regard.' As a result, 'they found themselves under the peremptory orders and instructions of those superior courts.' So they were now placed in an impossible position. 'They had the orders of one court, whose powers to instruct them in matters ecclesiastical they knew to be undoubted. They had a prohibition by another court, issued on the ex parte demand of a party apparently having no title to ask it, whose jurisdiction in such a matter,... they had at least as much cause to doubt.'[4]

For their part, the ministers made statements which fell rather short of an outright apology.[5] The Lord President was only partly impressed. The interdict must be obeyed, and the question as to title was at the present time immaterial. He warned the offending ministers that 'the ordinary punishment for disobedience to the law by breach of interdict is imprisonment', but nevertheless satisfied himself in pronouncing on them merely 'the solemn censure of the Court'.[6]

There was a postscript to this case. In 1841, Clark was again before the Court, demanding that his claim should be sustained that the Presbytery ought to have taken him on trials, regardless of any veto by the parishioners. James Moncreiff was one of the two counsel appearing for the Presbytery, and it was probably no surprise that they lost the case. In their judgement, their Lordships found 'that the rejection of the pursuer by the said Presbytery, as presentee aforesaid, without making trial of his qualifications in competent and legal form, ...expressly on the ground that the said Presbytery cannot ...in respect of a veto of the parishioners, was illegal and injurious to the patrimonial rights of the pursuer, and contrary to the provisions of the statutes and laws libeled.'[7] Another nail had been driven into the coffin of the Veto Act.

From then on there was really no chance of success in trying to reject ministers who were deeply unpopular with their congregations, on the basis of the Act. Patrons and their presentees made effective use of Court of Session interdicts to thwart the decisions, not only of presbyteries, but even of the General Assembly itself. The most notorious, but not the only example, was that of the Strathbogie Interdict of February, 1840.

The events leading to the issuing of the Interdict were complex in the extreme, and arose out of a dispute over the presentation of a minister to the parish of Marnoch, in the Presbytery of Strathbogie, to replace the long serving and popular William Stronach, deceased. The patron in this case was the Earl of Fife, who presented one John Edwards, the minister of a neighbouring parish, and who had earlier served as the assistant minister at Marnoch. But so unpopular had he been with the local parishioners, that at their request he had been dismissed the year before Stronach's death. Not surprisingly, for the patron to attempt to foist Edwards on them a second time did not go down well, and of the 300 heads of families in the parish, only one, the village inn-keeper,[8] signed the necessary 'call', and 261 vetoed it. Consequently Edwards' presentation, on the instruction of the General Assembly in 1838, was rejected by the Presbytery. Rather than provoke any further dissension, the Earl through his legal representatives presented David Henry, Edwards' successor as assistant minister, and who was well liked by the congregation. For the moment all seemed to be well.[9]

John Edwards, however, decided to pursue his claim to the position and succeeded in persuading the Court of Session to issue an interdict forbidding the Presbytery to proceed with Henry's induction. In their turn the Presbytery took the case to the General Assembly, which at that time was anxious to reach some kind of agreed accommodation with the Government. Consequently in July 1839, the Assembly issued an instruction that the Presbytery should obey the interdict, and not proceed with the induction of Henry. The Presbytery decided to comply, resolving that 'The Court of Session having authority in matters relating to the induction of ministers, the presbytery do delay all procedure until the matter be legally determined.'[10] For its part the Court of Session was disinclined to let the matter rest, and now issued a decision in Edwards' favour, ordering that the Presbytery give him a trial, and if he proved to be qualified for the post, then to go ahead and induct him. Lord Moncreiff, who had of course been one of the judges in the Auchterarder case, now in a minority judgement which Cockburn regarded as the best exposition of his side of the case,[11] warned that the Court should not interfere in these matters. He was outvoted, and in Strathbogie the Presbytery, or rather seven out of the twelve ministers in the Presbytery, duly gave Edwards his trial and inducted him before a hostile crowd, thus incurring the displeasure of the Church itself.

In December, the Commission of the General Assembly suspended the seven from office for 'insubordination', and described the Court of Session's involvement as an 'unwarranted encroachment'. They further set up a committee to make alternative arrangements for the provision of Sabbath services in the parishes of the suspended ministers. The response of the Court of Session was to issue a new interdict, preventing any minister from entering the churches, churchyards, or schoolhouses of the seven parishes to conduct religious services. The Church, still it would appear anxious to avoid an open war between church and state, decided that the services should be held in the open air. Once again the Court refused to accept a compromise – and proceeded to issue the 'extended' Strathbogie Interdict forbidding any minister to enter any of the seven parishes to conduct religious services, without the permission of the Court.

This was an interdict too far. In effect the Court was claiming the power to decide where in Scotland the Church could or could not conduct religious services. In January, Lord Moncreiff's eldest son, the Rev. Henry Wellwood Moncreiff, published his open letter to Lord Melbourne, urging Parliamentary intervention in the conflict. 'The argument', he wrote, 'by which it is attempted to show that the Church must yield to the Court of Session's interpretation of the statutes, even in relation to her spiritual functions, necessarily leads to an entire destruction of all the independent rights which were thought to have been secured in 1690 and 1707, and to a prostration of the Church beneath the supremacy of the Court of Session.' 'The Church', he went on to claim, 'had received a promise from your Lordship and the Government that the patronage of the Crown will be administered in accordance with the principle of the Veto Act.' What he understood by that undertaking was simply that 'before presenting to any parish, the government will take steps of some kind with the view of ascertaining the feelings of the people, or the acceptableness of the proposed candidate, as they have been accustomed to do since 1834.' But the present situation, he argued, now called for some general measure to be enacted by Parliament 'Protect the people from intrusion,' he urged, 'and I believe the Church will be satisfied.'[12]

In February of the same year, Chalmers and the Evangelicals held a public protest meeting, and Chalmers warned his audience that the infamous interdict was only the beginning – that the danger for the future was that the Court would seek to dictate not only where the Church could preach, but what it could preach, and under what conditions it could administer the sacraments.

Despite all this, it would be a mistake to imagine that the public in general, or the Church as a whole, supported Chalmers' position. Many Whigs, recalling his wooing of Tory support for the church endowment scheme, took some pleasure in the Church's predicament. Many Tories condemned the 'non-intrusionists' as socialists and radicals. Many in the Assembly argued that the church should withdraw its suspension of the seven ministers, and even apologise to the Court. Anxious to find a way out of the impasse in which he found himself, Chalmers decided to approach the Government, in the person of Lord Aberdeen. Initially Aberdeen was sympathetic, though critical of the Veto Act, but later he refused to accept a bill drafted by Chalmers which would have affirmed the sovereignty of the Church in matters spiritual, and its authority to administer the Veto Act. Negotiations between Chalmers and the Tory government were abandoned.[13]

The approach to Lord Aberdeen, and its disappointing outcome, was the subject of a lengthy and important letter from Lord Moncreiff senior to his great friend and professional colleague, Andrew Rutherfurd in February, 1840. Initially, Moncreiff had understood that Lord Aberdeen 'had been willing to secure the rights of the Church Courts exclusively to take cognisance of all the objections of the people, and to consider the effects of a Dissent of a majority or the great body of the people, whatever the grounds of the objection – only reserving appeal to the General Assembly, but excluding all interference by the civil Court.' This, in Moncreiff's view, would bring the matter back to where it stood before the passing of the Veto Act, a situation he could have lived with. 'If a better rule could not be got, I think that this would sustain the principle of non-intrusion, and be safe for the people in the present state of the Church.'

But much to his dismay, he now understood that 'Ld. Aberdeen's whole movement was essentially different from the understanding with him here – As far as I now understand, his proposal would be fatal to the case of the people, and in fact place the Settlement under the control of the Court of Session....If this goes on, the Revolution Settlement for Scotland, which rested mainly on the liberties of the Church, is at an end.'[14]

The final act then, or almost the final act, came with the issuing by the Court of Session of the Strathbogie Interdict, described by James Moncreiff as 'the culminating point of the downward career'. The interdict was, again according to Moncreiff:

universally disobeyed, but this only showed the more clearly that the stolid counsels which the Moderate party and the Government had followed had broken down the ancient bulwarks of the Church – as to have no option but legislation or disruption. The sagacious advisers had brought the strife to this successful issue, that the orders of the Supreme Civil Court were treated with absolute indifference, and were ostentatiously violated by the most venerated ministers in the land; and no one said them nay.

He acknowledged that Aberdeen had made some effort to mediate between the parties, and 'a more honest or trustworthy man could not be', but the problem was that at the time Aberdeen had been very much under the influence of his friend John Hope, the Dean of the Faculty, 'a man of fair ability but stronger will: an old member of the General Assembly, who could not brook the ascendancy of the Evangelical party where he had so often led their adversaries to victory, and without whose intervention, in all probability the law of 1834 would never have been challenged.'[15]

It was difficult – perhaps impossible – for Westminster politicians to grasp the seriousness of the issues in the minds of the Scots. 'It was widely believed,' wrote Wilson Bain in 1977, 'that Government Ministers, whether under Lord Melbourne or, from 1841, Sir Robert Peel, could not understand the magnitude of those disputes in Scotsmen's eyes. A remark such as that of Lord Cockburn about the Auchterarder case – "Scotland won't hear the last of this …for the next century"[16] – appeared to be incomprehensible to many members of Parliament, who could not grasp the intricacies of Scottish theology, nor Scottish attitudes to patronage, and to the independence of Church from State.'[17] There were in any case widespread fears amongst Westminster politicians that support for the non-intrusionists might threaten the future of the established Church in Scotland, and by implication, that of England as well.

Two more parishes and presbyteries found themselves having to explain their behaviour to the Court of Session before the final debacle in 1843. One of these – the Culsalmond case – once again revolved around the complaint of a presentee who had been denied admission to a parish, and one – the Stewarton case, raised new objections to the powers of the General Assembly to enact its own laws. Cumulatively, they made the existing relationship between the Church and the Court increasingly untenable.

The Culsalmond case of 1842, in which both Bell and James Moncreiff were employed as counsel for the respondents, involved some of the familiar ingredients of previous cases, but also raised some new issues.[18] The minister at the centre of the proceedings was one William

Middleton, a presentee to the parish, whose admission was at first dealt with by the Presbytery according to the regulations laid down by the Veto Act. On this occasion, a majority of parishioners did indeed dissent from his admission, but unusually, the Presbytery, by a majority, decided to ignore their dissent, and admitted Middleton regardless. A complaint was taken by the minority on the Presbytery, and representatives of the parishioners, direct to the Commission of the General Assembly, which ordered the parties to appear before it. In the interim, Middleton was forbidden to officiate in the parish.

In arriving at their initial decision to admit, the Presbytery had noted that the protests against his admission had been founded on the Veto Act, which had been declared to be *ultra vires* the Church and illegal. At a meeting on 11th November 1841 arranged to proceed with Middleton's induction, a further protest was lodged by the agent for the parishioners, raising special objections to the appointment, but these were ignored.[19] The matter was then referred to the Commission of the General Assembly, which issued the interdict against Middleton, prohibiting him from acting as minister of the parish. But by issuing the interdict, the Commission itself now came under the scrutiny of the Court of Session. Was the interdict legal, and indeed was the Commission itself a judicature, with the power of issuing interdicts?[20] The appellants, or more accurately the suspenders, as they sought the suspension of the interdict, argued that the only ecclesiastical courts recognised by statute were the Assembly itself, the synods, presbyteries, and kirk sessions. There was no mention of the Commission in any statute, nor was there any statutory mention of the Assembly's power to delegate its judicial authority. Counsel for the defendants, or respondents, claimed that the statutes recognising the jurisdiction of the Church did indeed recognise its power to delegate. In the end the Lord President, on behalf of the Court, suggested that that issue was so important that it should not be decided without a full debate involving all the judges.[21] The view of Lord Fullerton that the Court of Session had no power to review or suspend 'a purely ecclesiastical judgement pronounced by an ecclesiastical court' was brushed aside, as was the argument of the respondents that the Presbytery had acted improperly in refusing to listen to the special objections raised against Middleton. The Court accepted the Lord President's opinion that the Commission had acted illegally in founding their decision to interdict Middleton essentially on the Veto Act, and ordered the suspension of the interdict.[22]

Finally the Stewarton case, in which Moncreiff also acted as counsel for the defenders, differed from the previous cases in that it arose from the provisions, not of the Veto Act, but the Chapels Act of 1834.[23] It was similar to those, however, in that it resulted in the Court of Session again striking down an act of the General Assembly as being *ultra vires,* and to that extent added to the frustrations of the Evangelicals in the Assembly already smarting at the fate of the Veto Act.

The Chapels Act, it should be explained, arose out of the extensive population changes in Scotland already referred to – that is the massive expansion of the urban population of Scotland spawned by the industrial revolution. This led inevitably to a situation under which very many people belonged to no parish, and had no access to any church. In theory, this problem could have been resolved by creating new churches under the provision of the 'Act anent the planting of Kirks' of 1707, but that act required the consent of landowners, and this was not always easy to secure. As an alternative, many communities had simply raised funds themselves to build churches and provide the ministers' stipends. These new churches were known as 'chapels of ease'. A problem remained, however, in that the ministers of these chapels of ease found themselves at a disadvantage in comparison with ordinary parish ministers. They had no kirk session, and were not eligible to sit in the local presbytery. The Chapels Act was intended to address this problem recognising the status of chapels of ease as *quoad sacra* churches, thus enabling their ministers to be enrolled in the presbytery, and to sit in all the courts of the Church, including the Assembly itself. The Act was bound to be controversial, since many of these ministers were young, active, and fervent supporters of the Evangelicals. It is no surprise to find that, in 1833, the Moderates had successfully defeated a proposal to resolve the problem, and even less of one that the Evangelicals, once they had secured a majority in the Assembly in 1834, followed up the Veto Act with the Chapels Act in May.[24]

The Chapels Act provided that all ministers of the Associate Synod might be admitted to full communion with the Church of Scotland, subject to certain rules provided for the observance of the presbyteries. In August of 1839, the minister and congregation of the parish of Stewarton, in the Presbytery of Irvine, applied to be received into union with the Church of Scotland under the terms of the Act. On the 6th, the Presbytery duly admitted the Rev. James Clelland to the status and privileges of minister, added him to the roll of the Presbytery, and he took his seat. However, the patron, one William Cuninghame, and other heritors, decided to oppose any division of the parish, the allocation of a parish district, or a seat on the Presbytery for Mr Clelland, and so in March 1840 they successfully sought an interim interdict from the Court of Session, preventing the Presbytery from creating a new parish, and preventing Clelland from taking his seat. Not surprisingly, Clelland and his supporters fought back with a complaint to the Synod of Glasgow and Ayr, which was upheld, and when the patron in turn appealed to the

General Assembly, the Assembly supported the Presbytery, and instructed them to proceed 'according to the laws of the Church'. Interestingly and significantly, they also instructed them 'to insert express words in the deliverance by which they allocate a territorial district to the Church in question, *limiting the effect of the same to matters of spiritual jurisdiction and discipline, which alone are implied in....such allocation under the existing laws of the Church.*' [My italics] It seems obvious that this wording was included in an attempt to avoid the danger of the Act being struck down as affecting the civil rights of the patron. If so, it was to prove futile.

There followed a period of some confusion, as Clelland decided to give up his charge and left for England, while his successor, the Rev. James Latta, soon died. But in 1843, the patron sought Court of Session approval for the interim interdict to be made perpetual, claiming at the same time that the 1834 Act was *ultra vires*.

> It was unconstitutional and illegal in the General Assembly.....on the pretext of erecting new parishes *quoad sacra*, to alter the constitution and increase the numbers of a presbytery, which was a recognised court, possessed of certain jurisdictions, both civil and ecclesiastical, affecting the civil rights of heritors and parishioners within the bounds of the Presbytery.[25]

For their part, lawyers for the Presbytery, including Bell and James Moncreiff, tried to argue once more that this was a matter over which the Court had no jurisdiction. 'The matters in regard to which the interdict was sought, were of proper ecclesiastical cognizance, within that province, which, by statute, had been conferred exclusively on the church.' Whereas, 'the Court of Session, though equally supreme in its own province, was equally limited thereto; and its province was certainly limited to matters civil.....It was *ultra vires* of the civil court to renounce any order, ordaining an ecclesiastical judicatory, such as the Presbytery of Irvine, to disobey the superior Church judicatories, to which alone, by the law and constitution of the country, the Presbytery was subordinate.'[26] Brave words, or perhaps, in the light of previous judgments of the Court of Session, and indeed of the House of Lords, foolhardy.

But the decision in the Stewarton case, as Stewart Brown has pointed out, posed an immediate and practical threat to the Evangelical position. The Chapels Act, as we have seen, enabled ministers in the *quoad sacra* churches to be members of the General Assembly. Now the Court of Session not only declared the Chapels Act to be illegal, but as a consequence ordered that all *quoad sacra* churches be deprived of representation in church courts. As most of the churches in question had been built during the church extension campaign, the decision meant that the Non-Intrusionists would be deprived of their majority in the forthcoming Assembly.[27]

James Moncreiff himself, as events moved inexorably towards the crisis of 1843, had been ordained as an elder of St George's Church in Edinburgh, and was a member of the General Assembly in both 1842, representing Dalkeith, and in 1843, representing Hamilton.[28] Even more to the point, at the General Assembly of 1842 he was appointed a member of a special Commission set up by the Church designed to avoid its present difficulties getting out of hand. The Register of the Acts of the General Assembly for 1842 records that: 'The General Assembly has taken into consideration the state of the parishes hereinafter mentioned, and the necessity of making some special provision for the settlement and superintendence thereof, and for the management and ordering of certain other matters hereinafter mentioned...'[29]

The parishes brought under the supervision of this Commission included Marnoch in the Presbytery of Strathbogie, Auchterarder, Lethendy in the Presbytery of Dunkeld, and Culsalmond in the Presbytery of Garioch – all parishes where the dispute over the appointment of ministers had resulted in cases being brought before the civil courts. The powers of the Commission were extensive. They were to cooperate with the Presbyteries within whose boundaries these parishes were situated 'in the settlement and superintendence of the said parishes, and the making provision for the supply of the ordinances of religion, and the exercise of discipline and the ordering of all ecclesiastical matters therein.' They were empowered and instructed 'to advise and direct the said respective Presbyteries in all their proceedings thereanent with full power to the said Commissioners of themselves to [do] and perform.'

Moreover, almost as an afterthought, the Assembly decided to transfer to the Commission the duties previously assigned to the Non-intrusion committee.[30] In short, the General Assembly was assuming, via this Special Commission, direct ecclesiastical control over the four Presbyteries, and over the parishes for which they were responsible.

Quite what role Moncreiff himself fulfilled in this company is not on record. He was of course a relatively junior member of a very large committee, which consisted of 46 ministers and 26 laymen. Membership included many more powerful figures than he – Chalmers himself, for example, as well as the then Moderator. We find also that the quorum was set at five, of whom at least three had to be ministers. On the face of it, an advocate still in his very early thirties was unlikely to play a very prominent part in the activities of the Commission. But as it turned out, nor did anyone else. The very next item on the agenda of the Assembly was to call for the draft of the *Declaration and Claim of Right* to be presented to the Queen, approved by the members without a vote.[31] Not very surprisingly, there is no record of the Commission ever having presented a report of their proceedings prior to the Disruption.

The experience rendered Moncreiff highly critical of both sides in the dispute. It remained his firm belief that 'if either side had believed in the honesty of the other, there was no reason whatever why we should not have come to a successful result. I was also impressed by the comparative want of force and knowledge of affairs that some of my colleagues evinced.' In his opinion, 'If old Sir Harry, or Andrew Thomson had been there, the course would have been easier.' The differences between the two sides were not insurmountable. 'But I had doubts whether either side would have been sorry to see the conference break up. On the one hand, I think the Moderate party, and those who advised them, did not think that the Non-Intrusion party would bring matters to a crisis. .... On the other hand, the Non-Intrusionists had at that time no mind to consider anything: and were nervously afraid that any symptom of a desire to agree should be misconstrued or misunderstood.[32]

In Moncreiff's view, failure to find a sustainable solution was the result of serious mistakes and misunderstandings on both sides of the argument. The Moderates, for example, appear to have been persuaded, by the defection of a group of forty ministers from the Non-Intrusion party, that opposition to the Government position was crumbling. 'Before this untoward movement of the 'Forty'', Moncreiff explained, 'there had plainly been a disinclination on the part of the Govt., and I assume on the part of their advisers here, to risk a catastrophe, which the witless incident of the Strathbogie Interdict, whatever the contempt it had met with, had made almost inevitable.' But he was also critical of many of those who were on what he characterised as 'our side'. 'As the crisis approached,' he noted 'some advanced enthusiasts contemplated a disruption without dismay, and almost with satisfaction. The Court of Session had shown how far a State Church might be impeded in its pursuit of the spiritual welfare of its people; they thought it might not be amiss to be free.'

At the time, he believed, this enthusiasm for an exodus, 'had but a slender following,' but was supported by 'the more venturesome and ambitious members of the party. The Strathbogie Interdict was in effect, and was meant to be, a denial of the spiritual jurisdiction of the Church of Scotland in any sense. But it rested on no authority of weight, and the absolute immunity accorded to those who disregarded it, evinced that the Moderate party held it a false move, as it was.'

At the same time, Moncreiff seems to have had little sympathy for those hotheads on the Evangelical side who actively sought to put the issue publicly to the test. 'Such', he stated firmly, 'was not my view. I saw it with alarm. But with such impressions in operation on either side, it is not wonderful that our councils did not result in unanimity. The advisors of the Govt.', he believed, 'laboured under two disadvantages. They underestimated the courage of the clergy, and the religious convictions of the people. They did not believe that either would encounter personal loss in such a cause. They awoke a year later in a much wiser frame of mind.'[33]

Nor, apparently, had the Government paid adequate attention to the steps being taken in advance of the crucial General Assembly meeting, to deal with the financial consequences of a massive walk out of ministers. In November 1842, Chalmers had addressed a great Convocation of the clergy at St George's Church, and later at Roxburghe House, at which he unveiled his proposals for what he called a 'Sustenation Fund', to provide for the salaries of disaffected ministers, in the event of a disruption. His aim was to raise one hundred thousand pounds in the first year, money which could only have come from sympathetic members of the laity. The first to respond to this call was Charles Cowan, a wealthy businessman and a relative and close associate of Thomas Chalmers. On the morning of the November meeting, Cowan and Chalmers had breakfasted together, and after the meeting, Cowan invited to his house a number of his fellow elders to consider how to respond to the Chalmers plan. In the event only three of them actually turned up, but those three signed a statement binding themselves to contribute to the fund. A second meeting called by Cowan in December attracted a much larger attendance, and from then on Cowan busied himself in discussing more financial plans for the Church.[34] Some might have been reassured by this activity that the material consequences of leaving the established church were less suicidal than they might have been.

And so the Assembly met, in May 1843. The *Claim of Right* agreed by the General Assembly in the previous year, but already rejected by a vote in the House of Commons,[35] was laid on the table in the presence of the Royal Commissioners on the 18th May.[36] The outcome by this time was inescapable. '474 ministers of the Church', wrote Moncreiff later in life, 'demitted their offices, left home, manse, glebe, stipend – all the Associations of family and friends – and went forth in confidence of prevailing, risking all worldly possessions, but with the applause not only of Scotland, but of Europe. Such was their answer to the Strathbogie Interdict.'[37] In 1846, Moncreiff lauded the departing ministers as 'the very flower of the Church', and declared that

'The Free Church carried with them, with hardly an exception, every name which could have lent strength to her deliberations or added reputation to her body.'[38] And if, three years later, his judgement had become rather more circumspect, it was still positive. The dissenters' views, he wrote, 'may have been well or ill-founded, but the movement was picturesque in its manliness and self devotion.'[39]

Throughout the Ten Years' Conflict, the position of the Moncreiffs, father and sons, had been clear and consistent. Lord Moncreiff senior had proposed the Veto Act, and thereby supported the right of parishioners to refuse to accept undesirable nominees, even if he would not go so far as to advocate the popular election of ministers. He had sided with the minority on the Bench in the Auchterarder and Marnoch cases, and in the latter warned his fellow judges not to interfere in Church affairs. Yet the break up of the Church in 1843 took a huge toll, coming as it did only days before the death of his much loved wife at the beginning of June. Although he, along with his two elder sons, Henry and James, left the Church of Scotland and joined the Free Church, he was deeply saddened by Henry's decision in particular. 'And now', he wrote to Brougham on the 20th June, 'in times of the most poignant distress, I have the additional unhappiness laid upon me that my own eldest son....has found himself impelled by the imperative voice of conscience, to announce his intention of retiring from the Church to which he was devotedly attached, and for the present making a shipwreck of all his worldly enjoyments and prospects in life.'[40]

It has to be said that Henry, since his grandfather's death the only ordained minister in the family, never lost his belief in the rightness of his decision. More than thirty years later he published two substantial works – the *Vindication of the Free Church Claim of Right,* a volume of just short of 300 pages, covering the historical, scriptural, and juridical foundations of the Church's stand, and *The Free Church Principle*, a further defence of those who broke with the established Church in 1843, including of course his own father.

Throughout this period, our Moncreiff's personal position was equally clear and consistent. While identifying himself with the 'middle party', rather than the secessionists, he not only wrote briefs for the presbyteries which had rejected their patron's nominees, but also took an active part in the public meetings associated with the patronage issue. Following on from the House of Lords decision in the Auchterarder case, Moncreiff spoke at a meeting in support of a proposal that Parliament be asked to pass a measure to prevent the intrusion of unacceptable ministers, since it was now only too clear that the authority of the Assembly alone would be insufficient to resolve the problem.[41]

He also made active use of his friendship with William Gladstone, then a rising Member of Parliament, to persuade the Government to intervene to resolve the impending crisis. In February and again in March of 1841 he had written letters to Gladstone highly critical of the Court of Session decisions, and floating the idea of Parliamentary intervention by way of an Act regulating patronage, though his preference was still for the warring parties to unite to settle their differences 'before the immediate prospect of a serious convulsion engulfs them'.[42] Writing again in mid-May, only a few days before the fateful meeting of the Assembly, he warned that the secession of the disaffected ministers would certainly take place on the following Thursday, and 'beyond all question it will be a secession of hundreds, and I shall be glad if the number is under 400, which I believe is within the mark.' The only solution he now believed was direct Parliamentary intervention and that with immediate effect. Writing 'more from a sense of duty than from any hope of benefit', he urged that 'if Lord Aberdeen really means to pass a measure in the terms he alluded to in the Lords on Tuesday, then it was the height of impolicy – I may say imprudence not to announce it at once.' 'The announcement of a bill in the House of Commons might I have little doubt delay – and the passing of it avert the crisis, but otherwise I say at once it is past hope, and the train of evils consequent on it which may befall this land, no-one can tell.'[43] Yet it is difficult to understand what Moncreiff is referring to here. Lord Aberdeen's speech to the Lords on Tuesday 9th May did express the desire of the government to see an end to the dispute, and further claimed that it was prepared to avert a disruption 'by any means in their power', but at the same time he offered no solution to the problem, and expressly supported the House of Lords decision to declare the Veto Act illegal.[44] No action of course was taken.

Moncreiff should not have been surprised, if indeed he was, by the reluctance of government by whatever party to intervene to resolve the impending crisis, and their stubborn refusal to accept the non-intrusionist position on the specific issue of patronage, and the larger issue of the relationship between church and state in Scotland. As Ian Machin has explained, 'the policy of whigs and liberal conservatives was one of reviving the establishment and at the same time making concessions to other denominations. Desire to uphold the establishment was unlikely…to embrace so sacrificial a measure as the non-intrusionist demands, namely the virtual elimination of the state in spiritual government, while at the same time retaining the temporal advantages of establishment.'[45] Lord Melbourne for one was consistently hostile to any concession to non-intrusionist demands. 'I do not know how I could reconcile it with my conscience', he once wrote, 'to take the part of any

Church or of anything ecclesiastical anywhere in opposition to the law.'[46] An attempt had been made by Lord Aberdeen in 1840 to bring in legislation, but his bill would have rejected an outright congregational veto in favour of allowing presbyteries to consider objections to a presentation made by members of a congregation. The Non-intrusionists rejected the bill, and in July Aberdeen himself decided to abandon it. Given Melbourne's stated objection to the Non-intrusionist demands on principle, it was not to be expected that the Whigs would now espouse their cause – not least because of the party's reliance on support of both dissenters and Moderates at the forthcoming election. And so it went on. In the 1841 session of Parliament, an attempt was made by the Duke of Argyll, a conservative, to bring in a bill which would have given the right of veto to all male communicants over the age of twenty-one, but it became a casualty of the parliamentary dissolution. Neither party, indeed, could see any electoral advantage in supporting non-intrusion at the certain cost of alienating more powerful interests. For most of the time, in any case, party leaders were assured that if a disruption did occur, it would involve only a small minority of ministers. In August, 1841, John Hope had assured Aberdeen that 'the result of [a disruption] will be most inconsiderable...there are not six or ten [ministers] who would secede.'[47]

Once the Disruption had taken place, Moncreiff publicly castigated those landowners who refused to allow the Free Church sites for its buildings,[48] though later was able to note with satisfaction 'that in a country not proverbial for riches and very proverbial for providence, they have provided almost every parish with a residence for the pastor.'[49] Ecclesiastical freedom, he declared, was 'a cause to which every valued association, whether public or personal, devotes me, and which will be the very last which, whether in cloud or sunshine, I shall ever be tempted to desert.'[50] These views on religious freedom, and the spiritual independence of the Scottish Church, were principles to which he did indeed adhere for the rest of his life. In 1870, from his position as Lord Justice Clerk, he asserted that 'The jurisdiction of the Church Courts as recognised judicatories of this realm rests on a similar statutory foundation to that under which we administer justice within these walls.'[51] Like his father before him, he supported 'an entirely independent spiritual jurisdiction' for the Church in which the State had no business in intervening.[52]

'And so ended the "Ten Years' Conflict",' Moncreiff wrote in his *Reminiscences*:

> but the honours of war lay with the technically vanquished. All that was best of religious earnestness and popular confidence joined the Exodus. All the missionaries went with them – the preachers to whom crowds

flocked, Chalmers, Candlish, Gordon, Guthrie, and Robert Buchanan, and many more threw in their lot with the Free – the liberated church. Prosperity met them at every turn. Their voluntary coffers were filled. Churches and manses sprang up, exceeding in quality those which with tears their wives and children had left. The 474 charges represented by the outgoing ministers had in 1863 increased to 800. The fund raised for the sustenation of the ministry was in 1843 £366,219.[53]

Moncreiff was not alone in glorying in the outcome of the Disruption. As the *Free Church Magazine* declared with some satisfaction, if also with some pardonable exaggeration, in early 1844:

> It is a notorious fact, and one openly confessed by friends of the Establishment, that the best ministers have left it…It is a notorious fact, that the really good elders, the men of spiritual character…have…gone out of the Establishment. It is a notorious fact that almost the whole of the Sabbath School teachers, throughout the land, who belonged to the Establishment before, left it at the Disruption, and carried with them the great body of the young whom they had under their instruction. It is a notorious fact, that the people who have gone out are the most faithful in their attendance on public ordinances, most liberally contribute to missionary and other objects, and are the most distinguished for their love of Scripture truth.[54]

There is a postscript. As we have seen, all three Moncreiffs (though interestingly not James' father-in-law, Robert Bell) had seceded from the Church of Scotland soon after the Disruption, and James never again belonged to an established church. Yet he continued in later life to regret the whole affair as unnecessary, brought about by ignorance on the part of Government, and stubbornness on the part of Non-Intrusionists. 'I mourned,' he wrote, 'over [the] disruption of the Established Church of Scotland, for I thought the Government of that time threw away the best, most popular, and cheapest institution in Europe. I have ceased to belong to an established Church.'[55] In the fullness of time of course, long after his generation of the family had passed away, the wounds were healed and the Church at least partially reunited, but it took almost a century for this end to be accomplished. Cockburn's prescient forecast, that Scotland wouldn't hear the last of this for the next century,[56] proved to be remarkably close to the mark.

Chapter 7
The Trial of the Chartists

1848, the year in which three leaders[1] of the Chartist movement in Scotland went on trial before the Court of Session on charges of conspiracy and sedition, has been characterised as the 'Year of Revolution.' In Europe, a wave of popular unrest swept through several countries, driven by resistance to oppressive regimes and economic disasters. France, the German States, the Austrian Empire, Belgium, Denmark, and Poland, were all affected in some degree. A prime casualty was the constitutional monarchy in France, too close to Britain for comfort, as the regime of Louis Philippe was forced to make way for the Second Republic, headed by Louis Napoleon. In Britain itself, many feared that the Chartist movement, dedicated to what were seen at the time as revolutionary demands for political reform, represented a serious danger of armed insurrection, and a threat to the monarchy.

Few then or since have summed up the situation more effectively and succinctly, if not impartially, than Henry Cockburn, friend and colleague of the Moncreiffs, father and son, in his *Examination of the Trials for Sedition which have hitherto occurred in Scotland.*

> 'In some respects', he wrote in characteristic style, 'the times were not very unlike those of 1793 and 1794.[2] Besides the chronic sedition that adheres naturally to the practice of the Constitution, considerable masses of the people were under a violent attack of the acute complaint. This access was chiefly brought on by continental contagion. What the French call a republic had been recently set up in their country; almost every throne in Europe had been shaken or overturned by popular convulsion; Ireland was in rebellion; there was great mercantile distress in Britain; professional demagogues had not neglected the occasion, and these various excitements had brought out the idiots called Chartists not only into seditious oratory, but into displays of treasonable organization.'

'These circumstances,' he noted, 'crowded the English courts with political prisoners; but as only four individuals were prosecuted here [i.e. in Scotland] it at least cannot be said that there was any eagerness in resorting to the terrors of the law.'[3]

While receiving some inspiration perhaps from the continent, the principal stimuli to the Chartist movement were home grown. To a large extent it was a response to the chronic economic distress, felt most acutely in Ireland, but prevalent also throughout Britain. As Moncreiff himself noted some twenty years later, 'We all remember with pain the dark times, the darkest hour before the dawn, with commercial distress at home, scanty work and bad wages for the men.'[4] Equally important was the widespread sense of betrayal felt amongst the working class at the failure of government to follow through on the Great Reform Act of 1832 – an act which had extended the franchise to the commercial middle classes, but very definitely stopped short of extending it further down the social scale. What was to a large extent, therefore, a protest against cruel economic circumstances, was expressed in the form of demands for political and constitutional change. Hence the 'People's Charter' – a document drawn up by William Lovett, the leader of the London Working Men's Association, but widely adopted by the movement at large, setting out the specific agenda for reform – universal adult male suffrage; annual parliaments; payment for MPs; no property qualification for MPs; the secret ballot; and equal electoral districts. The fact that many of these reforms were subsequently adopted, and are in our time taken wholly for granted, should not blind us to the fact that in their day they were widely regarded as the harbingers of revolution.

Nor should the fact that many of them were later incorporated into the constitutional arrangements of the country persuade us that Chartism in the short run was anything but a failure. It was eventually brought down primarily by internal dissension, too close an involvement with Irish politics, and the refusal of government to be intimidated. It is one of the ironies of the situation that just when, in 1848, the revolutionaries in France were congratulating themselves on their successes, the Chartist movement appeared to have run its course. Part of the reason for this was the failure of the movement to achieve the status of a truly national, rather than a collection of regional movements, and the example of Scotland and Scottish Chartism is an interesting case in point. Nevertheless, in Scotland the movement was not yet defunct, and 1848 saw a brief revival[5] of popular enthusiasm for the cause, which was to lead by the end of the year to the arrest and trial of a small number of its leaders.

In his study of Scottish Chartism published in 1953, L.C. Wright argued that there were significant differences between the Chartist movements on either side of the border, and these differences were to be explained by significant differences in the economic situation in Scotland compared with England. The Industrial Revolution in England had begun to stall, mass unemployment was rife, and the high points of Chartist agitation tended to coincide with high points of unemployment – in 1839, 1842, and 1848. In Scotland in the same period the economy was relatively buoyant, and unemployment was never as intense or a widespread as in England at this time. Scotland, Wright explained, was embarking on the second phase of its Industrial Revolution, with the development of its coal and iron industries. Following the repeal of the

Corn Laws in 1846, food prices were falling (though this is disputed by some historians)[6] and there was comparatively little unrest in Scotland, as there had been in England over the issue of poor relief – principally because poor relief had never been of much significance in Scotland. What might have been a factor leading to disaffection in Scotland – the influx of large numbers of Irish immigrants, was, if anything, neutral, since they were largely content with the higher wages they could earn in Scotland. Politically their great hero was Daniel O'Connell, while Chartism's great Irish demagogue was O'Connell's great opponent, Feargus O'Connor.[7]

The effect of all these factors, Wright argued, was that 'Scottish Chartism steered a different course from the English form, one of enlightenment, rather than disruption.'[8] Wright's interpretation has met with some serious challenges in recent years, most strongly from Hamish Fraser, in his *Chartism in Scotland,* published in 2010. Fraser criticises Wright for the latter's narrow range of sources, his failure to make adequate use of the Chartist press, and his over reliance on Whig documents. These failings have led Wright, Fraser claims, to underestimate the seriousness of Chartist agitation in Scotland.[9] We might approach these arguments with some caution. Whig commentators, like Cockburn and Moncreiff himself, offered some shrewd insights into how the Chartists were regarded in at least some quarters in Scotland. Fraser's own treatment of the Ranken trial is remarkably perfunctory, and compares unfavourably with the account by Alexander Wilson, written more than thirty years before.[10]

On the other hand, it is true that for a time there was considerable mass support for Chartism in Scotland, at least in the larger towns and cities like Edinburgh, Glasgow, Aberdeen, Dundee, and Dumfries. And in three of these, Edinburgh, Dundee, and Aberdeen, there was support also for the creation of a militaristic organisation – the National Guard – whose function was to be, by means of armed insurrection, to tie up English forces, and so enable the Irish to deal with the garrison in Ireland. At the end of March, 1848, a meeting was held in the Adam Square Hall in Edinburgh to form a Metropolitan National Guard 'for the defence and protection of the metropolis of Scotland', which was to consist of four divisions each with 21 officers and 400 men. It is also true, however, that this event marked the high point of enthusiasm for Chartist agitation in Scotland outside Edinburgh. Plans were laid for a series of meetings to be held simultaneously on the 12th June in the major cities. Those in Glasgow and Aberdeen were poorly attended, and while the march to Magdalen Green in Dundee did take place, it was without any serious disruption. Only in Edinburgh did the 12th June event pose a significant threat to authority. Processions were forbidden, and troops and special constables were deployed. At Bruntsfield Links a substantial crowd, variously numbered from nine thousand to twenty thousand, gathered to hear rousing speeches from the political leaders of the movement in Scotland – John Grant, Henry Ranken and Robert Hamilton.

It was what was said at this and some other gatherings which led to the arrest of these three[11] in August, and their subsequent trial in November on charges of conspiracy and sedition. Not surprisingly, the trial aroused a good deal of public interest. On the first day, Tuesday 7th November, 1848, the court, according to more than one account, 'was crowded to excess.'[12] The proceedings were also reported in several newspapers both north and south of the border.[13]

The charges as set out in the indictment recorded in the *Justiciary Reports* were very detailed, but in essentials they claimed that 'the said John Grant, Henry Ranken, Robert Hamilton, did...wickedly and feloniously, combine and conspire....with other persons to the prosecutor unknown, calling themselves Chartists, to effect an alteration of the laws and constitution of the realm...not peaceably and lawfully, and loyally, but by force and violence, or by armed resistance to lawful authority.' They were further charged that they did 'wickedly and feloniously, and seditiously, resolve and agree to form a body, to be called the National Guard, and to be provided with arms, to be used for the illegal and seditious purpose of effecting, by force and violence, or by armed resistance to lawful authority, the said alterations of the laws and constitution of the realm.'[14]

There are, however significant differences between this account of the charges, and those contained in Lord Cockburn's personal account, and for reasons which will become clear, notice has to be taken of those differences. In the latter, referring to the charge of sedition, Cockburn outlined the facts underlying the charge: 'that certain persons called Chartists had combined to effect certain alterations of the laws and constitution of the realm by force; that a meeting of these persons and their adherents was called for the 12th June, 1848....that this meeting was held on Bruntsfield Links; that the prisoner Grant presided; that he and the other two prisoners had spoken...that all these speeches were seditious, and had not only been uttered *"wickedly and feloniously"* but had been "INTENDED *and calculated to excite popular disaffection, commotion and violence, and resistance to lawful authority"*.'[15]

What was it then that the speakers had said to lay them open to these charges? According to the account in the *Glasgow Herald*, Hamilton, at a meeting held on the 28th April in the Adam Square Hall, had said that he did not see why a revolution could not take place here as well as in France, and that on the 20th July on the Calton Hill, had declared that at one time he would have been satisfied with the charter, but now would not be satisfied with anything less than a Republic. He urged the 'young and spirited men of Scotland' to go to Ireland to help the Irish people, and that 'pikes were easily made'. Grant, Hamilton and Ranken at the great gathering at Bruntsfield Links had all, it was alleged, supported a motion to form a National Guard. Hamilton for one had urged those present to 'organise themselves into clubs and sections, and to provide themselves with guns and bayonets' to achieve their objectives. Grant's role had principally been to chair the meeting, and to declare the resolution on the National Guard to have been adopted. As for Ranken, the fullest account of his contribution is that of Henry Cockburn in his study of trials for sedition in Scottish courts already mentioned.

Much of what Ranken had to say could hardly be described as inflammatory, and consisted initially of a declaration 'that it is our intention not to rest satisfied...until the peoples' charter is the law of the land, being fully convinced that justice can neither be obtained nor preserved, unless the people are put in possession of their rights, which are clearly laid down in that document.' In order to bring that about, it would be necessary to 'create a feeling that will ultimately compel our oppressors to relinquish their grasp, which we are satisfied will be ere long, for we are determined that while there is misery for the inmates of the cottage, there shall be no peace for the inmates of the hall.'

It was at this point that his words took on a more overtly threatening aspect – warning that 'the science of chemistry has entered the workshop, and the working men could provide themselves with as deadly weapons as Warner's long range[16]......If it was to be a struggle for life and death, if it was to be destruction,...then you hoped and trusted that the working men would be true only to themselves, and only abstain from all acts of aggression until they were roused by the oppression of their oppressors.'

More serious still, Ranken was further charged with having advised the people, in terms very like those employed by Hamilton: 'to organize into clubs and sections, and to provide themselves with arms', and urging that 'the young and spirited men of Scotland should go to Ireland and help the Irish people....At one time you would have been satisfied with the charter as the law of the land, but that now you would accept nothing less than a republic.'[17]

Moncreiff himself had been drawn into this situation by being approached, along with fellow advocates Grahame, Logan and Lorimer, to defend the three leading Chartists – John Grant, Henry Ranken, and Robert Hamilton – against the charges of conspiracy and sedition. At the time, Moncreiff asserted later, he 'willingly complied with the Chartists tried for sedition in 1848, who asked me to become their counsel. Ever since I have had a very warm heart to the working man.' Wilson Bain has commented that Moncreiff's defence of the Chartists served as 'one of the most significant [cases] for understanding his personal views.'[18] But how far he actually sympathised with their cause we have real reason to doubt. In a remarkably candid passage in the *Reminiscences*, he declared robustly, 'Not that politically I cared in the least for their "six points". We should have been better off now, without even the diluted infusion we have accepted.'[19] In particular, as we know from the account of his remarks in the House of Commons in June 1853 on a proposed bill to introduce the secret ballot into British political practice, he was opposed in principle to the secret ballot, as being antagonistic to the fundamentals of free government. Secret voting, he contended was perfectly fitted for despotic governments, such as Spain and Tuscany, but was 'entirely repugnant to a popular constitution such as ours.' The proposer of the Bill, Henry Berkeley, had argued that no man had the right to know how any other had voted. Moncreiff disagreed – 'for he thought that, even if the establishment of vote by [secret] ballot were to take place – even if it did prevent intimidation, it would at the same time remove the proper check which public opinion exercised over every man's vote.'[20]

Moncreiff's own engagement in the Ranken trial, he insisted, was strictly professional, but since the trial raised some constitutional points of interest, and excited much public attention, then 'in these times, when day and night are made hideous by howls of "coercion", it may be wholesome to remind some Caledonian wiseacres what this trial was about.'

It was important to point out, as he did, that in Scotland there had never been a 'Coercion Act'. 'No civilized country in the world requires any special authority to punish criminally resistance to laws enacted by the Supreme Authority. That the person resisting disapproved of the law is a plea fit for Bedlam only.' Moncreiff's client, Henry Ranken, had been accused of having used language 'calculated or intended to excite disaffection among the people, and disobedience to the law'. If such a charge had been proved, then clearly it would have constituted a criminal offence. But in the event, the jury convicted Ranken only of having used language 'calculated' to incite disaffection, and negatived the word 'intended'. So the question arose as to whether such a verdict amounted to the crime of sedition. It was a question which Moncreiff did his best to exploit in the course of the trial.

If Moncreiff had little sympathy with the political agenda of his Chartist clients, he had a good deal of sympathy with the men themselves. 'I took much interest in the case', he wrote later, 'and in my clients, for it gave me an insight into one phase, at least, of the working man's mind. These orators were self educated men. They met once a week to discuss such works as Locke, and Reid, and Hume: and very intelligent they seemed to be, when they were not haranguing at the Calton Hill at Edinburgh.'[21] Or as Lord Cockburn himself put it: 'the prisoners were all respectable men, and, except as politicians, sensible.'[22]

This almost respectful attitude to the prisoners was characteristic of the proceedings as a whole. What Cockburn also remarked on particularly was the approach to the case by the Court, and the remarkable lack of prejudice against the accused, which he contrasted starkly with what had been the case half a century before: 'If any one who had heard the trials of 1793 and 1794, and had then left this country, had come back, and been present at this trial, it would not have been easy to have convinced him that he was again amongst the same people.' What was now so different was not so much the degree of mistimed political extravagance with which the prisoners were charged and which they represented....*But the total change in the tone and air of the public, and far more of the court, would have amazed and pleased him.*' [My italics] In Cockburn's opinion what had happened in the interim was that 'The people had gained great reforms, and a vast increase in power. Proscription, consequently, for political offences was at an end. A far better instructed attachment to the Constitution, including even its monarchy, was combined with infinitely greater political toleration. No part of the scene would have impressed him so much with the feeling of novelty as the speeches; each of which, including the judges' charge, seemed determined to exceed the other in popularity of doctrine.'[23] Here, of course, we are presented with a prime example of the Whig perspective on contemporary politics which we have been warned against by historians such as Hamish Fraser. But what we are concerned with here is not so much how to divine the real character of Scottish Chartism in the late1840s, as to reflect and explain the judicial treatment of their accused leaders.

At the time the *Caledonian Mercury* also congratulated the authorities on the restraint they had shown towards the Chartist agitators, pointing out that there had been no attempt 'to check these misguided men, or to interfere with them, so long as their proceedings, however violent and exaggerated, could by possibility come under the limits of free discussion. 'For weeks and months,' the *Mercury* continued, 'they carried on an agitation, holding open air meetings, congregating masses, and making excited appeals to their passions at a period when society was naturally alarmed at such demonstrations....Still there was a reluctance to interfere with meetings professedly called for political discussion, and it was not until the leaders began to talk of organizing an armed resistance to the laws that they were arrested to answer a criminal charge.'[24]

Even counsel for the prosecution, James Craufurd, was praised by the paper for his 'highly temperate address', and Cockburn likewise singled out speeches by Craufurd[25] and Moncreiff as characterising the low key approach to the trial. In Cockburn's opinion, Craufurd's 'was the best address that ever was delivered for the Crown to a jury in a Scotch trial for sedition. It was able, fair, and temperate; strong for a conviction, but liberally constitutional in public principle, and above all it was superior to the paltriness of inflaming, instead of allaying any prejudices the jury might be supposed to be under the influence.'

Most remarkable was Craufurd's explicit advice to the jury not to convict the prisoners on the basis of their political beliefs. He continued to insist that they were 'well entitled to hold these opinions, and to associate in order to maintain and advance them by all legitimate means – that is by addresses to the Crown, petitions to parliament, public meetings orderly conducted, argument, reasoning, entreaty and remonstrance.' This was not, he emphasised, 'a prosecution for opinion, and whether the changes desired by the Chartists would be wise or salutary, conducive to the public welfare or consistent with public security, is no question for you or any of us to consider.'[26]

Moncreiff's own address to the jury was in similar objective vein, contrasting the present proceedings with those of days gone by, and at the same time going out of his way to congratulate Craufurd on the tone of his speech. He compared the present proceedings with those trials he had studied in preparation for today's case, and was struck by the contrast 'in the tone of constitutional moderation in which the prosecution has been conducted, with prosecutions not yet forgotten, and still too recent to be stamped and characterised with the reprobation they deserve.' There had been times, he reminded the court, 'when verdicts have been returned under circumstances of public prejudice, in which the voice not of law merely, but of reason and sense was drowned in overpowering terror; verdicts which filled some, at least, who pronounced them with undying regret; and have stamped an indelible stigma on the times they characterise. I am under no apprehension of that kind today.'[27] He was satisfied that he would get a fair hearing from the court, and the defendants a fair trial.

It would be easy to dismiss these words as the common currency of the defence advocate currying favour with the men (they were of course all men) of the jury on behalf of his client. But as far as the behaviour of counsel for the prosecution was concerned, Moncreiff's description of its moderation, as we have seen, was accurate. And in the course of his case, Moncreiff himself demonstrated skills of advocacy beyond mere fair speeches. He was quick, on more than one occasion, to challenge some piece of evidence advanced by the prosecution as 'incompetent', and which ought therefore, to be disregarded. For example, when a witness called John Eikings was asked by Craufurd if he had heard Robert Hamilton advocate the use of arms at a meeting on Calton Hill, Moncreiff objected that the indictment against Hamilton and the others had not included any reference to such a meeting. 'The pannels', he insisted, 'were entitled to hold that the occasions and words set forth in the indictment were those alone on which the prosecutor was entitled to rely. It might lead to the greatest injustice if it was allowed that other meetings and other words than those libelled [i.e. cited] might be proved. It was incompetent to prove intention of conspiracy, without giving notice of the occasion in respect of which the proof was offered.' On this occasion the question was not pressed further.[28] He was not always so successful. When James Brownlee, a sergeant of police who had been present at the Bruntsfield meeting, was asked if Henry Ranken on that occasion had advised the people to get arms in order to procure the charter, Moncreiff tried again to have the evidence ruled inadmissible on much the same ground – that 'when an indictment for sedition libelled particular expressions in proof of the crime, it was incompetent to prove any general statement not included in the libel'. This time his objection was overruled.[29]

More telling, probably, was Moncreiff's examination of the witness P. Anderson, a tailor, who had been the secretary of the Edinburgh Chartist Association. Anderson was opposed to the use of violence, and when a motion was put by Henry Ranken to a meeting of the Association, calling for a further meeting to consider the propriety of forming a National Guard, Anderson had resigned. Under Moncreiff's cross examination, Anderson made it clear that Ranken had disagreed with the man known as 'Brigadier General' McKay, the prime mover behind the formation of the National Guard. He, Anderson, had always understood Ranken to be 'what was called a moral force Chartist' – that is 'an individual opposed to anything except persuasion for the purpose of obtaining any object'. Moreover Anderson had understood that at the meeting in question, Ranken had been opposed to the formation of the Guard, and so his motion calling for a public meeting to discuss the issue was in fact designed to put a stop to the proposal.[30]

Moncreiff had worked hard to present his client in the best possible light. His final address to the jury on Ranken's behalf took nearly two hours to deliver, and was designed to show that there was nothing criminal in holding to Chartist opinions, or in the language Ranken had used to defend them. Chartism was, he insisted, 'a code of politics quite as respectable in itself as any held by any other body of men. A man was as much entitled to uphold the six points of the Charter, as any other individual was entitled to hold his opinions, whatever these might be.' It had been alleged that Ranken had spoken in favour of organisation and of clubs, but when was there an organisation which was not organised into clubs and sections? And he pointed out that back in 1794 it had been found almost impossible to get a single man for the jury who was not connected with some club or other.

Moncreiff was prepared to admit that some of Ranken's language had been extravagant, but at the centre of it was 'the assertion of a doctrine truly constitutional; for when he talked about the people being illegally attacked, and the Government depriving them of the independence of action or speech contrary to the constitution, he only spoke what those who founded the liberties of Britain spoke frequently before', and he cited the examples of Charles James Fox, and Earl Grey. At the conclusion of this persuasive address, we are told, 'there was considerable applause, which was instantly checked by the judge'.[31]

His next intervention very nearly resulted in the complete collapse of the case against Ranken and Hamilton, and almost certainly had an effect on the leniency of the sentence. Towards the end of the proceedings, the jury withdrew for a mere half hour before returning a verdict of not proven on the charge of conspiracy against all three defendants, and further finding John Grant not guilty on the charge of sedition. When it came to the charge of sedition against Robert Hamilton the jury found him 'guilty of using language calculated to excite popular disaffection and resistance to lawful authority', and by a majority of one, found Henry Ranken guilty of using similar language.[32] This statement may seem clear enough to a modern audience, but it was not enough for the court, since it did not include the all-important word contained in the original indictment of 'intended', that is 'using language *intended* and calculated...'. The presiding judge, the Lord Justice Clerk, made the mistake of trying to clarify the situation. 'Now to make your verdict correct, you should determine whether they are guilty or not guilty of sedition to any extent you please. You may say, for example, that they are guilty of sedition in so far as they used language calculated to excite popular disaffection and resistance to lawful authority.'

'That is what we mean, my Lord.'

'In using the word *calculated*,' the Chancellor [foreman] of the jury was asked, 'do you mean to leave out the word "*intended*", or does your verdict mean to embrace both?'

The answer cannot have pleased him.

'We mean purposely to leave out the word "intended",' was the response.

So in its final form, the verdict was even less unequivocal than it might have been. 'The jury find Robert Hamilton guilty of sedition, in so far as that he used language calculated to excite popular disaffection and resistance to lawful authority; and by a majority find Henry Ranken guilty in the same terms.'[33]

Moncreiff was not one to let the opportunity slip out of his grasp. 'The primary question was, what did the jury signify?' The original indictment had charged the defendants with using language both 'calculated' *and* 'intended' to produce a particular result. But then the word 'intended' had been purposely deleted by the jury – that must surely mean that the language was *not* intended to produce that result Intention was the essence of the crime. If the defendants were being tried merely for using reckless language, that was no crime *per se*. If the original indictment had included *calculated* only, but not *intended*, that would not have amounted to sedition. Logically, the verdict negatived the terms of the indictment.[34]

It was a brave attempt, and clearly threw the court into some disarray. Up to this point, the case had been heard before just three judges – the Lord Justice Clerk, Lord Medwyn and Lord Moncreiff. Now, the whole court was summoned to debate the question. Cockburn recorded the discussion in some detail, since as it turned out, his own was the only voice to support James Moncreiff's position: 'The argument in support of the objection,' he noted, 'came, in substance, to this:- That the verdict was uncertain, or was defective as a ground for punishment,' since 'every Scotch indictment, *without any one exception*, has set forth either general wickedness and feloniousness of mind as the foundation of the charge, or some particular evil intention.' In the present case the indictment had included both, 'for it first asserts that all the acts were done "*wickedly and feloniously*", and then specifies the particular sort of wickedness to have consisted in a design to produce the very mischief for which the seditious acts are said to have been both "*intended* and calculated".' In other words, in the original indictment 'evil intention' had been made an essential part of the crime, and yet 'the verdict, especially when combined with the explanation which must be taken as part of it, did not merely not convict of any criminality of mind, but virtually acquitted of it.'[35]

Cockburn was clearly in sympathy with this argument, but nevertheless recorded the contrary view with equal care. What this amounted to was that the judges, with the exception of himself, effectively ignored the uncomfortable decision of the jury to remove the word 'intended', and decided that 'there was no legal necessity for always establishing [the] exact design in all cases of sedition: that any *malus animus,* including under this a criminal disregard for the consequences is sufficient.' Despite then the fact that 'the jury had negatived the evil intention libelled, they had not negatived all *malus animus*, for they had convicted the prisoners of *sedition*....and that the plain meaning, and the only correct construction, was, that in so far as the prisoners had used language calculated to excite popular disaffection and resistance to lawful authority, they had incurred all the guilt, whatever it may be, that is essential to the commission of sedition.'

As Cockburn commented, somewhat sourly, 'This answer was satisfactory to the whole court, except to myself.'[36]

A rather more convincing explanation of the judges' ruling was provided by Lord Moncreiff, James' father, who had expressed himself satisfied that the verdict was 'a good and effectual verdict', and one 'on which some sentences ought to pass, as moved by the Public Prosecutor'. 'If the jury had supposed or meant that they were finding the prisoners *not guilty*, they no doubt would have said so.' As it happened it fell to Lord Moncreiff, as one of the three judges trying the case, to propose an appropriate sentence. Having laid aside the charge of conspiracy, of which the defendants had been acquitted, he turned to the question of sedition. Here he obviously found himself in some difficulty – his remarks now condemnatory, now conciliatory. In the end his view of the situation owed more perhaps to the potentially dangerous consequences of the seditious speeches, than the niceties of law.

The jury, he noted, had found the prisoners guilty of the charge of sedition, and even in the modified terms of their verdict, that implied a certain criminal intention.

> ....it is impossible, I say, for any man of sober and calm mind, looking to the interests of the country, not to see that they are seditious in the character which the Jury have given them, namely that they were calculated to excite popular disaffection to the Government, and to excite resistance to lawful authority.....It would be a sad matter indeed, if the delivery of such speeches in large assemblies of persons, one of these assemblies in a room consisting of six, seven, or eight hundred persons, and another in an open field in Bruntsfield Links, where some thousands were present, were to be allowed, where the language of these speeches was of dangerous tendency to the best interests of the country.

Yet he found the duty of punishing *these* prisoners difficult and distasteful. 'Undoubtedly it is very painful to move a sentence against such persons as the pannels at the Bar, who appeared in other respects to have been respectable individuals.' Then, recalling himself to his responsibility, he changed his tone. 'But we must discharge our duty to the country. The law must be put in force; and the court cannot permit such things to go on without punishment; and when the Jury have found prisoners guilty of seditious speeches, it is the duty of the Court to pronounce such a sentence as to show to others that similar practices cannot be permitted with impunity.'

By this time the defendants must have been thoroughly bemused. Were they going to face long prison sentences, or be let off with a caution? The next part of the speech must have reassured them, up to a point. 'It is a great consolation to me,' Lord Moncreiff continued, 'to think that now, as the case stands before us, it is a very mitigated case of sedition', and he went on to acknowledge the fact that the jury had effectively removed the charge of intention from the indictment. In the circumstances the sentence he proposed, 'cannot be thought of by any portion of the community to be a severe punishment in such a case; and I am willing to believe that it must appear to every person of sober understanding to be as lenient as the Court can pronounce. The sentence which I propose is, imprisonment for each of the prisoners for a period of Four Calendar Months.'[37]

Lenient indeed! According to Cockburn, most intelligent people who had sat through the whole trial were convinced that the outcome should have been convictions of conspiracy against all three prisoners, and of sedition against Ranken and Hamilton.[38] He himself believed that the language used at the 12th June meeting, especially by Hamilton, was 'not only plainly seditious, but it was by far the most seditious that ever had been charged against any Scottish prisoner'. Yet when he consulted Lord Campbell, a member of the Cabinet, for his personal opinion on the validity of the verdict, Campbell replied that in his view the verdict ought to have been considered as one of acquittal. 'He thought that in principle it was just the English abortive verdict of "guilty of publishing only".'[39]

So in the end, leniency was the order of the day. Even the Lord Justice Clerk, who, we are told, had been seriously unimpressed with all the speeches of counsel, went out of his way when pronouncing sentence to deal courteously with the defendants. 'I would fain hope and trust, and I express it with sincerity, that, from your demeanour – I have gathered it one way or another, I cannot tell how – but I have gathered throughout the course of this trial, from your whole manner and demeanour, that it is not likely that you will rush wantonly and recklessly into the use of such language as you did upon the cases libelled.'[40]

Earlier in that same year, riots in Glasgow, wrongly ascribed by some to Chartist influence, had resulted in a large number of arrests, and the sentence of one convicted leader, George Smith, to eighteen years transportation.[41] Compared with this, and with the expectations of many who were present, the defendants in the Edinburgh trial got away extraordinarily lightly. Why was that? Was it because of their demeanour in court, which convinced even the Lord Justice Clerk that basically they were harmless? Was it because, as Cockburn commented, that a mild sentence would deprive them of all sympathy, and avoid the creation of martyrs? Was it because by this stage, there was a general understanding, shared by the jury, that support for Chartism, in Scotland at least, was on the wane? Or was it due to James Moncreiff, and the persuasiveness of his argument that once the jury had deleted the word 'intended' from the charge, all that was left was the accusation of using inappropriate language? Any advocate in his position, who had secured such a result, might be forgiven for taking a good deal of the credit for himself.

There was an intriguing postscript. Some 'twelve or fourteen years afterwards', Moncreiff wrote in his memoirs:

> while Adam Black and I were members for the City, at a somewhat stormy meeting, a man sprung up on the platform – said as he passed 'Don't name me' – and made an admirable speech in our support. It was one of the convicts of 1848, which, I do not say. I thanked him afterwards, and expressed my surprise at the moderation of his sentiments. 'Ah,' he replied, 'it makes all the difference when a man has to heed for his children.' I found afterwards that he had been prosperous in his trade, and was a master manufacturer.[42]

The Rev. Sir Harry Moncreiff Wellwood

Sir James Wellwood Moncreiff

Robert Bell

Eleanor Jane Bell

Lady Isabella Moncreiff

Moncreiff addresses the jury in the trial of
Madeine Smith

Tullibole Castle

15 Great Stuart Street

**15 Great Stuart Street
Interior**

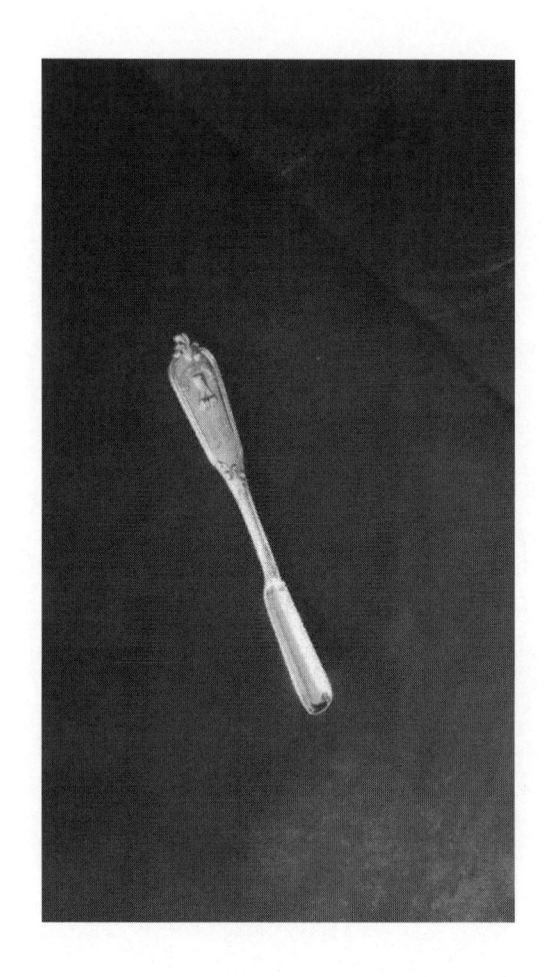

Marrowbone Spoon

III

Lord Advocate

Chapter 8
Minister for Scotland

I - In Parliament

In April 1851 James Moncreiff was appointed Lord Advocate of Scotland in the Liberal government of Lord John Russell at the unusually young age of 39. At the time he recorded in his personal notebook his pride in the achievement – he was the youngest Lord Advocate so far that century – but also his anxiety at the task before him – 'I have much to fear,' he wrote, 'and little heart to start with.'[1] No doubt it was a daunting task for a young lawyer with so far no parliamentary experience, yet he was to fill the post with distinction over most of the next twenty years, in the Aberdeen coalition government and under two more Liberal Prime Ministers – Palmerston and Gladstone – until he finally left politics to go on the Scottish Bench as Lord Justice Clerk in 1869.[2]

That Moncreiff was able to fill the post of Lord Advocate for so long was both a tribute to his skill as a politician and a manager, and a reflection of the dominance of the Liberal party throughout the United Kingdom for much of the period. This dominance had come about largely through the weakness of the Conservative opposition in Parliament and in the country, damaged though not killed by the electoral changes contained in the 1832 Reform Act, and further divided by Peel's repeal of the Corn Laws in 1846. After 1832 the Liberals were seen as the party of progress, reform, and commitment to free trade, widely supported in Scotland, while the Tories appeared as obstacles to change. Consequently, between the Reform Acts of 1832 and 1868, Conservatives won only seven seats at general elections. Yet the Liberal hegemony had its drawbacks. The very weakness of the Conservatives in turn weakened Liberal party discipline, and divisions developed between the Whigs – broadly content with the reforms of 1832, and the middle class Radicals, who were avid for further reform, staunch free traders, and hostile to the entrenched privileges of the Established Church. 'Not surprisingly,' wrote Tom Devine, 'these fissures became apparent at elections, when contests were often fought, not between Liberals and Conservatives, but between Liberals of different views on issues as varied as church disestablishment, trade union rights, and electoral reforms.'[3] From time to time Moncreiff, despite sharing at least some of the political beliefs of the Radicals, was to part company with them over such issues as the franchise and the secret ballot. Relations between himself and Duncan McLaren – a leading Radical and sometime Lord Provost of Edinburgh – were particularly fraught. They clashed over a number of important issues – the reform of education, and the campaign to bring back the office of Secretary of State – but also over relatively trivial but corrosive matters, like the Edinburgh Annuity Tax

Moncreiff was, however, fully conscious and appreciative of the great political changes which had followed on from the 1832 reforms. During the four years from 1830 to 1833, as he wrote many years later, 'the world was full of political change, nowhere more striking than in Scotland. It was a political Carnival; all so new.' Prior to the passing of the Bill, 'A real watershed election was hitherto unknown on this side of the Tweed......There was not a pretence or a spark of popular election in the parliamentary representation of those days in Scotland.' But after 1832 the Conservatives 'were obliged to see their old supremacy obliterated, and those over whom they had ruled for a quarter of a century, rulers in their turn. The voters in the counties were known as Freeholders – that is proprietors holding their land feudally from the Queen. Those who did not so hold, and a large proportion of the owners of land did not, had no voice. But the astuteness of the lawyers had invented a means of legalising a vote without legalising land, and a large manufacture of such qualifications was prevalent.' [This was the notorious 'faggot vote', of which more later]. As for the burghs, the Member was elected by the Town Councillors, 'but as they elected themselves, the popular element was still more thoroughly excluded. The election of the Member for the Burghs was determined by the majority of votes on a day fixed; and when things ran close, instances were not rare of a recusant Baillie being kidnapped and detained until after the election. Such was our free British Constitution in the days when I was twenty.'[4]

It was the Reform Bill, he affirmed, which had transformed the community socially as well as politically. 'I feel still something of the exultant throb which filled my frame when I thought that altho' they had waited so long, the steadfast asserters of popular rights, the men who in the *Edinburgh Review* had braved the persons of power, and defied the scorn of its underlings, were, after long years, to be rewarded.'[5]

And rewarded they were. An important consequence of the transfer of power from Tories to Whigs was the parallel transfer of patronage. While previously it had not been impossible for a Whig to be raised the Bench, as Moncreiff's own father had been in 1829, it was nevertheless the case that before 1832 judgeships, and the senior legal posts of Lord Advocate and Solicitor-General, almost invariably went to Tory nominees. As Moncreiff noted, with the exception of the year 1806, the office of Sheriff had uniformly fallen to Tory lawyers since 1784, and on the occasion of George IV's famous visit to Scotland in 1822, one of the political papers published a mock list of presentations to various offices, including the names of nine Whig advocates on being made sheriffs.[6] But now the appointment of Whigs to high legal office could become the norm. Francis Jeffrey was appointed Lord Advocate, and Henry Cockburn Solicitor-General.

In 1851, then, Moncreiff himself had become a beneficiary of Whig patronage. The second important factor leading to Moncreiff's appointment was a series of events over which he had no personal control, but which opened up useful vacancies in the legal hierarchy. In 1850 Francis Jeffrey, now Lord Jeffrey, died, and the then Solicitor-General, Maitland, was raised to the Bench in his place, while Moncreiff became Solicitor-General. Then in the following year Moncreiff's own father died, and while this was a cause of great sadness in the family, the outcome was that the then Lord Advocate, Andrew Rutherfurd, moved on to the Bench, and a mere nine days after the death of his father, Moncreiff took Rutherfurd's place as Lord Advocate.

It was of course true that the pool of talent available for these positions was severely limited – confined as it was to senior members of the Faculty of Advocates. This was to become a major element of criticism of the post of Lord Advocate in subsequent years, but at the time of Moncreiff's appointment the choice of possible candidates was effectively limited to only two or three rising stars in the Whig legal firmament – which included Moncreiff himself, and Andrew Murray Dunlop, the author in the early 1840s of the *Claim of Right*. Moncreiff's own family connections both with the party and with the Bench can hardly have been a hindrance.

Then there was the factor of Moncreiff's personal ambition and desire to make his mark in politics. For more than ten years before his appointment, he had enjoyed a growing legal practice. But for him the practice of the law was never quite enough – a career in politics beckoned. Given his parentage and the circumstances of his upbringing, surrounded as he was by his father's Whig friends and colleagues, this was hardly surprising though not inevitable – none of his siblings became politicians, or at least not professionals. For him, as he explained in his memoirs, his ambitions were limited to three – to sit down in the House of Commons after a speech amid cheering from all parts of the House; to sit as President one of the Divisions of the Court of Session; and to sit on the red benches of the House of Lords. 'I have known them all,' he wrote. 'The first was the best.'[7]

The office of Lord Advocate to which Moncreiff was appointed in 1851 was the most senior government post in Scotland at the time. Since the abolition of the Secretaryship of State after Culloden in 1746, the

Lord Advocate had become in effect the Minister for Scotland, (in 1867 W.E. Baxter, M.P for Montrose Burghs, was to describe him as 'the political dictator of Scotland'[8]), and as such he wielded considerable powers, though still, after 1827, being answerable to the Secretary of the Home Department in the Cabinet. In practice the Home Secretary delegated almost all his responsibilities for Scotland to the Lord Advocate, and he, in turn, delegated some of them to the Solicitor-General for Scotland and the Advocates-Depute, to the Scottish Lord of the Treasury, and to various administrative Boards sitting in Edinburgh.

Writing in 1888, John McLaren, one of Moncreiff's successors as Lord Advocate and son of Duncan McLaren, identified his professional responsibilities as first, the administration of the Department of Criminal Investigation and Criminal Prosecution; second, advising other government departments such as the Law Officers; third, advising on Scottish patronage; fourthly, the preparation of bills relating to Scotland, and the charge of such bills in the House of Commons, and finally 'public correspondence'.[9] Despite the fact that by 1888 Scotland now had a new Scottish Secretary, who might have been expected to have taken over some of the responsibilities of the Lord Advocate, McLaren's description of his principal duties did not differ greatly from Moncreiff's own experience of the office.[10]

Appointment as Lord Advocate was only the first step. It was expected that the appointee should also secure election to the House of Commons. Indeed, on those rare occasions when this did not happen, as in the case of Moncreiff's Tory friend John Inglis, the practical difficulties of carrying out the responsibilities of the job were considerable. Accordingly, in 1851 Moncreiff presented himself for election to the seat of Leith Burghs, traditionally the political home of Whig Lord Advocates. Although he was standing unopposed, that did not mean that he could avoid public meetings with the electorate, in Newhaven, Portobello and Leith itself, or avoid some rough handling from hecklers, many of whom objected to always having to have the Lord Advocate as their member. 'It was most insulting,' as one speaker put it, 'that Leith should be the pocket borough of Parliament House.'[11]

Others were less than happy that Moncreiff and the new Solicitor-General, John Cowan, were both Free Churchmen. The *Dundee Courier*, amongst other newspapers, commented critically on the great speed with which the election for Rutherfurd's successor had been arranged, saddling the electors of Leith Burghs for the fourth time in succession with a Whig Lord Advocate for their representative. 'What mysterious bond is it that indissolubly links a great mercantile and sea-faring constituency like Leith with a silk gown and a powdered wig, and tacks it like an appendage which cannot be wanted to the trappings of a government official?'[12] For his part, Moncreiff shrewdly made use of his family's name and reputation 'as a guarantee of my attachment to liberal principles, and regard for the people of Scotland'.[13] He made it clear that he stood for a policy of free trade, and was in favour of a further but limited extension of the franchise. He condemned the bribery that had occurred at recent elections, especially at Aylesbury, but 'was not yet inclined to go to the length of supporting vote by [the secret] ballot'.[14] Broadly speaking these were all political principles to which he continued to adhere for the rest of his career in Parliament.

The great obstacle, as he saw it, to a still wider extension of the franchise was the lack of a moral standard, not just amongst the electorate, but more particularly amongst candidates. 'An end,' he insisted, 'must be put to the influence, bribery, and treating now prevalent, before the franchise can be so widely extended as I should like to see it.'[15] It was at least partly for this reason that in the coming years he put so much emphasis on improvements in education, and the establishment of a national education system for Scotland.

On the subject of education, which was to bulk so large in his reform agenda over the next two decades, Moncreiff 'was anxious to see the parochial schools opened up, by the removal of [religious] tests, and placed altogether on a more liberal basis'. But interestingly, again in the light of his subsequent campaign for educational reform in Scotland, he replied cautiously, even one might say equivocally, to a question from one John Murray as to whether he was in favour of 'the scheme of national education which had emanated from certain members of the Free Church?' All he was prepared to say on this occasion was that 'he was not pledged to this or any other plan, but was open to consider whichever might be the most suitable to the wants of the country'.[16] Evidently he had already learned the political art of dealing with unwelcome questions.

Moncreiff's political principles were and remained for the rest of his life essentially those of 'Old Edinburgh Whigs' like his father and his father's friends. They are expressed in his many political speeches and public addresses. In 1871 he published an essay on 'Politics' in his 'novel', *A Visit to my Discontented Cousin.* This work was not so much a piece of fiction as a collection of twenty-five essays, many of them previously published in *Fraser's Magazine,* well known, oddly enough, as a Tory publication. The essays are loosely tied together by the fictional account of a visit by the narrator Pemberton, a London lawyer, to his second cousin Dagentree, at the latter's country estate. Subjects included in this collection range from fishing to photography, and may be taken broadly to represent Moncreiff's own views on these subjects, though often with a satirical twist. The essay on 'Politics' therefore turns out to be not so much a political *apologia pro vita sua,* as a light-hearted debate on party politics and political morality between the more idealistic Pemberton and his cynical cousin. To Dagentree, political life is 'concentrated selfishness', while Pemberton tries in vain to persuade him that 'the field of exertion is a noble one – the ends, when rightly estimated, the purest and most elevating of which the intellect is capable'. Dagentree will have none of it. 'Men enter the House of Commons,' he insists, 'much as the recruit enters the army. A bit of blue ribbon, the sound of a drum, a shilling, and a pot of beer are the component parts of the patriotism of the British Grenadiers.'[17]

Not surprisingly, Moncreiff duly found himself elected for the constituency of Leith Burghs, and thanked the electors with a suitably patriotic speech. 'I trust,' he told them, 'that when I go to London I shall never forget my native land, or forget that I am a Scotchman. Gentlemen, I love my country, I feel my heart beats more warmly as I tread its mountain sides….along its clear and crystal streams…for that country it is indeed an honour to work.'[18]

And he began on that work with commendable speed. The election took place on the 14th April, and barely one month later Moncreiff was on his feet in the House of Commons to deliver his maiden speech on the Ecclesiastical Titles Assumption Bill – an issue to which he had already referred in his address to the electors of Leith.[19] The promotion of this Bill was in reality an act of political opportunism on the part of Lord John Russell, who was becoming concerned that his Liberal administration was beginning to lose its original impetus after five years in power. The occasion for the Bill was an attempt by the Pope to re-establish a Catholic hierarchy in England, complete with titles for dioceses. The debate provided Moncreiff with an excellent opportunity to represent the views of himself, his nation, and its religion. He would never persecute Roman Catholics, he promised; he would try to organise the best state education for their children, but he never doubted the error of their faith. In this same speech, he took the opportunity to affirm his loyalty to the Whigs, 'who had founded their political reputation on having fought the battle of tolerance in its darkest times', his loyalty to the Queen, whose position as Head of the Church of England would be undermined by Vatican interference, and his loyalty to the Protestant faith. 'The old spirit of Scotland', he told the House, 'has become far more tolerant, but he was satisfied it had become not the less Protestant.'[20]

As Omond commented many years later, no first speech could have been made in more favourable circumstances.[21] It was to be the first of very many such speeches, by no means all on Scottish subjects. Hansard lists nearly 450 speeches he addressed to the Commons between

1851 and 1869 – his most prolific year by far being the last. Nor were his remarks limited to Scottish affairs – they ranged from education to the outbreak of rinderpest on the Isle of Man; from conspiracy to murder to the prevention of the sale of obscene books; from intestacy to smoke nuisance abatement. Some topics stand out as being of particular importance, either as being of special interest to himself, such as his plans for a national education system for Scotland, or because of their wider significance in the political history of the period, such as his proposals in 1860 for further electoral reform.

Over the years Moncreiff became known as an outstanding speaker, in Parliament and in public, and throughout his career was to be in great demand to address public bodies of all kinds. Moncreiff's political masters were well aware of his oratorical gifts – his eloquence, the breadth of his knowledge, his ability to think on his feet – and frequently called on him to address the House on subjects which were neither Scottish nor narrowly legal. As he himself claimed, between 1859 and 1866, 'there were few of the important imperial debates in which I was not asked by the Govt. to intervene.'[22] When the government was faced with a hostile motion in the House over the fall of Kars in the Crimean War, Moncreiff was made its spokesman, and the motion defeated.[23] And again, when the government sought an elegant address to compliment Speaker Dennison on his re-election after the 1867 Reform Act, Moncreiff duly obliged.[24] Indeed, such was the esteem in which Moncreiff was held by Lord Palmerston for one, that if Dennison had in fact retired in 1865 as some expected, it was Palmerston's reported intention to propose Moncreiff as the next Speaker.[25]

Of the areas of responsibility identified by John McLaren, probably the most important for any Lord Advocate was that of drawing up legislation to do with Scottish affairs, and then piloting bills through the House of Commons. At one point Moncreiff claimed that he had promoted one hundred such bills in Parliament, and although that was certainly an exaggeration, the number and range of his proposed enactments was impressive by any standards. They covered topics in criminal law, administrative law, international law, the law relating to marriage and divorce, to the poor, and of course the inevitable Edinburgh and Canongate Annuity Tax. The battle over this last was to drag on for much of his parliamentary career, and involve ever worsening relations between himself and Duncan McLaren.

In later chapters we will consider Moncreiff's attempts through legislation to create a national education system for Scotland, to reform the unpopular law on bankruptcy, and to respond to calls for the assimilation of Scots and English law. Like most politicians Moncreiff won some battles and lost others, and there were several instances, such as educational reform, and reform of the electoral system, when the final victory had to be left to his successors. But even in these cases, his attempts to achieve his objectives, despite being unsuccessful, tell us a good deal about the man, his political views, and the political obstacles he faced.

A good case in point is provided by his Electoral Reform Bill of 1860. On the first of March, 1860, Moncreiff came to the House with a Bill for the reform of representation in Scotland closely modelled on, but not identical with, current proposals for England.[26] The principal feature was to extend the franchise in Scotland by means of an occupation franchise of £10 in the counties and £6 in the burghs. The key innovation, however, and the principal distinction from the English plans, was the simplification of electoral registration in Scotland, based on the Valuation Rolls. This would entail dispensing altogether with the registration machinery of the 1832 Act, including the Registration Court.

Moncreiff was well aware of the potential dangers of reducing the monetary threshold for the franchise. Prior to, and indeed for some time after the Reform Act of 1832, there had been something of a minor industry in the manufacture of what were known as 'faggot votes'. According to William Ferguson, faulty draughtsmanship in the 1832 Act had left untouched the legal entitlement of the 'superiority' in a property to divide his rights into £10 units of value, and to assign each of these to well-disposed nominees, who were thereby entitled to vote. Furthermore, in the Scottish legal system where feudal inheritance remained strong, ownership of the superiority was quite separate from physical ownership of land or property, and was quite often retained when selling off land.[27] This abuse was particularly prevalent in Scotland, with its widely scattered landed population.

It also seems to have been practised particularly effectively by Tory landowners. According to Hutchison, the main period of vote making was between 1835 and 1839.[28] Yet as late as February 1880, the *Scotsman* published a list of 260 new Tory faggots for Mid-Lothian alone, somewhat contrary to the spirit of the Ballot Act of eight years earlier, which had introduced the secret ballot into British politics for the first time.[29] If by any chance it was not completely obvious which party a given faggot voter would support, then it was regarded as perfectly legitimate to try to find out. In August 1879, one William Anderson wrote to G.H. Garrie, to ask whether the latter could give him any information as to the political views of Mr Benjamin Sutherland, a baker and tenant of the Duke of Buccleuch. 'If not, perhaps you would be kind enough to give him a call and let me know the result.'[30] Legal battles were fought in the Registration Courts, as political parties sought to have the entitlement to vote of their opponents annulled. In 1870, members of the Liberal party tried to disenfranchise a Mr W.G. Roy, a tenant and joint lease holder with his brother of a house in Kew Terrace, on the ground that he was not in personal occupancy and did not reside there. Roy's response to this was to claim that one room of the house was exclusively his, and was filled with books, articles of furniture etc. belonging to him, and that he had free access to all of the house. The Sheriff supported Roy's claim. In the same session he also dismissed objections by Liberals to the enrolment of certain gentlemen, qualified to vote in respect of feu duties payable to them by the Duke of Buccleuch. The problem was that the duties related to land sold by the Duke to the North British Railway Company. Nevertheless, the Sheriff ruled that since the men in question were still in possession of feu duty to the amount of £10 upon the subjects on which they were originally enrolled, they were entitled to remain upon the roll as voters.[31]

Back in 1860, Moncreiff's proposed Bill would have reduced the monetary threshold for the franchise still further, and inevitably increased the opportunities for the manufacture of votes. He sought to deal with this problem by insisting that for all freeholds below £10, a residence requirement should be enforced. However, the bill ran into opposition on a number of fronts. Within the ranks of Scottish Liberals it aroused disappointment that Scotland was to receive only two more Members of Parliament – one for the city of Glasgow, and one for the four Scottish universities together. William Baxter argued in the House with some force that on the basis of population and taxation combined, the country was entitled to an increase of nineteen additional Members. Sir John Pakington, Member for Droitwich, objected to the fact that the method of registration in Scotland, as he called it a 'rating franchise', had not been adopted for England as well. Sir James Fergusson, another thorn in Moncreiff's Parliamentary flesh, but much less effective than Baxter, seemed to arguing on the one hand that the Bill promised enfranchisement to the working class, but without providing the means to achieve it, and on the other, that he was opposed to the extension of the franchise to the working classes *en masse*. Only the *intelligent* working men should be enfranchised.

When it came to the Committee stage of the Bill, Moncreiff enjoyed himself at length in ridiculing Fergusson's argument that the Bill should not be proceeded with on four distinct grounds – that it did not deal with reform in the three kingdoms in a single Bill; that the issues could not be properly considered at morning sittings when the House was wearied of the subject; that reform could not be considered even in the next session, 'because they might then be in troublous times'; that it could not be considered at all by what he called a 'moribund Parliament'. 'But if that argument,' Moncreiff pointed out, 'were carried out to its legitimate result, no Parliament could ever pass a Reform bill. For, according to his reasoning, a Parliament which passed a Reform Bill was doomed and moribund by that act.'[32]

Moncreiff might have won that exchange, but he lost the Bill. In June it was withdrawn – partly through lack of time, and partly because some 250 MPs had declared in favour of postponement until the next session. Yet for our purposes, the Bill and Moncreiff's speeches in support of it give us useful insights into his own thoughts on politics, and electoral reform, especially with regard to the question of the representation of the working class. Picking up on Fergusson's remarks about the dangers of enfranchising the mass of the working classes, Moncreiff made it very clear that he did not share that distrust. Perhaps recalling his contacts with the Chartist leaders in the 1840s, he spoke positively of this section of the populace, which he asserted 'embraced a great variety of interests, and a great portion of ability, industry, honesty, and intelligence', and suggested that 'the upper portion of the working classes would bring to the exercise of the franchise an intelligence and an interest in political affairs which perhaps they would not find among many of those embraced in the present constituency'.

He dismissed the fears of the Opposition that the extension of the vote to the working classes would swamp the old constituencies, since it was vain 'to suppose that the working men would band themselves together for one candidate, or for the promotion of certain peculiar ideas'. It was much more likely that they would simply 'go with the classes above them, and ... would be split into parties by differences of opinion, just as the constituencies are at the present moment. The traditions of this country', he asserted, 'led people to look to the upper ranks, and it was a mere chimera to suppose that by this Bill they were opening the floodgates of democracy, and undermining the foundations of the Constitution'. Nor was he much impressed by scares of trades unions and strikes, 'for it was not the reckless portion of the working classes, but the intelligent among them, who were members of these associations'.[33] It is easy with the benefit of hindsight to dismiss these views as unrealistic and naïve. Here was the authentic voice of the mid-century Scottish Liberal – the same voice which opposed the introduction of the secret ballot on grounds of the highest principle.

On more than one occasion, Moncreiff gave full and thorough consideration to the whole question of the merits and demerits of the secret ballot. Writing in the *Edinburgh Review* in 1860 on the second edition of Mill's *Thoughts on Parliamentary Reform,* he quoted with evident approval Mill's critique of the Ballot, from the perspective of almost three decades since the passing of the Great Reform Act of 1832. 'The operation of the Ballot is,' Mill argued, 'that it enables the voter to give full effect to his own private preferences, whether selfish or disinterested, under no inducement to defer to the opinions or wishes of others, except as these may influence his own.' It followed that 'secrecy is desirable in cases in which the motives acting on the voter through the will of others are likely to mislead him, while, if left to his own preferences, he would vote as he ought'. But equally it followed that where the voter's preferences were likely to lead him in the wrong direction, then the feeling of responsibility to others may keep him on the right path, then 'not secrecy, but publicity should be the rule'. What had changed since 1832, in Mill's opinion, was that back then, the main evil to be guarded against was potential coercion by landlords or employers, but now the much greater source of evil was 'the selfishness, or the selfish partialities of the voter himself'.

Moncreiff by no means disagreed with this opinion, but the great strength of his review article was that he went beyond the theoretical pros and cons of the secret ballot, to consider its consequences in practice. He conceded that if the ballot could be relied on to end electoral corruption, then it was 'entitled to a most favourable reception from all lovers of liberty'. But he offered a number of different scenarios, where the secrecy of the ballot might not be effective. Where an agent, for example, is given a sum of money to spend on the voters, with the promise that if the agent's candidate is elected, then more money will come his way. Or where a man has lent money to the electors, and then made it known that, come the election, the debts would be called in, unless the debtors are prepared to support his candidate. Or the ship-owning member, who 'has been in the habit of consolidating his interest...by many judicious orders for ship stores to the free and independent electors who deal in these commodities'. 'He cannot, indeed, be sure how Tompkins votes. But he can be quite sure how Tomkins speaks and acts.' Tomkins will be expected to speak on his behalf, act on his committee, and make it quite clear how important it is that he should be returned. 'And Tomkins stands so deservedly high in the borough that these services are more valuable than his vote, and are not too highly rewarded by the contract for supplying the new steamer on the stocks.' What he does not explain, of course, is how in circumstances such as these an open ballot would somehow remove these pressures on the voter.

Possibly a more defensible argument against the secret ballot was his claim that under such a system, Parliament would have to surrender all right of scrutiny of elections. 'If we are to have secret voting, the dropping of a ball or a ticket into a box must end all enquiry.' The consequence of this, he argued, 'would be a course of systematic and inscrutable corruption infinitely worse that any of the evils the Ballot is intended to cure'. 'Nor let it be forgotten that while on the one hand we are about to destroy the power of inquiry, with the other we propose to inaugurate a system of voting which has its own new and special tendencies to corrupt dealing.' Accepting that in the great majority of cases, the system would provide reasonable security, and that the results would generally be fair and honest, he observed that: 'There is no machine which the wit of man ever contrived, which the wit of some other man will not contrive to evade.' Under an open system of voting, the accuracy of the results could easily be checked. 'But what are we to do if things go wrong under the Ballot? We are at the mercy of the box, and of those who keep it. If the box is out of order, or its keepers out of honesty, we are helpless.'[34] And before we presume to condemn these opinions as undemocratic or out of tune with the times, let us consider how often, around the political world, in the twenty-first century, questions have been raised as to the fairness and legitimacy of elections, even with allegedly secret ballots.

Six years later, in December 1866, on the eve of the passing by the Disraeli Conservatives of the 1867 Reform Act, Moncreiff returned to the subject of the franchise, and the fundamental principles of Whiggism in an address to the electors of Edinburgh, his then constituency. Identifying himself as one of the Old Whigs, he cited the opinion of Charles James Fox, that 'the best plan of representation is that which will bring into activity the greatest number of independent voters, and that that is defective which would bring forth those whose situation and condition take from them the power of deliberation.' This dictum set the basis but also the limits of nineteenth century Liberal policy on popular representation, as expounded by Moncreiff. In 1832, he argued, the franchise was fixed on 'the principle that what you require in the voter is honesty, independence and intelligence, and that the men who could give an honest, independent and intelligent vote were the men to whom the franchise ought to be extended.' That raised the question of course as to how to identify such men, and once identified, how to ensure that they were given the vote. Moncreiff's answer to this question was, not surprisingly, to tie eligibility for the franchise to either the possession of property, or the occupation of it – not, he argued, because the vote should be enjoyed only by the propertied classes, but because these qualifications were 'tests or indications of the fitness of the voter....The line was so drawn only because it was thought that on that line and above it would be found a class of voters of whom it was reasonable to expect that they would in general be capable of giving an honest, independent and intelligent vote.' As the population progressed, especially in terms of education, and social conditions improved, so this improvement should be reflected in the extension of the franchise by lowering the value of the property qualification.

What Old Whigs like Moncreiff nevertheless set their faces firmly against was the doctrine of manhood suffrage, and he carefully absented himself from a meeting in the Corn Exchange in Edinburgh at which he expected the issue of manhood suffrage was to be promoted, and at which McLaren was to be the main speaker.[35] When Moncreiff did speak on the subject of electoral reform, it was to support the extension of the suffrage to those who had shown themselves to be responsible citizens – and denied that any man had an inherent right to political power – 'it is vested in the community and not in the individual.' In an address in Edinburgh's Music Hall in 1866, he referred to the work of 1832 as a 'Reformation – a cleansing of the stables to render them fit for habitation and efficient for their purpose. What is now wanted is an enlargement and extension merely. No doubt constitutional anomalies still adhere – some inequality in the distribution of seats, some disparities in electoral members...But these are exceptional details...The best plan of representation' (once more echoing Charles James Fox) 'is that which shall bring into activity the greatest number of independent voters.'[36]

Moncreiff's views on the electoral system, the secret ballot, and manhood suffrage, were unlikely to appeal to his Radical opponents inside, and outside, the House of Commons. Yet one could argue that the differences were more of degree than of kind. Moncreiff's view of the franchise was simply that the vote should be extended only to those fitted to exercise it responsibly. His prescription for identifying such people was a property qualification. Radicals in British politics at the time, when they spoke of manhood suffrage, meant something less than universal adult male suffrage – there was usually a qualification of some kind attached to the concept. The two qualifications commonly associated with 'manhood suffrage' were 'registered and residential'. According to Eugene Biagini, these were intended to have a restrictive character which was 'socially focussed and precise'.[37] As 'Littlejohn' explained in the *Weekly Times* of 11th March, 1866, 'no true reformer would desire to clothe with political power the man who is unfitted to wield it right'. The class he had in his sights, to be excluded from the franchise, was the 'agricultural labourer of Dorsetshire and Suffolk in his present degraded state'.[38] All this is not to deny that Moncreiff remained opposed to manhood suffrage on principle, and divided from the Radicals in his own party on this issue, and indeed on others.

The one such matter which caused him more difficulty with them than any other was over his repeated attempts to resolve the long standing question of the Edinburgh Annuity Tax. To give its full title, the Edinburgh and Canongate Annuity Tax, was a 'source of much bad blood and a thorn in Moncreiff's side for many years'.[39] The levy dated back to the early years of the seventeenth century, and was paid by the occupiers of shops and houses in the city for the purpose of providing stipends for its clergy. The tax was highly unpopular, particularly amongst those who were opposed to state support for religion, but refusal to pay the tax on grounds of principle led to multiple prosecutions, followed by the forced sale of the offender's personal possessions. Back in 1836 one T. Russell published a pamphlet entitled *The Annuity Tax or Edinburgh Church-rate, Opposed to the Law of God and therefore not Binding on Man.* Unfortunately, the authorities in Edinburgh failed to agree.

As early in Moncreiff's tenure as Lord Advocate as April, 1851, Edinburgh Town Council had sent a deputation to London to protest against the tax, and in a meeting with Moncreiff and Sir William Gibson-Craig, the leaders 'strongly urged' that the Government should agree to refer the issue of the tax to a recently appointed committee on the matter of the Church rates. Moncreiff and Gibson-Craig responded positively, and promised to arrange a further meeting with Home Secretary Sir George Grey, though when it took place, Grey asked that the protesters to put the ground of their complaint in writing, for submission to a specially convened committee.[40] One of the principal objections to the tax was that all lawyers, as members of the College of Justice, were exempt. As Duncan McLaren told the Select Committee in 1851, 'the exemption comes to this: in Edinburgh the aristocracy are all lawyers; they occupy the highest rented houses, and they are exempted; they are the parties who chiefly remain in the Established Church. The poor, and what we call the shopocracy, have almost all left the Church. The effect therefore is, that the annuity tax is levied in Edinburgh on the poor for the support of an establishment for the rich.'[41]

Despite the fact that Moncreiff himself, though certainly a lawyer, was not, of course, a member of the Established Church, and despite the fact that over the next few years he laboured valiantly to find a solution to the Annuity Tax problem, relations between himself and McLaren continued to be antagonistic. They were not improved either by Moncreiff's powerful defence of the *Scotsman* newspaper in a notorious libel suit brought against it by McLaren,[42] in which he accused McLaren of bringing the action not to clear his name, but 'to gratify vindictiveness' and 'to vent want of success in spleen'.[43] Moncreiff's speech to the jury lasted some two and a half hours, in which he argued that a verdict against the newspaper would damage the freedom of the press. In the end the jury found in McLaren's favour, though Moncreiff succeeded in having his claim for £1000 in damages reduced to £400.[44]

But there is no doubting his commitment to finding a solution to the tax issue. In July 1853 he moved the second reading of a Bill which would have abolished exemption, reduced the number of ministers in the capital from eighteen to fifteen, and replaced the tax with a municipal rate of 3%. In the end the Bill lapsed, but not before it had been attacked from diametrically opposite directions. J.B. Smith suggested that the number of ministers should be reduced to six, and Colonel Blair that there should be no reduction at all.[45] A second attempt at a compromise failed in 1857, but success finally came in 1860, with an Act which specifically abolished the Annuity Tax (and in the process doing away with the lawyers' exemption), set ministers' salaries at £600 a year, and made alternative arrangements for raising the money to pay for them.[46] In December of that year, Moncreiff spoke of his relief and gratification that he 'had been instrumental in passing the Act which terminates the Annuity Tax forever', but his speech was frequently interrupted by 'an unusual attempt to obstruct…free discussion, and public agitation after the Act came into force continued'. Some objectors to the Act had their property seized and sold at the town cross. Some others went to prison. But as Omond shrewdly commented, 'a good deal was heard about tender consciences and religious scruples. But it was well known that the cause of the movement was the determination of the leaders to capture both seats for Edinburgh from the Whigs.'[47]

McLaren for one had no good words to say about the Act, which, according to one of his biographers, he had condemned as the worst measure that had yet been offered. McLaren's own objections to it seem to have been financial rather than founded on religious scruples. Under the terms of the Act, seat [pew] rents had been set at the 'paltry sum' of £1600, whereas he had stated publicly that he would wash his hands of any scheme that assessed seat rents at less that £2,500. Others objected to the admittedly curious arrangement whereby the Act also included provision for a police rate. Long after 1860, therefore, agitation, based on principle or political advantage, continued to grow. In the general election of 1865, both Moncreiff and McLaren were returned as Members of Parliament for Edinburgh, and each engaged in some public manoeuvring to offload the problem on to the other. After the election result was known, Moncreiff made a speech in which he declared that 'Mr. McLaren first introduced me to the subject [of the Annuity Tax] in 1853. I have now done my best with it, and I now return it to him from whom it came'. If McLaren thought he could do any better, then he, Moncreiff, promised that 'as far as my assistance and co-operation go in anything that is just and equitable, they shall not be found wanting'.[48] McLaren retaliated by declining the offer of assistance on the ground that as a new MP it would be an impertinence on his part to propose the repeal so soon of a Government backed enactment. He did however, introduce Bills into the House of Commons in 1867 and 1868 to deal with the tax issue, but without success.[49] The ultimate resolution of this long drawn out and often tedious wrestling match was an amending act of 1870, pushed through by Moncreiff's successor as Lord Advocate, George Young – an act which addressed only financial issues and completely ignored any questions of conscience.[50]

In the general election of 1859, Moncreiff had stood successfully for one of the two Edinburgh parliamentary seats. But by the middle of the next decade the Radicals were now in a position to threaten Moncreiff's hold over the constituency. In the general election of 1865 McLaren came top of the poll with 4,354 votes, as against Moncreiff's 4,148, while his fellow Whig, Adam Black, lost his seat altogether. According to the *Weekly Herald and Mercury*, the defeat of Black and the 'virtual' defeat of Moncreiff were attributable, not to the issue of electoral reform, but rather as 'a protest against the iniquitous conduct of Mr Black and the Lord Advocate in the matter of the infamous clerico-police tax'.[51] It would soon be time to move on. In an address to his constituency committee before the 1868 election, Moncreiff explained his decision not to stand again for Edinburgh. The Reform Act of the previous year, he pointed out, had increased the number of voters from ten to twenty seven thousand, and 'the reason that has induced me to come to the resolution mainly, I may say solely, is that I do not feel that the task of canvassing in a contested election such an enormous body of voters is one which I ought to undertake'.[52] This was perhaps a little disingenuous. In 1865 he had retained his Edinburgh seat by a scant three or four hundred votes, and in the run up to the 1868 election, the opposition against him in the city was well organised. He accepted nomination for the new constituency of Glasgow and Aberdeen Universities, and was returned with a majority of 47 votes. In the following year he resigned his seat in the Commons for a seat on the Scottish Bench.

II – In Parliament House

'Arrived at Edinburgh the Lord High Chancellor of Scotland, the Lord Justice General, the Lord Privy Seal, the Privy Council, and the Lord Advocate, all in one post-chaise, containing only a single person.' This description of the multi-functions of the Lord Advocate of the day in an unnamed English newspaper was intended to be ironic.[53] In his authoritative study of Scotland's history in this period, Tom Devine has identified the Lord Advocate's key responsibilities as being in the areas of policing and law enforcement, and as tangible evidence of Scotland's powers to govern itself.[54] These areas were indeed among the primary responsibilities of the office of Lord Advocate in his governance of Scotland, but the reach of the office stretched very much further than this remark would seem to imply. In addition to his important role as the prime mover of a high proportion of parliamentary bills affecting Scotland, the Lord Advocate wielded extensive powers of patronage, though confined for the most part within the spheres of the law and academia, while from his office in Parliament House in Edinburgh he intervened in a great many aspects of Scottish life. A rapid trawl through the accumulated papers of the Advocate's Department, collected in the National Archives of Scotland, produces material on universities[55] and schools[56]; the Patent Office[57] and the Lunacy Board[58]; the Court of Session[59] and Sheriff Courts[60]; trades and manufactures[61]; marriage with deceased wife's sister[62]; police[63] and constables[64]; fisheries[65] and foreshores[66]; not to mention religious issues, education, and legislative proposals on many of these subjects and more. Correspondence between the Lord Advocate's office and officials in the Home Office in London similarly reflect the great variety of subjects discussed between them – laws relating to the burial of the dead[67]; the practice for arrestment for debt in Scotland[68]; the establishment of a new circuit court in Dundee[69]; civic disturbances in Dunfermline[70] – and so it goes on. As it happens, the great majority of items in these files are of a routine nature – indeed most of the correspondence is addressed to the Lord Advocate's office rather than originating from it. As such the material can tell us little about Moncreiff's own views on policy issues. But cumulatively, they provide a graphic demonstration of the breadth of his responsibilities, which went far beyond legal matters only. And although the responsibilities of the office inevitably reduced his opportunities for appearing personally before the Scottish courts, in later chapters we shall see how, during his terms as Lord Advocate, Moncreiff was called upon to act in a small number of very high profile cases.

The Lord Advocate's powers of patronage were amongst the most visible in his armoury, and inevitably amongst those most likely to arouse jealousy and criticism. His judicial appointments, we are told, included Lords Colonsay, Cowan, Deas, Handyside, Benholme, Neaves, Ardmillan, Mackenzie, Ormidale, Barncaple, and Mure, as well as twenty-four sheriffs.[71] We need to be clear that these appointments were not made solely on the Lord Advocate's personal authority. The usual procedure was for Moncreiff to make a recommendation to the Home Secretary, and while in most cases his advice would be acted on, there were one or two occasions when it was ignored. In 1851, for example, the first year of his stint as Lord Advocate, he had written to Sir George

Grey recommending the appointment of George Deas as Solicitor-General for Scotland, and 'gave my opinion without qualification against Handyside. It is a very unpleasant thing to do, but my conviction is that apart from any claims in other quarters, Handyside is not sufficient for the office.'[72] He was therefore very annoyed indeed to be told by Lord John Russell that on the advice of Lord Minto, Deas had been rejected, and Robert Handyside appointed.[73] This was an exceptional example, but it rankled. Many years later, in his *Reminiscences,* Moncreiff returned to this incident to attack the 'Camarilla' who had intrigued to prevent Deas' appointment. 'I did not know at the time, but the object of their assiduity was to exclude me. They had a Tory Lord Advocate under the garb of a Peelite, ready to supersede me.'[74] But in the great majority of cases his advice would be accepted, and this led inevitably to accusations of overweening power. Some Scottish members of Parliament 'kicked against the species of Caledonian autocracy, which they thought was in danger of being set up through his long experience and eminent qualities', and a committee was created to review the method of these appointments, though his obituarist protested that every selection was justified by results.[75] The *Glasgow Herald*, on the other hand, by the time of Moncreiff's retirement from the bench, was becoming increasingly critical of his record.[76] 'We are free to confess', ran an editorial, 'that in the quarter of a century during which Lord Moncreiff held the office of Lord Advocate there were many appointments and many exclusions which called forth the disapproval of fair-minded men, and which, indeed, were criticised with severity by the few writers for the press who had courage and knowledge sufficient for the task.' The paper grudgingly acknowledged that as Lord Advocate, Moncreiff 'sought upon the whole to do his duty, and did it tolerably amid many temptations and difficulties'. Nevertheless he was roundly criticised over the appointment of Advocates-Depute, which he seemed to regard as a matter for his own personal decision, in which the public had 'but a secondary and remote concern'. The result was, 'as there was a traditional rule that these officials were entitled to be promoted to vacant Sheriffships, that the country was saddled with that curious and not very admirable class of local judges once known in Parliament House slang as 'Moncreiff's Sheriffs'.[77]

In addition to legal and judicial appointments of this kind, Moncreiff's powers of patronage also extended to the appointment of academics to vacant chairs in Scottish universities, though as before the final decision lay with the Secretary of State at the Home Office. Throughout the 1850s and 60s, the Lord Advocate's office in Edinburgh was the recipient of more than thirty applications for and recommendations to professorships in the sciences, medicine, philosophy, divinity, languages, and English literature. By the late eighteen-fifties, the process had become standardised – that is applications and recommendations generally took the form of a single covering letter accompanying a printed pamphlet or brochure containing copies of references. Candidates would naturally seek support from those they believed to have influence in the appropriate quarters. Thus Mr George Liveing, a candidate for the chair of Natural Philosophy at Marischal College in Aberdeen, was sponsored by William Wellwood Stoddart, a relative of James Moncreiff, although Stoddart was actually acting on behalf of an unnamed friend and had no personal knowledge of Mr Liveing.[78] Or there was the example of Mr Stewart Munro, a landed proprietor and a constituent of the Member for Caithness, George Traill. Munro had served in the 83rd Regiment in India, where he had been in charge of a large depot at 'Kurrachee', which had provided him with ample experience of treating soldiers for gunshot wounds and other injuries, but was now himself in poor health, and anxious to secure the chair in Military Surgery in the University of Edinburgh. In a letter to Traill, who was to be his sponsor, Munro wrote that 'If you can obtain the appointment for me, I will feel deeply indebted, and will do my utmost in securing three or four votes, along with my own for you, should you wish it, at the next Election. The appointment,' he went on, 'will likely be given over by Sir George Grey to the Lord Advocate for Scotland, and as I am most anxious to get it, I hope you will do what you can…' Mr Traill duly obliged.[79]

The Lord Advocate's powers of patronage, then, were subject to final authorisation by the Secretary of State, though again the evidence suggests that Moncreiff's advice was usually acted upon. Much the same could be said of his role in the oversight of the police and policing. But this was a much more complex area of government, in which many other officers, committees, and agencies could play a part. Nor was Moncreiff's intervention, when he did intervene, always either effective or beneficial. In October 1861 he was sent two Memorials, from the Commissioners of Police of the Burgh of Thurso, and from the ratepayers of the Police District of Wick. The complaint in each case was the same – that the Commissioners of Supply for Caithness had assessed these two police districts inequitably when compared with the assessment of 'landward' districts. Moncreiff duly looked into the complaints, and reported to the Secretary of State that in his opinion they were well founded. The problem was what to do about it, and he advised Sir George Grey that the only direct means of influencing the Commissioners of Supply open to him was to instruct the Treasury to withhold some or all of the allowance for the pay and clothing of the police in Caithness. In practice this was difficult to justify, since the police in this county had been reported as being 'in a state of efficiency'. All he could suggest then was that the Commissioners should be advised of his opinion as to the soundness of the complaint, in the hope that they would be persuaded to redress the grievance, and Sir George Grey followed Moncreiff's advice.[80]

In response, the Commissioners did indeed make some small concessions on minor points, but left the source of the principal grievance unaddressed. The two districts affected thereupon declared that they would opt out of the county system of policing, and set up their own.[81] This brought into play the choleric Sheriff of Caithness, Sir Dingwall Fordyce, who saw the actions of the local Police Committee as a direct challenge to his authority as Sheriff to deploy the police 'in any part of the County, whether townward or landward'. The Committee, he declared, had greatly exceeded their powers in giving instructions to the Chief Constable as to the deployment of the force – this should be a matter for the Chief Constable himself, but 'subject to such lawful orders as the Sheriff may see fit to give'. Fordyce further pointed out to Moncreiff that they were now at the beginning of the herring fishing season, 'always a very anxious time for the preservation of the peace. If I as Sheriff am not to have the power of directing the employment of the county police in Wick and Pultneytown, where riots usually occur, it may be utterly impossible for me to provide for the preservation of peace and good order, save and except by the employment of the military from Edinburgh, which would be much to be regretted, and which is always so expensive.'[82] He then instructed Procurator Fiscal McLennan to write to the Chief Constable, and make it clear to him that as Chief Constable he was bound to obey the orders of the Sheriff with regard to the deployment of his police force, 'at such times and in such circumstances as the Sheriff may deem right and expedient, notwithstanding any directions of the Police Committee, and if you fail to obey such directions of the Sheriff you will do so at your peril'.[83]

For his part, the Chief Constable remained unimpressed. With, one suspects, a good deal of inner amusement, he wrote back in August 1863, to admit that he was fully prepared to obey the orders of the Sheriff, 'provided that, in the event of the police being required to act in Wick or Pultneytown, both of which places have separate police forces, and are not assessed for the county police, I receive a written order from you or your Substitute to that effect'. He also demanded to be given a 'guarantee for the payment of the constables so employed, and for the substitutes for the protection of the county which may be denuded of police when withdrawn, and also for any expenses or damages consequent of any of the county police being injured or killed in the execution of their duty when employed in any of these towns when under your orders'.[84]

It seems almost superfluous to quote from the Sheriff's furious response, full of passages underlined, rejecting the Chief Constable's conditions and insisting once again that 'You will clearly understand that you must obey my orders, and those of my Substitute...'[85] Further, it would be satisfying to be able to record that at this point Moncreiff stepped in and banged some heads together. Not so. The last reference to the debacle we have in the records is a letter from Moncreiff to Mr H.A. Bruce, MP, of 7th January 1864. Referring to Bruce's letter of the previous October, itself transmitting a letter from Col. Kinloch, the Inspector General of Constabulary, as to whether he was to recognise the recently established Police force in the Royal Burgh of Wick as legally constituted, Moncreiff was of the opinion that the magistrates of the burgh were indeed entitled, under the terms of 25 & 26 Vict. c.101,[86] to establish such a force. With a Pilatian flourish, he blandly informed Mr Bruce that 'The existence of separate police establishments within the Parliamentary boundaries of Wick is no doubt inconvenient, but it rests with the various police authorities to put an end to it, and the Secretary of State has not the power to coerce them.'[87] Not only then were the Lord Advocate's powers to intervene in a local dispute in Scotland shown to be limited, so also were those of the Home Secretary.

The extent of the responsibilities of the Lord Advocate for the management of Scotland undoubtedly put the holder of the office under great pressure – not least because of the need to be travelling regularly between Edinburgh and London. As Omond explained, Moncreiff usually went up to London in mid-February, and remained there, apart from a short Easter break, until the end of July. Even so, he was constantly travelling between England and Scotland. Once in Edinburgh, 'after a busy day at the Parliament House, often contending against that redoubtable antagonist Mr George Young, the Solicitor-General for Scotland, he would rush home to 15 Great Stuart Street, where he sometimes had to work till it was time to drive off to Waverley station in order to catch the night express to London. Reaching King's Cross in the grey dawn, he had a long morning at the Lord Advocate's office in Spring Gardens. Later that day there might be a meeting with some troublesome deputation from Scotland, or an appeal case, till it was time for the House of Commons.'[88]

This was a punishing schedule for any man. The sheer physical strain of frequent journeys between Edinburgh and London, let alone the pressures of the job itself, had destroyed the health of Andrew Rutherfurd, Lord Advocate for only nine years between 1839 and 1848. Moncreiff lasted for nearly twenty. John Inglis, Moncreiff 's close personal friend, and himself Lord Advocate for two very brief periods in 1852 and 1858, is said to have regarded his own elevation to the post 'as most Lord Advocates do, with mingled feelings'.[89] Or as Henry Cockburn once put it, even more bluntly, 'No sane man takes the position of Lord Advocate except to be well quit of it.'[90]

The punishing schedule was just one part of the price to be paid by the incumbents. Although as a practising advocate Moncreiff continued to appear in a number of high profile cases before the Court of Session, inevitably his law practice, which had been extensive, suffered, and with it his income. 'A family to maintain,' wrote Omond, 'a house in Edinburgh, a house in London, a house in the country in Scotland, election expenses, and a vast amount of miscellaneous expenditure which could not be avoided, injured the fortunes of a man who never had time, nor indeed much aptitude, for method or care in managing his private business.'[91]

Even Moncreiff himself, called upon to defend his office from attack in Parliament, confessed that 'in point of emoluments or prospects, it does not hold out any very golden or glittering temptation. A counsel in a large practice is not a gainer by accepting the position I have the honour to hold, and there is no prospect opening beyond it. There is no promotion, no peerage to look forward to. There are none of the prizes which are within the reach of the law officers of England and Ireland.'[92] As the biographer of John Inglis pointed out, there was a considerable discrepancy between the salaries of the Lord Advocate and his English opposite number, the Attorney-General – the one being paid £3,000 a year, and the other £10,000. In addition, 'the Lord Advocate is banished from his practice, except such fees as he may get in Scotch appeals, which are now comparatively rare. Even the Parliamentary bar, where the fees are largest and where the Lord Advocate would be certain of representing one side or the other, is closed against him as a member of the House.'[93] It is only fair to point out, however, that in 1859 the Treasury gave instructions for Moncreiff to be paid £850 on top of his annual salary, as compensation for the loss of patent fees.[94]

As well as distracting him from potentially lucrative professional pursuits, the pressure of work to some extent interrupted his literary activities. Back in 1846 when he was 35 he had published a volume of poetry, entitled *Morning and other Poems,* evidently much influenced by Gray's *Elegy*.[95] As the pressure of work increased, some projects, such as his proposed life of Cockburn, and an historical romance set in the 1690s, had to be put on one side and were never completed. Quite early in his professional career he had been invited to contribute an article on Francis Jeffrey to the first number of the new *North British Review,* and in all wrote some ten or eleven pieces for it, but none after his election to

Parliament in 1851. Nevertheless he was throughout his life a regular contributor to other journals such as the *Presbyterian Review* and the *Edinburgh Review*.

It has to be admitted that Moncreiff's literary strength lay not as a poet or a novelist, but as a reviewer, essayist, and above all, as we have seen on many occasions, as a public speaker. His three articles on Macaulay's *History* were particularly perceptive, and while not uncritical of the author's overly complex style, commended his 'masterly adaptation of known facts to a connected and systematic view of the history they comprise – and the bearings of the history on the future fortunes of the country.'[96] The review greatly gratified the author, who wrote to a friend that 'I should like Moncreiff to know how much pleasure he had given me'.[97] Wilson Bain has drawn an interesting comparison between the articles Moncreiff wrote for the *North British Review* before 1851 – 'clearly the work of a younger man' – and those for the *Edinburgh*, arguing that years of experience in government made him less critical of his political opponents. As an example Bain cites Moncreiff's comments at age 33 on Tory Lord Chancellor Eldin, of whom he wrote 'he passed through a career of unbroken influence, without doing one good deed for his country, nor a measure of humanity'.[98] By 1870, when he came to write an article for the *Edinburgh Review* on 'Earl Russell's Speeches', he was prepared to be more understanding. Though still highly critical of the trials of sedition of the 1790s, he was willing to concede that more allowance should be made for Tory Ministers. 'In self defence the gravity of the peril was great, and it remains a question whether under any circumstances or any government, we could have kept terms with France.'[99]

If he now had less time for writing, he still found some time for public speaking at which he was acknowledged to be an expert. Most of Moncreiff's public lectures and addresses, like the Law Reform and Bankruptcy lecture were, as might have been expected, on legal subjects. Several of these will be discussed in the next chapter. But there were also some matters of contemporary interest which had no legal aspect, yet which Moncreiff felt moved to address in public. One such was his lecture to the YMCA in 1867 on 'The Relation of Recent Scientific Inquiries to the Received Teaching of Scripture', in which he demonstrated his familiarity with Sir Charles Lyell's *Principles of Geology*, Thomas Chalmers' sermons on science, and Darwin's *On the Origin of Species*, and sought to find ways in which to reconcile aspects of scripture with contemporary scientific theories of the origins of the world. In this he was only partly successful. On the creation of the world in six days, he explained that a 'day' might mean any length of time 'as applied to an act of miraculous creation', since 'as the sun, moon and stars do not [appear] until the fourth of these periods, the word "day" could not have been intended to denote one revolution of the earth on its axis.'[100] As for the theory of natural selection and the survival of the fittest, he adopted the ridiculous example of a pig on its way to become an elephant – there would at some stage be a half-pig and a half-elephant, but the elephant would eliminate his half-brother.[101] In case this example is read as reflecting Moncreiff's outright dismissal of Darwinian theory, or more likely his complete misunderstanding of it, it is worth noting that in the *Visit to My Discontented Cousin,* Pemberton is made to describe Darwin as 'a very masterly analyst...who has certainly shown that the principle of natural selection exists, and has shown that it is at least possible that species may have originated in that way'.[102]

Even before he became Lord Advocate Moncreiff had been extremely busy and increasingly successful in his profession. Naturally after 1851 the pressure on his time and energies was much greater. But it would be misleading to suggest that he had no time at all for recreation, and that the lot of a Lord Advocate at this time was one of unceasing drudgery. There was the summer recess, when he and his family, like his father before him, could retire to the country. In the autumn, we are told, he engaged in fishing, shooting, and golfing at St Andrews or North Berwick.[103] He had a great love of the Scottish countryside and Scottish countryside pursuits, especially fishing for trout. In an essay on Trout-Fishing in his novel of 1871 he wrote: 'Trout-fishing, with the artificial fly, be it known to you, and to all like heretics and scoffers, is the most exciting and most soothing, the highest in art, the most mechanical in action, and yet the most relaxed of human enjoyments....Go where you will, with rod in hand, wherever you find a trout, you will find nature also in her most genial and loveliest mood.' Familiar with the works of Isaac Walton, he did not find Walton's style of fishing much to his taste. '...to tell the truth, I have misgivings as to that fishy oracle. He was a Cockney sportsman after all, and pursued his craft in dull sleepy waters, and would watch his float bobbing up and down, much bemused in country beer, as his verses testify.' Moncreiff's preference was for the streams of the North, and especially the waters of 'glorious Loch Laggan'. His description of the scenery around the Loch must strike a chord with anyone who has come upon the lochs and mountains of Scotland at their most majestic:

> The setting sun shed a flood of purple light on the more purple heath which coloured the hill slopes, illuminating the long western vista of mighty gorges, at the end of which, in a liquid mist, loomed the monarch of Scottish mountains. The yellow birch, with its silver stem, fringed all the lake, and straggled up the broken cliffs. The ground was carpeted with bright orange ferns, which clustered round the gray granite boulders,

and there, like a sapphire set in topazes and pearls, lay the broad blue waters, streaked by a long silver arrow of light.[104]

Perhaps he did have some skill as a poet after all.

Ever since the days of his childhood and youth, and the family's summer retreats to Eldin House, Moncreiff had had a great love of the outdoors, but he could also appreciate and enjoy less physical and more intellectual pursuits. Though not himself a performer, he was very fond of music, especially opera. If, and it is not too big an 'if', we are to assume that the character of Pemberton in Moncreiff's novel is the alter ego of the author himself, then what do we make of his essay 'A Discourse on Music'? On the one hand Pemberton is critical of those musical snobs who insist on perfect silence while the musicians are playing, when he would much prefer to continue his conversation with his 'pretty neighbour'. 'It is all very well for you', he rants, 'hideous hypocrite of the drawing room, knowing not one note of music from another, to stand with foolish looks, forcing your rebellious lips into the mockery of a rapturous smile.....I, who am an honest man, hold my tongue, as I would in any other solemn assembly, but to pretend that I like being interrupted when my pretty neighbour is waxing sociable and pleasant, I should disdain'. Moncreiff is teasing the reader, as he does so often in the character of Pemberton. The happiest hour he, Pemberton, ever spent at the opera, he claimed, 'was during the second act of Faust, when the charming Titiens was a substantial Marguerite, and I was fast asleep. Nor think that I heard not the music. I heard it every note, but so sublimated and commingled with my dreams as to produce the perfection of enjoyment.'[105]

At times, Moncreiff provides a more serious account of his love of opera and opera singers. 'I have heard Rubini and Tamburini, and Lablache; I have seen Taglioni and Duvernay; I have heard Malibran and Pasta, and Grisi, when she was in the early dawn of her glorious power. I have heard Catalani sing "God Save the King", and Braham sing "Sound the Alarm". But all I have ever heard, on stage or off it, yields in my memory to the second night of Jenny Lind's first engagement in London.' The first night had apparently gone off well enough, but she had been nervous and failed to do herself full justice. On the second evening, again, she began nervously, but encouraged by a hearty round of applause, 'broke into the second verse with a burst of inspired power that carried herself and every one before it. Silent were the audience – silent as death, till the strain concluded.' Then they rose to their feet, and men 'strained over the sides of the boxes and gallery to catch the bewitching and bewildering beauty of the fresh and unaccustomed tones. When the last notes ended, there was one simultaneous long-drawn breath, then such a concentric [sic] yell of cheering as, I believe, had never been heard within those walls before.'[106]

Moncreiff's nearly two decades as Lord Advocate were demanding, satisfying, frustrating, varied, and deeply rewarding. While it might hold out no 'golden temptation' of profit or a peerage, 'its great recommendation', he once explained to the House, 'is that it holds out the most honourable object of ambition – the opportunity for using power for its only true and legitimate end, the advantage of the nation. It offers the highest and truest reward of patriotism – the consciousness that one is placed in a position where, by diligence, one may be of use to one's day and generation.'[107] These remarks were delivered in 1864, eleven years after his first attempt to achieve his greatest political ambition – the creation of a national education scheme for Scotland. And as it turned out, no amount of diligence could completely overcome the obstacles placed in the way of realising that goal.

Chapter 9
Nationalism v. Anglicisation

In recent years a lively debate has developed among historians of Scotland about the nature of Scottish identity in the Victorian period, and the extent to which both it and Scottish autonomy had become eroded and compromised through an ever closer association with England within the large union.[1] Linda Colley, for example, in her *Britons: Forging the Nation,* argues that not only did the Act of Union produce a British state, but it also began the process of creating a homogeneous British society.[2] Graeme Morton, in his *Unionist-Nationalism*, has described this as 'a very problematic assumption'. While he accepts that after about 1760 a process of Anglicisation did occur, resulting in 'a commonality between Scottish civil society and English civil society', he questions whether this process could have resulted in the creation of a unitary British nation.[3] Indeed it is difficult for anyone living in Scotland in the twenty-first century to accept the Colley thesis without serious qualification.

In the early 1850s, when Moncreiff first took up office as Lord Advocate, Scotland was experiencing a new phase in Scottish nationalist aspirations, with calls for the undertakings contained in the Act of Union to be honoured. The movement drew support from both Conservative and Radical sectors, and took organisational form in the National Association for the Vindication of Scottish Rights, launched in 1853. While the Association was short-lived, in one important sense it set the agenda for the next thirty years, with its demand for the recreation of the office of Secretary of State, abolished a century earlier. Moncreiff, as the chief law officer of Scotland, was bound to take a view on this campaign, not least because the demands for a Secretary almost invariably were accompanied by attacks on the office of Lord Advocate. As 'Minister for Scotland', he had no sympathy for the imposition, as he saw it, of a wholly unnecessary higher tier of government.

Yet at much the same time a contrary trend had emerged, amongst those whose interpretation of Scottish national interests was very different. This movement, finding strong support among the manufacturers and traders in the west of the country, saw advantage to be gained from a closer association with England, and the opportunities that it offered for commercial access to the Empire. This led its supporters to argue for the assimilation of English and Scots laws – at least in the areas of commercial and maritime law. The movement also produced organisations to promote its objectives – the leading such institution being the Glasgow Law Amendment Society, formed in 1851. Again, from his position as the most senior law officer of Scotland, and with his responsibility for formulating and promoting legislation on Scottish affairs, Moncreiff was bound to take a view on the advantages and disadvantages of assimilation.

I – A Secretary of State for Scotland?

In the late 1840s and early 1850s in Scotland criticism of the union with England became increasingly widespread. Arising in the first instance with the failure of government to carry through important Scottish legislation in the form of the Marriage and Registration Bill and the Public Health Bill, the feelings of discontent soon led to a range of demands for reform of the relationship with England, though not at this time for disunion.[4] In 1850 Dr James Begg, a leading Free Church minister, published a pamphlet entitled *A Violation of the Treaty of Union the Main Origin of our Ecclesiastical Divisions and other Evils,* in which he blamed the English and the Act of Union for the parlous state of his native country. The picture he drew of the Scotland of his day was certainly a depressing one, including an increase in crime and drunkenness, the poor state of the universities, extreme poverty, mass emigration, and the failure to deal with educational reform and other social problems. These he blamed primarily on ecclesiastical divisions, themselves 'mainly caused by a deliberate violation of the Treaty of Union on the part of England',[5] and that this violation was part of a deliberate policy to subordinate Scotland to England. When it came to specific suggestions for reform, he called for the recreation of the office of Secretary of State for Scotland supported by a Council of Scotsmen, or failing that, a legislative body of their own in Scotland to deal with purely Scottish questions.[6]

Begg's arguments found fertile ground amongst Radical politicians and the United Presbyterian church, and an organisation representing the political wing of the dissenters, entitled the Scottish Central Board for the Vindication of the Rights of Dissenters whose first chairman was Duncan McLaren. They were joined in their campaign by Tory romantics, like the historical novelist James Grant, who in 1852 had published a series of letters and articles in the Scottish press, on the theme of 'Justice in Scotland'. Like Begg, he saw the interests of his native country being neglected by the government in England, and 'a shamefully partial system of government which lavishes all on the sister kingdom, and nothing, absolutely nothing on Scotland'.[7] Also like Begg, Grant called for the creation of a Secretary of State and a Scottish Privy Council, as well as the complete reorganisation of the system of representation in Scotland. In what may seem today as a bizarre move,

Grant and his brother John embarked on a public campaign focusing on heraldic issues – with a petition to the Lord Lyon King at Arms to suppress incorrect quarterings on flags flown by government departments, and on the new florin coins. This attracted huge popular support, as well as that of the Tory Earl of Eglinton, best known as the host of the neo-mediaeval Eglinton Tournament of 1839.[8] It was Eglinton who had presented the petition to the Lord Lyon, and who now became the President of the National Association for the Vindication of Scottish Rights. Once again, Duncan McLaren was a leading member of the Association, and James Grant one of its two secretaries.[9]

McLaren had long been a fierce critic of the office of Lord Advocate, though his first biographer, J.B. Mackie, insisted that this antagonism was in no way inspired by personal animosity towards Moncreiff himself. McLaren took particular exception to the fact that the holders of the office were invariably drawn from the upper ranks of the Scottish Bar, and regarded their professional pre-eminence not as a positive qualification for public service, but as a serious disqualification, given the heavy demands it made on the time and energies required for the efficient discharge of their Ministerial duties. Indeed he could see no justification for the limitation of state service in this way to one single profession, and held that 'political prizes in the form of Ministerial position and influence should be open to the best men of all classes and professions'. He found the existing system to be extremely inefficient, since, in his opinion, the Lord Advocate was 'overladen with private business which detained him in London, and which claimed, for the multiplicity of clients, much of the time and talent that State service needed'.[10]

The National Association, or the Scottish Rights Society as it became known, was launched in May 1853 at meetings in Edinburgh and Glasgow, which attracted thousands of supporters. Its publication, an *Address to the People of Scotland,* listed a number of grievances. These included claims that the heraldic emblems of Scotland had been degraded; that Scottish revenue was being largely spent in England; that Scotland was underrepresented in Parliament; that a number of Scottish offices had been abolished with nothing put in their place; and that Scotland needed to have its own Secretary of State. The essential differences between Scotland and England were set out in detail. 'Within our own borders we were to have our own laws and institutions, and our own local administration of law, a local ecclesiastical polity different from that of England, and, in fact, a national existence as a people quite distinct from that of England. We were to be united with England, but not merged into England.' Sentiments which would not be out of place today.

Part of the solution to the problem they saw as requiring a change in the system of Scottish administration – in particular the appointment of a Scottish Secretary. Indeed at the launch meeting of the Association in Edinburgh on 11th November 1853, McLaren moved the first resolution calling for the appointment of a Scottish Secretary of State to handle Parliamentary business, and attacked the office of Lord Advocate as having been, since 1828, 'merely an assistant to the Home Secretary'.[11] In its *Address* the Association had declared that the need for a Scottish Secretary 'will be apparent to all who understand that the Lord Advocate is unable to attend to the treble duties of advisor to the Crown, or public prosecutor and superintendent of the whole criminal proceedings; of Secretary of State and framer of bills for a country daily increasing in wealth, population and legislative business, and of attendance to his private practice, which he cannot be expected either to forget or forgo.' It was absurd to suppose that 'the mere fraction of the man's time, however able, is sufficient to govern the most industrious country in Europe, or that every Lord Advocate must infallibly be a statesman, and fit to undertake the vast amount of legislation appertaining to such a country as Scotland.'[12] . At the time, the *Address* was strongly attacked in the press, and the movement might well have collapsed had it not been rescued by a supportive article in *Blackwood's Magazine* by William Aytoun, which focused solely on the issue of the Secretary of State.[13]

This appraisal by the National Association of Scotland's position vis-a-vis England was revisited by Lord Eglinton in a speech at the Association's banquet in 1854, when he compared the governance of Scotland unfavourably with that of Ireland. While Ireland enjoyed a separate government, with a Lord Lieutenant and his staff of officers, in Scotland the equivalent was only the Lord Advocate, both subordinate to the Home Secretary and with a much narrower range of responsibilities. Eglinton's answer to the problem was once again the appointment of a Secretary of State with a seat in the Cabinet – only by this means could Scottish interests be realistically protected.[14]

The National Association survived for only a few short years. The outbreak of the Crimean War, and the upsurge of nationalism which it provoked, has been cited as one reason for its demise in 1856. But it also suffered from the fact that it embraced both old-fashioned Tories like Eglinton and Aytoun, together with dyed-in-the-wool Radicals like Duncan McLaren. In an open letter to McLaren in 1854, Moncreiff's older brother, Sir Henry, argued that although he agreed with all the main points in the *Address,* he did not see how any reformer could join such men when they were opposed to everything the Radicals stood for, such as free trade, parliamentary reform, the separation of church and state, and non-sectarian education.[15]

Henry Cockburn, a leading Whig lawyer, was originally dismissive of the Association's manifesto. Or as he put it in the second volume of his *Journal,* 'the names were respectable, but it was all trash'.[16] Cockburn was typical of many Scottish Whigs of his generation in wishing for a greater rather than a lesser degree of Anglicisation. He had welcomed the change of 1827 when Prime Minister George Canning had placed the management of Scottish affairs in the hands of his English Home Secretary, and according to Michael Fry, he wanted to make Scotland as much like England as possible.[17]

On one point only did he share the views of the National Association – that the Faculty of Advocates should no longer have a monopoly of the government of Scotland. Nor, as a lawyer himself, did he have much faith that it would be anything short of a miracle if an able and experienced lawyer appointed to be Lord Advocate also possessed the qualities of a capable governor and statesman. 'I can conceive even a Lord Advocate being a good general Scotch manager; but this must be so very rare it may be considered visionary.' He pointed out that while a peer cannot be Lord Advocate, he nevertheless might be a great administrator. 'Why should he not administer Scotland?' Whereas 'a Lord Advocate may be, and since 1800 has been, ignorant and in every way incapable, and raised to that office solely for his party services. Why should he have the government of the country as an appendage of his party position?'[18] One would hope that Cockburn was not referring here to his friend Moncreiff.

If the Association proved to be short-lived, nevertheless it left an important legacy in its demand for the appointment of a Secretary of State for Scotland, a demand which surfaced within and outside Parliament again and again until finally conceded in 1885. The obverse side of that particular coin, however, took the form of sporadic attacks on the office of Lord Advocate, with Moncreiff from time to time having to defend both his office and himself from such attacks.

In June 1858, the Radical Member for Montrose Burghs, W.E. Baxter, complained that insufficient consideration had been given to the Police Act and the Lunacy Act, the defects in which were now the subject of amending bills brought in by Lord Advocate Inglis, who had replaced Moncreiff after the 1857 election. The amendments were required, Baxter claimed, 'simply because the late Lord Advocate [Moncreiff], whom he quoted as having said that his political, apart from any other duties, were enough for only one man – had not sufficient time to attend to them while they were passing through the House. At the most critical period of the session, he was absent at the trial in Edinburgh of

Madeleine Smith.' The Lord Advocate, Baxter declared, was 'the dictator of Scotland in political matters', and moved that an Under-Secretary of State should be appointed to perform the political duties at present attached to the office of Lord Advocate. While on the one hand Baxter was careful to praise the actual holders of the office in recent times, he was highly critical of the office itself.

'The system was so inconvenient', he claimed, 'so anomalous, and so liable to be abused, that it was wonderful that it was conducted with so little ground of complaint.' While he would 'proceed to state what were the duties of the Lord Advocate...his description of them must necessarily be imperfect, because gentlemen who had themselves held that high office had frequently declared that they were unable to name all the functions of the office'.

The Lord Advocate was a member of the Faculty of Advocates, and was almost invariably the most distinguished man of his political party for the time being, and as a consequence had the largest private practice before the Court in Edinburgh. He was Attorney-General for Scotland, and public prosecutor for Scotland. All great offenders in that country were prosecuted by the Lord Advocate before the High Court of Justiciary in Edinburgh, and minor offenders by his subordinates in the local courts. They had in Scotland no grand jury and no coroner's inquest. The Lord Advocate therefore had the sole right of deciding who was to be prosecuted for any offence. He might also dismiss any prosecution, and he might in some instances punish without a trial.

Baxter cited Lord Cockburn as stating that the Lord Advocate, in certain circumstances, could imprison an individual for twenty years without being called to any account. 'The Lord Advocate also had a large practice in appeal cases before the House of Lords in London, and he was the Scotch law adviser to the crown. Were these duties not quite sufficient to occupy the time of any man? But in addition he was the political monarch and dictator of Scotland; he had the entire charge of all legislative business affecting Scotland, and he was the sole organ of his Administration in either House of Parliament.'[19] The attack drew forth from Viscount Duncan an equally robust defence, pointing out that Moncreiff while Lord Advocate had passed a great many important measures through Parliament, and on top of that 'had sacrificed a large portion of his time and considerable emoluments in order to do his duty to his country'.[20]

In 1864, Sir James Fergusson raised the question once again in Parliament, complaining that 'the duties which come within the practice of the Lord Advocate are so diverse...Scotch business is generally postponed until morning sittings become the Order of the Day, or it comes on at one or two in the morning.'[21] But even he was careful to praise Moncreiff personally, and differentiate between the imperfections of the post, and the conduct of its incumbent. In particular he commended 'the manner in which [he] has from time to time met the objections to…measures which he had introduced, and the favourable opportunities he has given for their discussion…I do not believe that there was ever a Lord Advocate who sacrificed so much of his time…to his public duties, but he discharges the duty of Secretary of State and Privy Councillor.'[22]

In a lengthy and devastatingly effective speech, Moncreiff carefully dissected and rebutted Fergusson's charges, beginning by identifying 'the elements of the objections to the existing state of things. First it is said that the Lord Advocate is a lawyer, and cannot be in the House of Commons when he has a practice in Edinburgh. The second assertion is that the Lord Advocate, having other vocations, has not the time for introducing measures of that magnitude which he ought to attempt. Thirdly we are told that the manner in which bills are prepared, proposed, and considered in the House is not satisfactory. The fourth is that the political functions of the Lord Advocate are such as ought not to be exercised by a practicing lawyer.'[23]

Each one of these complaints was answered and dismissed. Wisely Moncreiff deliberately chose to deal with Fergusson's points, not in the abstract, but as personal criticisms which he could rebut from personal experience – in effect turning the debate into a confidence motion. Certainly he was a practising lawyer, but during the session of Parliament he had 'substantially to throw his professional business to the winds'. He then went on to give a detailed account of his arrangements for the Parliamentary year. 'My usual course had been this. I have come up to London in the second or third week in February, and remained until the 20th March. Sometimes I may have borrowed a day or two after that date when the Court of Session rises for the jury trials; but never, so far as I am aware, to the detriment of public business. I have always been in my place after Easter, and have remained at least until the 20th July; and then, when the Scotch members are generally more intent on preparations for the 12th August than on legislative action, I have sometimes gone down to Scotland immediately.' He identified only two exceptions to this proceeding – when he conducted the prosecution of Madeleine Smith in June 1857, and when he attended the trial of the 'Pampero' – the ship built on the Clyde for the Confederacy in the American Civil War.

The second charge – that he as Lord Advocate did not have enough time to devote to the introduction of important legislative measures, could be easily refuted. Here he was on even stronger ground, and made the (greatly exaggerated) claim that during his term of office so far, one hundred bills which he had introduced had passed into law.[24] Indeed he admitted, tongue in cheek, that over-legislation was not desirable, and 'occasionally we have been in danger of that evil'. He then identified Acts of which he was particularly proud, such as the Act of 1853 abolishing the religious tests imposed on professors in the lay Chairs in Scottish universities, which, he declared, 'laid the foundation for the great measure of University reform passed in 1858'. Yes it was true, he had to confess, and we can imagine him shaking his head in mock repentance, that no measure of any great consequence had been passed in 1855. But what about the Education Bill of that year? Was it lost because the Lord Advocate failed to introduce it in time? It had been introduced into the Commons, he reminded his audience, on the 23rd March, and after long and searching criticisms read a third time on the 12th July. 'All I can say is that if the same liberal spirit had pervaded in another place, we should have been relieved of a great many of the difficulties which now impede the course of education in Scotland.' In 1861, as Lord Advocate, he had succeeded in bringing about the abolition of religious tests for parochial schoolmasters. 'In that measure we laid a foundation on which a great work may yet be raised…a large and comprehensive system of national education.' And so it went on. The list of enactments for which he had been responsible included the Registration Act, the Valuation Act, the Bankruptcy Act, Acts for establishing county police and regulating lunacy. He could claim with some justice that 'we have not shirked or slurred over our work'.

'Then it is said that the Bills are imperfect…The proper way of judging laws was to look to their effect. Do they benefit the class on whose behalf they have been passed? Do they remedy the evils at which they have been aimed? I contend that the measures we have carried will stand that test.' He had to agree, though, that the system of approving draft legislation itself introduced delays and imperfections. 'One cannot sit down and write an Act like an essay. It is subject to all sorts of alterations during its passage. If the machinery furnished by the House of Commons for framing laws is not scientifically precise, that is the price we have to pay for constitutional government.' Taking the ill-fated Education Bill of 1855 as an example, he traced its Parliamentary progress from that first reading in March. He was then asked to defer the second reading to give time for the country to 'have an opportunity of expressing an opinion with regards to its provisions'. There was a further delay while the views were sought of the Commissioners of Supply and the General Assembly of the Church of Scotland. The second reading eventually took place half way through June. 'We go into Committee and the paper is crowded with Amendments. I know that a Standing Order has been passed in another place not to take a second reading of any bill after the 30ᵗʰ June. Consequently I am obliged to accept Amendments without having a fair opportunity of considering them…or lose the Bill.'

'The last objection is that the Lord Advocate, being a practising lawyer, has too many functions to perform.' Moncreiff accepted that in England those functions were carried out by several different officials, but merely pointed out that in comparison, Scotland was not a very large country. She needed a separate official, however, because of the differences in the legal system. Under the present arrangements, he was satisfied 'that the criminal system of Scotland works admirably both for the discovery of crime and the protection of innocence.' The great advantage of the post of Lord Advocate was that he could get information quickly from his advocate-deputes and procurator fiscals. 'A Secretary of State in London would have to apply to the Lord Advocate for information at every turn', with the effect that 'the Lord Advocate would exercise the same power, but with diminished practice'.[25]

Moncreiff had more than made his point, and the motion was withdrawn for lack of support. In due course, as the amount of Scottish business grew in range and complexity, there was bound to be renewed demand for change, though change did not take place until long after Moncreiff had left the House of Commons for the Scottish Bench. As late as 1881, the Dean of the Faculty of Advocates in Edinburgh wrote to Mr. Gladstone to ask whether there was any substance in the rumour that there was to be an alteration in the powers and duties of the Lord Advocate, and that 'if the change that was rumoured was of the same character as that which had been suggested in former years', the views of the Faculty would be found stated in *Hansard,* in the speeches of Lord Advocates Inglis and Moncreiff. To this the Prime Minister, through his private secretary, responded that he had no knowledge of the matter, and referred the Dean to the Home Secretary. The Dean's letter, quoted at length in the *Glasgow Herald,* pointed out that the appointment of someone 'under the name of a Scotch Secretary' between the Lord Advocate and the Home Secretary, 'so far from promoting, would be an impediment to public business'. The reasons he gave were much the same as Moncreiff himself had put before the House years before – that since much of the business of a Lord Advocate had to do with the framing of bills on Scottish subjects, it needed a trained lawyer to see them through. If someone other than a lawyer were appointed Secretary for Scotland, all that would happen would be for the Lord Advocate of the day to spend much of his time instructing his superior in Scottish law. In any case, the Dean concluded, it appeared that the Government had in fact no plans to make such a change which, he suggested, 'is one promoted by a number of Scotch members, each one of whom has a high sense of his own fitness for such an office as a Scotch Secretary'.[26]

Even as late as January 1884, comment in the Scottish press on the subject was highly sceptical. On the 17th, the *Dundee Courier and Argus* referred back to the efforts of the Scottish Rights Society on the subject, concluding that if the movement for a Scottish Secretary failed, 'there is nothing to show that Scotchmen generally would beak their hearts about it, ...any more than such results followed on the collapse of the similar agitation of the Scottish Rights Association'.[27]

The occasion for this less than enthusiastic comment was the holding of a meeting in Edinburgh to discuss Lord Rosebery's plan for an independent Scottish Office, at which there was widespread cross-party support for a Scottish Secretary. Later that year a bill was introduced into Parliament to create the post of Secretary of State for Scotland, and although due to the change of government it was not proceeded with, in the following year the Conservatives, by agreement with the Liberals, introduced a similar measure, and the bill was duly passed.[28] The first incumbent was the Duke of Richmond and Gordon who, in his letter of acceptance, told the Prime Minister, Lord Salisbury, 'You know my opinion of the office, and that it is quite unnecessary.'[29]

We should not be surprised that this change met with no support from Moncreiff himself. In his view, the whole point of the office of Lord Advocate was that the holder of it was an expert in areas closed off to most other people. 'He represents,' he wrote after his final retirement from active politics, 'a community with laws and institutions divergent from those with which the large majority of members of Parliament are familiar, and on his personal knowledge of these his influence depends. For this reason the revived Secretary of State for Scotland is no very direct gain to the affairs of that country, whether in the Commons, the Lords, or the Cabinet. He does not know the work at first hand, and seldom is in office long enough to learn it.'[30]

II – The Assimilation of Scots and English Law

The eighteen-fifties, then, witnessed a resurgence of Scottish nationalist sentiment, and demands for a redefinition of the relationship with England. At the same time there was a strong body of opinion with very different views and aspirations. In the west of Scotland in particular manufacturers and merchants saw great advantage in developing closer economic ties with England and the Empire. They believed that this goal would be facilitated not by driving England and Scotland apart, not by preserving and enhancing distinctiveness, but by an assimilation of their respective legal systems. In 1851 these interests formed the Glasgow Law Amendment Society. Once again, this development had direct implications for the Lord Advocate. A major responsibility of his office, as we have seen, was to promote and carry through Parliament laws relating to Scottish affairs. The question was – what position would Moncreiff take on this issue? Would he co-operate with the proponents of assimilation, or, as a trained Scots lawyer and leading member of the legal profession, stand firm in defence of Scotland's distinctive legal traditions?

It is certainly true that, from the later eighteenth century onwards, closer ties between the two countries had developed. The middle and upper classes in Scotland were quick to appreciate the advantages of closer ties with England – commercial, social, and, to some extent, legal. According to H.J. Hanham, educated Scots became self conscious about the prevalence of Scotticisms in their speech; Scots lawyers had difficulty in making themselves understood in the House of Lords; wealthy Scots began to feel that a Scottish education would put their children at a disadvantage in the struggle for life, and began to send them to English schools and universities. Textbooks were produced to teach English to the Scots, almost like a foreign language. Elocutionists, like Thomas Sheridan, visited Edinburgh to give lessons in English pronunciation.[31] As we saw earlier, Moncreiff's own mother insisted that her children speak with an English accent – a rule of which Moncreiff himself evidently approved. While he had been educated in Edinburgh, he sent sons to Harrow and Oxbridge. At university he had joined the Speculative Society, one of whose aims was to train young lawyers in the idiom of the south.[32]

There was of course a powerful commercial driver behind the trend in favour of Anglicisation – that is the rapid economic development of Great Britain in the age of manufacturing and overseas trade within and beyond the British Empire, from which Scottish interests greatly benefited, and because of which cities like Glasgow multiplied in size. 'A great deal', wrote a contributor to the *Law Magazine* in the autumn of 1853, 'remains to be done in order to perfect the Law Merchant.' It was not simply a matter of reforming the mercantile law of England and Scotland, 'but that, situated as these two countries are towards each other, a difference in their respective legal systems as to matters of commerce is in itself an evil, and sufficient to justify a general remodeling.' What was being proposed, therefore, was 'to assimilate the commercial regulations of both countries', so that, 'by communicating to each other the peculiar excellencies of both, a commercial system may be produced...so framed as to be of general application throughout the United Kingdom'.[33] As I.G.C. Hutchison has explained, business and professional men in the west of Scotland were less interested in an assertion of Scottish distinctiveness than working towards a closer assimilation with England.[34] This attitude led to the creation of the

Glasgow Law Amendment Society, which drew particular attention to areas of Scottish law which in their view compared unfavourably with English law, and urged remedial action. A similar organisation was planned for Edinburgh, while in Aberdeen and Dundee the magistrates and Town Councils had agreed to co-operate with the Society's objectives.[35] Where the Society differed markedly from the National Association was in the calibre of its supporters. It first meeting was attended by three former Lord Provosts, three future MP's, the Dean of the Faculty of Procurators, and the heads of the three most important banks, while the leading business institutions in the city, the Chamber of Commerce and the Merchants' House, worked with the Society to devise its strategy.[36]

Alan Rodger has described the members of this movement as essentially 'practical men, rather than romantic supporters of a native legal system of whose doctrines they would usually be entirely ignorant'. If they were convinced that there was a case for adopting some aspect of English law, they saw this not as a defeat for Scots law, 'but as a step in the creation of that British commercial law which would help them sell their goods, and to be carried on British railway companies, or on British ships, to British markets at home and overseas'. These businessmen therefore became strong advocates of the movement to assimilate the commercial laws of England, Scotland, and Ireland.[37]

Economic and social changes, the Society argued, had created a situation where Scottish laws, 'however just and expedient in a poor community and a rude state of society are, to say the least, of questionable propriety in the present social conditions of the people of this country'.[38] Discrepancies between English and Scottish mercantile law led to serious practical difficulties. Decrees issued in one country could not be enforced in the other; a non-domicile could not sue in the other country's courts. The law of bankruptcy was seen as badly out of step with that of England. 'The time has therefore come', the Committee of the Society concluded, 'when the laws of the two divisions of the Island should be gradually assimilated.'[39]

Moncreiff himself was well aware of the process of industrialisation which had taken place in Scotland, and broadly accepted and approved of it. In one of his earliest contributions to the *North British Review,* he was highly critical of those who, as he put it, 'sit sadly down.... and lament the progress of human industry, the success of daring enterprise, the wonderful fertility of man's design, and the singular triumphs of practical science and art', an attitude which he condemned as 'contemptible for its weakness and puerility as it is sinful and debasing'. 'These shallow moralizers should remember that the scenes over which they mourn are not the results of the spirit of enterprise and invention which are implanted in our breasts, but are the types of a great duty imperfectly performed.' What he did acknowledge was that the process had put new responsibilities on government. Great cities had sprung up where small villages had previously stood; the rise in the urban population had brought with it the creation of the third estate, as well as the development of educational opportunities which earlier generations had had no access to.[40] A more thorough-going exposition of the Whig interpretation of history would be hard to find.

Writing in 1993, Colin Kidd argued that it is 'one of the unsubstantiated legends of Scottish history' that after 1707 and the loss of its parliamentary autonomy, 'the distinctiveness of Scots law provided a compensatory basis for national identity.' This view he associated in particular with modern Scottish legal nationalists, but conceded that it was 'not entirely a retrospective invention'. And he went on to say that 'a more subtle version of this thesis is the claim that the spirit of Scots jurisprudence is...cosmopolitan and open to European influences; by contrast, the English common law tradition has been insular and vulgarly nationalist.'[41] As we shall see, this view captures almost exactly the attitude to Scots and English law projected by Moncreiff in very many of his public addresses on legal subjects. So that while on the one hand he understood and accepted the societal changes brought about by industrialisation, and on occasion accepted, on purely pragmatic grounds, the value of adopting some aspects of English law and legal procedure, that is not at all the same as saying that he was in principle in favour of wholesale assimilation of the laws of the two countries.

Throughout his career, Moncreiff delivered a number of public addresses on legal subjects, and almost invariably compared the English legal system unfavourably to the Scots, which he robustly claimed had far more in common with European law. In one such address in 1870 on the occasion of the opening of a new course of law lectures in Edinburgh, he spoke at length on the connections between Scots law and that of the great continental systems. The Scots lawyer, he told his audience, 'recognises the common freemasonry in the language, the institutions, the reasoning, the habits of thought which pervade the systems and breathe in the writings of the continental jurists'. Conscious of the fact that Latin was no longer the common medium of the world, he pointed to a new jurisprudence being developed in France and Germany, which had given to the legal world great stores of learning on the subject. For that reason he urged the students in his audience to learn European languages, especially German, confessing that he personally had 'felt the want of German in the course of my legal investigations the greatest possible drawback, and I am certain that the next generation will feel it even more keenly than ours'.[42]

By comparison he described English law as 'an anomaly', and criticised it for lacking 'that coherence, that symmetry, that reasoning from general principles to particulars, which is characteristic of our own system and that of many of the Continental systems.'[43] While disdaining to claim any special euphony for Scottish legal language, he could not resist a dig at the English counterpart, for 'our English neighbours, who think everything barbarous which does not belong to them, and everything civilised which does, have the most barbarous legal nomenclature in the World'.[44] Yet it would be only fair to point out that three years earlier, in a lecture to the Scots Law Society, he had come to very different conclusions. On that occasion he had conceded that the law of England played a central role in the administration of mercantile law, and that 'the two countries, although nominally distinct, are really so identical in their interests and transactions, that no Scots lawyer can be thoroughly trained without in some measure meeting this difficulty.' He went so far as to assert that if he were to begin his professional life all over again, he would do his best to master English jurisprudence.[45]

While very much aware of the strength of the argument for a closer integration of mercantile and commercial law, it is not altogether surprising to find that initially and privately he was not a keen advocate of the policy. In a letter to his close personal friend and professional colleague, Andrew Rutherfurd, in February 1853, he explained that the Prime Minister, Lord Aberdeen, had agreed to set up a Royal Commission for the assimilation of the mercantile law of the two kingdoms. He now urged Rutherfurd to intervene, and to write to Lord John Russell 'impressing on him the absolute necessity of proceeding more cautiously in this matter of assimilation, than they show in some quarters any inclination to do.'[46] Yet by the autumn of that year he had evidently been won round, or at least to some extent. An article in the *Law Magazine* of 1853 noted that Moncreiff had been consulted about the setting up of the Commission, and that it had his full concurrence. In a speech at Leith on 1st September, he spoke in positive terms about the work of the Commission, which he expected would 'lay the foundations of a general system of jurisprudence, which, in the course of time, will be worked out to a consummation'.[47] At the same time, he explained to his constituents that the process of assimilation 'is not to be produced by merely taking one system and putting it upon other countries, but by the adoption of those parts of each system which are better than others.' He was particularly critical of those who assumed that 'Scotch law was only to be reformed by parties on the other side of the Tweed', and claimed that 'if gentlemen who are anxious to preserve the nationality of Scotland would exert themselves a little to prevent our legal system from being – I don't say vitiated, but altogether upset by crude and rash importations from the other side of the Tweed – I think they would be doing a very great service to their country. (Applause)' He took the opportunity, as he was to do again on many public occasions, to insist upon the superior character of Scots law as against that of England. 'We have in Scotland a system which, as far as machinery goes, as far as the principles and philosophy of it goes…is far superior to the English system'. While the latter had some virtues to commend it – it had done great things for the liberty of the subject, 'it is full of strange and odd and unaccountable fictions, and is altogether different from the simple philosophical system which we possess among ourselves.' As a result, it was much easier to reform the law in Scotland, without making radical changes in its principles.[48]

Such was the warmth of Moncreiff's defence of the legal system in Scotland, and criticism of that of England, that he was accused by the reviewer in the *Law Magazine* of having 'unconsciously caught the anti-Anglican prejudice' which he had himself denounced elsewhere in his speech. But this judgement misses the point. Moncreiff was not opposed to law assimilation in principle. He fully understood the advantages of assimilating commercial laws as an aid to expediting commercial intercourse. What he was opposed to was the unthinking importation of English law into Scotland simply by *force majeure*.

Moncreiff was also perfectly well aware that in addition to a common interest in areas such as mercantile law, there was the constitutional fact that ever since the early 18th century, appeals from the Scottish courts had been heard by the House of Lords in London. As he put it, 'the present constitution of our appellate jurisdiction necessarily infuses year by year an Anglican element into our Scottish system.'[49] He even had some appreciative remarks to make about the House of Lords, and claimed that Scotland had derived many advantages from its jurisdiction. At the same time he could not but help to make the point that the system would work even better if the judges bore it in mind that 'in these cases it is the law of Scotland only which the House is called upon to administer, and that the law of England is at almost every turn not only not identical with but repugnant to it.'[50] What he seems to be calling for was for Scottish appeals to be handled on the same basis as appeals to the Judicial Committee of the Privy Council from the colonial courts, where it was a settled principle that the law lords sitting on colonial appeals did indeed direct their judgments in accordance with the law of the colony from which the appeal came. In an empire which included so many countries with so many different legal systems, any other approach would have been unworkable.[51]

Where this principle was disregarded, it could lead their lordships to an unsound decision, and Moncreiff cited the example of *Duncan v.*

Findlater[52], which had to do with the liability of trust funds for the consequences of accidents caused by the negligence of trustees. The Court of Session, naturally adhering to the principles and authorities of the law of Scotland, held that the trust funds *were* liable, only to have their decision overturned by the House of Lords on an analogy of the law of England. Salt was then rubbed into the wound, as 'much grave ridicule and sharp remark was directed against the erroneous opinions of the Court below'. In the end, he was happy to record, the law lords got their comeuppance, as in a later judgment Lord Westbury ruled that the appeal judges in *Duncan v. Findlater* had even misunderstood the law of England; that the Court of Session had been quite right, and had in fact decided in conformity with what the law of England then was, and always had been.

Interestingly – indeed surprisingly – in those various cases where Moncreiff did agree to incorporate features from English law and practice into Scottish law, we find that very few, with the important exception of the bankruptcy law, happened to be in the field of commercial or maritime law. Some dealt simply with matters of procedure, when it appeared to him on purely pragmatic grounds that there were practical advantages to be gained, even in the face of opposition and criticism. A prime example was the Court of Session Act of 1868,[53] designed to streamline the business of the Court. Back in 1850, Moncreiff and John Inglis had been joint architects of a plan to do away with the cumbersome and time-consuming requirement for written pleadings before the Court,[54] and in the process incurred the wrath of the Faculty of Advocates, and all those who had been in receipt of substantial fees for their production. According to Inglis' biographer, J.C. Watt, the 1868 Act likewise prompted a storm of criticism from interested parties. 'Long established traditions were shaken, prejudices had to be dislodged, the fears of honest unbelievers respected, and a jealousy of Anglican terminology humoured.' There were outbursts from all sides at 'the anglicising of the Court', while both Moncreiff and Home Secretary Sir George Grey were violently 'assailed with invective for asserting....that the practice and mode of procedure required to be made more simple, certain, and expeditious'.[55]

Perhaps this particular example of anglicisation touched a nerve because it affected, in the case of the Court of Session, a notable national institution. Or more prosaically, it may just have been a reaction on the part of Scottish lawyers to loss of income. In his 1865 Address on Law Reform and the Bankruptcy Laws, Moncreiff recalled his earlier attempts to reform the procedures of the Court on the model of improvements introduced in Westminster Hall and the Court of Chancery. Referring to the Scotsman's pride in his country's history, he remarked that 'now and then an exaggeration of this spirit breaks out in unreasoning fear and loud outcry at the apprehension of the invasion of English institutions. It is the quill and not the arrow of the Southron which is the subject of alarm – not the blue bonnets but the white wigs against whom the Border is to be defended – an incursion of hostile and hungry lawyers on the sacred domain of the jurisprudence of Scotland....The fiery cross was displayed instantly to sound the alarm.'[56] Discretion being the better part of valour, he had felt it wiser to withdraw.

It is a measure of this deep hostility to the adoption of English forms into Scottish legal procedures that Moncreiff's obituarist, normally flattering to his subject, singled out for criticism this attempt to 'engraft upon our procedures some of the forms in vogue in Westminster'.[57] And yet there were occasions when he was being urged by other interests to do just that – usually though not always for reasons of efficiency – as when MPs urged him to adopt English and Irish forms in the Annual Report on Scottish Statistics in order to facilitate comparisons.[58] Or there might be rather less disinterested motives, when some Scottish Members tried to persuade him to adopt English legislation to remove the Irish poor back to their native country.[59]

These were relatively trivial matters. The same cannot be said about two of his most important attempted reforms – the one ultimately unsuccessful, at least in the short run, and the other quite the reverse. The first of these, discussed in the previous chapter, was the Bill for the reform of representation in Scotland which Moncreiff introduced into the House of Commons in March 1860 – a Bill closely modeled on, though not identical with, current proposals for England.[60] As we have seen, the Bill came under attack from many different sides and was eventually withdrawn. But if Moncreiff's attempts to reform the franchise in Scotland were unsuccessful, the same cannot be said about one of his major legislative achievements – the Bankruptcy Act of 1856 – described in his obituary as possibly the most complete code in the statute book, 'the best testimony to its excellence being the slight nature of subsequent amendment'.[61] But here again the issue of assimilation with English law arises. It also highlights the differences over that issue between lawyers and accountants, especially in Edinburgh, on the one side, and the west of Scotland commercial and industrial interests on the other.

The initiative for change initially, however, emanated from England, and in 1852 and 1853 a committee of London merchants published two *Reports* in which they advocated the unification of the law on bankruptcy, and increased local judicial control over the administration of bankrupt estates. These proposals found favour with the Glasgow Law Amendment Society, and also the West of Scotland Society for the Protection of Trade, who therefore welcomed a Bill promoted by Lord Brougham in September, 1853, incorporating the London Committee's recommendations. Rather less enthusiastic were members of the accountancy profession in Edinburgh, where the previous law on bankruptcy – the Bankruptcy (Scotland) Act – had served the interests of the city's accountants, lawyers, and merchants. According to Stephen Walker, bankruptcies, along with judicial factories and registered companies, were the most lucrative and significant sources of an Edinburgh chartered accountant's workload in the period from 1854.[62] Agitation grew to oppose the likely re-introduction of Brougham's Bill.

But if such agitation were to be successful, it would have to do more than present a case based simply on self-interest. As Walker and Lee have put it, instead the accountants reverted to what has been called 'the most successful political ideology in human history – the antithesis of the harmonisation of international law and the removal of institutional hindrances to cross-border trade – nationalism'.[63] Interestingly, John Grant, brother of and co-author with James Grant, one of the founder members of the National Association for the Vindication of Scottish Rights, was an accountant by profession.[64]

So the campaign against the London Committee's proposals, and against Brougham's Bill, combined an attack on specific details of the legislation with a nationalist attack on this attempt to impose the English system of bankruptcy administration on Scotland. One Samuel Raleigh, for example, a member of the Society of Accountants in Edinburgh, argued that opposition to the proposals was not motivated by any selfish desire to protect the income of trustees, but rather by a perception that the assimilation of the bankruptcy law would ride rough shod over the Scottish character and Scottish legal traditions. The 'violent and wholesale substitution' of the Scottish system of bankruptcy by the English, and the consequent introduction of alien legal institutions with no tradition in Scotland, would disrupt the whole judicial process north of the border.[65]

By 1854 the campaign against assimilation had gathered sufficient public support, and the support of the Lord Advocate himself, to mount a challenge to Brougham's Bill. In the debate in the House of Lords in March 1854, Brougham tried to argue that his Bill 'had the sanction of all classes in England and Scotland who were interested in the question', and in particular that of the mercantile interest. Opposition to it, he claimed, was restricted to self-interested lawyers and accountants, while the lack of support from the Lord Advocate could be dismissed as arising from his natural sympathy for the Edinburgh-Parliament House view.[66] The Bill passed its second reading in the House, but Scottish opposition and a marked lack of enthusiasm in government circles meant that it got no further.

It was now time for Scottish interests to take the initiative, and devise their own proposals for reform. In February 1853 the Edinburgh General Committee on Bankruptcy was formed, representing not just accountants but also lawyers and merchants, and its Sub-Committee produced a report. Then in 1854 Moncreiff himself invited the Faculty of Advocates to prepare a report on the Scots bankruptcy law, and it was this document, together with some features of the Sub-Committee's report, which provided the basis for the 1856 Act.[67] In March 1856, Moncreiff stood up in the House of Commons to move the second reading of his Bankruptcy (Scotland) Bill, and was able to assure the House that it had the support of 'the general community of Scotland', including town councils, chambers of commerce, and the societies for the protection of trade. Consisting of 176 clauses, it was partly an exercise in consolidation, and brought together nearly all the statutes passed on the subject since the beginning of the century. But there was much that was new. For one thing, it did away with the distinction between bankruptcy and insolvency. It abolished the office of Interim Factor – originally designed to take temporary charge of bankrupt estates, but one that had come in for a good deal of adverse criticism. The Bill now provided that Sheriffs, as well as the Lord Ordinary, should have the power to provide for the protection of bankrupt estates. In addition, there would be an accountant in bankruptcy, whose job it would be to make sure that estates were properly wound up, and prevent maladministration and fraud.

At the same time, Moncreiff could not resist reminding the House that 'Two years ago there had been considerable agitation in this country, and partially in Scotland, for an assimilation of the bankrupt laws of the two countries' and a great deal of pressure had been used 'for the purpose of importing into Scotland the general principles of the English law of bankruptcy'. But now, having taken the time to consult 'the great body of professional and mercantile men', he had come to the conclusion that 'the Scotch law of bankruptcy was much better, and it was also much cheaper than the bankrupt law of England'.[68]

All this helps to explain the triumphalist tone of Moncreiff's 1865 address to the Scottish Trade Protection Society. With a certain relish, he lambasted those in Scotland had sought after:

> of all morbid cravings imaginable, the English bankruptcy law. We loudly demanded, in the paroxysm of the disease, why the blessing of official assignees were not bestowed upon us – we went into fits about a court of Bankruptcy, and filled the air of Parliament with the wailings of Glasgow commerce, bereft of its place among the nations, and left an

outcast in our cold northern air, uncherished by commissioners, and unprotected by registrars. Kindly English friends were good enough to fan the flames, enlighten our ignorance, and point out the way in which our grievances might be redressed; little pamphlets were written, little speeches were spoken, and a great bill was prepared, which was to heal the afflicted spirit of Scotland, and cure its bankrupt woes.

Fortunately, the Scots soon came to their senses, and when those 'senses had entirely returned, we passed an Act on bankruptcy, which, by no means perfect, has been well and successfully administered. (Applause)' All this obviously went down well with an audience which appreciated the wit of the speaker and the fun poked at their 'kindly English friends' and their gullible Scottish colleagues.[69]

There is no doubt that the 1856 Act[70] was a marked improvement on its predecessor. One measure of its success was that it remained on the statute book virtually unamended for almost sixty years until 1913.[71] A further measure of that success was that in 1864 a House of Commons Select Committee recommended the introduction into England and Wales of the Scottish system of paid creditor elected trustees. In introducing a Bankruptcy Bill in the House of Commons in April 1869, the Attorney-General explained that one object of the Bill was to reduce the expense of bankruptcy administration in England, where it was sometimes as high as 75% of the estate. In Scotland it was typically only 12-13%. 'These figures pointed strongly to the expediency of adopting as far as possible the Scotch system'.[72] Sadly we have no record of Moncreiff's reaction to this news.

How then are we to assess Moncreiff's role in advancing or resisting the process of assimilation? As we have seen, again and again in public addresses he celebrated the virtues of Scottish law and the Scottish legal system, deprecating the English system and those who sought to import aspects of it into Scotland. Initially at least he urged caution to the Commission on Assimilation in 1853. And yet in practice he was perfectly willing to incorporate procedural features from south of the border into the Scottish courts where he felt they represented an improvement, and was roundly criticised by his obituarist for so doing. He perceived some benefit, but also some disadvantage, arising from the appellate jurisdiction of the House of Lords in Scottish cases. The Bankruptcy Act of 1856, arguably the greatest legislative success of his career as Lord Advocate, incorporated some minor features of the English system, while departing from it in its essential principles. That the Attorney-General of Great Britain should then decide to adopt the Scottish system over the English provides a fitting accolade to Moncreiff's pragmatic approach.

Chapter 10
Reforming Scotland's Education

I - Towards a National Schools System for Scotland?

Throughout his long term of office as Scotland's Lord Advocate, Moncreiff addressed himself to many different causes and reforms. But few issues engaged his attention more deeply than that of reform of the system of education in Scotland – in both schools and in universities. Indeed the two were closely connected in his mind – partly because he could see little progress being made in these areas so long as entry to the teaching profession was constrained by religious tests, but also because he understood the need for improvement in educational standards. As we have noted earlier, he also saw a connection between improvements in popular education and the extension of the franchise. His efforts were met with some real successes – most notably over the tests and teachers' salaries, and some real failures – his attempts to create a national system of education were regularly defeated. But if he did not always get everything he wanted, he did much to prepare the way for his successors.

We have already seen how, in mid-nineteenth century Scotland, the party political system had been weakened in two ways. As in England at the same time, the disarray of the Conservative party over Corn Law repeal left the Liberals in a commanding position. But this apparent strength had allowed divisions to develop within the party itself, essentially between Whigs and Radicals, as repeal removed the principal issue which had held the two factions of the party together.[1] And there was another major factor at work in Scotland which had no counterpart south of the border – the political fallout from the Disruption of 1843. A major characteristic of Scottish politics from the late 1840s onwards was the role of religion in political affairs, and this impacted directly upon the debate on educational reform. In effect a new voting bloc was being formed, consisting of the non-established churches – the Free Church and the Voluntaries – which came together in 1845 through the formation of the Evangelical Alliance – an anti-Catholic organisation. While key differences remained between the partners in this enterprise over state support for religion, they could find common ground in opposition to the Maynooth Grant. In 1846 the Edinburgh committee of the Alliance published *An Address to the Electors of Scotland,* ascribed to one of its leaders, Robert Candlish, which emphasised the importance of returning evangelical Protestants to Parliament, in the cause of opposing Popery. This document alarmed Whig party managers, who feared the importation of religious questions into national politics, and their fears were largely justified. In the 1847 election, in constituencies where there was a substantial proportion of Free Church or Voluntary voters, Whig candidates were either defeated or had their majorities severely reduced. In the election of 1852, Whigs had been largely driven from city seats. As Cockburn noted of the contest in the capital, the striking characteristics on all sides were the 'prevalence and intensity of our bigotry', and that 'the religious element was more powerful than the political'.[2] This religious element was to be a significant force in the campaign for the reform of the Scottish educational system.

In May 1843, at the very first meeting of the General Assembly of the Free Church following the Disruption, the Church's Education Committee set out the principles upon which future education policy should be founded. 'The functions of any Church, and especially any Church which aspires to be national, cannot be considered to be completely fulfilled till provision is made for the training of the children and the young persons connected with it, from the lowest elementary school to the first institutions of science and learning.'[3] The key phrase here was 'aspires to be national'. Free Churchmen saw their institution as the only truly legitimate Church of Scotland, and as such it was their bounden duty to provide their own schools system on a national basis. Not that there was complete agreement that this should be the priority. There were those who argued that the new Church should not cut itself off from the existing national educational heritage. There was no real doctrinal difference between the two churches, and parochial schools run by the established church taught the Bible and the Shorter Catechism. Free Church parents should not be prevented therefore[4] from sending their children to these schools, so long as there was no attempt to denigrate the Free Church, while in the meantime attempts should be made to make the career of schoolmaster open to Free Church candidates. In any case, some argued, the new Church would have quite enough to cope with financially, without the enormous cost of building new schools.

Despite these reservations, the Church Education Committee, under its new and energetic convener, Dr Candlish, set out a plan in 1846 to build 1000 new schools. Not long after, the Privy Council Education Committee came forward with a scheme to provide government funded grants for school building – a scheme which sparked off a debate within the Free Church as to whether or not the Church should accept such grants. One group, led by James Begg and Thomas Guthrie, argued that it should not. What they looked forward to was a truly national system of elementary education in Scotland – even to the extent of including within it the old Church of Scotland parochial schools and any new ones to be built by the Free Church. As Donald Withrington has explained, their preference was for an extended state-endowed system, based on the old parochial provision, and managed by local committees with no religious tests applied to them. The problem of denominational differences they hoped to solve by setting particular times of day for religious instruction, with the option of parents to withdraw their children from these sessions.

From the standpoint of James Begg and his supporters, in accepting the Privy Council grants for itself, the Church would be perpetuating the sectarian character of school education in Scotland. But Candlish refused to accept this argument. For him the flaw in the plan for a national system of education on the Begg model was not that it was national – but rather that it could not guarantee the proper religious character of education. At the time Candlish succeeded in opposing this plan, but many of its features were to surface again in the 1850s, in the two Bills proposed by Lord Melgund in 1850 and 1851, and in the several bills which Moncreiff himself was to put before Parliament to create his vision of a national system of education for Scotland. Indeed, according to J.D. Myers, the failure of Moncreiff's proposals may have been due not just to opposition from the Moderates and their allies, but also to the 'calculated machinations' of Candlish and his supporters.[5]

At much the same time, the Church of Scotland, as the established church, was determined to protect its position in relation to elementary education. The situation in Scotland when Moncreiff entered politics was one in which school education, at the level of parishes at least, was still firmly under the Church's control. This control was exercised by a variety of means, including the appointment of teachers in parish schools, presbyterial inspections, and above all the religious test, to which all aspiring teachers were required to subscribe. Fearing the possibility of disestablishment, the Church was determined to preserve the status quo against all comers. Back in 1844 – just one year after the Disruption – the General Assembly had drawn up a document entitled 'Protests, Declarations, and Testimony on the Subject of National Education', in which it was insisted that control of the parish schools by the Established Church must be maintained.

In addition to the parish schools, there were the denominational schools – Episcopalian and Roman Catholic, in receipt of Privy Council grants which they were unwilling to give up – and also, since the great Disruption of 1843, a good many Free Church schools. We have seen that not far short of five hundred ministers left their parishes in 1843, less well known is the fact that between six and seven hundred schoolteachers had similarly left their schools and joined the Free Church. The religious test for schoolteachers effectively debarred such teachers from positions in parish schools, despite the fact that they were themselves Presbyterians, with no real doctrinal differences from their Church of Scotland brethren. As Moncreiff himself put it rather neatly in 1851, 'The effect of the tests was simply to exclude many who differed in nothing from the Established Church except in not belonging to it.'[6] For some years after the Disruption had forced the Free Church to develop its own schools, it was anxious to keep them, but eventually the financial pressures became too much and it put its weight behind the idea of a national system.[7] Also worth mentioning were the United Presbyterians, who were not opposed in principle to the idea of state education, but were opposed to the right of the state to support religious teaching. Any truly comprehensive plan for a national system of education for all Scotland's children would somehow have to reconcile these very different positions, but from Moncreiff's perspective, the one essential condition for achieving his objective was to bring about the abolition of the religious test.

By the early 1850s the deficiencies of the existing state of Scotland's educational provision could no longer be ignored. Under the law as it then stood, each parish had to have a school provided by the local landowner, under the control of the established church. Demographic changes brought about largely by the process of industrialisation meant that in some urban areas as many as 40% of children were left uncatered for by the existing educational provision. Some attempts had been made to make up the shortfall by providing private schools, but the quality in these schools was notoriously uneven. In the parochial schools, as we have seen, the religious tests meant that all teachers had to be members of the Church of Scotland, thus excluding both Catholics from the profession, and the large number of teachers who had joined the Free Church at or since the Disruption. There was a growing desire for a school system which was national, non-sectarian, and without compulsory religious instruction. These were the goals adopted by the National Educational Association of Scotland, formed in 1850, with the objective of creating a 'general system of education, on a sound and popular basis, and capable of communicating instruction to all classes in the community'.[8]

The NEAS attracted support from a variety of interests and individuals, including the Voluntaries, with their commitment to non-sectarian and secular education, and opposition to state support for religious instruction. More surprising was the support of the Free Church. As we have seen, after the Disruption, the church had pursued a strategy of trying to undermine the position of the Church of Scotland as the national church by setting up its own schools throughout the country, and at the same time providing employment for those teachers who had joined the Church after 1843, and so forfeited their careers. This policy had been only partially successful. Provision of schools by the Church covered only about two thirds of congregations, with a concentration of schools in the Highlands, and a relative under supply in the Lowland areas. The cost of maintaining these schools placed an unsupportable burden on the finances of the Church, to the extent that the salaries of Free Church teachers had to be reduced by one third. From the point of view of the Church, therefore, to adopt the plan for the establishment of a national education scheme had many advantages. It would solve the financial problem and safeguard the employment of its teachers. At the same time it would undermine the claim of the Church of Scotland to be *the* national church.

So, rather than sweep away the existing parochial schools system, the NEAS saw it as the foundation of the new, though with significant changes. Instead of relying on the financial support of the old heritors, there would be a school rate, and a school committee elected by ratepayers. These local committees would be in a position to assess the educational needs of their localities, and found new schools. The longer term plan was for this system to absorb the denominational schools, for which there would no longer be a need for state subsidies, while the parish schools would lose their sectarian character through the abolition of the test, and the removal of supervision by the presbyteries. As R.D. Anderson has pointed out, the most contentious issue raised by the proposal for a national education system was what religious instruction was to be provided, if schools were to be in the hands of the public authority, rather than in those of the church.[9]

Almost from his first appearance in the House of Commons, Moncreiff embarked on a decades-long campaign to create a national system of school education in Scotland. In only his second House of Commons speech, in June 1851, he supported Viscount Melgund's second and unsuccessful Schools Bill, and he went on to introduce several more Bills of his own on the subject. Despite his efforts, only two of these found their way on to the statute book – an Act of 1857 settling teachers' salaries[10], and the Parochial and Burgh Schools Act of 1861[11]. And it was not until three years after his retirement from politics in 1869, that the 1872 Education Act finally secured for Scotland the national system of education he had dedicated himself to achieve.

The object of Lord Melgund's 1851 Schools Bill was to withdraw the parochial schools system from the control of the Church of Scotland, and impose a policy of purely secular education in new national schools. Moncreiff used the occasion to outline his own approach to the problem. 'There was a great necessity,' he claimed, 'for an enlarged means of education in Scotland…a national system of education that shall be really and truly sufficient for the needs of the country.' It was not enough to tinker with the existing situation by giving Government aid in the form of grants to other denominations while leaving the parish schools as they now stood – it would still be necessary to provide for the enormous mass of educational destitution in the country which the parochial schools could not reach. What was needed was a system of education 'which is national, not merely in theory but in reality, and which is adapted to the wants, and founded in the affections, of the people'.[12] At the same time he raised a question which was to preoccupy his thoughts on school and university education for a decade – the existence of the religious test for teachers. In arguing for the abolition of the test, the effect of which, of course, was to close off the profession to members of the Free Church as well as to all denominations and sects other than the Church of Scotland itself, he denied that he was attacking the Established Church. He had no wish to witness her decline – quite the reverse. Nor did he wish to undermine religious education, but there could not, he claimed, 'be a more miserable safeguard for the religious instruction of the people than this system'. In the event Melgund's Bill failed to pass with an overall majority against it of just twelve votes. Yet in Moncreiff's own opinion, despite its imperfections, 'it contained the outline of what might become a good national measure'.[13]

In an uncharacteristically alarmist outburst when introducing the first of his own Bills in 1854, Moncreiff warned fellow MPs of the dangers facing the country if no action was taken. Education, he argued, was no longer simply a matter of philanthropy or religious duty, but 'a question of self defence. If we do not encounter and overcome the ignorance of the people, the ignorance of the people will overcome us.' He went on to assert that there existed, 'in the very heart of our social system, in the very centre of our mighty cities, and at the very base and root of this immense community, what I do not err in terming a savage and barbarian race, tied to you by no sympathy, bound to your institutions by no common link.' 'We shall never deal with this question rightly,' he continued, 'except on the assumption that there exists at the very foundation of society a flood of deep, unfathomed, pestilential waters, which, unless prompt measures are taken, any upheaving [sic] of our social system may cause to burst their barriers, and sweep us and our boasted institutions to destruction.'[14]

In a more objective vein, he claimed simply that the state had a duty to discharge in educating its citizens, and that voluntary action had clearly failed to meet the educational needs of Scotland's expanding urban population. Leaving the parish schools unchanged, and giving government aid to the denominational schools, would not, he argued, 'solve the enormous mass of educational destitution....which the parish schools would not reach'.[15] Looking back on this issue from the perspective of the 1880s, Moncreiff recalled that 'it was plain that a great risk was gradually accumulating from the insufficiency of the old fabric to meet the new wants of the community'. He had long held the opinion 'that it was discreditable to the Nation that education was not universal', and had 'no sympathy with the old fallacy that the State should only aid voluntary efforts, a futility which has borne some pernicious fruit,....and I was among a number of those who held that if every child were educated many of our social and political problems would be solved.'[16]

As it turned out, the NEAS was to have only a limited life, and soon succumbed to internal pressures. But the essentials of its vision were kept alive by others, including Moncreiff, and Lord Melgund, whose two unsuccessful Bills in 1850 and 1851 were largely inspired by the NEAS programme. At this early stage, the Free Church opposed the Bills, primarily because of their opposition to a purely secular education system, though, as we have seen, Moncreiff, himself of course a prominent Free Churchman, spoke in the House of Commons in 1851 in Melgund's support. By the time Moncreiff put forward his own initial two Bills in 1854 and 1855 the Free Church had changed its tack, and the 1854 Bill also attracted support from the United Presbyterians. Since almost by definition this ensured the hostility of the Established Church, Moncreiff was assured of a rough parliamentary ride.

Nevertheless, by 1853 the auguries on the subject of educational reform in Scottish schools appeared to be more favourable, and it was becoming increasingly difficult to pretend that all was well with the state of elementary education in Scotland. On the subject of the religious tests, Moncreiff was confident that he had the support of the Whig party in Scotland.[17] On the larger question of the reform of elementary education, even the Church of Scotland Education Committee had registered its 'utmost anxiety about the thousands of children in our midst who are growing up in a state of ignorance and crime', admitting at the same time that the Church had run out of money to do anything about the problem.[18] The Free Church by now had come out in support of Moncreiff's proposals – at least in principle. And there was a pressing practical problem which required immediate action – the settlement of parish schoolteachers' salaries. Under an Act of 1803, the salaries of parish school teachers were in a sense 'index-linked', in that they were tied to the current price of oatmeal. 'Such salaries,' the Act decreed, 'never being less that the value of one Chalder and an Half, and not more than two Chalders for the next Twenty-five years, and so *toties quoties* at the end of every Twenty-five years for ever...'[19] Unfortunately for Scottish parish schoolmasters, the price of meal had been going down – threatening an unintended and unacceptable 25% cut in teachers' pay. As the fiftieth anniversary of the passing of the Act approached, supporters of educational reform planned to use the need for legislation on pay as an opportunity to press for other more far-reaching reforms, while many in the Established Church were determined that the issues of pay and reform must be kept separate and distinct. Church of Scotland Synods set up committees with the avowed aim of monitoring proposed educational legislation, and petitioning against any relaxation of the religious tests in both Schools and Universities.[20] A 'Declaration by Justices of the Peace, Commissioners of Supply, and Heritors', supported by 35 Scottish peers and 1,800 members of the gentry, represented 'the subscribers' strong opinion to be that, except for the purpose of meeting defects in its workings and increasing its efficiency, the present system of parochial schools ought not to be interfered with, and that their connection with the Church of Scotland ought to be maintained'.[21]

In order to justify the reforms set out in his Bills of 1854 and 1855, Moncreiff had to explain what was wrong with the existing system of presbyterial control of parochial education. 'The present system of superintendence and management of the parochial schools,' he told the House, 'has been found greatly defective and ought to be altered and amended.' Yet at the time he lacked the necessary factual evidence to support this claim, which was not to be forthcoming until the publication of the Report of the Argyll Commission ten years later, and therefore had to rely on assertion rather than on proof. 'The question,' he suggested, 'is whether the superintendence by the Presbytery be or be not efficient. Over a full century, it was in most cases little better than a name.' At the same time he had to concede that owing to competition from the Free Church since 1843, 'there has been increased vigilance [by presbyteries] of late years, and the parish schools are probably more efficient than for many years. But times of lethargy may come again, and the results will be as before.'[22] In Scotland, this kind of language was taken by some not as fair criticism, but as an insult. One James Johnstone MP wrote to Moncreiff that 'Scotland was sensitive to insult – [you] insulted the Church of Scotland and its management of parish schools.'[23]

Nevertheless, to begin with, there was a good deal of support for the Bill from both the Free Church and the Voluntary churches, which held a series of public meetings in its support, and as Fox Maule commented to Andrew Rutherfurd, 'if he can get the Voluntaries to accept it cordially, he will have a good chance of carrying it'.[24] But as Ian Hutchison has explained, a weak point of the Bill was that it could be seen as simply a way of subsidising the Free Church by shifting the cost of maintaining its own schools to all ratepayers, while at the same time effectively restricting schoolmasterships to members of either the Established or the Free Church, who alone could deliver Bible teaching. In an attempt to cater for the principles of the Voluntaries – opposed as they were to state sponsored religious instruction – clause 27 of the 1854 Bill stated that while specific times of day were to be set aside for this purpose, parents would be free to withdraw their children from these sessions. But the value of this concession as a means of keeping the Voluntaries on board was effectively undermined by the statement that no extra charge would be imposed for the children's attendance. This meant that in effect the cost would be borne by all ratepayers, regardless of their religious affiliation. By March of 1854, the United Presbyterians in particular had turned against the Bill, and their Synod in May declared that from now on it would be strongly opposed by the Church. The Lord Provost of Edinburgh, Duncan McLaren, to be Moncreiff's nemesis on so many issues in the future, was broadly in support of the 1854 Bill, at least in principle, though he objected to the composition of the proposed Central Board as containing too many university professors and not enough representatives of the burghs where so many of the new schools were to be created.[25]

There were other provisions of the 1854 Bill which attracted particular criticism. A central proposal was for the creation of a Board of Education for Scotland.[26] In a letter to the Hon. A. Kinnaird, M.P., J.C. Colquoun declared that the Board was 'the great issue which makes it the worst measure proposed within my experience to Parliament'.[27] And in a Memorandum on the same subject: 'It is in full operation in Holland, France, Prussia, and Germany…its results manifested in 1848 in infidel teachers, socialist doctrines, licentious schools, and a turbulent multitude.'[28] Extravagant language, perhaps, about a measure which would simply have transferred the general superintendence of parish schools from the Presbyteries to the Board. But many saw this as very much more than a mere administrative change – rather the beginning of a process of the secularisation of education in Scotland. In the Commons, F. Scott complained that the examination of schoolteachers under the terms of the Bill would not include religion,[29] while even a Free Church member alleged that the Bill 'practically orders public schoolmasters into a great secular corporation'.[30]

According to Wilson Bain, Moncreiff regarded the removal of superintendence by the Presbytery as less important than removing the religious tests for parish schoolmasters, but in any case he denied that 'by removing limitations on the power of election and vesting the management of schools in the heritors and ministers, subject to the General Board, instead of the Presbytery, we [are] weakening the guarantees for Religious Instruction…nor was this conceived in a spirit of hostility to the Church itself'.[31]

Opposition to the 1854 Bill was such that the measure failed to achieve a second reading. If Moncreiff's second attempt in the following year was to fare better, changes would have to be made. Most of these affected the membership of the proposed Board of Education. In its 1854 form, the Board had included government members and representatives of outside bodies, such as the universities. Now the membership was to include the Lord Provosts of Edinburgh, Glasgow, Aberdeen and Perth. In the Commons, Moncreiff was obliged to substitute for the Lord Provosts 'four persons...one elected from each of the four Town Councils' – a sensible enough alteration. More significant was the removal of the Lord Advocate himself and the Solicitor-General for Scotland from the membership, and the addition of four persons, one each elected by the Commissioners for Supply, and the counties of Aberdeen, Inverness, Renfrew and Ayr. The overall effect of these changes would have been to weaken Government influence and strengthen the forces of opposition to change.[32]

In many other respects the Bills of 1854 and 1855 were very similar though not identical. Both proposed set hours for religious instruction, which would have allowed dissenting parents to withdraw their children from that part of the curriculum – condemned by both the Established Church and the Free. Both made specific provision for teachers' salaries – an item which divided the two Churches. At one point in the Commons debate in May 1854 Moncreiff let his irritation show through. 'He could not see how human ingenuity could have framed it to have subscribed for more assistance. If he had listened to the Established Church, he would have had all the rest of Scotland opposed to him; if he had listened to the secularists, he would have had the Free Church, the Established Church, and the great majority of that House opposed to him.'[33] Both Bills made provision for a retirement allowance for teachers, and for their living accommodation and a schoolhouse. Above all, both abolished the religious test.

The abolition of the test, as we have seen, was the one issue on which Moncreiff would never give way. His position had little to do with religion as such, whatever his opponents might allege. He sought efficiency for the national educational system. To debar large numbers of well qualified (and Presbyterian) individuals, from the teaching profession, simply on the grounds that they did not belong to the Established Church, was a great waste of talent. As Moncreiff declared in a Memorandum to the Cabinet in February 1855, 'no measure...(should) perpetuate exclusion of two-thirds of the community in the constitution of schools which ought to be national. Nor do I see that, after the course adopted last season, it would be possible for Government in consistency to leave this defect unremedied.'[34] But this issue, as Bain has rightly pointed out, was the sticking point for most of the Bill's opponents. Henry Baillie, MP for Inverness-shire, spoke for many when he charged that the Bill 'contained no clause which gave the slightest security to the people that education ...would be religious education. No religious test must be required from the schoolmaster, who might be a Roman Catholic, or a member of any other religion, or no religion at all.'[35] Surprisingly the clause abolishing the test was not removed at the Committee stage, but it was amended to substitute for the test a declaration by the school teacher than he would teach nothing contrary to the interests of the Established Church. In the end, the Lords consigned the whole Bill to the dustbin. As Willis Pickard has pointed out in his biography of Duncan McLaren, a curious feature of the debates on a national education system for Scotland was the almost complete lack of any discussion of the curriculum, apart from the issue of religion.[36]

One practical reason for the failure of the Bill was the lack of Parliamentary time. The Lords had recently adopted a rule by which they refused to consider the second reading of any Bill after the 30th June and this Bill fell foul of that rule. 'The real cause of defeat,' Moncreiff complained after the event, 'arose from suitable time not being allowed by the Government for discussion of the Bill' – a problem he claimed was a common feature of the handling of Scottish business in Parliament. 'In Bills affecting Scotland, in which none but Scotch members take an interest,' he asserted, 'the business may generally be conducted satisfactorily without serious encroachment on Government time. But whenever a Scotch measure occurs which the opposition as a body treat as a party question, its defeat be almost certain unless it be brought on proper Government nights.'[37]

But defeat, as he made clear at the time and later, was not simply a matter of the lack of priority being given to Scottish Parliamentary business, but rather to the strength of English opposition to it. 'The measure of last year,' he told his government colleagues, 'though it gave rise to great difference of opinion, did not owe its defeat to [Scottish] opposition, either in the House or in the country. On the contrary, the division showed conclusively that the feeling of the Scotch members and of Scotland was strongly in favour of it. The division showed 36 Scotch Members for the Bill to 14 against, not a single Burgh Member voting against it, and those from the counties equally divided.'[38] On the other hand, opinion amongst Scottish Members of the Lords was much less favourable. In April 1854, thirty-three Scottish peers had signed a petition against the Bill. And as the Earl of Eglinton pointed out in the course of the debate on the 1855 Bill, of the sixteen representative peers, fifteen were opposed to the Bill and the sixteenth was in India.[39]

But Moncreiff continued to lay the blame for the defeat of the Bill squarely, if not altogether fairly, at the feet of the English Members. In his 1886 address on the occasion of the opening of the Kent Road Public School in Glasgow, he returned to the charge. When he first entered Parliament in 1851, he told his Glasgow audience, there was no national system in England, and no desire for one. The established Church maintained its own schools, supported financially by state grants distributed by the Privy Council, and was 'jealous of any proposal which would admit anyone else to a share in their management'. The Nonconformists, on the other hand, were opposed to any national system, 'on a kind of blended feeling between objecting to public money being spent for any such purpose, and the difficulties about religious instruction'. No support for a national system in Scotland could be expected from south of the border, since 'the average English mind looked with suspicion on all such projects, thinking they were matters the parsons ought to settle, and seeing no reason why, if England had weathered so many centuries without a national system, it should begin to have one then. In short, what with Church of England exclusiveness, Nonconformist dislike, and general apathy both in country and borough, the prospects for any efficient legislation for England were very far from hopeful.' It was to take a further twenty years before 'this mass of inert obstructionism or direct hostility could be cleared away'. Within Parliament, it was almost impossible to arouse any interest in the subject amongst English members, 'while our Scotch system was looked on as a provincial exotic, which could have no importance on the other side of the Tweed'.[40]

It was certainly true that Moncreiff had failed so far to enlist the support of English Members to any great degree, and as Scotland under the electoral law then obtaining was underrepresented in Parliament, support from south of the border was essential for success. Another possible problem was Moncreiff's tactical error in bundling too many controversial changes into a single Bill – an error he determined to avoid in the next stage of his campaign by drawing up proposals for three new Bills. His plans were set out in a Memorandum to the Cabinet in March, 1856. The first Bill would leave the level of teachers' salaries unchanged, but by abolishing the test would seek to open the profession up to all denominations. The second would deal with the financing of education in Scotland – the costs to be shared between landowners and ratepayers, and with the administration of education – the creation of a Board of Inspectors under the direction of a Minister of Education. The third, which would have created a temporary Parliamentary Commission to oversee the workings of a national system of education, with power, amongst other things to determine what new schools might be required, was not to be introduced unless and until the first two had been carried.

In introducing the first two Bills in the Commons in April 1856, Moncreiff did his best to disarm potential opposition. He went out of his way to conciliate the supporters of parochial schools, and made it clear that he did not seek to interfere with the judicial powers of the Presbyteries over schoolteachers accused of heretical teaching, or their powers to examine teachers, provided the latter were members of the Established Church. His success was no more than partial. Both Bills passed their second reading in the Commons by a healthy majority, only for the Lords to delete the all-important clause abolishing the test. Both Houses set up committees, but by May 1857 the whole process had run out of time, and the Bills lapsed. All that Moncreiff managed to salvage from the wreck was an Act of 1857,[41] which made provision for the salaries of parish schoolmasters – though still on the old system dating from 1803 where the level of salaries was based on the average price of oatmeal.

There followed a hiatus, during which, from February 1858 to April 1859, Moncreiff was out of office. Then, more or less fortuitously, an opportunity was presented for a new initiative in the campaign for the reform of Scottish education, in the form of a Court of Session judgement in what came to be known as the Elgin case.[42] The decision of the Court in the Elgin case was that a schoolmaster in a burgh (i.e. not a parochial) school must nevertheless take a religious test, and be subject to examination by the Presbytery. The reaction amongst Town Councils, who had for many years been responsible for the running of burgh schools with minimal interference from the Presbyteries, and from burgh schoolmasters, who had not formerly been required to take the test, was as might be expected. Complaints to Parliament against the decision and its implications for others poured in. Typical was the complaint from the Town Council of Glasgow, who explained that they had 'not taken into account the religious profession or denomination of any candidate, but have contented ourselves with ascertaining that the party was of irreproachable moral character, and best qualified'.[43] Nor were they accustomed to have their jurisdiction over the burgh schools interfered with by the Presbytery. Other Councils pointed out the consequences if a large number of well qualified teachers were now to be faced with the choice of subscribing to the test, or resigning from their positions. The decision of the Court, it was said, was 'hurtful to the feelings and in opposition to the desires of a great majority of people of Scotland, and highly detrimental to education'.[44]

Moncreiff at once saw an opportunity, and began to prepare the ground for a new campaign. He was in touch with schoolmasters, and with 'some of the leading Scotch members on the Conservative side of the House, as well as with those who have the confidence of the

Presbyterian Dissenters, and I think there is a probability of their substantially acquiescing in the following heads of a Bill:

1. The existing test be abolished
2. The patronage to remain with the Minister and Heritors as at present,
3. The examination of Schoolmasters, prior to admission, to be taken from the Presbyteries and transferred to an Examining Committee, to be nominated by the University Court in each of the four Universities…
4. Every schoolmaster on his admission to take the Declaration which is at present administered to every Professor, namely that he will teach nothing contrary to the Westminster Confession of Faith.'[45]

The Bill which Moncreiff presented to Parliament on 3rd June, 1861, and which was to be enacted as the Parochial and Burgh Schools Act[46], substantially followed the plan he had outlined in his Memorandum to Cabinet. The salaries of parish schoolmasters were set at a range from £35 to £70 per annum, and where an Inspector declared a teacher to be disqualified by reason of infirmity, age or negligence, he could be forcibly retired. If the teacher was not personally at fault, then he could receive a pension of not less that two thirds of salary. Clause 14 transferred the disciplinary powers of the Presbytery over parish schoolteachers to the civil authority in the form of the Sheriff. Clause 12 abolished the religious test, substituting only a certificate from the Examiners, and a Declaration that the schoolmaster would never teach opinions contrary to the Divine Authority of the Holy Scriptures, or to the Doctrines of the Shorter Catechism. In the words of A.L. Drummond and J. Bulloch, 'the main relevance for the Scottish churches lay in the fact that it transferred the power of examining new teachers from the Presbyteries to four Boards associated with the Universities, and that it ended the need to sign the Confession. Denominational inspection of schools by the Churches sponsoring them still continued, but (almost) the only control left to the Church of Scotland in the parish schools was the uncertain power of the local minister on the body which appointed a parish teacher.'[47] From Moncreiff's point of view, he had at long last succeeded in securing the abolition of the religious test, and 'thereby opened the door to the best men'.[48]

As Moncreiff had hoped, the passage of the Bill through Parliament, compared with that of its predecessors, was remarkably smooth. There were some murmurings that the inclusion of the Declaration was in practice a test by another name, but Moncreiff urged the complainants to accept the compromise.[49] At the Committee stage, Scottish Members forced an amendment to remove the power of the Presbytery to dismiss a teacher, its disciplinary powers reduced effectively to that of lodging a complaint with either the Secretary of State (in cases where a teachers had broken his religious declaration), or to the Sheriff (in cases of immorality or cruelty). But what Moncreiff had so far failed to achieve in this Act was his other great ambition for Scottish education – the creation of a truly national educational system

In 1861-2 a new threat to the education system in Scotland emerged in the form of what was called the Revised Code for educational grants, the brainchild of the then Minister for Education, Robert Lowe. Lowe was opposed in principle to the expenditure of state funding for the benefit of any other than those who could not help themselves, and was therefore out of sympathy with the kind of state supported national education system envisaged by Moncreiff and his colleagues, but the Code in any case was seen to be at odds with the conditions and objectives of Scottish education at large. For one thing, what grants there were for the support of education were confined to the education of children of the labouring classes. As we have seen in an earlier chapter, one of the great strengths of the education which Moncreiff himself had experienced had been the teaching of children of all social classes in the one institution. The Code was based on payment by results of annual examinations in six so called 'standard' subjects – which tended to encourage teachers to concentrate on basic educational skills, rather than the preparation for higher subjects as was the norm in Scotland. Moreover, the Code assumed all teachers were of the 'elementary' type – while they had to possess a government certificate to be qualified to teach, university qualifications were of no advantage. Moncreiff's policy all along was to strengthen, not weaken, the links between the schools and the universities.

Not surprisingly, the Code aroused furious opposition in Scotland. Part of the object of Moncreiff's next foray into educational legislation, the 1862 Bill, was to avoid the application of the Revised Code to Scotland, and, of course, to secure his main goal – the creation of a national system. His plan for this new Bill was explained to Cabinet in a Memorandum in December 1861, and the Bill itself introduced into the House of Commons on the 17th March, 1862. This time a General Council of Education would be created, but with only a 'general supervising power', together with a Commission with the authority to decide which existing schools were really necessary, and what new ones were required. Unnecessary schools would get no grant from the Council, necessary ones would be fully funded. Grants to denominational schools would be discontinued. But once again, as in

1854 and 1855, it was all in vain. Once again Moncreiff's plans were criticised on the ground of lack of evidence about the true state of Scottish schools, and he was forced to concede that 'since it was said that there was no educational destitution, or at least no proof of it, we came to be satisfied that without full enquiry into the educational state of Scotland it was no use to go on with this incessant knocking at the door of Parliament'.[50]

The next step then was to set such an enquiry in motion. In February 1864 Moncreiff told the House that he had proposed to the government that a Commission be issued to carry out a full enquiry into Scotland's schools, under the chairmanship of the Duke of Argyll, and the Argyll Commission duly pursued this task over the next three years. The Commission appointed a number of assistant commissioners to examine and report on the provision of education in a variety of areas, both geographical and educational, with their main Report being published in 1867 covering primary education alone. Its authors endorsed complaints against the Revised Code's support only of education for the labouring classes, but in other respects declared the Code to be sound, and recommended that it be put into effect.

That said, as R.D. Anderson has pointed out, the Commission's approach to proposals for educational reform was cautious, and while their recommendations largely followed Moncreiff's plans for a Board of Education with representatives from the universities, they left the existing parish school system essentially untouched. While the Commission did indeed look forward to the development of a national system of education, it should come about gradually, with local school committees initially supervising only new schools.[51]

The great achievement of the Commission, according to Moncreiff himself, was that it presented 'a statistical picture of education in Scotland as complete as ever was presented in any country'.[52] Armed with this wealth of evidence, and hoping to capitalise on the strength of feeling generated in Scotland by the Revised Code, Moncreiff and Argyll now moved a new Bill in 1867. Under its terms, a new national Board of Education sitting in Edinburgh would be created, representing the universities, burghs, and shires, with a few crown nominees. This body, whose relationship with the Privy Council Education Committee was left perhaps deliberately vague, was to be responsible for nearly all aspects of national organisation, and with direct oversight of the schools committees, set up to manage the new national schools. But the term 'new national schools' referred literally only to schools newly set up by the Board of Education where it was deemed necessary, leaving existing parochial, or 'old national schools', much as before, under the control of the Established Church.

Once again, the draft Bill attracted criticism from many different quarters. Some objected to the proposed creation of elected schools committees, which would leave control over rural schools in the hands of the 'lowest class of ratepayers, heads of families, and labouring men'. Others, like Free Churchman James Begg, complained that the Bill gave no assurance that religious education would be taught, while Begg and Duncan McLaren took issue with the proposed Board of Education, denouncing it as a Board 'of the closest and worst kind, and with powers more despotic than, we believe, it was ever proposed to give to any such tribunal in a free country'.[53] Then there was the inevitable objection from Voluntarists and secularists to the admission of denominational schools into a system of treasury grants – in their view the state should have no part in the support of religious teaching.[54]

.Mindful of the fate of earlier attempts, Moncreiff emphasised the element of continuity in the draft devised by the Commissioners. 'They intended,' he insisted, 'to keep things as they are [in] existing schools, because ….they are all wanted. All that is proposed in the first instance is that the superintending body shall see the schools efficiently conducted, and open to inspection.'[55]

In the event, however, as so often had been the case in the past, the Bill ran out of Parliamentary time, and it was not until 1869, after the election of the previous year had returned a large Liberal majority in Scotland, that a new Bill was prepared. In February Argyll introduced the Parochial Schools Bill in the Lords. While he claimed that the Bill was substantially the same as the 1867 Bill, there were some not insignificant changes, in response to the critics. The number of members on the Board in Edinburgh was cut from 14 to 10, with the university representatives down from 4 to 2, and the shire members from 3 to 2, with the 3 Crown members unchanged. The right to dismiss a teacher was removed from the local committees and reserved for the central Board, while the school committees were now to be elected on a broad ratepayer franchise, two thirds of the committee to be drawn from ratepayer occupiers, and one third from ratepayer landowners.

Even now, though, a combination of information, moderation, and conciliation was not enough. The debates on the Bill in the Lords and then in the Commons dragged on and on. Moncreiff offered concession after concession – on the central authority, on the local authority and on denominational grants. All in vain. Defeat finally came in the Lords, while Moncreiff himself quit politics to accept elevation to the Scottish bench as Lord Justice Clerk. From now on, others would have to carry the baton of reform of Scottish education.

Yet it remains a question: to what extent were the legislative achievements of Moncreiff's successors in this field of reform, merely building on foundations he had laid. After an initial defeat in 1871, the 1872 Education Act[56] was the work of Moncreiff's successor as Lord Advocate, George Young, and there is some evidence to suggest that in terms of basic objectives, as well as in some of the details, Young's Act owed a debt to the pioneering work of Moncreiff and his associates. For one thing, the 1861 Parochial and Burgh Schools Act, with its abolition of the religious test, had removed a major obstacle to the creation of a national education scheme. Schools in Scotland were now open to all Presbyterian teachers, and parish schools were left with only a few tattered remnants of the previously all-pervasive church supervision. Some specific clauses in the 1872 Act borrowed more or less directly from earlier Moncreiff proposals − clause 17 of the later Act divided Scotland into school districts, as had clause 8 of the 1854 bill. The so-called 'conscience clause', which permitted religious instruction only at set times, echoed and extended clause 27 of the 1855 Bill. As Wilson Bain points out, however, in one important respect Young's Act was less thorough going than Moncreiff's proposals in that it set up only a temporary Board in Edinburgh which would advise the Scotch Education Department in London, rather than the permanent Board located in Edinburgh specified in clauses 1-8 of the 1854 Bill.

Yet as Donald Withrington emphasised more than forty years ago, the 1872 Act, and the unsuccessful 1871 Bill which preceded it, were not a mere revision of the Bills of 1867 and 1869, and differed from them in certain fundamental respects. For example, neither of the Young Bills exempted parochial schools from the national system, rather they were intent upon 'procuring an efficient education for their children' for 'the whole people of Scotland'. No provision was made for a Board of Education sited in Edinburgh, where the landed interest and the Established Church would have exerted considerable influence. The heritors were no longer to have reserved places on the local school committees (now school boards), elections to which were based on a £4 franchise and open to men and women alike. Schooling was to be compulsory. Before the 1871 Bill was eventually withdrawn for lack of time (again), it had attracted some two hundred amendments.

Yet when Young returned to the Commons with a new Bill in February 1872, he had made almost no significant changes. The Privy Council sub-committee − the Scotch Education Department − was still to control the system in Scotland without an intermediate Edinburgh based General Board. The curriculum contained no formal provision for religious education. All parochial schools were to be transferred to the national system immediately. Although national schools were not to be confined to teaching elementary subjects, no money was to be made available for the higher class of education. Some concessions were made before the Bill passed in August – provision was made for a temporary Board in Edinburgh, and national schools were allowed to continue religious instruction according to use and wont, but only at the beginning or end of the working day. But at long last the objective of creating a truly national system of education for Scotland which Moncreiff had pursued assiduously for so long was finally achieved.

In fairness to Moncreiff, most commentators would concede that the political climate in 1872 was markedly different from the 1850s and 60s. Withrington points to the greater readiness of the Established Church and the Free Church to accept what was now being offered, while the secularists and Voluntarists were even more determined on disengagement of religious teaching from the schools.[57] The fact that the Education Act for England and Wales had been passed two years earlier blunted opposition in Parliament to the Scottish Bill, which no longer needed be seen south of the border as a dangerous precedent.

At the end of the day, the 1872 Act was a great achievement. It decreed compulsory education for all children to the age of thirteen, it set up School Boards throughout Scotland, and it established Moncreiff's long held dream of a national education system for his country. If Gladstone regretted the fact that Moncreiff had not been permitted 'to give the last hand to that legislative settlement of the question of Scotch Education which you have so energetically striven to achieve'[58], Moncreiff himself was generous in his praise for Young's success in bringing about 'the realisation of our most sanguine aspirations'.[59]

Yet the 1872 Act was not the end of the story of Moncreiff's contribution to educational reform. Shortly before his retirement from the House of Commons in 1869, he had succeeded in piloting through the House the Endowed Schools Act which became law in July – legislation which he believed, if it was a small matter compared with the issue of providing elementary education for all children in Scotland, nevertheless would be 'a magnificent foundation for...a full system of education, supported by public property, beginning with the lowest step and ascending up to the Universities'.

Given the limited scope of the Act in Scotland, this was probably too much to hope for, but the issue of endowed schools now began to command some attention from government, resulting in the appointment of three Royal Commissions, the second of which was chaired in 1878 by Moncreiff himself. What sparked this interest was the fact that the 1872 Act had not dealt with secondary education, apart from creating a special category of 'higher class' schools, which received no government grants and had to depend on income from fees. In 1872, then, a Commission under Sir Edward Colebrooke came out strongly in favour of the development of 'thoroughly equipped Secondary Schools...giving a really high class of Secondary education at reasonable fees, organised on the best principle, and managed and taught by an efficient staff of well-paid teachers'.[60] The Commission Report injected new life into the campaign for secondary education, and led to the creation of the Association for Promoting Secondary Education in Scotland, of which Moncreiff was a member. Then in 1878 he himself was appointed to chair a new Commission to advise on the implementation of the Endowed Institutions (Scotland) Act, and in particular how the Parliamentary grant for public education in Scotland might best be allocated to promote education in the higher branches of knowledge. The Commission produced three reports published in 1880-1, and while even Bain had to concede that these reports did not command wide acceptance, they do throw significant light on Moncreiff's own approach to education. He had always been critical of too rigid a separation between elementary and more advanced education. As the 1881 Report commented, while it endorsed the parish schools tradition, 'it is not only possible to combine thorough elementary teaching with instruction in the higher branches...but any separation of these subjects is detrimental to the tone of the school, and dispiriting to the master'. At the same time, Moncreiff appeared to be moving away from the Colebrooke emphasis on creating a strong secondary division. While new secondary schools might be needed in more populous areas, the Report concluded, this would not help the majority of rural children, and the aim should be as in the past to have a graduate in every parish, and provide financial support for the higher subjects.[61]

Like many politicians, perhaps most, Moncreiff's achievements in terms of legislation fell short of his personal ambitions – in his case for a national scheme of education for Scotland. But if his plans for such a scheme had to wait for his successors to be completed, he should nevertheless be credited with some notable advances – the abolition of the religious test, the resolution of the stalemate on teachers' salaries, the support of endowed schools.

II - Reform of the Universities

Moncreiff's approach to reform of Scotland's universities was closely connected to his ideas for educational reform at the schools level in two particular ways. The first, as we have already seen, had to do with his commitment to the abolition of the religious tests, and for reasons to be considered shortly, he found it much easier to achieve abolition in the case of the universities than he did for the schools. The second connection between the two in Moncreiff's mind was the need to develop the school curriculum so as to ensure that pupils were able to progress from school to university without the need for further elementary education, for example in Latin, before they were fit to embark on university level training proper.

There was in any case a widespread and growing understanding in the country that the case for university reform was becoming urgent. In Edinburgh University, for example, Moncreiff's alma mater, student numbers had been falling away dramatically since 1820. One reason for this was the abolition of religious tests for entrance to English universities, thus diminishing the attraction of Scottish universities from the point of view of English Nonconformists. Another key factor was the introduction of competitive entry to the civil service on the recommendation of the Northcote-Trevelyan report of 1853. Competitive entry examinations were not adopted for the home civil service until 1870, but they were introduced in the East India Company – the goal of many Scottish graduates – in 1855.[62] According to the *Edinburgh Review*, 'Of the many benefits which the Union had conferred on Scotsmen, the connection with the East India Company had been the most unquestionable.'[63] Experience showed that Scots tended not to do well in these examinations, due, it came to be understood, to the particular character and subject coverage of the Universities' curricula. The marking scheme for the EIC exams had apparently been devised by Macaulay, with an emphasis on English literature and history – subjects generally not studied in Scottish universities.[64]

The application of the test to university appointments went back to the late seventeenth century. Under the 1690 Act of Visitation of Churches, Colleges, and Schools, professors had to sign a declaration that they accepted the Westminster Confession of Faith and the Presbyterian system of church government. In practice, the operation of the rule had become limited to appointments to Divinity chairs, but after the Disruption of 1843 there was an attempt to revive the rule for all chairs, as a rather unsubtle means of ridding the universities of Free Churchmen. As a test case, an attempt was made, unwise as it turned out, to oust Sir David Brewster, a distinguished scientist and at the time the Principal of the United Colleges of St Andrews, though on that occasion the attempt failed.

Yet even within the Free Church itself, there were conflicting views about abolition of the test. In 1845 a group of MPs put forward a proposal to abolish the test for university professors in non-theological subjects.[65] As might have been expected, the move was opposed by Moderates in the Established Church, who were determined to reject any change in the law which gave the Church of Scotland its privileged position in national education, and which maintained the traditional link between the national church and the national universities. Dr James

Bryce warned his colleagues in the General Assembly in that year of the dire consequences of abolition, claiming that 'infidel professors will shut your classrooms against the pious youth of the country'.[66] Yet the bill was also attacked by leading Free Churchmen, including Robert Candlish, because they feared that it would weaken the connection between education and religion. What these men wanted was not abolition of the test, but its substitution of a test acceptable to themselves.[67]

In 1852, the year after Moncreiff entered the House of Commons, the whole question of the religious test for university professors raised its head again – when a vacancy arose at Edinburgh University on the death of one of his old professors, Professor John Wilson. The issue was further complicated by a bitter rivalry between Edinburgh Town Council, jealous of their rights of patronage over university chairs, and the University Senate. In the words of Inglis' biographer, J.C. Watt, 'It was unavoidable that the prevailing rancour of politics should embitter these disputes. The Town council was a nest of blind Radicalism and Dissent. The Senatus was unreasoning, Church and Tory.'[68] This time the issue involved a group of Free Church men, backed by the Town Council, who wanted to install one of their number, P.C. MacDougall, in the chair of Moral Philosophy at Edinburgh. Their opponents in the Established Church tried to use the test to keep out MacDougall, in favour of their own (arguably stronger) candidate, J.F. Ferrier.[69] Accordingly, the University Senate applied for an interdict against the Council presentee, although the test had been constantly evaded from Robertson's Principalship downwards.[70] Moncreiff supported the Free Church cause, primarily because he was opposed to the test on pragmatic grounds – that it kept out men of talent, was inappropriate for non-theological chairs, did not achieve its objectives, and was generally unpopular. As he pointed out to the House, the universities of Scotland were not ecclesiastical institutions, and they admitted students of all denominations. Opposition to the Bill, he claimed, came only from the Presbyteries and the Church Courts – those in favour included the cities of Edinburgh, Aberdeen, and Dundee, the convention of Royal Burghs, and the church judicatories of the Free Church and the United Presbyteries. 'The people,' he concluded, 'had no desire to maintain these tests.'[71] If they were to be retained at all, it should be only for theological posts.

Moncreiff moved the first reading of a Bill to remove the tests in February, 1852, and although the second reading was delayed until the June of 1853, its third reading was passed by a large majority – 196 to 17 – and the Bill became law in August. The speed with which Moncreiff succeeded in getting the test abolished in the universities contrasted sharply with the eight years it took to achieve the same result in the schools. This was due in part, according to Wilson Bain, to the fact that in 1852-3 Moncreiff had the support of the well respected Lord Aberdeen, rather than, as was the case in the proposed reform of the schools, the young and relatively untried Duke of Argyll. But another reason was that to get the Universities Bill through he had to make some significant concessions – most notably the substitution for the test of a declaration that the appointee would not use his position to subvert the Church of Scotland. Anyone accused of violating this declaration would be subject to disciplinary procedures which could result in dismissal. Professors of Divinity, and appointees to the Principalship, would still have to take the original test.[72]

Nevertheless, not everyone was happy with the proposal or its outcome. In the debate on the first reading, one Mr Scott, member for Berwickshire, had denounced the Bill as 'subversive of the character of the Scotch Universities', and prophesised that 'the scoffer, the atheist, the blasphemer...would be as free to occupy the chair of learning as the orthodox believer of a Christian creed. Was this the time when we should open the floodgates of infidelity and let loose a stream of pollution on the rising young?'[73] Even after the Bill passed the Commons, the Commission of the Church of Scotland denounced it as 'an unmerited and unwarrantable aggression on the rights and privileges guaranteed to the Church' by the Treaty of Union.[74] The Presbytery of Edinburgh went so far as to suggest that, if the Act were not to be repealed, then the Church should set up its own colleges, independent of the universities.[75] In 1869, looking back on these events from his position as the newly installed Rector of Edinburgh University, Moncreiff told his audience that 'it has been the most gratifying event to me in my public career that I was partly instrumental in placing the cope-stone on this fabric of national toleration...If any act in my public life has entitled me to this honour...it is the part I have borne in removing these pernicious encumbrances.'[76]

Nor was Moncreiff alone in pursuing university reform at this time. In Scotland there was a growing desire amongst graduates to have an effective voice in the governance of their own universities. In Aberdeen, reformers succeeded in persuading the professors in King's College to open up the election of the rector to graduates, and in Glasgow alumni created the Glasgow Association of Scottish Graduates. Prompted by the Association, Moncreiff drew up a Bill in 1857 which, if enacted, would have allowed for a government endowment of £20,000 a year, set up a national board of examiners, instituted a compulsory entrance examination for those wishing to graduate, and devised a graduation scheme incorporating BA and MA degrees in line with the recommendation of a report of 1830.[77] As it turned out, 1857 was also an election year, in which the Liberal government of Lord Palmerston was replaced by Derby and the Conservatives. Moncreiff likewise found himself replaced – by his old school friend John Inglis, whose ideas on university reform were very different from his own. Inglis' Bill of 1858 dealt primarily with matters of government, and was the origin of the now universal Court system in Scottish universities. Town councils, accustomed to the rights of patronage over professorial appointments, now had to share that right with university Courts in a seven man committee called the 'Curators of Patronage'. The real power over such matters as the creation of new chairs, changes to the curriculum, and provision of assistantships, lay in the hands of a temporary executive commission under the chairmanship of Inglis himself. Inglis was very much a hands-on chairman, or, as one commentator put it, Inglis 'was in fact the soul of the Commission, and [its] ordinances may be regarded as especially the product of his judgement and of his untiring attention to a mass of details'.[78] Moncreiff, by contrast, attended only about a quarter of the meetings, and most of those while out of office in 1858-9.

Indeed, although Moncreiff continued to have a close interest in university reform, and was a member of the next Commission in 1876, his actual influence in this area gradually diminished as the years wore on. Not that he was inactive. J.C. Watt tells us that although Inglis was nominally the chairman of the Commission, it was Moncreiff who actually did the work. But at the same time, Watt acknowledges that the Commission produced very little in the way of results. Moncreiff's main interest now lay in the relationship between educational standards in the schools and the universities, and he continued to oppose the establishment of university entrance examinations on the ground that what was really needed was an improvement in the standard and curricula at the school level. In 1869, in his address on being installed as Lord Rector of Edinburgh, Moncreiff made his position very clear. Noting that 'some have proposed a strict entrance examination', he objected that 'I look on that as tending simply to impoverish and depopulate the university without even touching the real evil. The remedy is to be found in raising the standards of our schools.'[79] Entrance examinations alone would merely give an unfair advantage to the better off.

Throughout his life Moncreiff had had a close association with the universities of Scotland. Himself a graduate of Edinburgh, he was president of the Association of Societies at the University in 1863, took part, as we have seen, in the Commissions of 1858 and 1876, was elected Member of Parliament for the Universities of Aberdeen and Glasgow in 1868,[80] and was elected Rector of Edinburgh University in 1869. For him, the university was very far from being an ivory tower, or a playground for a social elite. As a young man he had welcomed the fact that at the High School he had shared his education with boys from all social classes, and it was clear that he wanted the universities of Scotland likewise to be open to all. In his speech on installation as Lord Rector of Edinburgh he explained his vision of the university as 'the training school for the professional life in all its branches. Its object is not so much to send out accomplished scholars as to educate men for the practical business of life.'[81] Men very much like himself, in fact.

If one had to single out one area of policy as the closest to Moncreiff's heart, it would undoubtedly be that of education. Again and again he returned to the subject of creating a national scheme of school education. His vision was for an educational experience which would bring the social classes together and avoid the dangers of social dissension, to provide an effective education for all Scottish children, make the best use of available schoolmasterly talent, and smooth the path from school to university – the 'training school for the professional life'.

It cannot be denied that his success in achieving this vision was no more than partial, but it was certainly not negligible. The abolition of the religious tests in schools and universities was an essential step towards making the best use in future of able and qualified professors and schoolmasters. The latter were provided with adequate salaries, pensions, and accommodation. Endowed schools were put on a sounder footing by the Act of 1869. And if Moncreiff's primary object of creating a national system of school education had to wait for its realisation by his successor as Lord Advocate, then he for one was generous in his appreciation of that achievement.

Chapter 11
Madeleine Smith

The trial of Madeleine Smith in 1857 on a charge of murdering her lover, and her subsequent acquittal by a verdict of 'not proven', was certainly the most notorious and controversial of all the cases in which Moncreiff was ever involved as a prosecutor.[82] At the time it attracted huge public interest, reported on as it was by a wide range of newspapers on both sides of the border, from *The Aberdeen Journal* to *Trewman's Exeter Flying Post or Plymouth and Cornish Advertiser*, over the nine days of the proceedings.[83] Even today the case continues to excite interest, and over the years countless articles, books, novels, plays, television programmes, and at least one film have been written and produced to tell Madeleine's story anew for a contemporary audience.

This is hardly surprising, since it is a story which combines all the elements likely to intrigue the public. There was sex – the letters Madeleine wrote to her beloved, Emile L'Angelier, make it clear that sexual intercourse took place.[84] There were drugs – L'Angelier regularly took laudanum, munched poppy seeds, and allegedly took arsenic as well. There was the conflict of classes and nationalities – Madeleine was the daughter of a successful Glasgow architect of archetypal Victorian values, while L'Angelier was of French extraction from the Channel Islands, and a seedsman's packer earning £50 a year. There were clandestine meetings, and a great outpouring, especially on Madeleine's part, of passionate letters, most of which still survive today. Then there was the overriding fact of a charge of murder being levelled, not against a member of the criminal class, but the daughter of a prominent member of the professional elite in Scotland's second city. Finally there was the verdict – 'not proven' – leaving the whole matter open forever to the speculation that the verdict should in fact have been 'guilty'.

For the last century and a half, the truth of the matter has been no more than speculation, since until recently no new evidence had been produced to settle the matter one way or the other. In 2007 a new book was produced, claiming at last to have produced such evidence, though it would be more accurate to say that it examines old evidence in the light of modern psychiatry. This interpretation relies to a large extent on the characterisation of L'Angelier's personality as close to psychopathic, and the suggestion is that, driven close to the edge by Madeleine's rejection, he committed suicide, having first manipulated the evidence to point the finger at his former lover. For this author, the real mystery is – 'how could it happen that, for 150 years, the most obvious villain has been believed to be the victim, and the most obvious victim, the villain?'[85] To be sure, even at the time, there were those who believed that L'Angelier had committed suicide. In June 1857 the Procurator Fiscal of Dundee wrote to an official in the Lord Advocate's office in Parliament House, explaining that he had taken evidence from a number of witnesses who had spoken of L'Angelier's very changeable disposition,[86] which was clearly manic depressive, and his tendency to threaten suicide when disappointed in love. For her part, Madeleine maintained her innocence to the end of her life. From the point of view of the biography of James Moncreiff, however, whether Madeleine was actually guilty or innocent is not the real question. Of more direct interest are the issues of Moncreiff's handling of the case as Lord Advocate and prosecutor. Why, in the end, did he fail to secure a conviction?

The bare bones of the story are familiar enough. Madeleine lived with her parents, a sister and two brothers, in a fine stone built house in Blythswood Square in Glasgow. The Smiths also owned a large property at Row, called Rowelyn, which Mr Smith had personally designed, and to which the family repaired each summer. The Smiths were eminently respectable and of regular habits. During the week they were accustomed to hold dinner parties for friends and business associates; on Sundays they attended the United Presbyterian Church without fail, followed by family prayers at nine o'clock. Their eldest daughter Madeleine, described as 'a dark-eyed, handsome girl of twenty-one, with black hair and a fine complexion',[87] was being courted by a neighbour, William Minnoch, himself a prosperous businessman, and a partner in the firm of John Houldsworth and Company. On the 28th January, 1857, Minnoch asked her to marry him and she agreed, though no date for the wedding was set at that time. But early in March of the same year the Smiths travelled to Bridge of Allan, and stayed there until the 17th. Minnoch visited them there, and it was arranged that the wedding would be held in June. Altogether an unremarkable situation.[88]

That the situation was very far from being unremarkable soon became apparent. Returning to Glasgow, the Smiths were entertained to dinner at Minnoch's house on the 19th, and Madeleine and Minnoch met again at another dinner party on the 25th. The next day she disappeared, and after a search by Minnoch and one of Madeleine's brothers, she was discovered on a steamer at Greenock. She refused to explain her conduct, but promised that she would do so in due course if not pressed at the time. A few days later she told her fiancé that she had written to a Frenchman, asking for the return of some letters, and a few days after that she named him as Emile L'Angelier, who had been dead for a week, with rumours circulating about arsenic poisoning.[89]

The death of L'Angelier, it soon emerged, marked the end of what had been a passionate relationship between the two, during which they had pledged themselves to each other as man and wife. What had begun, as most relationships do, as a casual meeting between strangers, burgeoned into a serious love affair doomed, not surprisingly, by the refusal of Madeleine's father to countenance the match, but also by Madeleine's own gradual realisation that, after the kind of lifestyle she was used to, marriage on fifty pounds a year was hardly a practical proposition. Then there was another suitor, not just in the offing, but actually living in another part of the Blythswood Square house – William Minnoch, approved of by Mr Smith as a suitable husband for his daughter, and possessed of an annual income of some £4000. The outcome was a tragedy – the death of L'Angelier, the discovery of substantial levels of arsenic in his body, and the arrest of Madeleine, charged with his murder.

In the trial itself, held in Edinburgh in July 1857, James Moncreiff, now Lord Advocate, played a crucial role as counsel for the Crown, with his long term friend and contemporary, John Inglis, Dean of the Faculty, appearing for the defendant. And while speculation may continue to the end of time as to the soundness of the ultimate verdict, it is perhaps more interesting and fruitful to consider how these two leaders of their profession approached the business of the trial, and how their efforts led to that particular outcome.

It is fair to say that in mounting the prosecution, Moncreiff laboured under a number of disadvantages. The first was a general disinclination, which he may have shared, to hang an attractive and well bred young woman for the murder of a worthless foreigner. In the words of John Inglis' biographer:

> The pale but fresh firm face, set in the curtained bonnet of the day, the graceful figure, its lines traceable through the lace of a black mantilla, the lustrous eyes and the full quivering lips as she sat in the seat whence so many have gone to the scaffold, caused even strong men to quail at the mere apprehension of her doom. Guilty or innocent, she made them think, not of the crime or of the possibility that her hand poisoned the fatal cup, but of their own sisters and daughters. To hang her was impossible!'[90]

And as the *Glasgow Herald* of the day commented: '…we fervently trust that the cloud which at present obscures a most respectable and estimable household may be speedily and most effectually removed…The thought that a highly and virtuously bred young lady could destroy her sweetheart is almost too appalling for belief.'[91]

This was a sentiment which Inglis was to exploit to the full. But Inglis and Moncreiff shared a common problem when it came to explaining to their audience Madeleine's highly unladylike behaviour. Referring to the language of the letters she wrote to L'Angelier, Moncreiff declared that 'the language in which they are couched – the matters to which they refer – show so entire an overthrow of the moral sense – the sense of moral delicacy and decency – as to create a picture which I do not know ever had its parallel in a case of this sort.'[92] But Moncreiff was quite unable to disguise a degree of sympathy for the woman in the dock. 'Gentlemen, I never in my life had so harrowing a task as raking up and bringing before such a tribunal and audience as this the outpourings of such a despairing spirit, in such a position as this miserable woman was.'[93] As one recent commentator has observed, 'there was a certain ambiguity in Moncreiff's presentation of Madeleine's sexuality. He could not understand "where she had learned this depraved state of thought and feeling", but was more comfortable with the idea that Emile was responsible for her corruption.'[94] Both prosecutor and defence counsel found themselves putting much of the blame for Madeleine's plight on the unfortunate victim.

Moncreiff's own manner in presenting the case for the prosecution has been widely commented on for its moderation, restraint, and objectivity, though as Wilson Bain has pointed out, that low key approach could have been interpreted in different ways.[95] He quotes Henry Blyth as stating that 'it seemed to some that he had no real stomach for the task…and would not resort to rhetoric. Not for him the thundering denunciation of what he believed to be a falsehood, nor the pointed finger of accusation. He spoke quietly, expressed himself with moderation, …but when he had a point to make he made it loudly and with force.'[96] Some colour to the view that Moncreiff was reluctant to see Madeleine condemned is given by that part of his final address to the jury on the seventh day of the trial, when he declared:

> Gentlemen, I could have rejoiced if the result of the enquiry which it is our duty to make, and of the laborious collection of every element of proof which we could find, would have justified us on behalf of the Crown in resting content with the investigation of the facts, and withdrawing our charge against the prisoner.[97]

G.W.T. Omond, on the other hand, while offering a very similar description of Moncreiff's behaviour in court to that of Blyth, interpreted it as being 'in accordance with the traditions of the office [i.e. of Lord Advocate], seldom broken since the close of the seventeenth century. This tradition – the prosecutor must throw into the performance of his duties the ardour of an advocate but must exhibit the calm impartiality of the Crown, of which he is the representative – is so well understood in Scotland that if a Lord Advocate, or any of his deputies betrayed eagerness...they would have been thought guilty of a breach of professional decorum.'[98] J.C. Watt, writing in the early 1890s, makes a similar point. 'As prosecutor, he had to recognise the traditions of the Scottish school. For so humane is our jurisprudence that a prosecutor here is not allowed to adopt the persecuting methods which are followed elsewhere – in France for instance.'[99]

Bain makes the additional and perceptive point that very probably 'the custom of the office fitted the manner he personally favoured', and goes on to cite Moncreiff's own advice to his fellow legal practitioners that a speech should be 'clear, well reasoned, elegant and persuasive'.[100] It was advice he had himself followed in the prosecution earlier that same year of the Polish doctor, Dr Wielobycki, accused and then convicted of forgery. It was 'the testimony of all observers', remarked Moncreiff's obituarist in 1895. 'that as prosecutor Moncreiff sustained the best traditions of the Scotch system, in his judicial, restrained and eloquent performance in this capacity.'[101] (Though to quote J.C. Watt again, 'when occasion demanded, as it frequently did, on the platform and the hustings, 'Moncreiff was capable] of impassioned appeal and fiery declamation.'[102]) Finally, there was further contemporary comment from the *Journal of Jurisprudence*, reprinted in the *Glasgow Herald* on the 20th July, 1857. The Lord Advocate, the *Journal* commented, 'laboured under the disadvantage of being placed in an ungracious position, in directing all the crushing weight of the powerful machinery of the Crown against an unhappy girl, whose age, sex, and station – nay, whose passionate outpourings in the very letters which were the strongest testimony against her – secured for her everywhere a vivid sympathy.' It was acknowledged that to call for 'the doom of such a creature, guilty or innocent, was one of those painful tasks which those in an official position frequently must have the nerve to face.' In his discharge of that duty, Moncreiff was warmly commended. 'The whole conduct of the case for the Crown was a fine illustration of the humane manner in which the law of this country vindicates itself against those by whom it has been wronged. In the Lord Advocate's speech, this was especially observable. It was not that of an advocate representing only one side and one interest in the dread question which was placed in issue. On the contrary, it was pervaded throughout by a calmness and moderation, which, with its other qualities, gave it the character of an eloquence altogether judicial.'[103]

In the eyes, then, of all these commentators, Moncreiff's moderation in manner and address were wholly commendable, as being consistent with the traditions of the office and long standing professional practice. It does not seem to have occurred to any of them, however, to question whether it was the best way to win his case. As we shall see, no such scruples blunted the attack of defence counsel Inglis, as Dean of the Faculty the holder of another historic and highly respected office. As Peter Hunt commented in the nineteen-fifties, 'Moncreiff appealed to the head, Inglis appealed, and rightly so, to the heart as well as the head.'[104]

In appealing to the head, the Lord Advocate had planned his case with great precision. In order to win, he had to persuade the jury to accept, beyond reasonable doubt, the propositions contained in the original indictment, a lengthy document which may be summarised as amounting to three specific charges:

1) That on or about the 19th or 20th February 1857 the accused administered arsenic to Emile L'Angelier in a cup of coffee or cocoa, with intent to murder
2) That on or about the 22nd or 23rd February in the same year she likewise administered arsenic to L'Angelier with intent to murder, and
3) That on the 22nd or 23rd of March 1857 she murdered L'Angelier, again through the administration of arsenic.[105]

There was of course no question that the unfortunate L'Angelier had in fact died of arsenical poisoning. The post mortem had established that his body contained a large quantity – easily enough to cause death. Nor was there ever any serious suggestion that someone other than Madeleine, or L'Angelier himself in a bid to commit suicide, had administered it. In order to prove the Crown's case against Madeleine, Moncreiff proceeded steadily and painstakingly to establish, or try to establish, that she had had a compelling motive to kill her former lover, that she had possessed the means in the form of quantities of arsenic, and that she had had the opportunity to administer it to him.

Madeleine's motive for the alleged murder of Emile L'Angelier should now be clear, and it was set out in detail in Moncreiff's five hour long address to the jury on the seventh day of the trial, Tuesday the 7th July, 1857.

> 'These two persons met,' Moncreiff explained, 'they were introduced, I assume, clandestinely. After a time, it seems, an attachment commenced, which was forbidden by her parents. It is only right to say that the earlier letters of the prisoner at that time show good feeling, proper affection, and a proper sense of duty. Time went on; the intercourse was again renewed, and in the course of 1856, as you must have found, it assumed a criminal aspect. From that time down to the end of the year, not once or twice, but I have evidence to show, repeatedly, acts of improper connection took place. It will be necessary for you to take into your consideration that she had so completely committed herself by the end of

1856, that she was, I will not say in L'Angelier's power (he was in her power) but she belonged to him, and could with honour belong to no one else. But her affection began to cool, another suitor appeared; she endeavoured to break off her connection with L'Angelier by coldness, and asked him to return her letters. He refused, and threatened to put them in the hands of her father; ......It was then she saw the position she was in – she knew what letters she had written to L'Angelier – she knew what he could reveal – she knew that, if those letters were sent to her father, not only would her marriage with Mr. Minnoch be broken off, but that she could not hold up her head again. She writes in despair to him to give back her letters; he refuses.'[106]

This was an admirably crisp summary of the position Madeleine found herself in. A Victorian jury would have understood better than a modern audience the full horror of her situation. A young girl who had behaved as she had done would not only lose her current fiancé – but could never expect another man from her own social circle to even consider marrying her. The prospect of a lifetime of disgrace and spinsterhood loomed over her. How could that prospect be erased?

The prosecution's answer to that question was of course the she had, on three separate occasions, tried, and ultimately succeeded, to kill her former lover with arsenic. Arsenical poisoning was undoubtedly the cause of L'Angelier's death, but could it be shown that Madeleine had had arsenic in her possession?

In fact there was no difficulty on this point, since she had willingly testified to the possession of arsenic in her remarkably candid Declaration, made before the Sheriff-Substitute of Lanarkshire, Archibald Smith, immediately after her arrest. She had bought arsenic, she freely admitted, on several occasions. 'The last I bought was a sixpence-worth, which I bought in Currie's the apothecary's in Sauchiehall Street, and prior to that I bought other two quantities of arsenic, for which I paid sixpence each – one of these in Currie's, and the other in Murdoch the apothecary's shop, in Sauchiehall Street.' The arsenic had been used, so she claimed, as a cosmetic, recommended to her by a school friend, a Miss Guibilei, and the supply she had bought at Currie's on Wednesday 18th March had all been used up in a single application. Not very surprisingly she had kept her use of arsenic a secret from the rest of the family and when she purchased a supply from Murdoch's, she was not quite sure 'whether I was asked or not what it was for, but I think I said it was for a gardener to kill rats or destroy vermin among the flowers, and I only said this because I did not want them to know that I was going to use it as a cosmetic.'[107] Yet earlier in the proceedings, the prosecution had produced evidence, both from Miss

Guibilei (now Mrs Walcot), and from the Smith's own gardener, which flatly contradicted Madeleine's claims as to the use of the poison.[108]

By this stage, Moncreiff had successfully answered the first two questions as to motive and means. To establish opportunity was to prove much more difficult. Not surprisingly there had been no witnesses to the administration of the poison, and Moncreiff had to fall back on other forms of evidence to link together meetings between the two principals, and the ingestion of arsenic by the victim. One such piece of evidence was provided by a memorandum book, or diary, kept by L'Angelier, in which he recorded meetings with Madeleine in February 1857, and also noted occasions when he had been taken ill. The entry for Thursday 19th February, for instance reads:

'Saw Mimi (the pet name they both used for Madeleine)
a few moments.
was very ill during the night.'[109]

But when it came to the trial, the judges by a majority of two to one ruled the memorandum book inadmissible as evidence. According to one account written a century later, 'the ruling from the judges cut the ground from under the Lord Advocate's feet.' And again '...if (the entries) had been allowed in evidence, Madeleine must surely have hanged'.[110] Failure by the Crown to prove that the meeting on the 19th February had taken place, as well as its failure to prove that Madeleine was in possession of arsenic by that date, fatally weakened the first charge in the indictment of intent to murder on or about the 19th and 20th February, and later the Lord Justice Clerk was to advise the jury to return a verdict of Not Guilty on that charge. Even worse, from the prosecution's point of view, was its failure likewise to prove that Madeleine and L'Angelier had met before the latter's third and fatal ingestion of poison.

Moncreiff had succeeded admirably in demonstrating that Madeleine had had both the motive and the means to commit murder. The failure to complete the triangle, and demonstrate beyond reasonable doubt that she also had the opportunity, left the case of the Crown vulnerable from just the kind of attack defence counsel, John Inglis, was supremely qualified to mount. In a speech which has been described as 'the greatest ever heard in the High Court of Justiciary',[111] Inglis used a combination of meticulous argument and an appeal to the emotions to unpick the Lord Advocate's case, and ultimately save Madeleine from execution.

There were broadly three prongs to Inglis' attack. The first was to denigrate the character of L'Angelier, and portray him as a degenerate fortune hunter who had seduced an innocent young woman. 'We find him, according to the confession of all those who observed him then most narrowly, vain, conceited, pretentious, with a very great opinion of his own personal attractions, and a very silly expectation of admiration from the other sex...' And later: 'In the spring of 1856 the corrupting influence of the seducer was successful, and his victim fell...And how corrupting that influence must have been! – how vile the arts to which he resorted for accomplishing his nefarious purpose, can never be proved so well as by the altered tone and language of the unhappy prisoner's letters. She had not lost her virtue merely, but as the Lord Advocate said, her sense of decency.' And who was to blame for that? 'Think you that, without temptation, without evil teaching, a poor girl falls into such depths of degradation? No. Influence from without – most corrupting influence – can alone account for such a fall.'[112]

The second line of the Dean's argument was to cast doubts as to whether the arsenic L'Angelier had swallowed was in fact the same arsenic purchased by Madeleine. This was a risky line to take, but in it he was aided by the scientific evidence, or rather the lack of it. The arsenic purchased by Madeleine would, according to law, have been coloured with soot, but no traces of soot were discovered in the victim's body. This was in fact a less compelling argument than it might seem, since the investigating doctors had been given no instructions to look for traces of soot.[113]

Thirdly, and most effectively, Inglis was able to argue with some force that there was no evidence that Madeleine and Emile had met on the fateful day – Sunday 22nd March, when, it was alleged by the Crown, the final dose of arsenic had been passed from one to the other. This was an obvious weak point in Moncreiff's case, and Inglis exploited it to the full.

> Now, gentlemen, from half past nine to half past two o'clock – at least five hours – he [L'Angelier] is absolutely lost sight of; and I was startled at the boldness of the manner in which my learned friend the Lord Advocate met this difficulty. He says it is no doubt a matter of conjecture and inference that in the interval he was in the presence of the prisoner. Good heavens! Inference and conjecture! A matter of inference and conjecture whether, on the night he was poisoned he was in the presence of the person who is charged with his murder! I never heard such an expression from the mouth of a Crown prosecutor before...[114]

Moncreiff may have wondered if he should have taken up the offer extended to him by one Gerald Massey, the husband of a noted Edinburgh clairvoyant, who claimed that his wife had divined, through clairvoyance, that Christine Haggart, the Smith's maid, 'knows that L'Angelier was with Miss Smith on the night in question about 11 o'clock, and that Cocoa was made for him.'[115] Tantalisingly, according to a report in the *Glasgow Herald,* reprinted in the *Aberdeen Journal* on 15th July, on the previous Monday a witness from Glasgow had approached the authorities in Edinburgh, claiming to have important evidence. According to this person's statement, 'on a Sunday night about the time of L'Angelier's death, and between twelve and one o'clock on that night, he saw together two young persons, male and female, in the lane behind Mr. Smith's Blythswood Square house, uttering words of endearment, and that the young man was attired in a dress similar to that which is proved to have been usually worn by L'Angelier.'[116] Clearly, if this evidence had been available to the Court in the course of the trial, the outcome might very well have been different. We will return to this issue later.

That the outcome, despite the eloquence and skill of defence counsel, was no foregone conclusion, is evidenced by the fact that two out of the three verdicts were by majority decision: 'The jury find the panel not guilty of the first charge in the indictment by a majority; of the second charge not proven; and by a majority find the third charge also not proven.'[117]

Were these verdicts mistaken? Was Madeleine Smith in fact guilty? David Walker, in his multi-volume series on the Legal History of Scotland published at the beginning of this century, points out the impossible situation in which Madeleine Smith found herself, once the marriage to Minnoch was planned. If the letters she had written to L'Angelier came to light, as it seemed they must, she would have faced much more than social embarrassment. As we shall see in the next chapter on the Yelverton affair, Madeleine's relationship with L'Angelier exactly satisfied the requirements for an 'irregular marriage' under Scots law prevailing at the time, and for many centuries previously. Under the terms of what was known as a promise *subsequente copula*, where a man and a woman 'had exchanged promises to marry and thereafter had sexual relations on the faith of that promise, they were deemed then and there and thereby married, admittedly irregularly, but legally, validly, and irrevocably.'[118] It was only too clear from the letters which were read out in court that Madeleine had frequently addressed her lover as her husband, and regarded herself as his wife. They also had had sexual intercourse. With L'Angelier still alive, a marriage to Minnoch would have been bigamous, and herself liable to prosecution. 'A motive for killing him,' wrote Walker, 'was there, and she took steps to silence him.' Yet we should not forget the counter argument – that L'Angelier's killer may well have been himself, and all Madeleine's protestations of innocence were perfectly true. Even after the trial was over, Madeleine's lawyers were trying to get hold of the original of a letter referring to L'Angelier's habit of taking powders for various purposes, in an attempt to establish their client's innocence in the face an existing 'contrary impression in the public mind'.[119]

There is a postscript to this account of Moncreiff's role in the Madeleine Smith affair – in fact two postscripts. After the trial was over, Madeleine wrote thank you letters to a few of those who had provided her with support during the trial, including Miss Aitken, the Matron of Edinburgh Prison, and to Mr. Rose, the prison chaplain. The tone of the letters is remarkably unemotional – or would be remarkable if it had not become evident during the proceedings that Madeleine Smith was amazingly untouched by the whole affair, and her icy self-possession was remarked on by many. In her letter to Miss Aitken, Madeleine acknowledged that 'the feeling in the west is not so good towards me as you kind Edinburgh people showed me. I rather think it will be necessary for me to leave Scotland for a few months, but Mama is so unwell that we do not like to fix anything at present.' The letter continued: 'If you ever see Mr. Combe [the foreman of the jury] tell him that the pannel [sic] was not at all pleased with the verdict. I was delighted with the loud cheer the Court gave. I did not feel in the least put about when the jury were out considering whether they should send me home or keep me.'[120]

Madeleine's capacity for understatement is breathtaking.

It is known in the Moncreiff family that James Moncreiff himself was also the recipient of a letter of thanks from his erstwhile prisoner, though the actual letter unfortunately has since gone missing. Given what we know about Madeleine Smith, the fact that she wrote a thank you letter to her prosecutor is perhaps less surprising than it might have been.

There is no direct reference in Moncreiff's *Reminiscences* to the trial. There is, however, an interesting passage on the principle of the 'Not Proven' verdict – though in reference to a different case in which he was acting for the defence. Moncreiff approved of the existence of such a verdict, on the ground that what a jury in a criminal trial is being asked to decide is not whether the defendant is guilty or not – but simply whether the case against the defendant has been proved, or not proved.

> And yet you will hear self-satisfied critics other side of the Tweed sneering at what they call the Scotch verdict of 'not proven'. The only other country in the world which has any other form for a verdict of acquittal is England – a custom derided throughout Christendom. To say that a man is presumed innocent unless proved to be guilty, and that therefore the verdict on the failure to prove guilt should be Not Guilty; only proves the thickheaded blundering of the rule. The jury are not asked to decide on legal presumptions, but on a matter of fact: has it been

proved that the accused committed the crime? No other question is asked of a jury; and their proper answer can only be that it has been proved, or that it has not. Such I take it is the universal practice of civilized nations.'[121]

This position is wholly logical, but only when there is no provision also for a verdict of 'not guilty' – a situation which has not existed in Scottish criminal trials since the early eighteenth century at least. Otherwise, as in the sad case of Madeleine Smith, it is likely to be interpreted as meaning that the defendant was in fact guilty, but escaped the gallows for lack of sufficient proof to send her there.

Was that indeed the case here? Or was Moncreiff somehow responsible for the failure to secure a conviction? The answer has to be a combination of circumstances, in which Moncreiff's conduct of the prosecution was only one factor. Yes – his handling of the trial could be criticised for being too tentative – much less willing than his opponent Inglis was to go on the attack. In that he probably shared the feelings of his audience that it would be a terrible outcome if it resulted in the hanging of a personable young woman of the Glasgow elite. But there was also the awkward fact that no hard evidence could be found – at least not at the time – to prove that Smith and L'Angelier had been together on the occasion of his final ingestion of arsenic. The verdict in the trial of Madeleine Smith aroused great public interest at the time, and all the evidence is that it continues to do so in the present day.

And there is one final twist to the story, which may or may not be linked to the report in the Scottish newspapers that a witness had come forward after the trial to claim that Madeleine and Emile had been seen together in Glasgow on the night when it was supposed he had ingested the fatal dose of arsenic. According to members of the Moncreiff family, after the trial had reached its conclusion, James Moncreiff entertained both John Inglis, and the trial judge, Lord Hope, to dinner at Tullibole Castle. After the meal was over, the servants told Moncreiff that there was a man at the door who said that he had just walked from Stirling to Tullibole – a distance of about 20 miles – and that he had important information about the case. He was asked in, and explained that he was a sailor who had just returned from a voyage of several months, and had read in the newspapers about the result of the trial. Before he had sailed, and at a time which must have been that of Madeleine's last and fatal meeting with L'Angelier, he was walking across Blythswood Square very early in the morning to join his ship which was berthed at the Broomielaw. In the Square he came across Madeleine Smith coming up from the basement of one of the houses with a young man whose description matched that of L'Angelier. The sailor had been at primary school with

Madeleine, and stopped to talk with her. She appeared distracted, and the seaman went on his way.

The three lawyers questioned him, and came to the conclusion that he was telling the truth. They also realised that if he had given his evidence at the trial, then it would almost certainly have resulted in a guilty verdict. They sent the man outside while they discussed what should be done. In the end they each emptied their pockets of all their loose change, a sum totaling exactly twenty guineas, and gave this to the sailor, telling him to go away and not say a word to anyone about what he had told them.

Chapter 12
The Yelverton Affair

In December 1862, Moncreiff, still Lord Advocate, took on the case of Maria Theresa Longworth, a thirty year old English Catholic[1], who claimed to be the lawful married wife of an army major, the Hon. William Charles Yelverton, ultimately to become the heir of Lord Avonmore, an Irish peer. In some respects the case shared certain features with the Madeleine Smith affair. In both there had been powerful sexual passion; in both there had been rejection; and in both there had been a perceived discrepancy in social rank. But this was no murder trial, but rather a determined attempt by an intelligent and articulate woman to use the courts in Ireland, Scotland and England to confirm her marital status once and for all. In the end the attempt failed, but not before she had triumphed in both Dublin and Edinburgh. As her leading counsel before the Court of Session, Moncreiff was the architect of her Scottish success, though ultimately, along with the Solicitor-General for England, Sir Roundell Palmer, he faced defeat in the House of Lords.

The couple had first met by accident in 1852 as fellow passengers on the cross channel packet from Boulogne. Theresa Longworth was just twenty-two, the sixth child of a wealthy Manchester silk manufacturer, Thomas Longworth of Smedley House, returning home after a convent education in France. Yelverton was thirty three, a Brevet Major in the Royal Artillery, the third son, and one of several children, of Viscount Avonmore. By all accounts the Major was a dashing figure, and Longworth, if not beautiful was vivacious and intelligent. The attraction was immediate, strengthened on Longworth's side by Yelverton's thoughtfulness in escorting her home when her sister failed to meet her off the boat.[2] In June of the following year, when Longworth was in Naples to complete her education, she learned that Yelverton was now in Malta, and wrote to him asking him to forward a letter to a friend at Monastir in Turkey. From then on they continued to correspond, until they met for a second time in the Crimea in 1855.

The previous year Yelverton had been sent out to the Crimea on active service, while Longworth had returned home to care for her father. On his death, she herself went out to Galata with the French order of Soeurs de Charité, though she was not officially a member of the order, and while there Yelverton, stationed at Sevastopol, travelled to Galata to visit her. According to the account by Erickson and McCarthy, they each regarded this meeting quite differently – 'For her an acceptance of his proposal of marriage; for him the beginning of his plan to make her his mistress.'[3]

After they both returned to Britain, they continued to write to each other. Early in 1857, Yelverton was moved with his unit to Edinburgh at Leith Fort, while previously Longworth had also arrived in the city, where she took lodgings in St Vincent Street with a friend, Arabella MacFarlane, in the house of one Mrs Gemble. There Yelverton visited her almost on a daily basis, but again the two produced very different accounts of the visits. According to Yelverton, as he was to testify in court, he had sexual intercourse with Longworth at every opportunity, while she, supported by MacFarlane and Gemble, always insisted that the meetings were innocent. In a letter dated 20th June, but with no year identified, Longworth wrote to Yelverton's mother, the Viscountess Avonmore, that Yelverton

> began to visit us daily as my fiancé. We grew more and more attached. He had no patience to wait; I had no courage to destroy all hope. He declared that I was not only essential to his happiness but, that if he could not have the woman he loved, he was resolved to go headlong to perdition. But for his misery I would have retired to a convent. I was desespoirante. I wished to appeal to his uncle to free him; I wished to entreat your ladyship's advice. He did not like either plan. A secret union was thought of. We differed about the manner. He preferred a Scotch method. I, being a Catholic, could not consider any marriage as sacred unless performed in my own church. Nevertheless we did go through a ceremony together which he assured me was binding.[4]

The ceremony referred to here was neither the 'Scotch' method, a form of marriage which will be discussed in detail in due course, nor a Catholic one. According to her evidence, on the 12th April 1857, Longworth and Yelverton were at the St Vincent Street address, where they read together the marriage service of the Church of England, from the Book of Common Prayer belonging to Miss MacFarlane. Neither of them seems to have regarded this as of itself a binding marriage contract – indeed later in court Yelverton denied that it had ever taken place.[5] Longworth, for her part, refused, so she claimed, to give in to Yelverton's demands that they sleep together until their marriage had been blessed by a Roman Catholic priest. Instead she left Edinburgh and went home, until after several months of separation, Yelverton gave in, and agreed to take her to Ireland where, he told her 'all I required might safely be done'. In Ireland 'we had much difficulty finding a priest who would unite us. The permission of the Bishop had to be obtained, and upon Yelverton's declaration that he was not a Protestant, we were married in the Catholic Church last August, since which time I have lived in Scotland and in France as his wife. He has ever been most affectionate and devoted, his tenderness and kind disposition exceeding all my wildest dreams.'[6]

The Catholic ceremony referred to took place on the 15th August, 1857, in the chapel of Killowen, near Rostrevor. After permission had been sought and granted by the Right Reverend Dr. Leahy, Bishop of Dromore, the couple went through a service officiated by the local Catholic priest, Father[7] Benjamin Mooney, which Longworth regarded as a marriage service, while Yelverton regarded it as a mere sop to her conscience. From his point of view, however, it had the desired effect, and for several months thereafter the couple travelled around Ireland and Scotland as man and wife. In December Longworth went to live for a time with friends in Hull, a Mr and Mrs Thelwall. Yelverton visited her there, but then early the next year, 1858, they set off again to travel in France, where Longworth discovered she was pregnant. Yelverton left her to return to his military duties, while she struggled with a miscarriage and subsequent ill health. Before she lost the baby, however, she wrote to Father Mooney, asking for a copy of her marriage certificate, to ensure that there would be no problem over the baptism of the child. Mooney complied by sending what purported to be an extract from the marriage register, although according to one account, the marriage had not been entered in the parish books, and he had added the names of fictitious witnesses to the document.[8]

Then the whole situation began to fall apart. Yelverton's departure from France was abrupt and acrimonious. After the miscarriage, he had appeared for a time to continue to be affectionate and solicitous towards his 'wife', until, she wrote, 'a fortnight ago, when he suddenly told me he had been ruined, that I was the cause, not that I have ever had one sou from him, but have done my utmost to keep him from new debts. He believes I have betrayed his secret, it is utterly false, as investigation into the facts must prove. I am only anxious to help him by every means in my power. With time I can raise the capital required, until such time my own small income is at his disposal. I can manage without it, as I have no hope or interest in life apart from his.'[9]

Yelverton may well have been in financial difficulties at this time, and there are occasional references to his indebtedness in subsequent case reports.[10] Although he later became heir to the Avonmore estate and indeed subsequently inherited the title as fourth Viscount, at this time he was a younger son and only one of many siblings from the third Viscount's two marriages. In any case, there was something more than a temporary financial embarrassment involved here. On 26th June, 1858, Yelverton married Emily Marianne Ashworth Forbes, the youngest daughter of General Sir Charles Ashworth and the widow of Professor

Edward Forbes professor of natural history at Edinburgh University.. On the face of it, it did not appear that he married her for her money – her husband had not been well paid, and she had brought only a small dowry to that marriage. There was a powerful rumour, however, published in a number of newspapers at the time, that she had inherited the substantial sum of £50,000 from her late husband.[11] Poor Theresa Longworth's annual income was no more than £200.[12] According to Duncan Crow, Yelverton married Forbes not for her money, but because she was pregnant. In the circumstances a choice had to be made, and made quickly. 'The daughter of a general took precedence over the daughter of a Manchester silk manufacturer.'[13] Longworth learned of the marriage on the 29th.[14]

One can well imagine the effect of this information on Theresa Longworth. At about the same time (the lack of any date makes it impossible to be sure when the document was written) she received a letter, written in the third person, making it only too clear that any hope she might have had of a long term relationship with Yelverton was now out of the question. The letter reads as follows:

> Mr Yelverton[15] presents his compliments to Miss Longworth, and in reply to her questions informs her that all connection between Major Yelverton and Miss L. should now cease: and steps have accordingly been taken by that gentleman in furtherance of the wishes of his friends to carry out this resolution. No doubt when Miss L. considers this young gentleman's position she will naturally conclude that his friends do not wish to cast him off altogether – which had he continued to act contrary to their wishes they must have done. The arrangements with regard to Major Yelverton are now carried out, and this connection is now irrevocably ended. Therefore Mr Yelverton does entreat of Miss Longworth to consider her plans for the future that a passage shall be found for Miss Longworth to New Zealand as before mentioned, or to anywhere else she should wish, and arrangements made for certain payments to be made to her, as may be agreed upon.[16]

It is not difficult to imagine Longworth's feelings on reading this missive. Three years later, in 1861 – the same year as the first of the various court hearings which were to decide her fate once and for all, she published a semi-autobiographical novel – *The Martyrs of Circumstance*. In it she included a vignette describing the experience of a 'pretty, gentle girl' who had run away with 'a gay young officer, with nothing but his epaulettes, his pay, and his debts'. The couple had decided that it was out of the question for her to live in army barracks – they would find a picturesque cottage, with ivy growing over it, in which to begin their life together. Alfred, the young husband, duly set off in a search for such an idyll, but alas, 'unfortunately he found – not the ivy cottage, but a gay wealthy widow, who straightway became enamoured of his handsome whiskers, and conceived the idea of monopolising them to herself, by relieving him of his difficulties, and transferring his debts from his creditors to her own account'. 'Was there ever any mischief in the world,' the narrator concludes, 'that a rich widow was not at the bottom of it?'[17]

This was in the future. Longworth's immediate response was to resort to the law. Taking her case to the Procurator Fiscal in Edinburgh, she succeeded in having Yelverton arrested on a charge of bigamy, and lodged in the Calton jail until freed on bail of £1,000.[18] The charge was soon dropped for lack of evidence, but this did not deter several contemporary newspapers, and at least one modern commentator, from referring to the later court cases as bigamy cases, which of course they were not.[19] In fact, as one Member of Parliament[20] whimsically pointed out at the time, given the state of the law on marriage, it was legally possible for a man to have a wife in each of the three kingdoms.[21]

Next, Longworth approached the newly created Court for Divorce and Matrimonial Causes to seek restitution of her conjugal rights, only for the Court to conclude with Yelverton that it had no jurisdiction in the matter, as Yelverton's domicile was in Ireland, not England, while Longworth as his wife could have no domicile of her own.[22] It was now Yelverton's turn to go to law – approaching the Court of Session in Edinburgh to seek a declaration that he was not married to Theresa – while she for her part sought a ruling from the same Court that her marriage to Yelverton was valid. For convenience, the Court decided in July 1860 to join the two cases into one, focussing on the legality or otherwise of the marriage, but it was to take a further two years, until December 1862, before the conjoined case came before the Court, with Moncreiff now acting as leading counsel for Theresa.

In the meantime, Longworth had come to the view that her best hope now lay with the courts in Ireland. After she learned of Yelverton's marriage to Mrs Forbes, she went for a time to stay with her old friends in Hull, John Thelwall, a successful ironmaster, and his wife. Now he and Longworth devised a scheme whereby he would take Yelverton to court, ostensibly to recover a sum of £259:17:3 for board and lodging and other expenses incurred by his 'wife', Longworth, but actually to force a formal recognition of her marital status. Husbands were legally liable for debts incurred by their wives. If Yelverton could be proved to be liable for Longworth's debts, then logically it meant that she was his wife. A previous attempt at a very similar tactic, *Grant v. Yelverton,* had fizzled out in June 1860,[23] but Longworth and her friends were undeterred.

The case of *Thelwall v. Yelverton* lasted for ten days, from the 21st February to the 4th March, 1861. Coverage of the event in the national press was extensive, and the case aroused huge public and popular interest.[24] Undoubtedly Longworth was the heroine of the piece – seduced by a member of the hated landlord class, a Roman Catholic, and a woman of intelligence and resolve, who was more than capable of holding her own in the witness box. For his part, Yelverton equally well fulfilled the role of villain. The exchange between himself and Mr Sergeant Sullivan has become something of a classic:

> Do you think it a laudable thing to seduce a woman?
> Upon my honour, I do not.
> Upon your oath – I do not want your notions of honour.
> [Then:]
> Was she a gentlewoman in your opinion?
> I think, sir, that accomplishments, religion, and everything else must be added to gentle blood to give a proper definition of a gentlewoman.
> You must have gentle blood at all events, according to your definition?
> Exactly.
> And perhaps it is no harm to seduce a woman who has not that qualification?[25]

The outcome of the trial was pretty much a foregone conclusion. After deliberating for no more than an hour, the jury came back with a verdict in Theresa's favour, declaring that there was both a Scottish and an Irish marriage. The court erupted in scenes of wild enthusiasm, while Theresa herself delivered a short speech of appreciation, declaring that the verdict had made her an Irishwoman. Yet in fact the outcome was much less valuable in law than it appeared. As Duncan Crow explained, the case of *Thelwall v. Yelverton* was an action *in personam,* that is to say that it had reference to a specific person and not to the world at large. Although the only issue raised and tried in the Four Courts at Dublin was whether or not Yelverton was married to Theresa, the legal issue was whether or not Major Yelverton owed John Thelwall £259:17:3. The verdict decided that he did – but nothing more.[26]

It raises the question – why did Theresa and her advisers opt for this oblique approach to her marital status, rather than, say, directly seeking the restoration of her conjugal rights. There are two possible answers to this – the first is that she had already tried to get her conjugal rights restored in Scotland and failed, and second that, in such a trial, she could not have appeared as a witness. One outstanding feature of the Irish trial had been her consummate performance in the witness box.

And now, at last, the focus moved back to Scotland, where she was able to muster the formidable team in her support of both Lord

Advocate, James Moncreiff, and Solicitor-General Maitland. In the first instance, the case came before a single judge – the Lord Ordinary, Lord Ardmillan, before whom the combined talents of her counsel did not prevail. Ardmillan was not unsympathetic, but still found against her. 'For the conduct of the Defender', he concluded, 'there can be no excuse. But he was not the seeker, the seducer, or the betrayer of the Pursuer. The story of the pursuer, her charms, her talent, her misfortune, even the intense and persevering devotedness of her passion must excite interest, pity and sympathy. But she was no mere girl, no simpleton, no stranger to the ways of the world, no victim to insidious arts. She was not deceived; she fell by her own consent.'[27]

Ardmillan's decision aroused a good deal of hostile comment from the contemporary media. The *Caledonian Mercury* described it as an 'inexplicably one-sided, harsh, and inconsistent judgment'. Longworth was described as 'a lady of birth, education, and rare accomplishments', struggling against great odds and many disadvantages to vindicate her right and title to be the wife of Major Yelverton. The effect of the Ardmillan judgement, however, was to 'extenuate the perfidy and pollution of the "honourable" scoundrel who could vow before a minister of religion, and in the presence of High Heaven, to take Theresa Longworth to be his lawful wedded wife, and then, having accomplished his object, cast her off and embrace another, under the pretence that the whole ceremony was a sham.'[28]

It was not to be expected that Longworth would accept this judgment without complaint. Her appeal before the Inner House of the Court of Session was heard on the 19th December 1862 before three judges – the Lord President, Lord Curriehill, and Lord Deas.[29] As in Ireland, the case attracted great public attention, and we are told that on the day of the hearing, 'A large crowd of persons assembled this morning in Parliament Square, all eagerly desirous of gaining admission to the Court of Session.'[30] Moncreiff and Maitland conducted her case, seeking a declarator of marriage with Yelverton on two grounds – consent *de praesenti*, and what was called a promise *subsequente copula*. Consent *de praesenti* simply meant that the two had agreed to be man and wife by mutual consent – it being Theresa's claim that on the 12th April 1857 they had sat in her lodgings in St Vincent Street in Edinburgh, and read through the marriage service of the Church of England together. A promise *subsequente copula,* meant a promise to marry followed by sexual intercourse. One question for the lawyers to decide was whether this second mode of 'irregular' marriage required the *copula* to take place in Scotland. Then there was the ceremony performed by Father Mooney, the Roman Catholic priest, on the 15th August 1857 in Killowen chapel. Longworth was obliged to concede, however, that in view of the law forbidding the marriage of Protestants with Catholics in Ireland, that argument could not be pressed. But she insisted that as a Catholic she had scruples about a marriage not celebrated by a priest, and had on that account refused to cohabit with Yelverton until after the Irish ceremony. Afterwards they had lived as man and wife in Ireland, Scotland, England, and France. Against that, Yelverton denied that he had ever agreed to marry Longworth; that illicit sex between them had begun in Edinburgh and continued in Ireland before the Killowen ceremony; and that the latter was not in fact a true marriage ceremony, but merely 'a form in which the pursuer alone was interested, and that although it would leave him free, it would satisfy her conscience'.[31]

No-one doubted that under the law of Scotland as it then existed (and not abolished until 1939)[32] a marriage secured by either of the two methods under discussion would have been perfectly valid. The task for Longworth's counsel was to show that they had in fact taken place. There was no explicit evidence for the alleged ceremony held in St Vincent Street, which might have constituted a consent *de praesenti*. Curiously, it would have been easier to substantiate the marriage *subsequente copula*, if it could be shown that illicit intercourse had in fact taken place, as Yelverton asserted and Longworth denied, in Scotland. Lacking hard evidence or written proof of a promise of marriage, counsel had to fall back on inference and implication, in particular from passages in the letters Yelverton had written to Longworth when they were apart. For example, in one of her letters to Yelverton written when she was staying in England, Longworth had enclosed the marriage cards of a 'Mr and Mrs Shears', but without explanation. In reply Yelverton, apparently in the belief that it was Longworth who had married Shears, wrote; 'by your marriage you have earned my lasting gratitude, as on reflection I found I had placed myself in a false position in regard to you, and one of all others the most painful to me, viz., that I had promised to you to do more than I could have performed when the time came!' In a later letter, written after the parties had returned from Ireland, he referred again to promises made: 'I have never intentionally deceived you, and I have done more that I promised, at great risk.'[33] There was evidence to suggest that Yelverton had treated her as his wife, and had bought her a wedding ring before the Irish ceremony. Once at Killowen, he had told Father Mooney that 'there is no necessity for this, it has all been settled or arranged, but I will do it to settle the lady's conscience, or words to that effect.' What had already been 'settled or arranged'? An agreement to marry? Although Yelverton never told his family of the marriage, when the couple travelled together, they did so as man and wife, and on the occasion of their visit to Doune

Castle, he wrote their names in the visitors' book as Mr and Mrs Yelverton.[34]

Two of the three judges – Curriehill and Deas, were persuaded by counsel's arguments that a marriage between Yelverton and Longworth under one or other of the two possibilities did indeed exist. Curriehill described the gift of the ring as 'a significant symbol of acknowledgement of her as his wife.' Their having cohabited as man and wife in Ireland, 'cannot, I think, be entirely left out of view as acknowledgements by the parties they were so connected'. While the ceremony at Killowen could not be regarded of itself as having the legal effect of a marriage ceremony, 'yet it may have the different effect of being an acknowledgment of a prior marriage. Viewing the declarations (interchanged while the parties were kneeling at the altar) they contain unequivocal acknowledgements that the parties were husband and wife'.

As for the defender, Yelverton, to make his case, he should have established by evidence 'the falsehood of such solemn and unequivocal declarations. All he has done, however, is deny they took place....Putting together these unequivocal acknowledgements of marriage in Ireland, and the subsequent ones occurring in Scotland, England and France, I am of the opinion that they are sufficient to satisfy the rule of the law of Scotland, and that the marriage is established.' Even if he was mistaken, Curriehill believed that there was still ample evidence to substantiate a marriage *subsequente copula*.[35]

Deas agreed. After briefly outlining the law on the issue, he concluded that two of the defender's letters 'can be said directly to prove a promise'. There was a problem, of course, that although the defender claimed that intercourse had taken place in Scotland, and so could have been directly connected to the promise, Longworth denied this, and claimed they had not slept together until they were in Ireland. 'The first intercourse took place in Ireland, and although the parties returned to and cohabited in Scotland, the novel question arises, whether the intercourse upon returning to Scotland can be so connected with the promise as to make a marriage?' He concluded that it could, and that a marriage *subsequente copula* had taken place. He was also convinced that there was sufficient evidence to establish a marriage consent *de praesenti*

Only the Lord President disagreed. He could find no direct evidence to support the allegation of the interchange of consent, or of the reading of the Church of England service. 'One of the things most to be expected as an immediate consequence of marriage is consummation; but here there was no sexual intercourse while the parties remained in Edinburgh.' Neither Longworth's landlady, Mrs Gemble, nor Miss MacFarlane, her companion, had any idea that a marriage had taken place. In his view, the letters which passed between the parties 'are inconsistent with the supposition of their being at that time husband and wife'.[36] But the vote was two to one for Longworth. She had won her case. Once again, public sympathy was strongly in her favour. 'From morning till night,' reported the *Caledonian Mercury,* 'she is surrounded by visitors, who sympathise with her in so much as she has endured, and congratulate her on her success in so persistently vindicating her rights.' It is satisfying to note that her first action, on learning the outcome of the case, was to proceed 'direct to the residence of the Lord Advocate, who had so ably and effectively fought her case, and while tendering her cordial thanks, presented his Lordship a very handsome bouquet'.[37]

Amidst this chorus of approval, only *The Times* struck a discordant note. In a remarkably grumpy editorial, reprinted without comment in a number of Scottish newspapers, the paper inveighed both against the way in which the proceedings had been conducted, and the state of Scottish law on marriage which the proceedings had revealed. It took exception to the 'eloquence' of the judgments, as well as the 'partisan expressions of sympathy by the audience', but reserved its most biting criticism for the law of marriage in Scotland, 'that is so obscure that Judges cannot agree on it, and so ill conceived as to enlist men's sympathies against virtue'. The Scottish people apparently

> do not think that any form, or any publicity, or any registration ought to be a necessary condition to the most important contract into which two persons can enter...This notion is so barbarous, so unchristian, and so contrary to natural justice, that if the Scotch will have it so, all other nations ought to put them in a state of matrimonial quarantine, and confine the operation of their marriages to Scotland.[38]

Longworth had only a little while to savour her success. Yelverton appealed – this time to the House of Lords, where Moncreiff was again her champion. While the official report of the Court of Session case did not include any record of Moncreiff's actual words, the report of the appeal case reproduced his arguments in some detail. In the first place, he claimed, there had been a promise of marriage in Scotland; secondly, an interchange of consent in Scotland, and thirdly, a marriage in Ireland. 'The first two depended on the construction of the law of Scotland, and he contended that the promises and subsequent *copula* in this case constituted a Scotch marriage. The law of Scotland was the old canon law, by which consent, as in this case, was sufficient to constitute marriage. It was not necessary to show the time of the consent, but quite sufficient to prove that there had been a promise and subsequent *copula.*'[39] As in the case before the Court of Session, Moncreiff argued strongly that there was sufficient evidence to be found in Yelverton's letters to Longworth to prove that a promise of marriage had taken place.

Unfortunately for Longworth, not all the judges in the House were convinced, although some were. Among the latter was the Lord Chancellor, Lord Westbury, who fully accepted Longworth's claim that there had been a solemn exchange of consent between the two on the 12th April, 1857 – the occasion of the reading of the marriage service used by the Church of England. On the 12th July of the same year, Longworth had written to Yelverton: 'My ears ache to hear the "mia", though I am convinced you might say it with perfect truth now and for exactly three months past.' 'I regard this letter of the 12th July,' Westbury told the court, as full proof of the truth of the Respondent's chief allegation, namely, that there had been a marriage by mutual consent, or at all events a deliberate mutual sacred promise to marry entered into at Edinburgh on the 12th April, 1857.[40] Only one other of the five judges involved – Lord Brougham – agreed with Westbury. Lords Wensleydale, Chelmsford and Kingsdown did not. Longworth had lost again.

Many people might have accepted by this stage that there was no possibility of success in the face of a final determination of the issue by the House of Lords. Theresa Longworth was made of sterner stuff. As she had once written to Yelverton in happier days, 'the strongest and most prominent point of my character is the extreme tenacity of purpose, and, I may say, the incapacity to relinquish an object once fairly sought.'[41] Very true. In November, 1864, Yelverton presented his petition to the Court of Session, seeking to have the judgment of the Lords now applied. Longworth immediately lodged a note with the court, asking them instead to put aside consideration of the petition and allow her to enter a statement of new evidence which had only recently come to light. The Court refused, so she countered with a request that the whole case be referred to the oath of Major Yelverton. This was an unusual legal procedure by which, if the court had approved her request, Yelverton would have been obliged to state on oath whether or not she was his wife, and such a statement would have overridden the judgment of the House of Lords.[42] Despite the support of the Lord Advocate, by a majority of the judges of the Court of Session, permission was denied.[43] The grounds for their decision, which came in for a good deal of contemporary criticism, was that if Yelverton asserted under oath that he was indeed married to Longworth, it would inevitably affect the status of the former Mrs Forbes and her children, who were not parties to the current proceedings. A request by Longworth's counsel to have Mrs Forbes called as a witness was refused.[44]

By this stage, it must have been clear even to Theresa Longworth that her long campaign to have her marriage to Yelverton upheld by the courts would get no further. That certainly did not mark her abandonment of legal action, or the ending of her professional association with James Moncreiff. In 1865 she was again before their Lordships of the Court of Session – this time to sue the proprietors of the *Saturday Review* for libel, to the tune of £3,000. In the offending article based on the letters Longworth had written to Yelverton and read out in the course of the Dublin trial, the *Review* had sought to portray Longworth, Moncreiff claimed:

> as being one of the most abandoned of her sex...an adventuress, with a disreputable previous history...who pretended to be a *Soeur de Charité*, but who was in reality acting as a woman of bad conduct, who sainted and sinnered [sic] by turns, writing as no modest woman would write, scheming as no modest woman would scheme, with religious scruples which did not prevent her from provoking to sin.[45]

But not even Moncreiff's well practised eloquence could prevail. The case was heard before a jury who initially declared themselves evenly divided in their verdict. Told to go away and think again, they returned with a decision against Theresa by six votes to three. 'The hearty hissing which the jurors received in giving in their verdict in favour of the *Saturday Review*', commented an editorial in the *Caledonian Mercury*, 'may be taken as a general expression of the feeling which will prevail on the subject throughout the kingdom.'[46]

That was not at all the end of the story of Theresa Longworth, though it ended her association with Moncreiff and her other Scottish counsel. In none of his writings which have come down to us did he make any mention of this remarkable woman. And of course there was a postscript. Having been rejected by Yelverton, and had her claims to be his wife denied by the members of the highest court in the land, she simply ignored the lot of them, and called herself the Hon. Mrs Yelverton, or even, after her former lover succeeded to the title, Viscountess Avonmore.[47] And there was a final legal postscript. The Yelverton case had thrown into high relief the anomalous state of marriage law in the three kingdoms. Accordingly a Royal Commission into the question was set up and reported in 1869, making several references to Yelverton in the process.[48] The eventual outcome was the Marriage Act of 1870, which amongst other things removed the prohibition on the solemnisation of the marriage of Protestants with Catholics in Ireland.[49]

IV

Lord Moncreiff

Chapter 13
On the Bench……

Early on the morning of Monday the 20th September, 1869, Lord Justice Clerk George Patton left his house on the Glenalmond estate and disappeared. A massive search involving hundreds of volunteers produced no immediate result, until, on the Wednesday, a necktie and razor case were discovered on the bank of the river Almond, near a torrent known locally as the Spout of Buchanty. For the next three days the search was concentrated on the river itself, led by an experienced boatman, Joseph Malloch of Perth,[1] and eventually a body was found, about 100 yards further down stream. 'The appearance of the body,' the *Glasgow Herald* told its readers, 'was most revolting, there being a deep gash in the throat, bearing out the theory that before falling into the water his Lordship had endeavoured to end his existence by cutting his throat.'[2]

Patton had indeed committed suicide, and there was no great mystery about his reasons. Previously Solicitor-General for Scotland, he was appointed Lord Advocate in 1866. Like Moncreiff before him, he needed a seat in the House of Commons, and twice contested the constituency of Bridgewater, which, it was well known, required its candidates to be particularly well off. An official enquiry, indeed, into allegations of electoral malpractice in Bridgewater was already in progress, and questions were being asked in the press about Patton's possible involvement.[3] As the *Pall Mall Gazette* commented, 'No one can be blind to the possible effect on a delicate-minded and sensitive Judge of an impending examination as to bygone electoral expenditure, incurred perhaps at the time without sufficient consideration, or under some sort of compulsion, which might fix him with moral responsibility for corrupting and bribing, and thus bring doubt or discredit on his judicial office.'[4]

According to Omond, there was no doubt that Patton's own conduct was innocent. The same could not be said for some of his supporters. When Patton had stood for re-election on becoming Lord Advocate, we are told that:

> his friend Mr. George Thompson handed £2000 in notes to Mr Henry Westropp– himself unseated on petition after the election of 1865 – who exchanged them for gold at the Bank of England, and took the money to the Carlton Club, where he made it up into a parcel, and sent it out to a Mr. Lilly, an auctioneer and J.P. of Bridgwater, who was waiting in a cab outside. This money Lilly took down to Bridgwater, where he gave it to the agent Tromp, by whom it was disbursed in bribes.'[5]

Evidence before the enquiry showed that while Patton's published expenses for the two elections came to no more than £374, in reality this figure should have been more than £6,000, of which at least £1,900 had been paid out in bribes. As Omond had to concede, even if Patton had been unaware of what his agent was up to, 'it would be difficult to escape the imputation of having wilfully closed his eyes'.[6]

There was a bizarre twist to this affair. Amongst the papers in Tullibole Castle there is a letter to Moncreiff from William Gladstone when Prime Minister, referring to the death of Patton 'just announced', and offering Moncreiff the now vacant office of Lord Justice Clerk. This letter, however, is dated the 31st August[7] – some three weeks *before* Patton's actual disappearance. Any suspicions that Gladstone had merely misdated the letter are immediately dispelled by the existence of two further letters dated 27th September, and 1st October, 1869[8], referring back to his August letter. What seems on the face of it to be a baffling circumstance turns out to be explained as an unexpected coincidence. At the end of August George Patton's older brother Thomas did indeed die suddenly from a heart attack, while out grouse shooting on the Glenalmond estate. Thomas, as the owner of the estate, was known locally as the 'Laird of Glenalmond'. Younger brother George, as Lord Justice Clerk, bore the judicial title of 'Lord Glenalmond'.[9] It is not difficult to see how the confusion arose. But it is interesting to note that as soon as the erroneous report was became public, there was already speculation in the Scottish press that Moncreiff might be offered the post.[10]

This tragedy for Patton and his family was to have a dramatic effect on the life and political career of James Moncreiff. Abandoning the office of Lord Advocate and the House of Commons for ever, Moncreiff accepted the position of Lord Justice Clerk, head of the Second Division of the Court of Session. It was a post he was to hold for almost another twenty years, retiring finally in 1888, at the age of seventy-seven.

Moncreiff's decision to leave politics and go on the judicial bench was not quite as sudden as it appeared. He had been offered a judgeship the previous year by the Conservative administration, and been sufficiently interested in the offer to seek the opinion of his friend and ministerial colleague, Edward Cardwell. That advice had been decidedly ambivalent. On the one hand, Cardwell assured him that for him to accept a judgeship from the present government would not 'prevent our future Prime Minister from giving your claims upon your own party a perfectly fair consideration'. On the other, he was advised that he 'would add to those claims, if you continued on his behalf the contest in which you are now engaged for the Universities.' In either case, he was urged to get in touch with Gladstone himself, tell him about the offer, and seek his advice.[11] In the event the offer was not taken up, until in the following year, after the suicide of George Patton had been confirmed. Gladstone now wrote to Moncreiff to say that he had put the proposal to offer him the post of Lord Justice Clerk before the Queen, but that no step would be taken without Moncreiff's agreement, and followed this up with a second letter a day or two later seeking an urgent response. The week before that, on the 25th September, Moncreiff's friend Henry Reeve, the Registrar at the Privy Council Office, had written to him that 'I see by the Times of this morning that all doubt as to the fate of poor Patton is at an end. It is a most painful tragedy, and for many reasons must have been peculiarly painful and agitating to you, and one does not like to think of the mental torture this poor man must have undergone to arrive at so dreadful conclusion.' At the same time, Reeve experienced 'an extraordinary amount of satisfaction that you should at last have reached that haven of dignity and comparative repose, which no one has more completely earned than yourself.' Interestingly, Reeve, an astute senior civil servant with an ear very close to the political ground, further commented that 'You will, if I mistake not, leave the Commons without much regret.'[12] After some delay, this offer was accepted.

Four years later, in October, 1873, a further reward was offered and accepted, in the form of a peerage, gazetted on 1st January, 1874.[13] Again, for personal reasons, Moncreiff took the best part of a month, after discussing the offer with his family, to decide finally on acceptance. His reservations were principally financial. To support the dignity of a peerage was evidently a costly business.[14] As he explained in a letter to Gladstone at the end of October, that despite being able to claim some success in his profession, his 'nomadic Parliamentary life for 18 years was not favourable to the accumulation of a fortune'. Nevertheless, he would not have accepted it, 'had I not hoped that I may hold it and transmit it, if not with affluence, at least with honour and independence.'[15]

If indeed Moncreiff was keen to leave behind the political career he had been engaged in for the best part of twenty years, and take on the new responsibilities of the second most senior judge in the Scottish Pantheon, he was also aware that he did so at something of a disadvantage in having been, while engaged in the duties of Lord Advocate, only intermittently involved in the actual day to day practice of the law. In a speech delivered on his accession to the bench, he commented that despite his thirty-five years' experience of the law, he had been drawn away by 'pursuits and distractions alien to the profession', and would need the help and support of his fellow judges and former colleagues at the bar. Even the author of his obituary in the *Scottish Law Review* had to admit that his position as a judge was not made any easier by the fact that 'he had not figured to any great extent in the intenser phases of legal argument before the appeal Courts', and while as an advocate he had made a name for himself as a jury pleader with 'a large employment in that special branch', 'he had not had that continuity...of subtle reasoning about conflicting cases and complex principles which seems alone fitted to produce the greatest judges'.[16] Yet another disadvantage lay in the 'circumstance of succeeding at no great interval so great a luminary as Inglis', his long time colleague and friend.

Indeed, some years before his death, a semi-anonymous writer in the *Journal of Jurisprudence* marked Moncreiff's retirement from the Bench with a remarkable and highly critical appraisal – the word 'appreciation' seems out of place here. 'S.S.C' (it was the norm for contributors to the *Journal* to sign only with their initials) made a very sharp distinction between Moncreiff's judicial persona as Lord Justice Clerk, presiding over criminal cases in the High Court of Justiciary, and his role as Lord President of the Second Division of the Court of Session. Of his career as the first, he wrote, 'one can speak with almost unqualified approbation'. Moncreiff was thoroughly familiar with the criminal law, had had a long experience as Lord Advocate in its administration, an intimate knowledge of jury practice, a ready grasp of the salient points of evidence, and a wide knowledge of human nature, men, and of affairs. These were the 'qualities and acquirements which Lord Moncreiff brought with him from the Bar to the criminal Bench, and they combined to make him at once a thoroughly safe and admirably efficient criminal judge'.

Sadly, the same could not be said of his performance in the Second Division. The author wrote of the general dissatisfaction of the legal profession with the conduct of business within the Court. 'The complaints against the Division are that little justice is done to the arguments, and that there is no confidence that a case will be disposed of in accordance with the rules and principles which have generally commended themselves to lawyers.' He complained also of a 'system of constant interruption from, and conversation upon the Bench', by which 'the arguments of counsel are torn to tatters'. Moncreiff stood accused of being one of the worst offenders when it came to interruptions, and was also to blame for the unsystematic conduct of the Court's business. 'It is of great importance for the orderly conduct of the business of a court that its President should be thoroughly master of all the forms of process and rules of procedure. Of such forms and rules Lord Moncreiff remained to the last profoundly ignorant, and what regard was paid to them in his court-room was due entirely to his clerks.'

Up to this point these complaints could be explained, if not dismissed, as the outpourings of a disgruntled advocate who wanted to let off steam. The generosity of his praise for Moncreiff as a criminal lawyer, however, suggests that this appraisal is not simply an attack by a professional or political enemy. More worrying is the low opinion he evidently had of Moncreiff's command of the civil law. The author recognised, as indeed so did his subject, that when Moncreiff had come to the Bench, 'he was not a learned case lawyer'. He had never had a large Inner House practice; his parliamentary duties had kept him for a great deal of his time in London, and when he did come to Scotland on professional work, it was mostly in jury trials – 'no great schools of law'. This need not have been a serious problem. 'There have been judges who knew little law when they came to the Bench, who yet became most learned lawyers....But a learned lawyer Lord Moncreiff never became. He lacked that capacity for drudgery, and that quiescence of temperament, which such a course of study requires.'[17]

Not all commentators on Moncreiff's judicial performance agreed with this negative assessment. A spokesman for the Faculty of Advocates in 1888 commented most favourably on Moncreiff's relations with members of the Bar.[18] Moncreiff's obituary in the *Scottish Law Review*, while accepting that he had come to the Bench with something less than a detailed and profound knowledge of the law and legal principles, nevertheless commended him for his ability, after a few years of 'everyday contact with those cases and principles,...to pick up the threads of the law he had to administer. His ready grasp and above all his predominant good sense led him almost intuitively to true conclusions, truer, it is said, than those of others who were esteemed profounder lawyers.'[19]

A case in point was that of *Woodhead v. The Gartness Mineral Co.*,[20] over which Moncreiff had presided. In expressing his opinion on what should be the judgement of the Court, found himself in a minority of one against all six other judges, including Inglis. Yet only a few years later the House of Lords in *Johnson v. W.H.Lindsay & Co*[21] took a very different view from Moncreiff's colleagues, and the record of the latter case declares the decision of the Court of Session in the *Lindsay* case to have been 'disapproved'.

Both these cases had to do with the liability of masters, where a servant has suffered physical injury through the negligence of a fellow workman. They also raised the question of how that liability might be affected by the existence of 'common employment' and a 'common master'. Why these concepts were relevant to these cases was due to the fact that under the law of employment as it then stood, a workman who suffered injury in the normal course of his work had no redress against his master, unless the master himself had been negligent. As Lord Chief Justice Erle explained in *Hall v. Johnson*, it was an established principle in English law, but also in Scotland, Ireland and America, 'that a servant when he engages to serve a master, undertakes as between himself and his master, to run all the ordinary risks of the service, including negligence on the part of a fellow servant, who is acting in the discharge of his duty as a servant of him who is the common master of both.'[22]

Inglis' opinion in the *Woodhead* case, as reported, is confusing. On the one hand he seems to be arguing that where there are two workmen employed by a common master, and one through negligence injures the other, the master is not liable, because both employees have undertaken to run the risks of their employment. But he goes on to declare that 'it is not because the wrongdoer is, in a technical sense, the servant of the same master that the master is not answerable.' It is not because the injured and the injurer are both his hired and paid servants, but 'because he is not personally at fault, and has not warranted the injured workman against the perils of the work'.[23]

This interpretation of the law of employment went too far for the judges in the *Lindsay* case, since it seemed to imply that only where a complete stranger, not an employee, suffered injury, could the master be held liable. In this last case, workers were engaged in building a block of houses, some employed by the builders, Higgs & Hill, and some by W.H. Lindsay & Co, specialists in fireproof iron work. Poor Mr Johnson happened to be working on the ground floor, while some of Lindsay's employees were at a higher level, laying concrete. One of these, through his own negligence, dropped a bucket full of concrete on Johnson, who was later awarded compensation of £52:10s. A succession of appeals finally brought the matter before the House of Lords, where counsel for Lindsay tried to argue that both workmen involved were in effect working on common employment and for a common master, and cited the judgment in *Woodhead v.Gartness.* To no avail. Their Lordships reversed the judgement of the court below, and reinstated Johnson's compensation, while 'disapproving' the decision on the *Woodhead* case.[24] Moncreiff's independent opinion back in 1877 had been vindicated.

In the *Woodhead* case, Moncreiff had been in a minority of one. There was no such problem with regard to what was probably the single most high profile case in the whole of his judicial career – the prosecution for fraud in 1879 of the directors of the City of Glasgow Bank. Moncreiff presided over the case in the High Court of Judiciary in

Edinburgh in January and February of that year, supported by two other senior judges – Lords Mure and Craighill.

The failure of the City of Glasgow Bank with estimated debts of £10 million, announced in the press on 2nd October, 1878,[25] seems to have caught almost everyone by surprise. According to the Irish *Freeman's Journal,* 'The failure of the Glasgow City Bank for ten millions is a disaster as unequalled in magnitude as it was wholly unexpected.' The *Journal* went on to point out that according to the previous week's edition of the *Investor's Monthly Manual*, all the signs were that the bank was in a healthy state. Its stock was given as £1 million, the share price stood at £237 per £100, and it paid dividends of 12%. But now that the disastrous news had broken, there was general concern to avoid a widespread panic. While the other Scottish banks were unwilling to come to the Bank's assistance, they did announce that they would accept its notes in current circulation. The *Scotsman* hastened to assure its readers that 'the circumstances of the suspended bank were entirely exceptional, and that its status was not comparable with that of the other Scotch banks'.[26] How the unhealthy state of its affairs had been kept secret until now was difficult to explain, but the paper assumed that it 'was not before the minds of the shareholders, and can hardly have been known to the directors'.

The City of Glasgow Bank had first been established in 1839, with 779 subscribers and a capital of £656,250. It was its regular practice to publish the annual balance sheet for shareholders in June each year, and the accounts for June 1878 showed healthy deposits of £8,000,000 and the existence of 133 branches around the country. Capital, reserves, and undistributed profits totalled £1,600,000, and, as noted in the press, a dividend of 12% would be paid to shareholders. The announcement less than four months later that the directors had decided to close the bank naturally sent shock waves throughout not just the city of Glasgow, but across Scotland and beyond. It is estimated that hundreds of businesses were brought down by the bank failure, and the 1200 shareholders and their families, unprotected by limited liability safeguards, were made destitute. At a meeting of the liquidators held at the beginning of January, 1879, it was decided to pay a dividend of a mere five shillings (later raised to 6/8d) in the pound.[27] At the same time all six of the Bank's directors were served with indictments, and the trial date set for the 20th January.[28]

Before the trial could take place, sympathisers with the shareholders met to discuss ways of providing some financial relief for those affected. These schemes included a controversial plan for a lottery, designed to raise a total of £6 million, of which £3 million would go to the shareholders. They and their supporters saw this as the only way to solve their problems. At a meeting of 'influential men' in Glasgow, Sir James Watson referred to the bank failure as 'a national calamity, so ruinous to its innocent shareholders and their families, and so disastrous in its effects on the community at large, that it demands and justifies exceptional modes of relief'.[29] Others saw it differently, and the plan was roundly condemned in the pulpits[30] and the press of the day. 'Many people, we are sure,' asserted an editorial in the *Leeds Mercury*, 'must have been inclined to regard the first announcement of the proposed lottery in aid of the shareholders in the Glasgow City Bank as an ill-timed hoax. The suggestion of such a scheme was, indeed, so outrageous that it is astonishing that anyone could be found to discuss it seriously. Yet we now know that the proposal has been received with extraordinary favour in Scotland...'[31] The writer professed himself to be reassured, however, by the intervention of the Law Officers, from whom the promoters had received a discreet hint that what they were planning might well fall foul of the relevant legislation, and it is a fact that the scheme was shortly to be abandoned.[32]

In the meantime the directors and manager of the City Bank had been removed from where they were lodged in Glasgow Prison, and conveyed with elaborate secrecy to Edinburgh, and the Calton Jail.[33] The succeeding trial was to last for eleven days, in the course of which the incompetence or worse of the manager, Stronach, and his fellow directors was shown in high relief.

As we have noted, Lord Moncreiff presided over this trial, but his contribution to the eventual outcome was greater than that of a mere chairman of the proceedings. The issue of whether the directors, or some of them, were guilty of an actual crime, or merely of professional incompetence, lay at the heart of the affair. There was also a question as to whether they might in fact succeed in getting off scot-free on a technicality. Two days before the trial was due to open, the *Graphic* advised its readers of a rumour 'unfounded we hope, that the directors of the Glasgow City Bank are likely to be acquitted in consequence of a flaw in the indictment'.[34]

Indeed before the trial proper was allowed to get under way, one entire session was taken up by legal argument challenging the 'relevancy and non-specification' of the charges contained in the indictment. The following day, to a Court which 'was again crowded, but not inconveniently', Moncreiff returned to give his and his colleagues' decision on the issues raised by counsel for the defence. He explained to the court that the question he and his fellow judges had had to decide was whether the indictment contained facts sufficiently relevant to go to proof before a jury. Their conclusion seems to have been that while many of the questions raised by counsel for the defence involved 'considerations of very great weight', these should most properly be dealt with when they came to investigate the facts of the case.

The real issue, however, was the issue of criminality, in particular in relation to the first charge in the indictment. This first charge – that of issuing false statements and balance sheets – had been withdrawn by the Lord Advocate, and it was now argued that the charge of misrepresentation of the assets and liabilities was in a similar position, and ought to be deleted. The Court held, however, that 'the charges respecting the assets and liabilities were matters of proof, and not of relevancy, but there was no doubt that it would be necessary when the facts of the case came to be proved, to add to the illegality of the accounts charged, *some element of bad faith, or guilty knowledge, or of some fraudulent intent. This was an elementary principle, and was essential to establish the crime itself.*'[35] [my italics] It would not have been enough to base the charge simply on the obligation of directors not to allow overdrafts without security – 'unless there had appeared in the charge something alleging breach of faith'. Evidently the indictment itself was less than explicit on this matter of bad faith or criminal intent, and Moncreiff remarked that 'he could have wished that the charge had been more specifically expressed.....but on further consideration he found words in the indictment which might be taken to override all the facts alleged, and to raise the elements of bad faith throughout the whole of these transactions.....the charge was clear that the prisoners had made use of their character as directors to obtain advances in regard to moneys entrusted to them', and this was sufficient to justify an investigation by a jury'.[36] Without this conclusion, the case against the directors would almost certainly have collapsed before it came to trial.

It is worth noting in passing that in seeking out evidence for bad faith and criminality Moncreiff may well have been influenced by his uncomfortable experience twenty years earlier over the affair of the failure of the Western Bank. Back in October 1858 the Bank had gone bankrupt to the tune of almost £3 million, plunging many of its shareholders into financial ruin. At the time both Moncreiff and John Inglis, who had each held office as Lord Advocate in that year, were satisfied that under the law as it then existed, the directors of the bank had done nothing to make them liable to criminal prosecution. This view was severely criticised both within and outside Parliament. The *Caledonian Mercury*, for one, grew apoplectic at the thought that 'for all this deliberate wickedness, for all this gross and systematic deception, practised alike on the public and the shareholders, there is, in the opinion of the public prosecutors of Scotland, no punishment provided by the law, which pursues with inexorable severity the stealing of a turnip or the snaring of a hare.'[37] If a mistake had been made at the time, it was not one which Moncreiff was going to make twice.

And so the case got under way, the prosecution being conducted by the Lord Advocate and the Solicitor-General for Scotland, with fourteen 'legal gentlemen' appearing for the defence. The defendants faced a total of seventeen charges, including the misrepresentation of assets and liabilities, overdrawing private accounts, and the purloining of funds belonging to depositors. The directors had all made declarations before the Sheriff of Lanarkshire denying the charges, though the terms of their statements cannot have impressed their customers with their attention to the affairs of the bank. Mr Potter, who was to be sentenced to eighteen months imprisonment, claimed to have been deceived by the manager, Stronach. Robert Salmond claimed to have been absent when the last balance sheet was prepared, but signed it in the belief that it was a true representation of the position of the bank. Robert Taylor denied all misrepresentation or concealment. He attended all weekly meetings of the directors, and 'considered that by doing so he discharged his duty without himself examining the books'. Henry Inglis had been absent from board meetings through illness, but had complete faith in the bank officials. John Innes Wright, whose firm had received very large advances from the Bank, alleged that although he was a member of the board, he did not take an active part in the management but relied on the experience of his fellow directors. Robert Stronach, the manager, wisely declined to make any statement with regard to the charge of theft.[38]

We are told that upwards of one hundred and fifty witnesses were due to be called, but of these the most damning from the point of view of the defence were Dr Macgregor, an independent accountant called in by the directors to advise on the preparation of the balance sheet shortly before the stoppage, and one William Morrison, formerly a clerk at the bank, but since 1871 its chief accountant. It was one of Morrison's responsibilities to prepare the draft annual balance sheet for submission to the manager. In his evidence he claimed that for the June 1878 document, he had prepared the draft in accordance with the books of the bank, but then altered it under instructions from Stronach and Mr Potter. As a result, the amount of deposits declared in the public balance sheet of 1878 was given as £8,102,000, misrepresented to the tune of £740,000. The bank notes in circulation were incorrectly stated to the amount of £89,000. The outstanding drafts were falsely stated to the extent of £410,000. 'These understatements were made by the direction of Mr Stronach, the manager, and were marked on the abstract by red ink.'[39] And so it went on. The credit accounts were falsely stated to the amount of £3 million; the cash in hand overstated by £200,000. False balance sheets had been prepared not only for 1878, but also for the two previous years of 1876 and '77. The only small glimmer of light relief was afforded by Morrison's near namesake, William Morris, whose monthly task it was to prepare statements of credits given to one of the bank's largest customers, Smith, Fleming and Co. Sometimes these statements were accompanied by securities, sometimes not. In one particular case the security of an advance to the company had been six live elephants in Rangoon. (Laughter).

Dr Macgregor, as an outside consultant, had no need for concealment. He spoke of his meeting with the directors, at which the general affairs of the bank were discussed – a discussion in which Stronach took very little part, seeming to be 'entirely overcome'. Having carried out his investigation Macgregor concluded that several of the directors and some of the firms with whom they did business had largely overdrawn their accounts. In his opinion the bank was now hopelessly insolvent – the deficit according to his calculations being of the order of six and a half million.

And so the trial ground its way on for several more days. The Court heard from shareholders and depositors, from the prosecution and the defence. For his part the Lord Advocate announced on the 27th that he had withdrawn the charges of theft and embezzlement.[40] On January 30th, the Dean of the Faculty rose to speak on behalf of the defence – by all accounts a speech of great power, and one which had a greater effect on the jury than any other. According to the *Glasgow Herald,* the speech was 'courageous and skilful, and had the verdict been given immediately on the conclusion of his speech, the impression was that every one of the panels [defendants] would have been set free.'[41] The Dean was able to exploit weaknesses in William Morrison's evidence, upon which the prosecution had largely relied. 'As the case stands', the paper concluded, 'a great deal depends on the summing up of the Judge. It is freely said that a powerful charge made either in one direction of another would, as matters stand at present, take the jury along with it to a verdict either of "all guilty" or of all "not guilty", or at least "not proven".'

Moncreiff's address to the jury received widespread praise from the press. The *Sheffield and Rotherham Independent* described it as 'an able and exhaustive summing up of the whole case'.[42] The address lasted for four hours, and began with an admonition to the jury to put out of their minds the 'excited comments out of doors' occasioned by the fact that the failure of the bank had reduced hundreds of shareholders from affluence to poverty, and concentrate wholly on the facts given in evidence. Despite the length of the address, it succeeded in reducing the complexity of the case to a few simple propositions. According to him, the only charge now preferred against the prisoners was that they had falsified the balance sheets of the bank from 1876 to 1878, and that they had done so with a fraudulent intent to deceive the shareholders. For the jury to come to a decision on this issue, he put to them three simple questions – first, whether the balance sheets were false; second, whether the prisoners, or any of them, knew that they were false; and third, whether the circulation and publication of the balance sheets had been done with fraudulent intent. He further reduced the burden on the jury by suggesting that they concentrate on just two of the amounts in the balance sheets which were alleged to be false. 'He thought it would save the jury a great amount of trouble if they dismissed the idea of going through all the particulars of book keeping, and that it would be enough if they came to the conclusion that the balance sheets had been falsified in these particular amounts.' He made some criticism of Morrison's evidence, which had sometimes been confused and contradictory, but if his evidence was to be believed, then the accounts had been altered, and altered with intent to deceive.[43] Evidently the summing up succeeded in enabling the jury to come to a speedy decision. After retiring for just two hours, they returned with a verdict. 'We unanimously find Lewis Potter and Robert Summers Stronach guilty of all the charges as libelled; and John Stewart, Robert Salmond, John Innes Wright, Henry Inglis, and William Taylor guilty of using and uttering false balance-sheets or statements of the state of the City of Glasgow Bank.'[44]

Potter and Stronach were each sentenced to eighteen months imprisonment. The punishment would have been much more severe, Moncreiff explained, if the jury had found that the crimes they had committed had been carried out for personal gain, rather than, as had been argued on their behalf, for the benefit of the bank. The remaining directors, who had been convicted of uttering false balance sheets, but not actually of fabricating them, each received eight months. Even to some contemporaries, these sentences seemed over lenient. The *Economist*, for one, thought them to be inadequate, even taking into account the three months the directors had already served before the start of the trial. The *Statist* agreed. 'So far as the sentence goes, it would appear to be a safer thing to make away with six or seven millions of money, and thereby to filch from thousands of affluent families everything they possess in the world, than to pick a pocket of a few pence.'[45] It would have been interesting to know what the Dundee mill girl, whom Moncreiff had sentenced to eight years in prison back in 1870 for stealing a silver watch and some clothing from her landlady, might have thought of this outcome.[46]

It would be difficult to argue convincingly that in this case, as in that of Madeleine Smith, the Court had not been influenced in any way by the social position of the accused. There were times, however, when the dictates of the law ruled any softening of the sentence literally out of court. This was of course true of capital cases, the most notorious in Moncreiff's term as Lord Justice Clerk undoubtedly being that of Eugene Chantrelle, charged with the murder of his wife, Elizabeth, in January, 1878.[47] Chantrelle was a teacher of French who had married one of his pupils, with whom he had three children. The marriage had lasted for eight years, but by all accounts it was far from happy. Chantrelle, according to the indictment, had beaten her, accused her of adultery and incest, and threatened to shoot her or poison her, and 'that by his violence and threatening had put her in bodily fear of losing her life'.[48] She had indeed finally lost her life, and Chantrelle was charged with having murdered her by first drugging her with opium, and then gassing her by deliberately breaking the inlet pipe to a gas fire, and leaving her to die. As well as his malice towards her, without as far as it emerged any evidence of wrongdoing on her part, Chantrelle had taken out a number of insurance policies on her life amounting to over £2,000. As the *Leeds Mercury* noted, 'the social position of the parties, and somewhat peculiar circumstances surrounding the case have naturally invested the trial with great interest, not only in Edinburgh, where the Chantrelles were well known, but all over the country.'[49] On this occasion the 'social position of the parties' had no discernable effect on either the verdict or on the sentence. Moncreiff pronounced the sentence of death.[50]

In the very different but equally notorious case of the Glasgow Dynamite trial, Moncreiff likewise found himself bound to hand down a sentence which, whatever his personal feelings, he had no power to vary. Ten Irishmen from Glasgow were charged with blowing up three installations in the city – the Tradeston gasometer, the Possil Canal Bridge, and the Caledonian Railway shed. There was an important question of law involved here – when does an intention to carry out an unlawful act become a criminal conspiracy? In his charge to the jury Moncreiff drew a clear distinction between them, following the decision in the House of Lords in 1868 that 'a conspiracy consists not merely in the intention of two or more but in the agreement of two or more to do an unlawful act, or to do a lawful act by unlawful means. So long as such a design rests in intention only, it is not indictable, but when two agree to carry it into effect the very thought is an act in itself.'[51] In the event, the jury found five of the ten guilty of conspiracy, but stated their belief that the remainder were not fully aware of the intentions of their leaders, and recommended them to the mercy of the court. In the case of the first five, Moncreiff expressed regret that the accused should have brought themselves into the situation they now found themselves, but told them that 'there is only one sentence which it is open to me to pronounce under a conviction for the crime charged, and that is to be detained in penal servitude during the rest of your natural lives'. For the remainder, he explained to them that the jury had 'taken a very merciful and discriminating view of the circumstances as regards your respective cases. They have found you guilty of the common law charge, and have added the recommendation couched in very strong terms which the Court are bound to consider with great respect, and which may very fairly qualify the sentence which otherwise we might have pronounced. The sentence of the Court is detention in penal servitude for seven years.'[52]

This question, then, as to whether Moncreiff should be regarded as being particularly lenient or severe in his sentences was addressed in 1888, by the author of the unusually harsh criticism already noted in the pages of the *Journal of Jurisprudence*. On this particular issue the author felt that Moncreiff had managed to strike a happy mean between the two extremes, though in other respects, as we have seen, he found much to find fault with in Moncreiff's handling of civil cases.[53] There are in fact, as one might expect, examples of both leniency and severity to be found in Moncreiff's record, even as measured by contemporary opinion. One of his judgments which aroused particular popular anger at the time was his decision in 1883 to sentence the so-called 'Strome Ferry rioters' to four months in prison.

Strome Ferry was, and indeed still is, a small village on the west coast of Scotland. The fortunes of the village had been transformed in 1870 by the expansion of the Highland railway line, which now terminated at the local pier, and provided a huge stimulus to the local fishing industry, encouraging the railway company to begin to run a Sunday service. This move was hotly opposed by the local population, who disapproved of Sabbath working on religious grounds. The result was the Strome Ferry Riot of Sunday, 3rd June 1883, when a mob, numbered at its height at 200 and armed with barrel staves and bludgeons, tried to prevent the landing of fish from two steamships, the *Lochiel* and the *Harold*, and the loading of the fish on to the train. A small body of police tried to control the mob, but were heavily outnumbered and several were injured.

And so four of the rioters found themselves hauled up before the High Court of Justiciary in Edinburgh, charged with mobbing and rioting. It was clear that the jury had considerable sympathy with the rioters, and although they found them guilty, recommended them 'to the utmost leniency of the Court, on account of their ignorance of the law, and the strong religious convictions they hold against Sabbath desecration'.[54]

Moncreiff himself was clearly disposed towards leniency, but within limits. 'I am quite ready,' he told the Court, 'to give such effect as I am able to the grounds of recommendation on which the Jury proceeded. I am very far indeed from treating lightly any religious conviction on that subject.' At the same time he pointed out to the accused 'that for persons in your position to spend the day of rest from morning to night in illegal violence and unseemly behaviour was hardly the way to advance the cause you had at heart, or to inspire in others due respect and reverence for that sacred institution.' Nor, of course, could he or any judge accept ignorance of the law as an excuse for crime.[55] The defendants were sentenced to four months in jail.

The popular outcry with which the sentence was greeted must have taken Moncreiff very much by surprise. Not that everyone was critical. An editorial in the *Glasgow Herald* commended Moncreiff for taking pains to arrive at a just decision, declaring that 'the name and character of Lord Moncreiff afford a guarantee for as great a degree of leniency in this case as was consistent with justice'.[56] But the paper also reported that the accused had been told by two of their religious leaders, Dr Begg and William Balfour, that they were to be 'looked upon as being in the same category as the apostles of the Church and the great martyrs'. Some members of the jury were so worked up that they made representations to the Home Secretary, Sir William Harcourt, to review the sentence. The Free Church Presbytery unanimously agreed to memorialise the Home Secretary to mitigate the sentence.[57] In August, the Edinburgh Town Council likewise debated a motion on whether to approach the Home Secretary to review and reduce the sentence. The proposer, Mr Maxwell, claimed 'that there was a strong and universal feeling throughout the country that the sentence on the Strome Ferry rioters was unduly and unjustly severe'. The Provost, while not wishing to cast aspersions on Lord Moncreiff, commented: 'At the same time the best and wisest of men make mistakes, and he thought he had made a mistake in this case.' Given 'the character and aim of the men, and that they were not a criminal class… and considering the strong recommendation of the jury that the utmost leniency should be shown to them by the Judge, he thought the punishment was too heavy; and the Home Secretary would only act in accordance with the feeling of the country were he to agree to greatly commute the sentence.'[58]

Sir William declined.[59]

The Strome Ferry case, and indeed other cases discussed so far in this study, raise some obvious issues to do with class divisions and prejudices, as well as clashes between religious belief and vested interests. The point has been made that it would be difficult to argue convincingly that the class background of Madeleine Smith, say, or even more so of the Glasgow City Bank Directors, did not have some relevance to the outcome of their trials and the sentences imposed. This point is thrown into sharp relief when comparisons are drawn with cases from the Circuit Courts, and the sentences handed down for crimes of petty thievery. Some saw the verdict in Strome Ferry to be a clear reflection of the power of vested interests. In a letter to the *Dundee Courier and Argus* in August 1883, a 'Reformer', commented that if the rioters were ignorant of the law, they 'were certainly not ignorant of the Divine Law, which they stood so manfully up for. It will now appear to many, according to the ruling of the Judge, that the Fourth Commandment is not so binding after all, especially where the interests of the wealthy trading classes are at stake'.[60]

And finally – and it was indeed one of the last cases tried before Moncreiff in the High Court of Justiciary – there was the case of the so-called 'Deer Raid' in the Pairc district of the island of Lewis in November,1887, in which several hundred crofters took part.[61] While a considerable number of deer were indeed killed in the raid, its purpose was rather to draw attention to the plight of the inhabitants of the island, where large swathes of land, including many townships, had been cleared to make more space available for the deer. The organisers of the raid were arrested, and six men, including the local schoolmaster, charged with mobbing and rioting. Their case came up for trial in January, 1888 in the High Court of Justiciary, before the Lord Justice Clerk.[62]

Moncreiff's charge to the jury came in for a good deal of criticism from the press of the day,[63] while the outcome of the case was a publicity triumph for the islanders.[64] The legal issue involved was simply whether the raiders were guilty of nothing more than trespass, or, as alleged, of mobbing and rioting. In his summing up Moncreiff considered the first option, 'that this was only a mere poaching affair, and that the Day Trespass Act would have been quite sufficient to cover it'. This, he concluded, 'was an entire and absolute mistake', since the charge against the defendants was not one of trespass or poaching, but mobbing and rioting. Instead he quoted the opinion of one of his predecessors, Lord Justice Clerk Hope, that 'the essence of mobbing and rioting is (taking terms applicable to this case) the exhibition, demonstration, and use of the power of numbers to overawe, obstruct, impede and defeat those employed in the discharge of the duty entrusted to them'.[65] He evidently believed that this was an apt description of the Deer Raid. If so, then he patently failed to convince the jury, who took no more than half an hour to return with their verdict: 'not guilty as libelled'.[66]

So – how are the judges to be judged? Or in particular how are we to assess Lord Moncreiff's performance on the Bench in the light of his decisions, judgements, and sentences, and in the opinion of contemporary commentators. If inferior to Lord Inglis or Lord Watson in the extent and depth of his learning, he has nevertheless been commended for his ability to overcome that disadvantage through experience and intuition. All commentators agree on the elegance of his expression, his wide experience of the world of affairs, his understanding of human nature. The *Gartness* case demonstrated both the soundness of his views, and his independence of mind. By some of his contemporaries he was regarded as too harsh in his judgements, by others too lenient. But did he leave a legacy?

The really outstanding judges, it could be argued, are those whose interpretation of the law in particular circumstances, provides a precedent for future guidance and more general application. In at least once instance, that could be said of Lord Moncreiff

The case was that of *Campbell v. Ord and Maddison*,[67] heard before the Court of Session in 1883, and rather like the *Johnson v. Lindsay* case, had to do with liability for injuries caused by accident. In this instance, however, the injured party was not an employee, but a small boy – under four years old at the time of the incident – who had had his fingers badly crushed in the cogwheels of an oil-cake crushing machine, owned by agricultural engineers, Ord & Maddison. The machine had been placed on display in the weekly market held in a street called Tower Knowe, in Hawick. He and his seven year old brother had been playing in the street, and the accident to young Robert occurred when he unwisely put his fingers in the machine, and his brother then turned the handle to operate it.

The case came before the Court of Session twice in the same year. In July 1873, the issue was tried before Lord Moncreiff, with the father, on his son's behalf, seeking damages from the exhibitors of the machine. Early in the hearing, defence counsel demanded that Moncreiff direct the jury to the effect that in law Robert Campbell was to be held as having contributed to the accident for which damages were now being sought. Secondly, they demanded that he also direct the jury that if they were satisfied that the brother, Neil Campbell, had also contributed to the accident, then the pursuer was not entitled to recover damages. In both instances, Moncreiff refused to give this direction, and in the case of the first, made it clear that the question of contributory negligence was a matter of fact, not of law, and left the fact to the jury. The latter found for the Campbells, and awarded damages of £100.

Instead of launching an appeal against this verdict, defence counsel lodged a bill of exceptions, and demanded a retrial, essentially claiming that Moncreiff had misdirected the jury. This resulted in a further hearing, this time before four Court of Session judges, Lords Cowan, Benholme, and Neaves, as well as Moncreiff himself. All four came to the same conclusion – that Moncreiff had been right not to direct the jury as he had been pressed to do, but to rule that the question of contributory negligence was a matter of fact, and not of law. 'This,' stated Lord Cowan, 'as it appears to me, was the only safe and proper mode in such a case as the present, of leaving the question as to contributory negligence to the jury for their decision upon the facts in evidence before them.'

When it came to Moncreiff's turn to speak, not surprisingly he followed the same line, and as the case of *Campbell v. Ord and Maddison* has been cited or referred to on numerous occasions since, it is worth quoting his opinion at length.

> On the bill of exceptions, I am of the opinion that neither of the propositions I was asked to lay down is sound in law. The first is a proposition not of law but of fact. It would be as unsound to say as a proposition in law that this child was not capable of negligence as to say that he was. Negligence implies a capacity to apprehend intelligently the duty, obligation, or precaution neglected, and that depends to a large degree on the nature of that which is neglected, as well as on the intelligence and maturity of the person said to have neglected it. The capacity to neglect is a question of fact in the individual case.....I told the jury that this is a matter for themselves to decide – that a child of four years old might be guilty of negligence – and that it was for them to say whether such was the case here.
>
> In regard to the second exception it was impossible for me to lay down the law in the terms requested. The mere fact of the boys playing together did not, in my opinion, make one of them responsible for the act or the negligence of the other. Even if the proposition had been so worded as to combine the two boys in the act of setting the machine in motion, looking to the circumstance, I could not have affirmed it, for if the boy injured was not guilty of negligence in his own act, neither could he be so in respect of the act of the other.

Moncreiff,'s ruling in the *Campbell v. Ord and Maddison* case was a major contribution to the law regarding contributory negligence. According to the law as it now stands, that is since the Law Reform (Contributory Negligence) Act, 1945, where it has been established that a pursuer contributed to his or her own injury, then an appropriate reduction in damages is made. Prior to that Act, the effect of contributory negligence was much more severe – it exonerated the defender completely. In 1870, in *Grant v. Caledonian Railway Co.,*[68] the First Division of the Court of Session denied damages to a young girl aged six years and seven months who had been killed by a train while on an unmanned level crossing. While the decision in the case was by a majority of three to two, all the judges agreed that the unfortunate child should be regarded as if she were an adult. To quote Lord Ardmillan, for example: 'It is said that the little girl was between 7 and 8 years old. Now the fact that she was a young child is in my opinion of no importance. Either she was so young as not to be able to take care of herself, in which case she should not have been permitted to be there, and in that case the railway company are not liable; or she was, when accompanied by her elder brother, in a position to take care of herself, and if so, she was on an equal footing with other passengers crossing the line. We must deal with her just as if she were of full age.'

The importance of Moncreiff's formulation was that it required the court in such cases to consider two elements: the personal characteristics of the child, and the nature of the danger. In place of a blanket assumption that when it comes to questions of contributory negligence a child must be considered as an adult, the real question must be – did this particular child have the capacity to appreciate the particular danger to which he was exposed? *Campbell v. Ord and Maddison* has become the *locus classicus*, and the application of Moncreiff's formulation can be seen in much subsequent case law.[69]

Moncreiff's landmark ruling in the case of *Campbell v. Ord and Maddison* came a scant three years after his ascension to the Scottish Bench, and as such would appear to substantiate the view of the *Scottish Law Review* some twenty years later that, despite his initial lack of experience of the more arcane avenues of the law, he had indeed succeeded quite quickly in picking 'up the threads of the law he had to administer'.

And so at last, his time on the Bench came to an end. On several occasions in the early and mid-eighties there had been rumours of his increasing ill health and imminent retirement,[70] and these rumours became accomplished fact in October 1888.[71] Looking back on the almost twenty years of his judicial career, his obituarist in the *Scottish Law Review* brushed aside any criticism of his performance on the Bench, or his alleged lack of knowledge of the law.

> 'Many of his judgements give evidence,' he declared, 'of vast erudition, and contain excursions into curious byways of antiquarian law. But especially remarkable are they for a gleaming brightness of diction altogether rare in so turgid and technical a department of literature. This faculty...was the result of long years of sedulous training; and it accounts perhaps for his being at his best when charging a jury...No judge could be more impartial or more scrupulous to present the best features of both sides of a case. Then to the bar he never failed to extend respect, courtesy and patience.'[72]

Obituaries naturally tend to paint only a positive picture of their subject. As we have seen, not everyone who had dealings before Moncreiff as a judge would have accepted this view of his treatment of counsel appearing before him. He had been accused, in the pages of the

Juridical Review, of being less than attentive to the arguments of counsel in the Second Division, and rather too inclined to engage in private conversation with colleagues on the Bench. But that same critic found much to praise in Moncreiff's handling of cases in the High Court of Justiciary. Some of his judgments were criticised for their harshness, some for their leniency. At the same time, he deserved credit for educating himself in those branches of Scots law with which he was unfamiliar, and in one area at least – the law of negligence – making a lasting contribution to the subject.

Chapter 14
....and off it

In August 1875, the local Dundee newspaper criticised Lord Ardmillan, one of Moncreiff's colleagues, for entering into public debate on ecclesiastical issues, on the ground that he was disqualified from so doing by virtue of his judicial office. Ardmillan was compared unfavourably with Lord Moncreiff, as he now was, 'who has in his time been a greater politician than Lord Ardmillan, but who, although he has a seat in the House of Lords, is now seldom heard of except in connection with the performance of his judicial duties'.[1] Just as, in the 1850s and 1860s, the number of Moncreiff's appearances in Scottish courts had suffered from his political responsibilities, so now his judicial responsibilities had a similar effect on his political activities. But it would be quite wrong to portray him as now withdrawing from public affairs. In certain areas of public policy – typically to do with reform of the law and the courts – he continued to be active after leaving the House of Commons. His deep and abiding interest in education and religion continued to involve him in public debate and controversy for years to come, while both his eminence and his long experience of affairs led to a plethora of honours and public appointments. In 1869 he was elected Lord Rector of the University of Edinburgh, created a baronet in 1871, and raised to the peerage as Lord Moncreiff of Tullibole in 1874.

No serious reader of the public press over the next twenty-five years after his departure from the Commons could have characterised Moncreiff as some kind of recluse. In 1874 he chaired a session of the Social Science Congress, at which he also gave an address on Jurisprudence. His name was put forward in January 1875 for election as Chancellor of Glasgow University to stand against the chosen nominee of the professoriate, Sir William Stirling-Maxwell. The nomination was ineptly handled by a self-appointed committee of the Liberal party in Scotland, and eventually had to be withdrawn.[2] Over the years his name appears as Deputy Lieutenant and Justice of the Peace of Edinburgh; Deputy Lieutenant of Kinross-shire; trustee of an insurance company; founder member of the Cockburn Society dedicated to the preservation and improvement of the city of Edinburgh; as the arbiter of the Glasgow shipbuilding strike in 1877; as president of the New Club, and of the Royal Society of Edinburgh; as Honorary Colonel of the Edinburgh Rifle Volunteers; as Honorary President of the Scottish Cricket Union – a game of which, it will be recalled, he was a keen player in his younger days. He delivered lectures at the Royal Society of Edinburgh, the Scots Law Society, the Juridical Society, and many others.

With the exception, perhaps, of his role in the shipbuilding strike, where he found in favour of the employers, these were relatively undemanding and uncontentious appointments. In 1869, Moncreiff, as well as being elevated to the Scottish Bench as Lord Justice Clerk, had also been appointed to the Privy Council. In 1871 he became a baronet in his own right (not until 1883 would he inherit the family baronetcy on the death of his older brother, Sir Henry), and in 1874, as we have seen, he was raised to the peerage as Baron Moncreiff of Tullibole. As a member of the House of Lords, he soon became involved the debate on the proposal to substitute for the House of Lords as the final appeal court for Scotland and Ireland, the new Imperial Court of Appeal. On this issue Moncreiff adopted a simple pragmatic position. While he regarded the departure of the House of Lords with regret, he accepted the logic of the argument, that since under the Judicature Act of 1873 appeals from the English courts were now to be carried to this new Court, then it would make sense for Scottish and Irish appeals to be dealt with in the same way. He approved in particular of the undertaking that the existing intermediate arrangements for hearing appeals peculiar to Scotland would not be affected.[3] In the event, of course, the Judicature Act itself was amended by the incoming Conservative administration in 1876, and the appellate jurisdiction of the House of Lords restored.[4]

In 1881, Moncreiff was consulted by the then Lord Chancellor over the proposed Court of Session Bill, which sought to give to Parliament power to set the number of judges in the Court by statute. As the Lord Chancellor explained, the purpose of the Bill was to increase efficiency in the Court of Session, and avoid a situation where there was insufficient business to keep the Court fully occupied. He was able to show that the numbers of judges both in the Court of Session and the local courts were out of proportion to the population of the country, and in relation to the situation in England. Nevertheless, the proposal aroused great opposition from Town Councils and professional bodies in Edinburgh and Glasgow, who sent petitions against the Bill after its first reading in March.[5] Despite having been a member of the Royal Commission on the subject, which had concluded that the Court could not operate effectively with less than thirteen judges, when it came to the discussion in the Lords Moncreiff did not share these misgivings. After all he had had several years experience of the Court in operation He reminded the House that he himself had presided over one of the Divisions of the Court for seven years with four judges, and for five years with only three. In his opinion, 'three was the best number for expedition, and four was the safest and surest'.[6] Nevertheless, though he admitted that he had advised the introduction of the Bill by government in the first place, now that he had come to appreciate the strength of the opposition to it, he moved the adjournment of the Bill to allow time for further consideration. The effect of this delay was to lead to the Bill running out of time, and being abandoned. In that sense, as the *Dundee Courier and Argus* commented, the government 'have received a check, and apparently it is the Lord Justice Clerk who had been the instrument of it'.[7]

The proposals to reduce the strength of the Court of Session had evidently touched a nerve in Scotland, where the complaint was heard, neither for the first time nor the last, that the authorities south of the border lacked a proper understanding of the peculiar circumstances obtaining in the north. This was not mere chauvinism, however, and a good case could be made out for the very different, more varied, and more extensive roles fulfilled by the Scottish judges, which justified a higher proportion of judges to national population. Similar feelings – that the Scots were being disadvantaged unfairly in comparison with the English – surfaced over the Scottish Peerages Bill of 1882-3. This Bill was designed to address anomalies in the system of electing representative Scottish peers to sit in the House of Lords, and the issue arose in the first instance over the disputed Earldom of Mar. As the *Glasgow Herald* explained to its readers, the Bill embodied the recommendations of a Committee of which Moncreiff was the chairman. In the debate on the second reading, Moncreiff pointed out that when the Scottish peers meet at Holyrood to elect one of their number as their representative to discharge high duties in the British Parliament, there was absolutely no guarantee that those who vote are peers at all.[8] The final decision on recognition of Scottish peerages had been the Committee of Privileges of the House of Lords, and in the difficult Mar case, that Committee had consisted of three Lords, two of whom were English lawyers, and one, Lord Redesdale, was neither a lawyer not a Scotsman. 'It might have been expected,' the *Herald* complained, 'that even a group of English peers would have paid some respect to Scottish feeling, and have allowed some authority to Scottish documents and legal opinions.' This however was not the case. 'The most highly prized traditions of Scotland were ruthlessly trodden under foot; her most ancient Peerage was declared to be a "creation" of yesterday; the "Decreet of Ranking" was declared to be a series of blunders; the decisions of the Court of Session were ignored; and the Treaty of Union was quietly set on one side.'[9]

The Bill, if passed, would have involved the Court of Session formally in the process, by empowering it to examine petitions relating to disputed peerages, and report its findings to the House of Lords. The issue rumbled on for several months. In early 1883 the Lord Chancellor came forward with his own Bill to regulate the election of Scottish peers, and one which would not have given new powers to the Court of Session. Despite this, Moncreiff was broadly sympathetic to the Bill, since it would accomplish the objectives of his original Committee, by ensuring that a nominal roll of Scottish peers should be drawn up under the authority of the Court of Session, without giving the latter the power to determine the absolute right of a claimant to a peerage.

Moncreiff's contribution to the debate on the Scottish Peerages Bill was his last major speech in the Lords, but it certainly did not mark, or not yet, his final withdrawal from public affairs. For much of his career he had pursued two fundamental interests – the reform and development of Scottish education, and the welfare of the Presbyterian church, and these two issues continued to engage his support for as long as his health allowed. We have already discussed his role in the development of a national system of education for his native country, and how as Lord Advocate he tried again and again to achieve this objective, only in the end to be obliged to stand to one side as his successor in the post, Lord Advocate George Young, pushed through his Education Act of 1872. Moncreiff's final contribution to Scottish education came through his chairmanship of the Committee on Endowed Schools,[10] though once again it was left to his successor, Lord Burleigh, to finish the job.

Moncreiff had still been in post as Lord Advocate when Sir Edward Colebrooke had come forward with a proposal that a Royal Commission be set up to enquire into these schools. At the time, Moncreiff argued that the suggestion was premature: 'until you had settled the question of elementary education, it was premature to deal with the question of middle class education'.[11] Nevertheless, one of the last of Moncreiff's bills to become law was an Act of 1869, 'to make provision for the better government and administration of Hospitals and other Endowed institutions in Scotland'.[12] In his view, 'these endowments would be a magnificent foundation for...a full system of education, supported by public property, beginning with the lowest step, and ascending up to the Universities.'[13] Once the 1872 Education Act had reached the statute books, and the question of elementary education in Scotland had been settled for the time being, there was no further reason for delay. Three Royal Commissions followed, the first in 1872 chaired by Colebrooke, the second in 1878 chaired by Moncreiff, and the third in 1882, chaired by Burleigh.

As Lenman and Stocks pointed out a century later, the big problem which would-be reformers of the endowed schools system had to face, was the near impossibility of reorganising the endowments without in effect transferring charitable funds from the children of the poor to the children of the middle class. And indeed, the fee-paying schools which emerged[14] from the reforms were essentially middle class schools whose fees, though subsidised by the endowments, were still higher than could be afforded by most working class parents.[15] Moncreiff's remit, as chairman of the 1878 Commission, was to make recommendations to the Scotch Education Department as to how the Parliamentary grant for public education in Scotland should best be distributed to promote education in the higher branches of knowledge. To fulfil this objective, the Commission met on thirty-one occasions, of which twenty were chaired by Moncreiff, and considered three principal issues – what was the educational value of different specific subjects; the plan of examination laid down by the inspectors; and efficiency of teachers in public schools.

Moncreiff himself took an active part in the questioning of witnesses, and showed himself very concerned over the issue of fees, and how they affected school attendance. In reply to one of his questions, Dr Taylor responded that 'the present system does not succeed in securing …regular attendance…Small as was the school fee, it was a heavy burden on parents earning perhaps 10s or 12s per week….I can see no other cause sufficient to account for the [poor] attendance but the payment of fees.'[16] An equally important issue was the system of payment by results, a system introduced into Scotland with the adoption of the Revised Code a few years earlier. Professor Laurie, Professor of Education at Edinburgh University, was asked to comment on the difficulty 'that a master is tempted to confine himself, or put his whole strength out, on the subjects for which he will receive the highest remuneration'. This was a problem on which Moncreiff pondered in the important address he delivered at the opening of the Kent Road Public School in Glasgow in 1886. While he was by now accustomed to the principle of payment by results, 'Nevertheless this highly organised system of ascertaining periodically the amount of gain produced to the community in return for the price we pay for it, is not all to profit. The most valuable results of education are not produced in a year, nor can they become apparent on an examination or inspection. The results of education are for a lifetime; and what we really want to communicate is the love of knowledge.'[17] Few educationists today would quarrel with that last sentence.

In the event, despite all its hard work, the reports of Moncreiff's Commission did not achieve broad acceptance, and it had to be followed by yet another in 1882, under Lord Burleigh. Not for the first time, the work Moncreiff had started had to be brought to a successful conclusion by his successor. Nevertheless, as Wilson Bain argues, the Commission's

Reports included a great deal of valuable information, as well as useful insights into contemporary attitudes towards education on the part of professionals. A key conclusion illuminated the essential relationship between elementary and secondary education, and one very much in line with Moncreiff's own thinking over many years. 'It is not only possible to combine thorough elementary teaching with instruction in the higher branches, but...any separation of these subjects is detrimental to the tone of the school and dispiriting to the master.'[18] The Reports included statistical information which, amongst other things, provided 'on the whole, satisfactory evidence of the zeal and efficiency of the teachers and the attention of the scholars'.[19] With their particular interest in the efficiency of teachers, the Commissioners recommended that they should be encouraged to spend some time at a university, and an additional grant be awarded to teachers with both training college and university qualifications. Again, this was very much in line with Moncreiff's own view of the value of a university education, which he once described as a 'miniature of life itself'.[20]

Moncreiff's address at the opening of the Kent Road Public School in April 1886 was his last public utterance on the subject of education. As well as providing valuable insights into his lifelong interest in the subject, it brought together the related subjects, in his mind and in the minds of many of his generation, of education and religion. As we have seen in an earlier chapter, Moncreiff had been committed for all his political life, to creating a national system of education for Scotland – an objective which had continually been thwarted, in his view, by religious obstructionism. In England this had taken the form of 'Church of England exclusiveness, Nonconformist dislike, and general apathy both in country and borough'. In Scotland the situation was both similar and different – similar in that the Disruption of 1843 'had thrown the whole machinery out of gear', in that no one could be a school master who did not belong to the Established Church, but different in that 'solid religious difficulty was absent, and all both thought and taught alike'.[21]

It was consistent with Moncreiff's impatience with a situation where there were no doctrinal differences between the Established and Free Churches, that he (with brother Henry) vigorously opposed disestablishment of the Established Church, and also lent his support to a Bill in 1886 which sought to reunite the two. The issue of disestablishment had been raised from time to time over many years, but in the late seventies it was gaining some support even from some members of the Free Church, who, according to one account, 'have at present only one thing in view in ecclesiastical matters, and that being to get rid of the Established Church at all hazards'.[22] Sir Henry and brother James were strongly opposed to any such policy, recognising that if achieved both Churches would suffer the consequences. 'It is impossible,' Moncreiff is quoted as saying, 'to root out an old tree without disturbing the soil around it; and the abolition of the Established Church would bring with it many results, religious, public, and social, extending far beyond our subjects of controversy.'[23] It made sense, therefore, when in 1886 a Bill was put before the House of Commons to 'remove obstacles to the reunion of the Presbyterians in Scotland', that Moncreiff should write a letter in its support.[24]

Four years later we find him again intervening in the disestablishment question, by publicly offering his support to the recently formed Layman's League, which according to Lord Balfour of Burleigh, had been set up to oppose disestablishment and the secularisation of endowments, and to promote the reunion of the Presbyterian Churches. Although Moncreiff was disinclined due to his advancing years to engage in public agitation, he did write an extensive open letter to Lord Balfour, declaring that the recent proceedings in the General Assembly of the Free Church in these matters was not consistent with the statement of principles made at the time of the Disruption, and that he was not able to support them. In 1891 Moncreiff was a signatory, on behalf of the Free Church, of an appeal addressed to the Synod of the United Presbyterian Church to prepare the way towards a 'reunion of the scattered branches of Scottish Presbyterianism, without any sacrifice of honour or principle of any of the bodies into which the ancient Scottish Church is at present divided'.[25] Finally, when the Free Church Branch of the League held its conference in Edinburgh in May 1894, Moncreiff was by this time too ill to attend.[26] He died on the 27th of April of the following year. His efforts on behalf of the League, and his attempts to heal the divisions in Scottish Presbyterianism had been, as the *Scotsman* commented in June 1895, 'the last public movement in which his Lordship took an active interest.'[27]

The many obituaries which inevitably followed just as inevitably rehearsed Moncreiff's career, detailed his achievements, the posts he had held, and the honours he had received. They wrote of his love of politics, of his eloquence, whether in Parliament, at the hustings, or in court. They mentioned his role in the abolition of the religious test in Scotland's schools, and his many law reforms. The *Dundee Courier and Argus* described him, surely correctly, as 'among the foremost of lawyers and Liberal statesmen produced by Scotland in the present century'.[28]

And yet there was something missing. The *Glasgow Herald*, almost alone, regretted the fact the world had not seen the 'Autobiography' on which it was known he had been working in his retirement. The work, the paper was convinced, 'would doubtless, from the acknowledged literary skill of the writer, have formed a fitting and delightful sequel to the "Memorials" and "Journal" of Henry Cockburn – his friend and his father's friend – and would besides have given us a portrait of his subject, his contemporaries, and the political events of the Victorian era in which he was involved, such as a mere biographer might despair of delineating.'[29] We now know that this autobiography, or his *Reminiscences* as Moncreiff himself referred to them, were embarked upon but never finished. What remains of them, however, as we have seen from time to time in this biographical study, did much more than cover the political events of the Victorian era, and did indeed give us a portrait of the man. From them we discover a man with enormous energy and powerful intellect, a strong sense of family, a devout Presbyterian but no religious bigot, and a man who made lifelong friendships and commanded widespread respect. He also possessed a rare and wonderful quality – the ability not to take himself too seriously. Who, after toiling through these many pages of religious wrangling, political debate, court room dramas, and public performances, can ever forget the picture of the small boy in church with the family servants, no doubt numb with boredom, who suddenly took it into his head to jump on the back of his neighbour, and be dragged out in disgrace? If Moncreiff had not confessed it, no-one would ever have known.

Note on the *Reminiscences*

When Lord Moncreiff retired from the Bench in 1888, he began writing his memoirs, or as he himself described them, his *Reminiscences*. That this memoir existed was known to G.W.T. Omond, and is briefly mentioned in his book on the Lord Advocates of Scotland. According to Omond, the memoir covered the period from 1840 to 1870, but was never completed or published.

I have been very fortunate indeed to have been granted access to this document, which I have transcribed and indexed. (Page numbers given in endnotes in this biography refer to this typed version) In fact the memoir covers the period from Moncreiff's early life until the early 1850s, not long after he was appointed Lord Advocate. It is about 60,000 words in length, but with several gaps, and comes to an end abruptly after some two hundred pages. For the light it throws both on Moncreiff's early life, but also on many other episodes in his career, it is an invaluable resource.

List of Cases
(in chronological order)

Earl of Kinnoul and Rev. R Young against the Presbytery of Auchterarder (1838), Robertson, C.G., *Auchterarder Report,* 2 vols., 1838

Duncan v. Findlater, (1839) 6 Cl. Fin. 894, ER [7] 824

Presbytery of Auchterarder v. Earl of Kinnoull (1839), HL Macl. and Rob. 220

Rev. John Edwards against the Presbytery of Strathbogie, (1839), Session cases, 2 D. 258

Clark v. Stirling (1839), 1 D. 995

Presbytery of Strathbogie (1840), 2 D. 585

Edwards v. Cruikshank (1840), 2 D. 1830

Earl of Kinnoull v. Ferguson (1841) 3 D. 778

Clark v. Stirling (1841), 3 D. 722

Middleton v. Anderson (1842) 4 D. 957

Dewar v. Cruikshank (1842), 4 D. 1446

Earl of Kinnoull v. Ferguson (1843) 5 D. 1010

Cruikshank v. Gordon (1843), 5 D. 909

Her Majesty's Advocate v. John Gordon Robertson and others, (1842) Broun, vol. I, 152

Edwards v. Leith, (1843) 15 Scottish Jurist

Cuninghame v. Presbytery of Irvine (1843), 5 D. 427

Her Majesty's Advocate v. Cumming, Grant, Ranken, and Hamilton, (1848) Shaw's Justiciary cases, 1848-52, pp.27-8

R. v. Madeleine Smith (1857), Notable British Trials, 1949, Jesse F.T., (ed.)

Yelverton v. Longworth, (1862), Macpherson I, 161

Yelverton v. Longworth, (1864), Macqueen IV, 829-30

Her Majesty's Advocate v. Edward William Pritchard, (1865), Irvine's Justiciary Cases, V, 1865-7, pp.88-191

Hall v. Johnson, (1865) 3 H & C, 665

Grant v. Caledonian Railway Co, (1870) 9 M., 258

Campbell v. Ord and Maddison, 1873, Rettie I, 149-56

Woodhead v. The Gartness Mineral Co., (1877) 4 Sc. Sess. Cases, 4th Series, 469

Trial of Eugene Marie Chantrelle, (1878) Notable Scottish Trials, (Duncan Smith, A., ed.), 1906

Her Majesty's Advocate against Alexander Gollan and others, (1883) Couper's Justiciary Cases, vol. V, 1882-5, p.317

Lord Advocate v. Donald Macrae and others, (1888) White's Justiciary Cases, I. p.543
George Johnson v. W.H.Lindsay & Co., (1891) H.L. A.C., 371
Galbraith's Curator v. Stewart (No 2), (1998), SLT 1305

NOTES

Chapter 1

[1] Moncreiff, J. W., *Reminiscences,*(hereinafter *LMR*) p.4
[2] Moncreiff J.W., 'Sir Charles Bell', *Edinburgh Review*, April 1872, **p.4**
[3] Young, D., *Edinburgh in the Age of Walter Scott,* 1965, p.34
[4] *Dictionary of National Biography,* 2004 ed., vol. 38, p.605
[5] *LMR,* p.3
[6] The Moncreiff's other children were : Henry Wellwood, 1809-83; William, 1813-95; George Robertson, 1817-97; Thomas, 1821-63; Elisabeth, 1819-1908; Louisa Anne, 1832-77; Catherine Mary, 1825-1919. Listed in Moncreiff, F., and Moncreiffe, W, *The Moncreiffs and the Moncreiffes,* 1929, pp.170-1. However this list does not include James' older sister Nancy who died aged nine in 1819
[7] *LMR.,* p.6
[8] Murdoch, A., and Sher, R., *Learned and Literary Culture,* in, Devine, T., and Mitchison, R., (eds) *People and Society in Scotland,* vol. I. p.129
[9] Young D., *op. cit.,* p.113
[10] *Ibid.,* p.7
[11] *Ibid.,* p.10
[12] *DNB,* 2004 ed., vol. 38, p.604
[13] Cockburn, H., *Life of Francis Jeffrey,* pp.200-01
[14] See Chapter 3 - The Making of an Advocate
[15] Cockburn, H., *Journal, 1831-54,* p.261
[16] Cockburn, H., *Memorials,* p.259
[17] *Ibid.,* p.262
[18] *LMR.,* p.50
[19] *Ibid.,* p.17
[20] *Ibid.,* p.23
[21] *LMR.,* p.203
[22] Cockburn, H., *op. cit.,* p.272
[23] Grant, E., *Memoirs of a Highland Lady,* II (2006 edition), p.68
[24] *LMR.,* p.22
[25] *Ibid.*
[26] *Ibid.*
[27] *Ibid.,* p.53
[28] *Ibid.,* p.99
[29] *Ibid.,* p.51
[30] Lauder, Sir T.D., *Account of the Great Floods of August 1829 in the Province of Morayshire...,* 1830, p.396

[31] *Ibid.,* p.399
[32] Grant, E., *Memoirs of a Highland Lady, I,* p.130. A note at the bottom of this page explains that a *bout rimé* was a list of words that rhymed, which were then given to 'a Poet' whose task was to write a poem using the rhymes in the same order as they came in the list.
[33] Mrs Cuming, Mrs Lauder's mother, and at that time the owner of the house
[34] Grant, E., *op. cit.,* vol. I, p.128
[35] *LMR.,* pp.53-4
[36] Watt, J.C., *John Inglis,* p.227
[37] *Ibid.,* p.34
[38] Watt, J.C., *op. cit.,* p.227
[39] In his *Edinburgh in the Age of Walter Scott,* p.72, Douglas Young cites an incident to illustrate Sir Harry's political principles. According to Young, 'When Prince Charles Edward was in Edinburgh in 1745, the old minister prayed: "O Lord, this young man has come among us seeking an earthly crown – grant him a heavenly one."' One problem with this anecdote is that Sir Harry wasn't born until 1750.
[40] Cockburn, H., *op. cit.,* p.42
[41] *LMR.,* pp.34-5

Chapter 2

[1] Omond, G.W.T., *op. cit.,* p.55
[2] Bain, W.H., *The Life and Achievements of James Wellwood Moncreiff,* unpublished MA thesis, Glasgow 1977, p.3
[3] *Edinburgh Review.* April 1872, p.408
[4] Quoted in Murray, J., *A History of the Royal High School,* 1997, p.40
[5] *The History of Sanford and Merton* was a best-selling children's book by Thomas Day, a Unitarian minister, published in three volumes between 1783 and 1789. Day was much influenced by Rousseau, and the book is an attempt to present Rousseau's philosophical ideas to British children in fictional form.
[6] *LMR,* p.10
[7] The foundation stone of the Infirmary Street building was laid in 1777, to be replaced by a new building on the Calton Hill in 1829 – four years too late for Moncreiff. Murray, J., *op. cit,* p.47
[8] *LMR.,* p.10
[9] *Ibid.,* p.13
[10] Cockburn, H., *Memorials of His Own Time,* 1971 ed., p.3
[11] Murray, J., *op. cit.,* pp.27-8
[12] Cockburn, H., *op. cit.,* p.249
[13] *LMR.,* pp.11-12
[14] *Ibid.,* p.12
[15] *Ibid.,* p.13
[16] *Ibid.,* p.14
[17] Moncreiff, J.W., *Legal Education – An Address,* 1870, p.6

[18] *LMR.*, p.12
[19] *Ibid*, p.14
[20] *Ibid.*, pp.14-5
[21] Prebble, J., *The King's Jaunt,* 1988
[22] Pittoch, M.G.H., *The Stuart Myth and the Scottish Identity, 1638 to the Present,* 1991, pp.88-9
[23] *Ibid.* p.16
[24] Grant, E., *Memoirs of a Highland Lady,* II, pp.165-6
[25] 'Henry Brougham', *Dictionary of National Biography*
[26] Cockburn, H., *op. cit.*, pp.394-9
[27] *LMR.,* p.18
[28] *Ibid.*, p.12
[29] *Ibid.*, p.24
[30] *Ibid.*, p.25
[31] *Ibid,* pp.25-9
[32] Omond, G.W.T., *op. cit.,* pp.149-150
[33] *History of the Speculative Society of Edinburgh since its Inception in 1764,* Edinburgh, 1845, quoted in Morton, G., *Unionist-Nationalism,* 1999, p.90
[34] But see Cockburn, H., *Memorials,* p.74. Cockburn is describing the rivalry within the Speculative between the old Tories, represented by Charles Hope and David Hume, and the young Whigs led by Brougham, Jeffrey and Horner. 'This contest produced animated debates and proceedings, which did not occupy the society alone, but the whole College, and indeed all Edinburgh, for nearly an entire session.' Presumably by Moncreiff's time, the Whigs had ousted the older generation of Tories.
[35] *Ibid.*, p.150. c.f. the lines in Goldsmith's *Deserted Village*:
'In arguing too the parson owned his skill
For e'en though vanquished, he could argue still.'
[36] As one twentieth century commentator has remarked, looking back to the early days of the Society, 'The primary aim of the Spec., was to improve [its] members in public speaking and literary composition in the idiom of the south.' This desire to be intelligible in English professional circles arose from the experience of the first Scottish MPs at Westminster, whose speech when they went back home during the Parliamentary recess 'smacked of London both in locution and in intonation.' The change begun in this way 'spread throughout the eighteenth century, especially among those who set and followed the intellectual fashions. Indeed, one of the ambitions of progressive Scots in the century was to write and speak good English'. Clark, A.M., *History of the Speculative Society,* Bicentenary Edition, 1968, p.21. One is reminded of Moncreiff's own wish to speak pure English rather than Scots.
[37] *LMR.,* p.60
[38] *Ibid.*, pp.60-1
[39] Omond, *op. cit.*, p.15
[40] *Encyclopaedia Britannica,* 11th Ed., 1911

[41] *Scots Law Review*, XI No 126, June 1895. p.153. Omond also (op. cit. p.149) speaks of North's class in Moral Philosophy, and the fact that Moncreiff won the medal.
[42] Moncreiff to Rutherfurd, Private, 4th September, 1851. Rutherfurd Papers, f.261
[43] *LMR*, p.46
[44] Quoted in Omond, *op. cit.*, p.151
[45] *Ibid.*

Chapter 3

[1] Bain, W.H., *op. cit.*, p.13
[2] *LMR.*, pp.46-8
[3] *Ibid.*, p.54
[4] See, for example, his judgement in Campbell v. Ord and Maddison, 1873, Rettie I, pp. 149-56 The significance of this case as a precedent will be considered in Chapter 13 – On the Bench and After.
[5] *LMR*, p.46
[6] Omond, G.W.T., *op. cit.*, p.293
[7] Edwards, O.D., *Burke and Hare*, 1980, p.161
[8] *LMR*, p.46
[9] Edwards, O.D., *op. cit.*, p.iii
[10] *LMR*, p.47
[11] *Ibid.*, p.48. Richard Patch was tried for the murder by shooting of a Mr Bligh, and executed on 8th April, 1806
[12] Macdonald, Sir J.H.A., *Life Jottings*, 1915, pp.106-7
[13] *LMR*, p.48
[14] *Ibid.*
[15] Following conviction Burke was executed by hanging on 28th January, 1829, and his body later dissected in the anatomy theatre in Edinburgh University. MacDougal was released but hounded by angry mobs in Edinburgh, Stirling and Newcastle. It was rumoured that she emigrated to Australia, and died there in 1868. Similarly, Hare, though released, had to flee the mob, and was last seen in the vicinity of Carlisle.
[16] *Ibid.*, p.47
[17] Edwards, O.D., *op. cit.*, p.159
[18] Cockburn, H., *op. cit.*, p.45
[19] *Ibid*, p.48
[20] *Ibid*, p.54
[21] Watt, J.C., *John Inglis*, 1893 p.42
[22] *LMR.*, pp.54-5
[23] Moncreiff, J.W., *Legal Education – An Address*, 1870, p.8
[24] I am indebted to my colleague Ross Macdonald for this explanation of the choice of thesis title
[25] Bain, W.H., *op. cit.*, p.17
[26] *LMR.*, pp.79-80

[27] Quoted by Bain, W.H., *op. cit.,*ch.2 n.12. *A Visit to My Discontented Cousin* was published in 1870. To call it a novel is to use the word loosely – the work is in fact a collection of articles Moncreiff had written over the years for *Fraser's Magazine,* with some additional fictional material to provide a framework. It included articles on such subjects as Trout Fishing, and Politics, and we will meet it again.

[28] Bain, W.H., *op. cit.*, p.17

[29] *Scots Law Review*, 'Lord Moncreiff', vol. XI, no. 126, June 1895, p.156

[30] A kyloe was a breed of small long horned Scottish cattle

[31] *LMR.,* p.83

[32] *Ibid.*, p.84

[33] *Ibid*, p.70

[34] *Ibid.*, p.115

[35] *Ibid.*, p.116

[36] *Ibid.*

[37] *Scots Law Rev., op. cit.,* p.156

[38] Omond, *op. cit.,* p.153. *LMR,* p.116. One indication of Moncreiff's professional success is provided by the censuses of 1851 and 1861. Over that ten year period, the number of servants in the family employ grew from 6 to 10, without any increase in the size of the family

[39] Henry James, b. 24th April, 1840; Robert Chichester, b. 24th August, 1843; James William, b. 16th September, 1845; Frederick Charles, b. 15th October, 1847; Francis Jeffrey, b. 27th August, 1849; Eleanora Jane, b. 1835; Marianne Eliza, b. 15th September 1841. Moncreiff, F., and Moncreiffe, W., *The Moncreiffs and the Moncreiffes,* privately printed, 1929, vol. I, pp.170-4

[40] Hetherington, William Maxwell, 1852, *History of the Church of Scotland from the origins of Christianity to the period of the Disruption,, 1843,* 1852, vol. 2, p.394

[41] Burleigh, J., *A Church History of Scotland,* 1960, p.344

[42] For a list of cases, see Chapter 5, note 26

[43] Moncreiff put the number of ministers who left at the Disruption at 474. *LMR.,* p.131, though the figure most often quoted is 451. The latter figure is the number of ministers who left the Church immediately at the Assembly of 1843 – 474 was the total who left then and subsequently.

[44] For a fuller account of this case, see Chapter 7

[45] Watt, J.C., *John Inglis,* 1893, p.231

[46] Cockburn, H., *Examination of the Trials for Sedition which have hitherto occurred in Scotland,* vol. II, p.239

[47] Moncreiff's appointment was welcomed by Cockburn, who described him as being 'able professionally,; an excellent speaker; an intelligent and powerful writer; and a high–minded, honourable man, and of a capital breed.' Cockburn, H., *op. cit.,* p.261

[48] See Chapter 11

[49] See Chapter 12

[50] Session Cases, Macpherson I, 1862, pp.161-77

[51] *The Times*, 29th July, 1864
[52] 33 & 34 Vict. c.110, sec. 38
[53] Moncreiff, J.W., 'Jeffrey's Contributions to the Edinburgh Review', *North British Review*, 1844, p.252-84
[54] *LMR*, p.136
[55] *LMR*, pp.137-6
[56] Moncreiff, J.W., *A History of England from the Accession of James II*, vols. III and IV, by Thomas Babington Macaulay, *Edinburgh Review*, vol. 105, pp.142-81. See Paul Hopkins' *Glencoe – the End of the Highland War*, pp.3-4 for comment on Moncreiff's review. Hopkins writes: 'The collection was made available to the reviewer of Macaulay for the *Edinburgh Review*, who printed another selection of documents from late 1691 which would have made this view [i.e. that William was ignorant of the plan to punish the Macdonalds] untenable, or would have done, had they not been overlooked ever since.' I am grateful to Owen Dudley Edwards for drawing my attention to this item.
[57] The Wellesley Index of Victorian Periodicals lists 11 articles by Moncreiff in the *North British Review*, and 21 in the *Edinburgh Review*, between May 1844 and July 1891
[58] *LMR*, p.138

Chapter 4

[1] Contemporary accounts, such as Turner A., in *The Scottish Secession of 1843*, give the number of signers of the Deed at 451, while Moncreiff in his *Reminiscences*, written after 1888, put the total number of seceders at 474. *LMR*, p.131. This latter figure corresponds with the statement in Brown, T, *The Annals of the Disruption*, page 98, that 'The number of names affixed [to the Deed of Demission], including subsequent adherers, was 474.'
[2] Fry, ,M., *Patronage and Principle: A Political History of Modern Scotland*, 1991, p.52.
[3] Brown, S.J., 'The Ten Years' Conflict and the Disruption', in Brown, S.J., and Fry, M., *Scotland in the Age of the Disruption*, p2.
[4] *LMR*, p.131
[5] Brown, T., *Annals of the Disruption*, 2nd ed., 1893
[6] *Ibid.*, pp. 133-4
[7] Bain, W.H., *op. cit.*, p.22
[8] Brown, T., *op. cit.*, p.369
[9] *Ibid*, p.358
[10] *Ibid*, p.354
[11] Bain, W.H., *op. cit.*, p.21
[12] *LMR.*, p.126
[13] *Ibid*, p.127; Register of the Acts of the General Assembly, 1842, pp.5, 407. National Archives of Scotland, CH 1/1/90

[14] Moncreiff, H.W., *A Letter to Lord Melbourne on the expediency of the interference of Parliament in order to remove the present difficulties in the appointment of ministers.* Edinburgh, 1840.
[15] 10 Anne 12.
[16] Rodger, A., *The Church, the Courts, and the Constitution: Aspects of the Disruption of 1843,* p.7.
[17] Cockburn, H., *Memorials,,* p.139.
[18] [Lockhart, J.G.], *Peter's Letters to his Kinfolk,* iii, pp. 46-8. The Letters nowadays are attributed to a Welshman, one Peter Morris of Pensharpe Hall, Aberyswyth.
[19] Moncreiff Wellwood, Sir Harry, *A Brief Account of the Constitution of the Established Church of Scotland, and of the questions concerning patronage and secession,* 1833. p.94
[20] Cockburn, H., *Journal,* vol. 1, p.294
[21] Thomson, Andrew, DD., 11th July, 1779 - 9th February, 1831.
[22] Chalmers, Thomas, DD., 17th March, 1780 – 31st May, 1847.
[23] Drummond, A.L., and Bulloch, J., *The Scottish Church, 1688-1843,* p.212.
[24] Brown, C.G., *Religion and Society in Scotland since 1707,* p.20
[25] Cockburn, H., *Journal,* I p.183
[26] Drummond and Bulloch, *op. cit.,* p.184
[27] *Ibid,* p.230
[28] Brown, S.J., *Thomas Chalmers and the godly commonwealth in Scotland,* p.236.
[29] Thomas Chalmers to John Leermouth, 25th August, 1834. Quoted in Brown, S.J., *op. cit.,* Chap. 5, note 74.
[30] For a brief discussion of the role of the Lay Association of the Free Church of Scotland in founding the Province of Otago in the 1840s, see Olssen, E., *A History of Otago,* 1984, pp.31-3.
[31] Sir R. Peel to Thomas Chalmers, 24th January, 1835. Peel Papers, British Library Add. Ms. 40411, fol. 200. Quoted in Brown, S.J., Chap, 5, note 89.
[32] The pamphlet referred to here is almost certainly one entitled *A Word More on the Moderatorship,* published in 1837, by 'A Bystander'. In the library catalogue authorship is ascribed to James Wellwood Moncreiff, 1775-1851- that is Moncreiff's father. But given the fact that we are told that Lord Moncreiff did not deign to respond to Chalmers' attacks, and that his son did so through the medium of a pamphlet, it seems reasonable to ascribe authorship to the son. Cockburn noted in his *Journal* that 'Moncreiff published an excellent [pamphlet] some years ago against Chalmers, when the doctor took his fit over the Moderatorship. Cockburn, H., *Journal,* vol. II, p.71, footnote.
[33] *LMR.,* pp.123-4. As Callum Brown pointed out back in 1997, the common belief that Chalmers was the 'key inspirer and organiser' of the evangelical movement in Scotland was misplaced. According to Brown, Chalmers was 'too much a High Tory to understand or applaud the popular democracy unleashed,' and was 'forced reluctantly to back the policies on which the evangelicals "went out"'. Brown. C.G., *Religion and society in Scotland*

since 1707, 1997, p.27. This conclusion is borne out by the events here described. The role of Lord Moncreiff, and not Chalmers alone, in inspiring the unsuccessful 1833 Veto Act proposal has been totally overlooked by historians.

[34] See, for example, his 88 page pamphlet with the self explanatory title: *On the Evils which the Established Church in Edinburgh has already suffered, and Suffers still, in virtue of the seat letting being in the hands of the magistrates,* 1835.

[35] Black, A., *The Church its own Enemy,* 1835, pp.21-2.

[36] £15,168 and £50,548 respectively

[37] Brown, S.J., *op. cit.,* p.250.

[38] *Ibid.*

[39] *Ibid,* p.256

[40] *Ibid,* pp.256-63

[41] No copies of the manifesto have so far come to light. The substance of it is rehearsed in Chalmers, T., *A Conference with Certain Ministers and Elders of the Church of Scotland on the Subject of the Moderatorship of the General Assembly,* 1837, p.6.

[42] Chalmers, T., *op. cit.,* p.6.

[43] My italics.

[44] Chalmers, T., *op. cit.,* p.10.

[45] Bell, R., *Observations on the Conference of the Rev. Dr Thomas Chalmers, D.D., LLD, FRSE, with certain Ministers and Elders of the Church of Scotland,* 1837, pp.6-7.

[46] See note 30 above.

[47] A Bystander, *A Word More on the Moderatorship,* 1837, *passim.*

[48] *LMR,* p.122

[49] Brown, S.J., *op. cit.,* p.262.

Chapter 5

[1] *LMR,* p.123

[2] Rodger, A., *op. cit.,* p.3

[3] Candlish, Dr Robert S., 1806-73

[4] Quoted in Wilson, W., *Memorials of Principal Candlish,* pp.35-6

[5] *Ibid.,* p.41

[6] The Earl of Kinnoull and the Rev. R. Young against the Presbytery of Auchterarder, 1838. Robertson, C.G., *Auchterarder Report,* 2 vols., 1838

[7] Rev. John Edwards against the Presbytery of Strathbogie, 1839. Session cases 2 D. 258

[8] Acts of the General Assembly, 1842, Act XIX. *The Claim* had been drafted by Alexander Dunlop, an advocate with evangelical convictions, and a professional colleague of the Moncreiffs.

[9] *LMR.,* pp.117-34

[10] *Ibid.,* pp.117-8

[11] Scott, W., *The Heart of Midlothian,* 1924 ed., pp.652-3

[12] *LMR*, p.120
[13] Lord Moncreiff to Thomas Chalmers, 13th April, 1833[?] New College Library CHA 4.258.8. This letter is actually undated as to year, and is recorded in the Library catalogue as [1839] – the square brackets indicating uncertainty as to date. From the content it seems to be much more likely that it refers to the Assemblies of either 1833 or 1834. Professor Stewart Brown, Chalmers' biographer, in correspondence with the author, has suggested 1833 as the more likely of the two, and this is given further credibility by the fact that the 13th April in 1833 was a Saturday, and in 1834 a Sunday. Assuming that there were indeed postal deliveries in Edinburgh on Sundays in the 1830s, if Moncreiff had been writing on a Sunday, he would surely have said 'today or tomorrow'.
[14] Cockburn, H., *Memorials of His Own Time,* vol. 1, p.44
[15] Moncreiff, Sir H.W., *The Free Church Principle,* p.57
[16] Burleigh, J., *A Church History of Scotland,* p.344
[17] Rodger, *op. cit.,* I p.8
[18] Moncreiff, Sir H.W., *op. cit.,* p.45.
[19] Lord Moncreiff to Henry Brougham, 3rd March, 1833. Brougham Papers, 33,269.
[20] Lord Moncreiff to Henry Brougham, 5th March 1833, Brougham Papers, 33,271
[21] Lord Moncreiff to Henry Brougham, 31st May, 1833, Brougham Papers, 33,272x
[22] Robertson, C.G., *Report of the Auchterarder Case,* 1838, vol. 2 p.276
[23] Rodger, A., *op. cit.,* I p.8
[24] Moncreiff, Sir H.W., *The Free Church Principle,* pp.233-4
[25] Jeffrey to Cockburn, 22nd March, 1834. Adv. Ms. 9.1.10. f. 835 at f. 838r. National Library of Scotland. Quoted in Rodger, *op. cit.,* p.9
[26] Jeffrey to Cockburn, 27th March, 1834. *Ibid.,* f. 840r. In Rodger, *op. cit.,* p.9
[27] Rodger, *op. cit.,* p.8.
[28] Cockburn, *op. cit.,* p.61.
[29] List of cases: (* - Moncreiff as counsel; + - Bell as counsel)
    A. Veto Act cases
    Presbytery of Strathbogie (Parish of Marnoch)
    Presbytery of Strathbogie (1839) 2 D. 258
    Presbytery of Strathbogie (1840) 2.D. 585
    Edwards v. Cruikshank (1840) 2 D. 1830* +
    Dewar v. Cruikshank (1842) 4 D. 1446
    Cruikshank v. Gordon (1843) 5 D. 909* +
    Edwards v. Leith (1843) 15 Scottish Jurist

    Presbytery of Auchterarder (Parish of Auchterarder)
    Earl of Kinnoull v. Presbytery of Auchterarder (1838) *Auchterarder Report,* Robertson, C.G., 2 vols. 1838
    Presbytery of Auchterarder v. Earl of Kinnoull (1839) House of Lords, Macl. & Rob. 220

Earl of Kinnoull v. Ferguson (1841) 3 D. 778*
Earl of Kinnoull v. Ferguson (1843) 5 D. 1010+

Presbytery of Garioch (Parish of Culsalmond)
Middleton v. Anderson (1842) 4 D. 957* +
Presbytery of Dunkeld (Parish of Lethendy)
Clark v. Stirling (1839) 1 D. 995+
Clark v. Stirling (1841) 3 D. 722 *
Robertson, C.G., *Lethendy Report,* 1841.

B. Chapels Act case

Presbytery of Irvine, (Parish of Stewarton)
Cuninghame v. Presbytery of Irvine (1843) 5 D. 427. * +
Robertson, C.G. *Stewarton Report,* 1843

[30] Brown, S.J., 'The Ten Years' Conflict', in Brown S.J., and Fry, M., *Scotland in the Age of the Disruption,* p.10
[31] *LMR.,* pp.120-1
[32] *Ibid.,* p.124
[33] Earl of Kinnoull and Rev. R. Young v Presbytery of Auchterarder (1838). Robertson, C.G., *Auchterarder Report.* 2 vols., 1838
[34] Rodger, *op. cit.* p.11
[35] *Ibid.,* p.13
[36] *Auchterarder Report* I p.101
[37] *Ibid.,* p.107
[38] *Ibid.,* pp.385-6
[39] *Ibid.,* II, p.275-6
[40] *Ibid.,* p.282
[41] *Ibid.,* p.291
[42] *Ibid.,* p.353
[43] *Second Auchterarder Case.* Earl of Kinnoull v. Ferguson (1841). Session Cases. 3 D. 778
[44] *Ibid.*
[45] As noted earlier in Chapter 4, note 1, the number of signatories to the Deed of Demission at the time of the Disruption totaled 451, but over a period of time this figure rose to the 474 cited in Moncreiff's *Reminiscences.*
[46] *LMR.,* p.125
[47] Presbytery of Auchterarder v. Earl of Kinnoull (1839) English Reports, House of Lords. Macl. & Rob. 220
[48] 'An Act to restore patrons to their ancient rights of presenting ministers to the churches vacant in that part of Great Britain called Scotland.'

Chapter 6

[1] Clark v. Stirling (1839) 1 D. 955, No 226
[2] Rodger, *op. cit.,* p.23

[3] Clark v. Stirling, p.997
[4] *Ibid.*
[5] Rodger, *op. cit.,* note 176
[6] Clark v. Stirling, p.1022
[7] Clark v. Stirling, (1841) 3 D. No 130. p.722
[8] Machin, G.I.T., 'The Disruption and British Politics', *Scottish Historical Review,* vol.51, No. 151, April 1872, p.26
[9] Drummond, A.L. and Bulloch, J., *op. cit.* p.238
[10] Burleigh, J., *A Church History of Scotland,* p.344
[11] Bain, W.H. *op. cit.,* p.21
[12] Moncreiff, H.W., *A letter to Lord Melbourne...,* Edinburgh, 1840. pp. 144, 146
[13] For a very full explanation of the reasons why government ministers were reluctant to intervene in the growing crisis in the Church of Scotland, See Machin, G.I.T., 'The Disruption and British Politics, 1834-43', *Scottish Historical Review,* vol. 51, no. 131, April 1872, pp.20-51
[14] Lord Moncreiff to Andrew Rutherfurd, 22nd February, 1840. Rutherfurd Papers, MS 9700, No. 223
[15] *Ibid.*
[16] Cockburn, H., *op. cit.* vol. I. p.169
[17] Bain *op. cit.* p.23
[18] Middleton v. Anderson, (1842) 4 D. No 167. pp.957 ff.
[19] *Ibid.,* p.958
[20] *Ibid.*
[21] *Ibid.,* p.973
[22] *Ibid.,* p.1018
[23] Cuninghame and Others v. The Presbytery of Irvine (1843) 5 D. No 96, pp. 427ff.
[24] Rodger, *op, cit.,* p.10
[25] Cuninghame v. The Presbytery of Irvine, p.432
[26] *Ibid.,* p.437
[27] Brown, S.J., 'The Ten Years' Conflict', in Brown, S.J., and Fry, M., *Scotland in the Age of the Disruption,* p.19
[28] *Register of the Acts of the General Assembly,* 1842, CH1/1/90, p.5
[29] *Ibid.,* 1842, p.405
[30] *Ibid.,* 1842, p.410.
[31] *Ibid.*
[32] *LMR.,* p.128
[33] *Ibid.,* p.130
[34] MacLeod, A.D., *A Kirk Disrupted: Charles Cowan, MP, and the Free Church of Scotland,* pp.142-45
[35] Drummond and Bulloch, *op. cit.,* pp.242-3
[36] Moncreiff, H.W., *A Vindication of the Free Church Claim of Right,* 1877, p.vii.
[37] *Ibid.,* p.131. There is still some uncertainty as to the actual number of ministers who seceded. A list published in 1844 gave the figure as 451.

Drummond and Bulloch, *op. cit.,* p.249; Buchanan, R., *Ten Years' Conflict,* ii, pp.588-608
[38] *North British Review,* May, 1846, p.222
[39] *Edinburgh Review,* April, 1849, p.476
[40] Lord Moncreiff to Henry Brougham, 20th June, 1843, Brougham Papers, 33,317
[41] Omond. G.W.T., *op. cit.,* p.153
[42] Moncreiff, J.W. to Gladstone W.E., 24th February and 15th March, 1841. Gladstone Papers, Add. MS. 44357, ff. 279 and 303
[43] Moncreiff, J.W. to Gladstone, W.E., 13th May, 1843. Gladstone Papers, Add. MS. 44360
[44] *Hansard Debates,* HL., 9th May, 1843. Vol. 69, cols. 12-22
[45] Machin, G.I.T., 'The Disruption and British Politics, 1834-43.' *Scottish Historical Review,* LI, No. 151, April 1872, p.21
[46] Melbourne to Dunfermline, 20th April, 1841. *Melbourne Papers,* 416. Quoted in Machin, *op. cit.,* p.28
[47] Hope, J., to Aberdeen, 31st August, 1841, *Aberdeen Papers,* 43205, f. 186
[48] Omond, G.W.T., *op. cit.,* p.153
[49] Moncreiff, J.W., *Edinburgh Review,* April 1849, p.476
[50] Omond, G.W.T., *op. cit.* p.153
[51] Bulloch, A. and Drummond, *The Church in Victorian Scotland,* p.6
[52] Moncreiff, J.W., *Church and State from the Reformation to 1843,* p.108
[53] *LMR.,* p.132
[54] Quoted in Brown, C.G., *Religion and Society in Scotland since 1707,* p.21
[55] Moncreiff, J.W., *Address to the General Council of the University of Glasgow,* p.13
[56] Cockburn, H., *op. cit.* vol. I p.169

Chapter 7

[1] John Grant, Henry Ranken (sometimes given as Rankine), and Robert Hamilton. A fourth, James Cumming, was arrested and charged, but his trial was not proceeded with.
[2] At the time when Britain was at war with Revolutionary France in the 1790's, a number of trials for sedition took place in Scotland. See, for example, Cockburn's accounts of the trial for sedition of Skirving, (1793), and those of Margarot, Sinclair and Gerrald in Cockburn, H., *Examination of the Trials for Sedition which have hitherto occurred in Scotland,* 1888, vol. I, pp.222-92, and vol. II, pp.1- 150. Skirving, for example, was sentenced to transportation for fourteen years.
[3] *Ibid.,* vol. II, p.227
[4] Moncreiff, J.W., *An Address on the extension of the Franchise,* 1866, p.36
[5] For an account of this revival, see Wilson, A., *The Chartist Movement in Scotland,* 1970, Chapter 16: '*1848: a brief awakening.*' Also Fraser, W.H., *Chartism in Scotland,* 2010, Chapter 9.
[6] e.g. Woodward, E.L., *The Age of Reform,* pp.118-9

[7] Wright, L.C., *Scottish Chartism*, pp.5-19
[8] *Ibid.*, p.20
[9] Fraser, W.H., *op. cit.*, p.1
[10] *Ibid*, p.165-6; Wilson, *op. cit.*, pp.236-8.
[11] and also of James Cumming, a shoemaker. The case against Cumming was adjourned until after the conclusion of the trial of Grant, Ranken, and Hamilton, but given the outcome of that trial it was decided not to proceed with the case against Cumming. Cockburn, *op. cit.*, p.244. But according to the *Northern Star* of 28th November, 1848, the decision not to proceed was due to confusion in the Lord Advocate's office over two men with the same name. See Fraser, W.H., *op. cit.* p.166
[12] *Caledonian Mercury*, 9th November 1848; *Northern Star and National Trades Journal*, 18th November, 1848.
[13] As well as the *Aberdeen Journal, Caledonian Mercury, Glasgow Herald,* and *Scotsman* in Scotland, English papers, in the North and in London, also reported the case in varying degrees of detail. See, for example, *The Morning Chronicle, The Morning Post, The Examiner, The Liverpool Mercury, The Freeman's Journal and Daily Commercial Advertiser,* and the *Bradford Observer.*
[14] *Her Majesty's Advocate v. Cumming, Grant, Ranken, and Hamilton,* (1848) Shaw's Justiciary Reports, 1848-52., pp.27-8
[15] The capitals and italics are as in the original. Cockburn, *op. cit.*, p.230
[16] 'Warner's long range' was a device, the brainchild of a Captain Warner in the early 1840s, designed to blow up warships at a distance of up to five miles by using balloons carrying bombs. When Sir Robert Peel was asked in the House of Commons if the government intended to carry out a trial of the system, he demurred, saying that since the discussion of the subject in the previous year 'not a week had elapsed without his receiving letters from individuals offering to blow up ships on much more favourable terms than those proposed by Captain Warner.' [Reported in the *Morning Chronicle* of 20th March, 1845]. In the end a trial *was* conducted, presumably without using actual explosives, on Cannock Chase. It was a complete failure. [See *Freeman's Journal and Daily Commercial Advertiser*, 29th April, 1847] As the story of the 'long range' was widely reported in the national and regional press in the spring of 1847, it is fair to assume that the Chartist leaders were aware of that failure before they referred to the device at their rally in 1848. That fact may raise a query about the seriousness of the threat contained in this speech.
[17] Cockburn, *op. cit.*, pp.231-3
[18] Bain, W. H., *op. cit.*, p.210.
[19] *LMR*, p.146
[20] *Hansard Debates*, 3rd Series, H.C., vol. 128, 212, 14th June, 1853
[21] *LMR.,* p.147
[22] Cockburn, *op. cit.*, p.242
[23] Ibid., pp.242-3
[24] *Caledonian Mercury,* 20th November, 1848

[25] The prosecution should have been led by the Lord Advocate, Andrew Rutherfurd, but he was too ill to attend, so Craufurd took his place.
[26] Cockburn, *op. cit.*, p.234
[27] *Ibid.*, p.235
[28] *Justiciary Reports.*, p.51
[29] *Ibid*, p.53
[30] *Caledonian Mercury,* 16th November, 1848, *Glasgow Herald,* 17th November, 1848.
[31] *Morning Chronicle,* 16th November, 1848.
[32] Cockburn, *op. cit.*, p.237
[33] *Ibid*, p.238. The italics are in the original
[34] *Justiciary Reports.*, p.64
[35] Cockburn, *op. cit.*, p.239
[36] Cockburn, *op. cit.*, p.241
[37] *Justiciary Reports,* p.123
[38] Cockburn, *op. cit.*, p.237
[39] Wilson, A., *op. cit.,* p.240; Cockburn, H., *Trials for Sedition,* vol. ii, pp.226-43; Cockburn, H., *Journal,* vol. ii, pp.235-7
[40] *Justiciary Reports.*, p.123
[41] Wilson, A., *op. cit.*, P.221
[42] *LMR.*, p.148

Chapter 8

[1] Tullibole Collection, Box 21, TD77/34 at p.49
[2] Moncreiff held the office of Lord Advocate from April 1851 to May 1852; November 1852 to February 1858; from June 1859 to June 1866; and from January to October, 1869.
[3] Devine, T.M., *The Scottish Nation, 1700-2007,* p.281
[4] *LMR,* pp.110-11
[5] *Ibid.*
[6] *Ibid.,* p.112
[7] *LMR,* pp.111-2
[8] *Hansard,* 3rd Ser., H.C., vol. CLXXXVI, Col. 397
[9] In Hanham, H.J., 'The Creation of the Scottish Office, 1881-7', *Juridical Review,* 1965, p.238
[10] The office of Secretary of State for Scotland was created in 1885 by 48 & 49 Vict. c.61. According to J. Cairns, the Act reduced the responsibilities of the Lord Advocate to legal affairs only, but this change evidently did not take immediate effect. See Cairns, J., 'The Faculty of Advocates', in Smith, T.B., and Black, R., *The Laws of Scotland: Stair Memorial Encyclopaedia,* vol. 13, 1995
[11] Omond, *op. cit.,* p.157
[12] *Dundee Courier,* 11th April, 1851
[13] Omond, *op. cit.,* p.156
[14] *Glasgow Herald,* 11th April, 1851

[15] Omond, *op. cit.,* p.157
[16] *Glasgow Herald,* 11th April, 1851
[17] Moncreiff, J.W., *A Visit to My Discontented Cousin,* pp.164-6
[18] 'Lord Moncreiff', *Scottish Law Review,* June, 1895, p.160
[19] *Glasgow Herald,* 11th April, 1851
[20] *Hansard Parliamentary Debates,* 3rd Series, HC, [116] 1014, 15th May, 1851
[21] Omond, *op. cit.,* p.160
[22] *LMR,* p.196
[23] *Hansard, Parliamentary Debates,* 3rd Series, HC, 28th April, 1856, [141] 1684
[24] 'Lord Moncreiff', *Scottish Law Review,* June, 1895, p.162
[25] *LMR,* p.195
[26] *Hansard Parliamentary Debates,* H.C. 3rd Series, 1st March, 1860 [156] 2085-95,
[27] Ferguson, W., 'The Reform Act (Scotland): intention and effects, *SHR,* 45 (1965), pp.105-116
[28] Hutchison, I.C.G., *op. cit.,* pp.3-4
[29] *Scotsman,* 12th February 1880.
[30] Lord Advocate's Papers, GD224/133/11. William Anderson to G.H. Garrie, 30th August, 1879
[31] *Scotsman,* 5th and 11th October, 1870
[32] *Hansard Parliamentary Debates,* H.C., 3rd Series, 7th June, 1860 [159] 72-6
[33] *Ibid*
[34] Moncreiff, J.W., 'Secret Voting and Parliamentary Reform', *Edinburgh Review,* July, 1860, pp.266-75
[35] Moncreiff, J.W., *Extension of the Suffrage – An Address to the Electors of Edinburgh,* 10th December, 1866, pp. 10-15
[36] Moncreiff, J.W., *Ibid,* 1866, *passim*
[37] Biagini, E.F., *Liberty, Retrenchment and Reform,* p.268
[38] *Weekly News,* 11th March, 1866, quoted in Biagini, *op. cit.,* p.268
[39] Omond, *op. cit.,* p.165
[40] *Caledonian Mercury* 12th May, 1851
[41] McLaren's evidence before the Select Committee on the Edinburgh Annuity Tax, (1851), p.286
[42] In an editorial on the 1856 election, Alexander Russell had described McLaren as a snake, and accused him of being a member of an 'unholy alliance' in support of one candidate. Quoted in Bain, *op. cit.,* p.197
[43] Mackie, J.B., *The Life and Works of Duncan McLaren,* 1888, 2 vols., i. p.161
[44] In his biography of McLaren, Willis Pickard points out that even so, the £400 was four times what McLaren had been prepared to settle for privately. Pickard, W., *The Member for Scotland – The Life of Duncan McLaren,* p.141
[45] *Hansard, Parl. Deb.,* 3rd Series, HC, [129] 457, 461, 19th July, 1853
[46] 23 & 24 Vict. c.50, An Act to Abolish the Annuity Tax in Edinburgh and Montrose, and to make provision in regard to the stipends of the Ministers of that City and Burgh…..
[47] Omond, *op. cit.,* p.235

[48] Mackie, J.B., *op. cit.*, i. p.199,
[49] Pickard, W., *op. cit.*, p.183
[50] 33 & 34 Vict. c.87. And Act to amend the Annuity Abolition Act (1860)
[51] Quoted in Pickard, W., *op. cit.*, p.174
[52] Quoted in 'Lord Moncreiff', *Scottish Law Review*, June, 1895, p.159
[53] Quoted in Omond, *op. cit.*, p.215. The comment actually referred to one of Moncreiff's predecessors in the office, Charles Hope, arriving back home after defending himself in the House of Commons against a vote of censure for having acted in a manner 'oppressive, illegal and contrary to his professional duties.'
[54] Devine, T.M.,
[55] AD56/49
[56] AD56/57
[57] AD56/337
[58] AD56/218
[59] AD56/4
[60] AD58/24
[61] AD56/112
[62] AD58/129
[63] AD56/246
[64] AD56/247
[65] CR10/231, 232
[66] CR11/60, 61, 75, 283, 284, 285
[67] HO45/6069
[68] HO45/4791
[69] HO45/7773
[70] HO45/3135
[71] *Scottish Law Review*, p.167
[72] Moncreiff to Fox Maule, 21st June, 1851. Lord Advocate's Papers, GD45/14/685
[73] Moncreiff to Rutherfurd, 9th January, 1853. Rutherfurd Papers, f.297
[74] *LMR*, p.189
[75] 'Lord Moncreiff', in *Scottish Law Review*, June 1895, p.163
[76] See for example the paper's somewhat sour comment in April 1880, declaring that Moncreiff's 'long and tiresome domination over Scotch business is not remembered with universal gratitude, even by Liberals.' *Glasgow Herald*, 10th April, 1880
[77] *Glasgow Herald*, 18th May, 1880
[78] William Wellwood Stoddart to James Moncreiff, 7th March, 1856. Lord Advocate's Papers, AD56/49. No ref. number.
[79] Stewart Munro to George Traill, 18th Feb., 1856. George Traill to Lord Advocate, 25th Feb., 1856. Lord Advocate's Papers, AD56/49, No. 325
[80] Moncreiff, J.W. to H. Waddington, 2nd April, 1862. Lord Advocate's Papers, AD56/247

[81] Memorial of the Commissioners of Police of Thurso, 16th May, 1862. Minutes of meeting of Police Commissioners of Caithness, 30th June, 1863. Ibid

[82] Sir Dingwall Fordyce, Sheriff of Caithness, to Lord Advocate, 15th July, 1863. Ibid

[83] M. McLennan, Procurator Fiscal of Caithness, to Chief Constable, Alex Mitchell, 18th July, 1863. Ibid

[84] Chief Constable Mitchell to Sheriff Sir Dingwall Fordyce, 6th August, 1863. Ibid

[85] Sheriff Sir Dingwall Fordyce to Chief Constable Mitchell, 11th August, 1863. Ibid. This was not the only occasion during Moncreiff's term of office when war broke out between a Chief Constable and his Sheriff. In 1867 a similar dispute as to which of them was in overall charge of policing surfaced in Roxburgh over the issue of salmon poaching on the Tweed. AD56/248, *passim.*

[86] An Act to make more effectual provision for regulating the Police in Towns and Populous places in Scotland....25 & 26 Vict. c.101

[87] Lord Advocate to H.A. Bruce, MP, 7th January, 1864. AD56/248

[88] Omond, *op. cit.,* p.232

[89] Watt, J.C., *John Inglis,* p.146

[90] Cockburn, H., *Journal,* II. P.310

[91] *Ibid.,* p.232

[92] *Hansard Parliamentary Debates,* 3rd Series, HC [175] 1188, 3rd June 1864

[93] Watt, J.C., *op. cit.,* p.147

[94] Hamilton, G.A. to Lord Advocate, 20th July, 1859, Lord Advocate's Papers, AD56/31 No.875, and 30th April, 1867, No.8001

[95] The collection was published in 1846, but evidently written some years earlier. See Bain, W.H., *op. cit.,* p.239

[96] Omond, *op. cit.,* p.156

[97] *Ibid.*

[98] Moncreiff, J.W., 'Life of Lord Chancellor Eldon', *North British Review,* November, 1844, vol. 2, p.227

[99] Moncreiff, J.W., 'Earl Russell's Speeches', *Edinburgh Review,* April 1870, vol. 131, p.570

[100] Moncreiff, J.W., *The Relation of Recent Scientific Inquiries to the Received Teaching of Scripture,* 1867, p.10

[101] *Ibid,* p.10

[102] Moncreiff, J.W., *A Visit to my Discontented Cousin* p.177

[103] Omond, *op. cit.,* p.231

[104] Moncreiff, J.W., *A Visit....,* pp.38-9

[105] *Ibid.* pp.246-7

[106] *Ibid.,* pp.241-3

[107] *Hansard,* 3rd Series, HC, [175] 1188 3rd January, 1864

Chapter 9

[1] For a useful summary of this debate, See Devine, T.M., *The Scottish Nation, 1700-2007,* pp.285-6
[2] Colley, L., *Britons: Forging the Nation,* pp.128-9
[3] Morton, G., *Unionist-Nationalism,* pp.14-15
[4] Hanham, H.J., 'Mid-Century Scottish Nationalism', in Robson, R., *Ideas and Institutions in Victorian Britain,* 1967, p.151
[5] Begg, J., *A Violation of the Treaty of Union the Main Origin of our Ecclesiastical Divisions and other Evils,* 1874, p.4
[6] Smith, T., *Memoirs of James Begg, DD,* 1888, vol.II, pp.148-50
[7] Quoted in Hanham, H.J., *op. cit.,* p.157
[8] Eglinton has often been dismissed by historians as merely an eccentric, but for a more positive view, see, Tyrrell, A., 'The Earl of Eglinton, Scottish Conservatism, and the National Association for the Vindication of Scottish Rights', *Hist. J.,* Vol. 53, issue 01, March 2010, pp.87-107
[9] Hanham, H.J., *op. cit.,* p.160
[10] Mackie, J.B., *The Life and Work of Duncan McLaren,* 1888, p.122
[11] Pickard, W., *The Member for Scotland – The Life of Duncan McLaren,* p.127
[12] Quoted in Omond, *op. cit.,* p.185-6
[13] Hanham, H.J., *op. cit.,* p.166
[14] Tyrrell, A., *op. cit.,* p.100
[15] Moncreiff, H.W., *Scottish Rights and Grievances: Reasons for Declining to join the National Association for the Vindication of Scottish Rights,* 1854
[16] Cockburn, H., *Journal,* II, pp.300-1
[17] Fry M., 'The Whig Interpretation of Scottish History', in Donnachie, I. and Whatley, C.A., *The Manufacture of Scottish History,* p.80
[18] Cockburn, H., *Journal,* 11th April, 1854, pp.308-11
[19] *Hansard Parl. Deb.,* 3rd Series, HC. [150] 2118, 15th June, 1858.
[20] Watt, J.C., *John Inglis.,* p.170
[21] *Hansard Parl. Deb.,* 3rd Series, HC, [175] 1170 3rd June, 1864
[22] *Ibid.*
[23] *Hansard, Parl. Deb.,* 3rd Series, HC, [175] 1180, 3rd June, 1864
[24] This claim has been regularly repeated both by Moncreiff himself and subsequent commentators, but is certainly an exaggeration. A comparison between Moncreiff's speeches in the House proposing or supporting Parliamentary bills, and the actual record of laws passed during his term of office, though only an approximation, falls far short of the figure of one hundred.
[25] *Hansard, Parliamentary Debates,* 3rd Series, HC, [175] 3rd June, 1864
[26] *Glasgow Herald,* 3rd February, 1881
[27] *Dundee Courier and Argus,* 17th January, 1884
[28] 48 & 49 Vict. c.61
[29] Quoted in Hanham, H.J., 'The Creation of the Scottish Office, 1881 – 87', *op. cit.,* p.229
[30] *LMR,* p.190

[31] Hanham, H.J., *Scottish Nationalism*, pp.34-5
[32] Anon., *History of the Speculative Society*, 1968, p,21
[33] 'Scoto-English Law Commissions and Law Assimilations – Mercantile Law Reform.' *Law Magazine*, vol. 50, Aug.-Nov. 1853, p.320
[34] Hutchison, I.G.C., *A Political History of Scotland, 1832-1924*, p.93
[35] *Report of a Committee appointed at a preliminary meeting to consider and report on the proper Constitution of a Law Amendment Society in Glasgow, in connection with the London Society for promoting the amendment of the Law.* 1851. In *Law Review and Quarterly Journal of British and Foreign Jurisprudence*, November, 1851- February, 1852, p.204
[36] Hutchison, I.G.C., *op. cit.*, pp.93-4
[37] Rodger, A., 'The Codification of Commercial Law in Victorian Britain', *Law Quarterly Rev.*, 1992, vol. 108, p.571
[38] *Report of the Committee of the Law Amendment Society of Glasgow*, pp.5-7
[39] *Ibid.*, pp.8-10
[40] Moncreiff, J.W., 'Politics', *North British Review*, 1845, in Moncreiff, J., *Criticisms and Essays*, n.d., vol. 1, Tullibole Collection, p.288
[41] Kidd, C., *Subverting Scotland's Past*, 1993, pp.144-5
[42] Moncreiff, J.W., *Address on Legal Education,*, 1870, p.1 Alan Rodger rather unkindly questioned whether Moncreiff, who did not know German, actually meant what he said when he recommended that Scottish Law Students should learn the language. 'But the fact that he felt it appropriate to make the point in a public address to young law students is significant.' Rodger, A., 'Scottish Advocates in the Nineteenth Century: the German Connection', *Law Quarterly Review*, 1994 (Oct.) vol.110. pp.563-91, footnote 106
[43] *Address on Legal Education*, p.15
[44] Moncreiff, J.W., *The Education of a Lawyer*, 1867, p.10
[45] *Ibid.*, p.19
[46] Moncreiff to Andrew Rutherfurd, 23rd February, 1853. Rutherfurd Papers, f.321. We have already seen how Rutherfurd was consulted by Moncreiff's father over the Aberdeen government's attitude to the Veto Act. Both father and son had the highest opinion of Rutherfurd, whom James Moncreiff junior once described as 'the greatest public officer we have had in Scotland since Dundas.' Moncreiff's Notebook, Tullibole Papers, Box 21. TD77/34, p.23
[47] *The Scotsman*, 3rd September, 1853
[48] *Law Magazine, op. cit.*, pp.319-27
[49] *Education of a Lawyer*, p.20
[50] *Ibid.*, p.21
[51] On the operation of the Judicial Committee of the Privy Council as an appellate court for colonial appeals, see, Swinfen, D.B., *Imperial Appeal: The Debate on the Appellate Jurisdiction of the Judicial Committee of the Privy Council*, 1984, *passim*.
[52] *Duncan v. Findlater*, [1839] 6 Cl. Fin. 894, ER [7] 824

[53] 31 & 32 Vict. c.100
[54] 13 and 14 Vict. c.36 s.14. 'Be it enacted that it shall not be competent to the Lord Ordinary to direct Cases or Minutes of Debate or other written Argument to be prepared by the parties...'
[55] Watt, J.C., *John Inglis*, pp.243-5
[56] Moncreiff, J.W., *Address on Law Reform and the Bankruptcy Laws*, p.5
[57] *Scottish Law Review*, June, 1895, p.160
[58] *Hansard, Parliamentary Debates*, HC, 3rd Series, 2nd March, 1865
[59] *Ibid.*, 3rd June, 1862, [167] 291
[60] *Ibid.*, 1st March, 1860, [156] 2085-95
[61] *Scottish Law Review, op, cit.*, p.161
[62] Walker, S.P., *The Society of Accountants in Edinburgh, 1854-1914*, 1988, p.32
[63] Walker, S.P., and Lee, T.A., *Studies in Early Professionalism – Scottish Chartered Accountants*, 1999, pp.93-4
[64] Hanham, H.J., 'Mid-Century Scottish Nationalism', in Robson, R., (ed.) *Ideas and Institutions in Victorian Britain,* 1967, p.159, note 1
[65] Quoted in Walker and Lee, *op. cit.*, p.96
[66] *Hansard*, HC 3rd Series, 10th March 1854, p.588
[67] Walker and Lee, *op. cit.*, p.99
[68] *Hansard*, 3rd Series, HC, 1856, v.141, cc.22-3
[69] Moncreiff, J.W., *Address on Law Reform and the Bankruptcy Laws*, 1865, pp.6-7
[70] 20 & 21 Vict. c. 19
[71] Bankruptcy Act 1913, 3 & 4, Geo. V, c.20
[72] *Hansard*, 3rd Series, HC, 5th April, 1869, cols. 142-172. The debate resulted in the Bankruptcy Act, 32 & 33 Vict. c.71

Chapter 10

[1] Hutchison, *op. cit.*, p.62
[2] Cockburn, H., *Journal*, II, pp.284
[3] *Proceedings of the General Assembly of the Free Church of Scotland*, May, 1843, p.146; Quoted in Withrington, D.J., 'Adrift among the Reefs of Conflicting Ideals – Education and the Free Church, 1843-55', in Brown S.J., and Fry, M., *Scotland in the Age of the Disruption*, p.82,
[4] Withrington, D.J., *op. cit.*, pp.82-4
[5] Myers, J.D., 'Scottish Nationalism and the Antecedents of the 1872 Education Act', *Scottish Educational Studies*, iv, 1972, 73-92
[6] *Hansard Debates*, 3rd Series, [117] 420, 4th June, 1851
[7] Withrington, D.J., 'The Free Church Educational Scheme, 1843-50', *Scottish Church History Society Records*, 15, pp.103-15
[8] Cited in Kay-Shuttleworth, *Public Education as Affected by the Minutes of the Privy Council from 1846 to 1852* (1853), p.388
[9] Anderson, R.D., *Education and the Scottish People, 1750-1918*, p.50

[10] 20 & 21 Vict. C.59 – An Act Concerning the Parochial Schoolmasters in Scotland. See also note 39 below
[11] 24 & 25 Vict. c. 107
[12] Bain, *op. cit.,* chapter 4, note 2
[13] Quoted in Bain, *op. cit.,* p.51
[14] *Hansard Debates,* 3rd Series, [112], 77-8, 19th June, 1850.
[15] *Ibid,* 1851. See Bain, W.H., "Attacking the Citadel", James Moncreiff's Proposals to Reform Scottish Education, 1851-69. *Scottish Educational Review,* 1978-80, p.5
[16] Moncreiff, J.W., *An Educational Retrospect,* 1886, p.8
[17] Moncreiff, J.W. to Lord John Russell, 4th July, 1853, Aberdeen Papers, Add. MS 4301. 'As to the Tests', Moncreiff wrote, 'I send you what I think an admirable article from the Scotsman, a paper not much given to the Confession of Faith, ratifying my treaty on the subject in the strongest terms. This may be fairly taken as an index of the feeling of the Whig party in Scotland.'
[18] Myers, J.D., "Scottish Nationalism and the Antecedents of the 1872 Education Act", *Scottish Educational Studies,* Vol. 4, No 2 (Nov. 1972), p.78.
[19] Geo III. c. 54, cl. 6
[20] Bain, W.H., *Life and Achievements of James Moncreiff,* p.53
[21] *Declaration by Justices of the Peace, Commissioners of Supply, and Heritors,* Lord Advocate's Papers, National Archives of Scotland, AD/56/47/1
[22] *Hansard Debates,* 3rd Series, [130] 1161-2, 23rd February, 1854
[23] Johnstone, J., *A letter to the Lord Advocate on the Education Bill,* (1855) p.10
[24] Maule, F., to Rutherfurd, A., 27th February, 1854, Rutherfurd MSS, MS 9699, ff. 167-8, Quoted in Hutchison, I.C.G., *op. cit.,* p.76
[25] Pickard, W., *The Member for Scotland – The Life of Duncan McLaren,* pp.124-5
[26] Clauses 1-6 and clause 8 of both the 1854 and 1855 Bills
[27] Colquhoun, J.C., *A Letter on the Scotch Education Bill,* (1854) p.9
[28] Quoted in Bain, *op. cit.,* p.62
[29] *Hansard Debates,* 3rd Series, [137] 1005, 23rd March, 1855
[30] *Eighteen Reasons for rejecting the Lord Advocate's Bill,* 1855, p.2 . Quoted in Bain, *Life and Achievements...*p.65
[31] *Hansard Debates,* 3rd Series, [130] 1162, 23rd February, 1854
[32] Bain, *op. cit.,* p.60
[33] *Hansard Debates,* 3rd Series, [133] 293, 12th May 1854
[34] Sellar, A.C., and Maxwell, C.F., *Report on Lowland Parishes,* pp. XXXIII-IV
[35] *Hansard Debates,* 3rd Series, [137] 1914, 27th April, 1855.
[36] Pickard, W., *The Member for Scotland – The Life of Duncan McLaren,* p.125
[37] Moncreiff J.W., *Memorandum,* 22nd February, 1855, Lord Advocate's Papers, AD/56/47/2
[38] *Ibid.*
[39] *Hansard, Debates,* 3rd Series, HL, [139] 1046, 19th July,1855
[40] Moncreiff, J.W., *An Educational Retrospect,* p.9

[41] 20 & 21 Vict. C. 59 - An Act Concerning Parochial Schoolmasters in Scotland. By once again tying salaries to the average price of oatmeal, the Act did nothing to address the problem caused by the fall in this price since the last assessment in 1828. Its primary purpose was to solve a quite different problem - that created by the failure to carry out a new assessment in 1853 – twenty-five years after the last one – as required by the 1803 Act, 43 G. III c. 54. It therefore instructed Sheriffs and Stewards to carry out a new assessment of average oatmeal prices, which would be the basis for salaries from Martinmas 1859. This left the period 1857-59 unprovided for, so the solution was to continue on the basis of the 1828 figures until the new assessment came into force.

[42] *Presbytery of Elgin v. Town Council of Elgin*, 16th January, 1861, 23 D. 287

[43] *Memorial from the Town Council of Glasgow*, 3rd April, 1861, Lord Advocate's Papers, AD/56/47/2.

[44] *Memorial from Nairn Burgh Council*, March 1861, Ibid

[45] Moncreiff, J.W., *Memorandum to Cabinet*, Ibid

[46] 24 & 25 Vict. c.107. Bain has described the Act as 'perhaps James Moncreiff's most significant contribution to Scottish education.' Bain, W.H., *op. cit.*, p.108

[47] Drummond, A.L., and Bulloch, J., *The Church in Victorian Scotland, 1843-1874*, p.97

[48] Moncreiff, J.W., *An Educational Retrospect*, p.12

[49] *Hansard Debates*, 3rd Series, [164] 195, 2nd July, 1861

[50] Moncreiff, J.W., *An Educational Retrospect*, p.12

[51] Anderson, R.D., *Education and Society in Mid-Victorian Scotland*, pp.105-6. Argyll Commission, 2nd Report, pp. clxxiii ff.

[52] *Hansard Debates*, 3rd Series, [188] 344, 21st June, 1867

[53] *The Watchword*, No. 32, November, 1868. Quoted in Withrington, D.J., 'Towards a National System, 1867-72: The Last Years in the Struggle for a Scottish Education Act', in *Scottish Educational Studies*, iv., p.114

[54] *Ibid.*, pp.109-113

[55] *Hansard*, 3rd Series, [188] 344, 21st June, 1867

[56] Education (Scotland) Act, 35 & 36 Vict. c. 62

[57] Withrington, D.J., *op. cit.*, p.120

[58] Gladstone, W.E., to Moncreiff, 31st August, 1869. Tullibole Papers, Box 21, Envelope 1

[59] Moncreiff, J.W., *An Educational Retrospect*, pp.14-5

[60] Colebrook Commission, *Third Report*, p.191.

[61] Moncreiff Commission, *Special Report*, p.vii

[62] Anderson, R.D., *op. cit.*, p.64

[63] *Edinburgh Review*, January 1858, vol. 197, pp.90-1

[64] Anderson, *op. cit.*, p.64. To be accurate, the innovation was the work of a committee chaired by the President of the Board of Control, Charles Wood (later Lord Halifax). Macaulay wrote the committee's Report

[65] *Hansard Debates*, lxxx, (1845), cols 11-23, and lxxxii (1845) cols. 227-79

[66] *Macphail's Edinburgh Ecclesiastical Journal and Literary Review,* xi. (1851) p.326. Quoted in Withrington, D.J., 'Adrift among the Reefs of Conflicting Ideals? Education and the Free Church, 1843-55', in Brown S.J., and Fry. M., *Scotland in the Age of the Disruption,* p.89

[67] *Ibid.,* pp.87-9

[68] Watt, ,J.C., *John Inglis,* p.176

[69] Bain, *Life and Achievements…,* p.164

[70] Watt J.C., *op. cit.,* p.176

[71] *Hansard Debates,* 3rd Series, [120] 1235, 28th April, 1852

[72] This situation persisted until 1858, when by an amendment to a Bill introduced by John Inglis, the theological chairs and the Principalship were opened to members of all churches. In the following year Sir David Brewster, whom the Presbytery of St Andrews had tried to oust in 1843, was appointed to the Principalship of Edinburgh. Grant, A, *The Story of the University of Edinburgh,* vol. 2, p.96

[73] Omond, G.W.T., *op. cit.,* p.172

[74] *Acts of the General Assembly,* 10th August, 1853

[75] Omond, *op. cit.,* p.172

[76] Moncreiff, J.W., *Address on Installation as Lord Rector of the University of Edinburgh,* (1869) p.20

[77] Anderson, *op. cit.,* pp.65-6

[78] Grant, A., *op. cit.,* vol. 2, p.90

[79] Moncreiff, J.W., *Address…* p.31

[80] In an open letter to the electors of Aberdeen and Glasgow Universities on 8th July, 1868, Moncreiff was at pains to point out how his university reforms had led to higher salaries for academic staff. Tullibole Papers, Box 21, no.6

[81] *Ibid.,* p.20

Chapter 11

[82] Perhaps surprisingly, Moncreiff was not involved in the prosecution of Edward William Pritchard, accused and convicted of poisoning his wife and mother-in-law in 1865. The prosecution was led by the Solicitor-General for Scotland, George Young, later appointed to succeed Moncreiff as Lord Advocate in October, 1869.

[83] An online search of 19th century newspapers results in 169 items on the Madeleine Smith trial, between the 2nd and 20th July, 1857, from over 40 different newspapers. Of course there was a good deal of 'borrowing' of news between papers.

[84] 'I believe,' wrote James Pagan of the *Glasgow Herald,* in a letter to the Advocate's Department, 'I am not mistaken in assuming that portions of the letters are of an indelicate character. These, of course, we could not for our own sakes publish under any circumstances, but as the letters must be frequently referred to in the course of the trial, a copy, if it can be had at all, is most essential to the correct and very extended report of the proceedings which we contemplate.' Crown counsel declined the request.

J. Pagan to D. Mackenzie, 25th June, 1857. Advocate's Department papers, AD 14/57/255/10, no. 117

[85] Campbell, J.P., *A Scottish Murder; Rewriting the Madeleine Smith Story*, 2007, pp.211-16

[86] Procurator Fiscal of Dundee to D. Mackenzie, Advocate's Department, 28th June, 1857. Advocate's Department papers, AD14/57/255/10, no. 125

[87] Omond, G.T.W., *op. cit.*, p.193

[88] MacGowan, D., *The Strange Affair of Madeleine Smith*, 2007, p.112

[89] Jesse, F.T., (ed.), *Trial of Madeleine Smith*, Notable British Trials, 1949, pp.30-3

[90] Watt., J.C., *John Inglis*, 1893, p.85

[91] Hunt, P., *The Madeleine Smith Affair*, 1950, p.147

[92] Jesse, F.T., *op. cit.*, pp.190-91

[93] *Ibid.*, p.204

[94] Stevenson, M., *Madeleine Smith and the Theatre of Ambiguity*, unpublished M.Litt. thesis, University of Dundee, 2005

[95] Bain, W.H, *op. cit.*, pp.208-9

[96] Blyth, H., *Madeleine Smith*, p.142

[97] Jesse, F. T., *op. cit.*, p.179

[98] Omond, *op. cit.*, p.197

[99] Watt, J.C., *op. cit.*, p.86

[100] Moncreiff, J.W., *Legal Education – an Address*, 1870, p.6

[101] 'Lord Moncreiff', in *Scottish Law Review*, vol. XL, No. 126, June 1895, p.166. As in the Madeleine Smith trial, Moncreiff as prosecutor was pitted against John Inglis, Dean of the Faculty, for the defence. For a contemporary account of the Wielobycki trial, see the *Caledonian Mercury*, 9th, 10th, 12th, and 15th January, 1857

[102] Watt, J.C., *op. cit.*, p.87

[103] *Glasgow Herald*, 20th July, 1857

[104] Hunt, P., *op. cit.*, p.152

[105] Jesse, F.T., *op. cit.*, p.41-3

[106] *Ibid*, p.188

[107] *Ibid.*, pp.99-101; MacGowan, *op. cit.*, p.79-81

[108] Jesse, F.T., pp.103-4

[109] Quoted in MacGowan, D., *op. cit.*, p.94,

[110] Hunt,, *op. cit.*, p.110

[111] *Ibid.*, p.151

[112] Jesse, F.T., *op. cit.*, p.237

[113] *Ibid.*, p.260

[114] *Ibid.*, p.258

[115] Gerald Massey to Lord Advocate, n.d. Advocate's Department papers, AD14/57.225/10, no. 134

[116] *Aberdeen Journal*, 15th July, 1857

[117] According to the same edition of the *Aberdeen Journal*, 'after deliberation, there were five for a verdict of guilty; and ten for one of not proven. On the

question of an absolute acquittal, there was no diversity of sentiment whatever.'
[118] Walker, D.M., *A Legal History of Scotland,* vol. V1, *The Nineteenth Century,* pp.482-3
[119] Messrs. Ranken, Walker, and Johnston to Lord Advocate, 7th August, 1857. Advocate's Department papers, AD14/57/255/10, no. 4
[120] Quoted in Hunt, *op. cit.*, p.187
[121] *LMR.,* pp.84-5

Chapter 12

[1] Longworth was converted to Catholicism while a student at an Ursuline convent in France. Erickson, A., and McCarthy, Fr. J.R., *The Yelverton Case: Civil Legislation and Marriage,* Victorian Studies 14, March 1971, p.276 note 1
[2] *Caledonian Mercury,* 25th February, 1861.
[3] Erickson and McCarthy, *op. cit.*, p.275
[4] Longworth to Vicountess Avonmore, 20th June n.d. Yelverton Papers. National Archives of Scotland, CS46/1867/8/73
[5] See for example Yelverton's claims in the Court of Session case in 1862, when he denied that there had ever been an agreement to marry with Longworth. *Yelverton v. Longworth,* Court of Session cases, Macpherson I, 1862-3, p.161, No. 33.
[6] Longworth to Viscountess Avonmore 20th June, n.d. Yelverton Papers
[7] In all contemporary accounts, Mooney is referred to as 'Mr.', rather than 'Father', as might have been expected of a Catholic priest.
[8] Erickson and McCarthy, op. cit., p.277. The original of this document is preserved in the National Archives of Scotland. Yelverton Papers
[9] Longworth to Vicountess Avonmore, Yelverton Papers
[10] For example, the report in the *Liverpool Mercury,* 23rd February, 1861
[11] *Bradford Observer,* 28th February, 1861
[12] *Derby Mercury,* 27th February, 1861
[13] Crow, D., *Theresa – the Story of the Yelverton Case,* 1966, pp.171-2
[14] Erickson and McCarthy, op. cit., p.277
[15] Probably Yelverton's brother Frederick
[16] Yelverton Papers.
[17] Longworth, M. T., *Martyrs to Circumstance,* 1861, pp.175-7. Longworth published the book under the name of the Hon. Mrs. Yelverton.
[18] *Morning Post,* 11th March, 1858
[19] See, for example, Gill, R., *The Imperial Anxieties of a Nineteenth Century Bigamy Case,* History Workshop Journal, 57 (2004), pp.57-78, which describes *Thelwell* [sic] *v. Yelverton* as a case of bigamy. It was of course nothing of the kind, and in none of the succeeding cases was Yelverton ever tried on a charge of bigamy. We have seen that the Scottish authorities, who initially arrested him for bigamy, were obliged to drop the charge for lack of evidence. No doubt if the House of Lords had decided

that Theresa's marriage was valid, which it did not, then Yelverton would have been open to prosecution on such a charge.

[20] James Whiteside, M.P. Whiteside was also one of Longworth's legal counsel in Ireland

[21] *Hansard Parliamentary Debates,* 14 May, 1861, vol. 162, Third Ser. Col. 2,062

[22] *Law Times Reports,* Vol. I, New Series (1860) pp.194-7

[23] *Belfast Newsletter,* 14th June, 1860

[24] In addition to the extensive newspaper reports of the *Thelwall v. Yelverton* case, a full contemporary account was published by George Vickers, a London publisher: Anon, *The Yelverton Marriage Case, Thelwall v. Yelverton, Comprising an Authentic and Unabridged Account of the Most Extraordinary Trial of Modern Times, with all its Revelations, Incidents, and Details Specially Reported,* London, 1861

[25] Quoted in Crow, *op. cit.,* p.15

[26] *Ibid.,* p.238

[27] *Ibid.,* p.241

[28] *Caledonian Mercury,* 20th December 1862. There was much more in the same vein.

[29] *Yelverton v. Longworth or Yelverton,* Session Cases, Macpherson I, 1862-3, No. 33, 19th December, 1862, p.161

[30] *Morning Chronicle,* 20th December, 1862

[31] *Yelverton v. Longworth,* p.162

[32] 2 & 3 Geo. VI c.34. Section 5 enacted that 'No irregular marriage by declaration *de praesenti* or by promise *subsequente copula* contracted after the commencement of this Act shall be valid.'

[33] Quoted in *Yelverton v. Longworth,* p.164

[34] *Ibid.*

[35] *Ibid.,* pp.168-9

[36] *Ibid.,* p.174

[37] *Caledonian Mercury,* 24th December, 1862

[38] Reprinted in the *Glasgow Herald,* 23rd December, 1862, and the *Dundee Courier and Argus,* 24th December, 1862

[39] *Yelverton v. Longworth.* House of Lords Appeal Cases. Macqueen IV, June 1864, pp.829-30

[40] *Ibid,* pp.834-5

[41] Quoted in Crow, *op. cit.,* p.244.

[42] Crow, *op. cit,* p.245

[43] *Caledonian Mercury,* 11th March, 1865

[44] *Bradford Observer,* 16th March, 1865. Lord Deas dissented from the majority

[45] *Caledonian Mercury,* 6th December, 1865

[46] *Caledonian Mercury,* 7th December, 1865

[47] For example, on the title page of her novels.

[48] Parliamentary Papers, 32, 1868. *Report on the State and Operation of Laws in force in the United Kingdom with respect to constitution and proof of the Contract of Marriages and registration and other means of preserving*

evidences and also marriages of European British Subjects in India and colonies in Foreign Countries.

[49] Matrimonial Causes and Marriage Law (Ireland) Amendment Act, 1870. 33 & 34 Vict. c.110

Chapter 13

[1] Malloch was credited with having retrieved 17 bodies from rivers over the previous ten years. *Glasgow Herald,* 25th September, 1869

[2] *Ibid*

[3] For example, the *Daily News* commented on the 7th September that 'What the Lord Justice Clerk of Scotland spent at the two elections has yet to be ascertained.'

[4] Quoted in the *Glasgow Herald,* 25th September, 1869

[5] *Second Report on Bridgwater,* p.840, quoted in Omond, *op. cit.,* p.250

[6] Omond, *op. cit.,* p.250

[7] Gladstone to Moncreiff, 31st August, 1869. Tullibole Papers, Box 21, Envelope 1

[8] Gladstone to Moncreiff, 27th September and 1st October, 1869. Ibid

[9] *Dundee Advertiser,* n.d., quoted in the *Bradford Observer,* 1st September, 1869. Clearly an earlier issue of the *Advertiser* had included the mistaken report of George Patton's death. The *Advertiser's* rival Dundee journal, the *Courier and Argus,* took much pleasure in making sarcastic comments about the *Advertiser's* 'literary murder' of the unfortunate Patton. *Dundee Courier and Argus,* 31st August, 1869

[10] According to the above report in the *Courier and Argus,* as soon as Patton's supposed death was announced in the press, lawyers in Edinburgh had begun speculating on Moncreiff's chances of succeeding to the vacancy.

[11] Cardwell, E., to Moncreiff, 1st October, 1868. Tullibole Papers, Box 21, Envelope 2

[12] Reeve, H., to Moncreiff, 25th September, 1869. *Ibid.*

[13] Gladstone, W.E., to Moncreiff, 11th October, 1873, Ibid.

[14] In 1885, Moncreiff wrote to Gladstone to nominate his old friend Sir William Dunbar for a peerage, commenting that 'I understand also that his fortune is quite able to support such a dignity'. Moncreiff to Gladstone, W.E., 10th June, 1885, Gladstone Papers, Add. MS 44491 f. 81

[15] Moncreiff to Gladstone, W.E., 29th October, 1873, Gladstone Papers, Add. MS 44491, f.289

[16] 'Lord Moncreiff', *Scottish Law Review,* vol. XL, No. 126, June 1895, pp.168-8

[17] *Ibid.*

[18] Mackintosh, W., to Moncreiff. n.d. 1888, Tullibole Papers, Box 21, Envelope 2

[19] *Scottish Law Review,* as note 16

[20] *Woodhead v. Gartness Mineral Co.,* (1877) 4 Sc. Sess. Cases, 4th Series, 469

[21] *George Johnson, v. W.H. Lindsay & Co,* (1891) H.L., A.C. 371

[22] *Hall v. Johnson,* (1865) 3 H & C at p.595
[23] *Woodhead v. Gartness,* at p.178
[24] *Johnson v. Lindsay* at pp. 380, 385, 387
[25] See, for example, the brief notices in the *Sheffield and Rotherham Independent,* and the *Liverpool Mercury,* 2nd October, 1878
[26] Quoted in the *Sheffield and Rotherham Independent,* 3rd October, 1878
[27] *Belfast Newsletter,* 1st January, 1879; *Newcastle Courant,* 17th January, 1879
[28] In their original form, the indictments contained seventeen charges, and the documents in the case were said to amount to 'more than a waggon load.' *Sheffield and Rotherham Independent,* 25th January, 1879
[29] *Sheffield and Rotherham Independent,* 11th January, 1879
[30] For example the United Presbyterian minister Mr Inglis denounced the scheme as 'infamous gambling – the same vice which had brought on the sad calamity which the whole country deplored.' *Dundee Courier and Argus,* 14th January, 1879. At a meeting to raise money in a local fund, Mr Rathbone, MP, declared that 'the amount of misery which would be created in this country by a large lottery, if successfully held, would be far worse and far more permanent than any suffering caused by the Bank, because evil which affected the character of men lived much longer than any mere physical evil, and extended far deeper.' *Aberdeen Weekly Journal,* 14th January, 1879
[31] *Leeds Mercury,* 16th January, 1879. A similar scheme for a lottery to rescue shareholders was also mooted in the case of the West of England Bank. *Newcastle Courant,* 17th January, 1879
[32] *Birmingham Daily Post,* 18th January, 1879
[33] *Dundee Courier and Argus,* 17th January, 1879
[34] *Graphic,* 18th January, 1879
[35] *Belfast Newsletter,* 22nd January, 1879
[36] *Ibid.*
[37] *Scottish Law Review,* op. cit., p.166; *Caledonian Mercury,* 9th October, 1858
[38] *Ibid.*
[39] It was explained by the *Aberdeen Weekly Journal* on the 4th January, that the documents prepared for use in the court case were reproduced using lithography, which showed in detail the alterations and erasures alleged to have been made by the accused
[40] *Isle of Man Times and General Advertiser,* 1st February, 1879
[41] *Glasgow Herald,* 31st January, 1879
[42] *Sheffield and Rotherham Independent,* 1st February, 1879
[43] *Ibid.*
[44] *Daily Gazette,* 1st February, 1879
[45] Quoted in the *Pall Mall Gazette,* 8th February, 1879
[46] *Dundee Courier and Argus,* 2nd September, 1870
[47] Duncan Smith, A., *Trial of Eugene Marie Chantrelle,* (1878) Notable Scottish Trials, 1906, *passim*
[48] *Leeds Mercury,* 8th May, 1878
[49] *Ibid.*

[50] *Trial of Eugene Marie Chantrelle*, p.195
[51] *Glasgow Herald*, 22nd December, 1883
[52] *Dundee Courier and Argus*, 22nd December, 1883.
[53] 'Lord Moncreiff as a Judge', *Journal of Jurisprudence*, 1888, vol. XXXII, p.567
[54] *Her Majesty's Advocate against Alexander Gollan and others*, Couper's Justiciary Cases, vol.V, 1882-5, p.317
[55] *Ibid*, p.327. For a fuller account of this incident, see McConnell, D., *The Strome Ferry Railway Riot of 1883*, 1993
[56] *Glasgow Herald*, 27 July, 1883
[57] McConnell, *op. cit.*, p.24
[58] *Dundee Courier and Argus*, 3 August, 1883
[59] *Glasgow Herald*, 3 August, 1883
[60] *Dundee Courier and Argus*, 6 August, 1883
[61] For the background to the Deer Raid see Devine, T.M., *Clanship to Crofters' War*, chaps. 14, 15
[62] *Lord Advocate v. Donald Macrae and Others*, White's Justiciary Cases, I, p.543
[63] E.g., *Pall Mall Gazette*, 18th January, 1888. The *Gazette* was critical both of the substance and the manner of Moncreiff's exposition of the law: '...the Lord Justice droned and prosed away in a voice which was absolutely inaudible in the body of the court, and which could not be heard actually even by the jurymen at his lordship's right hand.'
[64] One outcome of the case was the setting up of a Government enquiry which substantiated newspaper reports of the plight of the crofters, and may well have discouraged future governments from extending further legal protection to deer forests. See the Lochs Community website for further details.
[65] *Her Majesty's Advocate against John Gordon Robertson and others*, (1842) Broun, I, p.193
[66] *Glasgow Herald*, 18th January, 1888
[67] *Campbell v. Ord and Maddison*, 1883, 1R, 149. I am especially grateful to my colleague, Mr Gordon Cameron, for drawing my attention to this case, and also explaining the significance of Lord Moncreiff's ruling.
[68] *Grant v. Caledonian Railway Co.*, (1870) 9 M., 258
[69] See for example, Lord Nimmo-Smith in *Galbraith's Curator v. Stewart (No. 2)* 1998, SLT 1305
[70] *Dundee Courier and Argus*, 17th September, 1881; *AberdeenWeekly Journal*, 12th June, 1885; *Aberdeen Weekly Journal*, 2nd October, 1888
[71] Lord Salisbury, writing to Moncreiff on the 29th September to mark the latter's retirement, refers to Moncreiff's 'doubtful health.' Tullibole Papers, Box 21, Envelope 1
[72] 'Lord Moncreiff', *Scottish Law Review*, June 1895, vol. XL, No. 126, p.170

Chapter 14

[1] *Dundee Courier and Argus,* 24th August, 1875
[2] *Glasgow Herald,* 15th March, 1875
[3] *Dundee Courier and Argus.,* 11th May, 1874. In Scotland appeals were initially heard by a single judge, the Lord Ordinary, and could then be carried to the Inner House of the Court of Session, with the final appeal being to the House of Lords
[4] Ensor, R.C.K., *England, 1870-1914*, pp.16-19
[5] *Glasgow Herald,* 23rd March, 1881
[6] *Hansard,* vol. 259, 1629, 22nd March, 1881
[7] *Dundee Courier and Argus,* 24th March, 1881
[8] *Glasgow Herald,* 25th July, 1882
[9] *Ibid.,* 11th April, 1883
[10] For a fuller account of Moncreiff's role as chairman of the Commission, see Bain, W.H., *op. cit.,* Chapter 8
[11] *Hansard,* H.C., vol. 196, 1444, 8th June, 1869
[12] 32 & 33 Vict. c.39
[13] *Hansard,* H.C., vol.197, 160, 17th June 1869
[14] *First Report of the Commissioners on Endowed Institutions in Scotland,* p.11
[15] Lenman, B.P., and Stocks, J., *The Beginnings of State Education,* p.101
[16] *Minutes of Evidence of the Commissioners,* vol. 1, p.147
[17] Moncreiff, J.W., *An Educational Retrospect,* p.24
[18] *Report of the Commissioners,* p.7
[19] Bain, W.H., *op. cit.,* p.160
[20] Moncreiff, J.W., *Address on Installation as Lord Rector of Edinburgh University,* (1886) p.6
[21] Moncreiff, J.W., *An Educational Retrospect,* pp.9-10
[22] *Dundee Courier and Argus,* 29th April, 1878
[23] *Ibid.*
[24] *Glasgow Herald,* 18th March, 1886
[25] *Glasgow Herald,* 30th April, 1891
[26] *Glasgow Herald,* 26th May, 1894
[27] *Scotsman,* 28th June, 1895
[28] *Dundee Courier and Argus,* 29th April, 1895
[29] *Glasgow Herald,* 29th April, 1895

Select Bibliography

Primary Sources

British Library

Aberdeen Papers: correspondence
Gladstone Papers: correspondence
Peel Papers: correspondence

Hansard's Parliamentary Debates

Law Reports

Couper's Justiciary Cases
Court of Session Cases
English Reports
Irvine's Justiciary Cases
Shaw's Justiciary Cases
White's Justiciary Cases

National Archives, London

Home Office Papers: correspondence
Russell Papers: correspondence

National Archives of Scotland

Acts of the General Assembly of the Church of Scotland
Lord Advocate's Papers: correspondence
Yelverton Papers: miscellaneous

National Library of Scotland

Rutherfurd Papers: correspondence

New College, Edinburgh

Moncreiff correspondence

Tullibole Castle

Moncreiff correspondence – Box 21
Moncreiff's manuscript *Reminiscences*
Moncreiff's manuscript notebook

University College, London
Brougham Papers: correspondence

Newspapers

Parliamentary Papers

Public and General Statutes

Secondary Sources

A.   Up to 1895

Address to the People of Scotland and Statement of Grievances by the National Association for the Vindication of Scottish Rights, (Edinburgh, 1853)
Assimilation Commission. *First Report of the Commission appointed to inquire and ascertain how far the mercantile laws in the different parts of the United Kingdom of Great Britain and Ireland may be advantageously assimilated.* Parliamentary Papers vol. XXVII, p.455
Assimilation Commission. *Second Report*............ Parliamentary Papers vol. XVIII. 1854-5, p.653
Bankruptcy and Insolvency (Scotland) Bill, 1853, with Paper of observations. House of Lords Sessional Papers vol. 3, 100-100a, 1852-3
Begg, J., *A Violation of the Treaty of Union the Main Origin of our Ecclesiastical Divisions and other Evils,* 1874
Bell, R., *Observations on the Conference of the Rev. Thomas Chalmers, DD, LLD. FRSE, with Certain Ministers and Elders of the Church of Scotland.* (Edinburgh, 1837)
Black, A., *The Church Its Own Enemy,* (Edinburgh 1835)

Brown, T., *Annals of the Disruption,* (Edinburgh, 1893)
Chalmers, T.C., *A Conference with Certain Ministers and elders of the Church of Scotland on the Subject of the Moderatorship of the General Assembly,* (Glasgow, 1837)
Buchanan, R., *The Ten Years' Conflict,* (Glasgow, 1849)
Cockburn, H., *Journal, 1831-54,* 2 vols., (Edinburgh, 1871)
Cockburn, H., *Memorials of His Time,* (Edinburgh, 1856)
Cockburn, H., *An Examination of the Trials for Sedition which have occurred in Scotland,* 2 vols. (Edinburgh, 1888)
Grant, A., *The Story of the University of Edinburgh,* (London, 1884)
Hanna, W., *Memoirs of the life and writings of Thomas Chalmers,* (Edinburgh, 1849-52)
Justice to Scotland, Report of the first Meeting of the National Association for the Vindication of Scottish Rights, (Edinburgh, 1853)
Irvine, A.F., *Report of the Trial of Madeleine Smith before the High Court of Justiciary......,* (Edinburgh, 1857)
Lauder, T.D., *An Account of the Great Floods of August 1829 in the Province of Moray and adjoining Districts,* (Elgin, 1830)
Law Magazine or Quarterly Review of Jurisprudence, (London, 1851-4)
London Committee of Merchants and Other Associated for the Improvements of the Commercial and Bankruptcy Law of Scotland, and the Assimilation of the laws of England and Scotland, *Report and Suggestions addressed to the Mercantile community of the United Kingdom,* (London, 1852)
Ibid, *Second Address to the Mercantile Community,* (Edinburgh, 1853)
Longworth, M.T., *Martyrs of Circumstance,* (London, 1861)
'Lord Moncreiff', *Scottish Law Review,* June, 1895
'Lord Moncreiff as a Judge', *Journal of Jurisprudence,* 1888, vol. XXXII, p.567
Mackie, J.B., *The Life and Work of Duncan McLaren,* (Edinburgh, 1888)
Moncreiff, H.W., *A Letter to Lord Melbourne on the Expediency of the Interference of Parliament in order to remove the present difficulties in the appointment of Ministers,* (Edinburgh, 1840)
Moncreiff, H.W., *Scottish Rights and Grievances: Reasons for Declining to join the National Association for the Vindication of Scottish Rights,* (Edinburgh, 1854)
Moncreiff, H.W., *The Free Church Principle, its Character and History,* (Edinburgh, 1883)
Moncreiff, J.W., *A Happy New Year,* (Edinburgh, 1862)
Moncreiff, J.W., *A Visit to my Discontented Cousin,* (London, 1871)
Moncreiff, J.W. *A Word More on the Moderatorship,* (Edinburgh, 1837)

Moncreiff, J.W., *Address on Installation as Lord Rector of Edinburgh University,* (Edinburgh, 1869)
Moncreiff, J.W., *Address on Jurisprudence and the Amendment of the Law,* (Edinburgh, 1860)
Moncreiff, J.W., *Address on Law Reform and the Bankruptcy Laws,* (Edinburgh, 1865)
Moncreiff, J.W., *Address on Legal Education,* (Edinburgh, 1870)
Moncreiff, J.W., *Address to the inaugural meeting of the Cockburn Association,* (Edinburgh, 1875)
Moncreiff, J.W., *Address on the Art of Pleading,* (London, 1860)
Moncreiff, J.W., *Address to the General Council of the University of Glasgow,* (Glasgow, 1868)
Moncreiff, J.W., *An Educational Retrospect,* (Glasgow, 1886)
Moncreiff, J.W., *Church and State, from the Reformation to 1843,* 1878
Moncreiff, J.W., *Criticism and Essays,* n.d.
Moncreiff, J.W., 'Earl Russell's Speeches', *Edinburgh Review,* April 1870, vol. 31, p.570
Moncreiff, J.W., 'Extension of the Franchise', *Edinburgh Review,* January 1866, vol. 123, pp.263-96
Moncreiff, J.W., *Inaugural Address to the Associated Societies of Edinburgh University,* (Edinburgh, 1863)
Moncreiff, J.W., *Legal Education,* (Edinburgh, 1870)
Moncreiff, J.W., 'Letters and Discoveries of Sir Charles Bell', *Edinburgh Review,* April 1872, vol. 135, pp.394-429
Moncreiff, J.W., 'Life of Lord Chancellor Eldon', *North British Review,* November, 1844, vol. 2, p.227
Moncreiff, J.W., 'Lord Jeffrey's Contributions to the Edinburgh Review', *North British Review,* vol. 1, May 1844, pp.252-84
Moncreiff, J.W., 'Politics', *North British Review,* 1845
Moncreiff, J.W., 'Secret Voting and Parliamentary Reform', *Ed. Rev.* 1860
Moncreiff, J.W., *The Education of a Lawyer,* (Edinburgh, 1867)
Moncreiff, J.W., *The Extension of the Suffrage – an Address to the Electors of Edinburgh,* (Edinburgh, 1867)
Moncreiff, J.W., *The Last Years of the Annuity Tax,* (Edinburgh, 1860)
Moncreiff, J.W., *The Relation of Recent Scientific Inquiries to the Received Teaching of Scripture,* (Edinburgh, 1867)
Moncreiff Wellwood, Sir Harry, *A Brief Account of the Constitution of the Established Church of Scotland, and of the questions concerning patronage and secession,* (Edinburgh, 1883)
Report of the Committee of the Glasgow Law Amendment Society, (Glasgow, 1851)

Robertson, C.G., *Report of the Auchterarder Case,* 2 vols., (Edinburgh, 1838)
Robertson, C.G., *Report of the Lethendy Case,* (Edinburgh, 1841)
Robertson, C.G., *Report of the Stewarton Case,* (Edinburgh, 1843)
Russell, T., *The Annuity Tax or Edinburgh Church-Rate, Opposed to the Law of God and therefore not Binding on Man.* (Edinburgh, 1836)
Smith, T., *The Memoirs of James Begg, DD,* (Edinburgh, 1888)
'The Late Lord Moncreiff', *Scots Law Times,* April, 1895
Vickers, G., *The Yelverton Marriage Case,* (London, 1861)
Watt, J.C., *John Inglis,* (Edinburgh, 1893)
Wilson, W., *Memorials of Principal Candlish,* (Edinburgh, 1880)

B.   After 1895

Anderson, R.D., *Education and Opportunity in Victorian Scotland,* (Edinburgh, 1983)
Anderson, R.D., *Education and the Scottish People, 1750-1918,* (Oxford, 1995)
Anderson, R.D., *Education and Society in Victorian Scotland,* (Edinburgh, 1989)
Bain, W.H., *The Life and Achievements of James Wellwood Moncreiff,* (unpublished M.Litt. thesis, Glasgow, 1977)
Bain W.H., 'Attacking the Citadel, James Moncreiff's Proposals to Reform Scottish Education, 1851-69', *Scottish Educational Review,* 1978-80, pp.5-14
Biagini, E.F., *Liberty, Retrenchment and Reform,* (Cambridge, 1992)
Brown, C., *Religion and Society in Scotland since 1701,* (Edinburgh, 1997)
Brown, C., *The Social History of Religion in Scotland since 1730,* (London)
Brown, S.J., *Thomas Chalmers and the Godly Commonwealth,* (Oxford, 1982)
Brown S.J., and Fry, M., (eds.) *Scotland in the Age of the Disruption,* (Edinburgh, 1993)
Burleigh, J.H.S., A Church History of Scotland, (London, 1960)
Cairns, J., 'The Faculty of Advocates', in Smith, T.B., and Black, R., *The Laws of Scotland: Stair Memorial Encyclopaedia,* vol. 13, 1995
Cameron, E., *Impaled upon a Thistle – Scotland since 1880,* (Edinburgh, 2010)
Campbell, J.P., *A Scottish Murder,* (Stroud, 2007)
Cheyne, A.C., *The Transforming of the Kirk: Victorian Scotland's Religious Revolution,* (Edinburgh, 1983)

Clark, T.A., *History of the Speculative Society,* (Edinburgh, 1968)
Colley, L., *Britons: Forging the Nation,* (London, 2009)
Crow, D., *Theresa – The Story of the Yelverton Case,* (London, 1966)
Devine, T.M., And Mitchison, R., *People and Society in Scotland, 1760-1830,* (Edinburgh,1988)
Devine, T.M., *Clanship to Crofters War – the social transformation of the Scottish Highlands,* (Manchester, 1994)
Devine, T.M., *Scottish Elites,* (Edinburgh, 1994)
Devine, T.M., *The Scottish Nation, 1707-2000,* (London, 1999)
Devine, T.M., *The Scottish Nation, 1700-2007,* (London, 2006)
Donnachie, I., and Whately, C.A., (eds), *The Manufacture of Scottish History,* (Edinburgh, 1992)
Drummond, A.L., and Bulloch, J., *The Scottish Church, 1688-1843,* (Edinburgh, 1973)
Ensor, R.C.K., *England, 1870-1914,* (Oxford, 1963)
Erickson, A.B., and McCarthy, J.R., 'The Yelverton Case – Civil Legislation and Marriage', *Victorian Studies,* 1971, pp.274ff.
Ferguson, W., 'The Reform Act (Scotland): intention and effects', *SHR,* 45. (1965), pp.105-116
Fraser, W.H., *Chartism in Scotland,* (Pontypool, 2010)
Fraser, W.H., *Scottish Popular Politics,* (Edinburgh, 2000)
Fraser, W.H. and Morris, R.J., (eds.) *People and Society in Scotland, 1830-1914,* (Edinburgh, 1990)
Fry, M., *Patronage and Principle,* (Edinburgh, 1987)
Fry, M., 'The Whig Interpretation of Scottish History', in Donnachie, I., and Whately, C.A., (eds), *The Manufacture of Scottish History,* (Edinburgh, 1992)
Gammage, R.G., *History of the Chartist Movement,* (London, 1969)
Gill, R., 'The Imperial Anxieties of a Nineteenth Century Religion Case', *History Workshop Journal,* 2004, 57, pp.58-78
Gordon, E., and Nair, G., *Murder and Morality in Victorian Britain – the Story of Madeleine Smith,* (Manchester, 2009)
Grant, E., *Memoirs of a Highland Lady,* (Edinburgh, 1898)
Hanham, H.J., *Scottish Nationalism,* (London,1969)
Hanham, H.J., 'Mid-Century Scottish Nationalism: Romantic and Radical', in Robson, R. (ed.), *Ideas and Institutions of Victorian Britain,* (London, 1967)
Hanham, H.J., 'The Creation of the Scottish Office, 1881-7', *Juridical Rev.*1965, p.238
Hartman, M.S., *Victorian Murderesses,* (London, 1977)
Harvie, C., *Scottish Society and Politics, 1707 to the Present,* (London, 1998)

Hopkins, P., *Glencoe and the End of the Highland War*, (Edinburgh, 1998)
Hutchison, I.G.C., *A Political History of Scotland, 1832-1914*, (Edinburgh, 1986)
Jesse, F.T., *The Trial of Madeleine Smith*, (Edinburgh,1927)
Kahn, E., 'The Yelverton Affair – a Nineteenth Century Sensation', *History Ireland*, 2009
Kidd, C, *Subverting Scotland's Past*, (Cambridge, 1993)
Lenman, B.P., and Stocks, J., 'The Beginnings of State Education in Scotland, 1872-1885', *Scottish Educational Studies*, 4, 1972, pp.73 ff.
Macaulay, W. B., *The Journals of Thomas Babington Macaulay*, (Thomas, W., ed.) 2008
McCaffrey, J.F., *Scotland in the Nineteenth Century*, (Basingstoke, 1998)
Macdonald, C., (ed) *Unionist Scotland, 1800-1997*, (Edinburgh, 1998)
MacGowan, D., *The Strange Affair of Madeleine Smith*, (Edinburgh, 2007)
McConnell, D., *The Strome Ferry Railway Riot of 1883*, (Dornoch, 1993)
Macdougall, N., (ed.), *Church, Politics and Society in Scotland, 1408-1929*, (Edinburgh, 1983)
MacLeod, A.D., *A Kirk Disrupted, Charles Cowan MP and the Free Church of Scotland*, (Fearn, 2013)
Machin, G.I.T., 'The Disruption and British Politics', *Scottish Historical Review*, vol. 51, No.151, April 1972, pp.20-51
Moncreiff, F. and Moncreiffe, W., *The Moncreiffs and the Moncreiffes*, (Edinburgh, 1929)
Morton, G., *Unionist-Nationalism*, (Edinburgh,1999)
Murdoch, A., and Sher, R.B., 'Literacy and learned culture', in Devine, T.M., and Mitchison, R., *People and Society in Scotland, 1760-1830*, (Edinburgh, 1988)
Murray, J., *A History of the Royal High School*, (Edinburgh, 1997)
Myers, J.D., 'Scottish Nationalism and the Antecedents of the 1872 Education Act', *Scottish Educational Studies*, 4, 1972, pp.73 ff.
Olssen, E., *A History of Otago*, (Dunedin, 1984)
Omond, G.W.T., *The Lord Advocates of Scotland, 1834-1880*, 2nd Series, (London, 1914)
Pickard, W., *The Member for Scotland- the Life of Duncan McLaren*, (Edinburgh, 2011)
Pittock, M.G.H., *The Invention of Scotland: The Stuart Myth and the Scottish Identity, 1638 to the Present*, (London, 1991)
Rodger, A., 'The Codification of Commercial Law in Victorian Britain', *Law Quarterly Review*, 1992, vol. 108, pp.570-90

Rodger, A.., 'Scottish Advocates in the Nineteenth Century: the German Connection'. *Law Quarterly Review*, 1994, v. 110, pp. 563-91

Rodger, A., *The Courts, the Church and the Constitution – Aspects of the Disruption of 1843,* (Edinburgh, 2008)

Schama, C., *Wild Romance,* (London, 2011)

Smith, M.H., *A Complete Report of the Trial of Miss Madeleine Smith,* 2009

Smout, T.C., *A Century of the Scottish People,* (London, 1986)

Southgate, D.G., *The Passing of the Whigs,* (Aldershot, 1993)

Stevenson, M., *Madeleine Smith and the Theatre of Ambiguity – The Dilemma of Sex and Power in 19th Century Scotland,* unpublished MA thesis, University of Dundee

Stewart, A and Cameron, J.K., *The Free Church of Scotland, 1843-1910,* (Edinburgh, 1910)

Swinfen, D.B., *Imperial Appeal, The Debate on the Appellate Jurisdiction of the Judicial Committee of the Privy Council,* (Manchester, 1987)

Tyrrell, A., 'The Earl of Eglinton, Scottish Conservatism, and the National Association for the Vindication of Scottish Rights', *Hist. J.,* vol. 53, issue 01, March 2010, pp.87-107

Walker, D.M., *The Legal History of Scotland,* (Edinburgh, 2001)

Walker, S.P., and Lee, T.A., *Studies in Early Professionalism – Scottish Chartered Accountants,* (Edinburgh, 1999)

Walker, S.P., *The Society of Accountants in Edinburgh, 1854-1914,* (New York, 1988)

Ward, J.T., *Chartism,* (London, 1973)

Whatley, C., *The Scots and the Union,* Second ed., (Edinburgh, 2014)

Wilson, A., *The Chartist Movement in Scotland,* (Manchester, 1970)

Withrington, D.J., 'Adrift among the Reefs of Conflicting Ideals', in Brown, S. J., and Fry, M., *Scotland in the Age of the Disruption,* pp.79-97, (Edinburgh, 1993)

Withrington, D.J., 'The Free Church Educational Scheme, 1843-50', *Records of the Scottish Church History Society,* xv, 1964, pp.108-10

Withrington, D.J., 'Towards a National System – the Last Years of the Struggle for a Scottish Education Act', *Scottish Educational Studies,* 4, 1972, pp.73 ff.

Woodward, E.L., *The Age of Reform,* (Oxford, 1954)

Wright L.C., *Scottish Chartism,* (Edinburgh, 1953)

Young, D., *Edinburgh in the Age of Walter Scott,* (Norman, Oklahoma, 1956)

Index

A

A Visit to my Discontented Cousin, 36, 121
A Word More on the Moderatorship, 58
Aberdeen, 3, 51, 93, 132, 135, 154, 172, 184, 185, 186
Aberdeen Journal, 188, 197
Aberdeen, Lord, 79, 80, 88, 89, 117, 156
Aberdour, 22
Act of Assembly of 1649, 66
Act of Union, 43, 46, 61, 63, 143, 144, 185
Act of Visitation of Churches, Colleges, and Schools, 1690, 183
Act on the Calling of Ministers, 67
Adam, Alexander, 17
Address on Law Reform and the Bankruptcy Laws, 158
Address to the People of Scotland, 145, 146
Aitken, Miss, 198
Alexandre, 13
Allan Hay, 13
An Address to the Electors of Scotland, 163
Anderson, P., 99
Anderson, R.D., 167, 178
Anderson, William, 124
Annual Report on Scottish Statistics, 159
Anti-Corn Law League, 42, 56
Ardmillan, Lord, 133, 207, 232, 235
Argyll Commission, 170, 178
Argyll, Duke of, 42, 89, 178, 179, 185
Aristotle, 27
Ashworth, Sir Charles, 203
Assimilation of Scots and English Law, 123, 143, 152, 153, 155, 156, 157, 159, 160, 161, 162
Association for Promoting Secondary Education in Scotland, 182
Attorney-General, 138, 148, 162
Auchterarder, 39, 60, 67, 68, 72, 84
Auchterarder case, 45, 62, 66, 68, 69, 72, 73, 75, 76, 77, 80, 87

Auchtertool, 22
Avonmore, Vicountess, 202, 212
Ayr, 172
Aytoun, William, 24, 146

B

Baillie, Henry, 172
Bain, W.H., 15, 31, 36, 80, 96, 139, 171, 172, 180, 182, 185, 191, 192, 239
Balfour, Lord of Burleigh, 241
Balfour, William, 229
Balliol College, 5
Bankruptcy (Scotland) Act, 160
Bankruptcy Act of 1856, 159, 162
Bannatyne Club, 8
Barncaple, Lord, 133
Barrier Act, 67
Baxter, William, 120, 125, 147, 148
Begg, James, 144, 164, 165, 179, 229
Bell, Benjamin Robert, 19
Bell, Isabella, 38
Bell, Robert, 38, 40, 45, 46, 53, 54, 57, 58, 59, 67, 69, 70, 75, 80, 83, 90
Benholme, Lord, 133, 231
Berkeley, Henry, 96
Biagini, Eugene, 129
Black, Adam, 54, 104, 132
Blackford, 13
Blackie, Professor, 3
Blackwood's Magazine, 26, 146
Blair, Colonel, 131
Blyth, Henry, 191
Board of Education for Scotland, 171, 172, 178, 179, 180
Boswell, Sir Alex, 19, 22
Braham, 141
Breadalbane, Marquis of, 42
Brewster, Sir David, 183
Bridgewater, 215
Brief Account of the Constitution of the Church of Scotland, 48
Brougham, Henry, 2, 15, 19, 21, 22, 25, 65, 66, 87, 160, 211
Brown, Callum, 49
Brown, S.J., 43, 55, 67, 83
Brown, Thomas, 44

284

Brownlee, James, 99
Bruce, H.A., 137
Bryce, James, 184
Buccleuch, Duke of, 124, 125
Buchanan, Robert, 90
Burke, William, 5, 31, 32, 33, 34, 35
Burleigh, Lord, 238, 239
Burntisland, 9
Butler, Reuben, 63

C

Calcutta, Bishop of, 4
Caledonian Mercury, 97, 207, 210, 212, 223
Calton Hill, 20, 94, 97, 99
Calton Jail, 222
Campbell v. Ord and Maddison, 231, 232, 233
Campbell, Lord, 103
Campbell, Neil, 231
Campbell, Robert, 231
Candlish, Robert, 61, 90, 163, 164, 165, 184
Canning, George, 147
Cardwell, Edward, 216
Carson, Aglionby, 16, 17
Castelreagh, Lord, 20
Catalani, 141
Catholic Disabilities, 7, 13
Catholic Emancipation Act, 49
Central Board for the Vindication of the Rights of Dissenters, 144
Chalmers, Thomas, 7, 13, 38, 43, 48, 49, 50, 51, 52, 53, 54, 55, 56, 57, 58, 59, 60, 61, 64, 66, 68, 78, 79, 84, 86, 90, 139
Chantrelle, Elizabeth, 227
Chantrelle, Eugene, 227
Chapels Act, 39, 67, 81, 82, 83
chapels of ease, 49, 50, 82
Chartists, 40, 41, 56, 91, 92, 93, 94, 95, 96, 97, 98, 99, 103, 104, 126
Cheape, Douglas, 35
Chelmsford, Lord, 211
Chief Constable, 136, 137
Christison, Alexander, 17
Church Accommodation, 54
Church Accommodation Committee, 51, 54
Church Extension, 50, 53, 56, 57, 58, 59
Church Extension Committee, 54

Church of Scotland, 2, 14, 39, 43, 44, 46, 47, 52, 58, 61, 63, 67, 82, 85, 87, 90, 150, 164, 165, 166, 167, 168, 170, 176, 183, 185
Church of Scotland Education Committee, 169
Church Patronage (Scotland) Act, 46, 69
City of Glasgow Bank, 220, 221, 222, 226, 229
Claim of Right, 43, 85, 86, 119
Clark, Mr, 75, 76
Classical Society, 23, 24, 27, 32
Clelland, James, 82, 83
Clerk, John, 8
Clerk, Peter, 68
Cockburn Society, 235
Cockburn, Henry, 2, 5, 6, 7, 8, 14, 16, 17, 18, 22, 33, 34, 35, 40, 41, 47, 48, 49, 64, 66, 67, 74, 77, 80, 90, 91, 93, 94, 95, 97, 98, 101, 102, 103, 104, 119, 138, 147, 148, 164, 242
Colebrooke Commission, 182
Colebrooke, Sir Edward, 181, 182, 238
Colley, Linda, 143
Colquoun, J.C., 171
Combe, Mr, 198
Committee on Endowed Schools, 238
Conference of Hungerford, 42
Confession of Faith, 61, 62, 176, 183
consent *de praesenti*, 207, 208, 209
Conservative Party, 26, 117, 118, 128, 143, 152, 163, 175, 186, 216, 236
Conyngham, Lord, 21
Corn Laws, Repeal, 93, 117
Court of Session, 2, 38, 39, 41, 45, 48, 60, 61, 62, 67, 68, 69, 70, 74, 75, 77, 78, 79, 80, 81, 82, 83, 85, 88, 91, 119, 133, 138, 149, 158, 175, 201, 205, 207, 210, 211, 212, 216, 218, 219, 231, 232, 236, 237
Court of Session Bill, 1881, 236
Cowan, Charles, 86
Cowan, John, 120
Cowan, Lord, 133, 231
Craig, James, 2
Craigellachie, 11
Craighill, Lord, 221
Craufurd, James, 98, 99
Crichton, Peter, 7
Culsalmond, 39, 60, 67, 84
Culsalmond case, 80

Cuninghame, William, 82
Cunningham, William, 59
Curriehill, Lord, 207, 209
Curtis, Sir William, 21

D

Dagentree, 121, 122
Dalkeith, 9, 84
Dalrymple, Lord, 42
Darwin, Charles, 139, 140
Day Trespass Act, 230
De Feudis, 35
Dean of the Faculty of Advocates, 2, 5, 33, 36, 41, 69, 80, 151, 190, 193, 196, 225
Deans, David, 63
Deas, Lord, 133, 134, 207, 209
Deed of Demission, 43
Deer Raid, 230
Derby, Lord, 186
Descartes, 27
Devine, Tom, 117, 132
Disestablishment, 55, 117, 165, 240, 241
Disruption, The, 14, 32, 39, 41, 43, 44, 45, 46, 48, 52, 60, 63, 73, 75, 85, 89, 90, 163, 164, 165, 166, 183, 240, 241
Disruption, The Annals of the, 44
Dissenters, 52, 55, 176
Docherty, Mary Ann, 33
Drummond A.L., and Bulloch J., 176
Dublin, 201, 206, 212
Dumfries, 93
Duncan v. Findlater, 158
Duncan, Viscount, 148
Dundas, John Hamilton, 21
Dundee, 68, 93, 133, 154, 184, 189, 235
Dundee Courier and Argus, 152, 230, 237, 241
Dunlop, Andrew Murray, 119
Duvernay, 141

E

East India Company, 4, 183
Ecclesiastical Titles Assumption Bill, 122
Edinburgh, 1, 2, 3, 5, 6, 7, 11, 13, 16, 19, 20, 23, 24, 28, 32, 45, 46, 51, 58, 67, 84, 93, 97, 120, 128, 129, 131, 132, 134, 136, 137, 138, 145, 146, 147, 148, 149, 151, 152, 153, 154, 155, 159, 160, 163, 172, 178, 179, 180, 184, 190, 196, 198, 201, 202, 205, 207, 209, 211, 221, 222, 227, 235, 236, 241
Edinburgh Academy, 24
Edinburgh Annuity Tax, 118, 123, 129
Edinburgh Chartist Association, 99
Edinburgh General Committee on Bankruptcy, 161
Edinburgh High School, 15, 16, 17, 18, 19, 23, 24, 27, 187
Edinburgh Review, 15, 27, 41, 118, 126, 139, 183
Edinburgh Rifle Volunteers, 235
Edinburgh Town Council, 51, 54, 130, 184, 229
Edinburgh University, 1, 2, 3, 17, 23, 27, 32, 33, 135, 183, 184, 185, 186, 204, 235, 239
Edinburgh, Lord Provost, 118
Education Act of 1870, 181
Education Act of 1872, 167, 180, 181, 238
Education Bill of 1854, 168, 169, 170, 171, 172, 180
Education Bill of 1855, 150, 169, 170, 172, 173, 180
Education Bill of 1862, 177
Education Bill of 1867, 178
Education Bill of 1872, 180
Education Bills of 1856, 175
Edwards, John, 77, 78
Edwards, Owen Dudley, 33
Eglinton Tournament, 145
Eglinton, Earl of, 145, 146, 173
Eikings, John, 99
Eldin Church, 9
Eldin House, 5, 7, 8, 9, 10, 14, 141
Eldin, Lord, 8, 139
Elgin case, 175
Endowed Institutions (Scotland) Act, 182
Endowed Schools Act of 1869, 181
English pronunciation, 3, 153
Episcopalians, 165
Erle, Lord Chief Justice, 220
Erskine, Henry, 5
Established Church, 43, 44, 46, 53, 61, 73, 90, 117, 130, 165, 166, 168,

169, 170, 172, 173, 175, 178, 180, 181, 183, 184, 240
Evangelical Alliance, 163
Evangelical party, 13, 48, 56, 57, 67
Evangelicals, 39, 43, 45, 47, 48, 49, 53, 55, 56, 58, 63, 69, 78, 80, 82, 83, 86

F

Faculty of Advocates, 1, 31, 119, 147, 148, 151, 158, 161, 219
faggot vote, 118, 124
Fala, 18
Ferguson, William, 124
Fergusson, Charles, 52
Fergusson, Sir James, 125, 126, 148, 149
Ferrier, J.F., 184
Fochabers, 11
Forbes, Edward, 204
Forbes, Emily Marianne Ashworth, 203, 205, 211
Fordyce, Sir Dingwall, 136
Forensic Society, 24, 25
Fox, Charles James, 100, 128, 129
Fraser, Hamish, 93, 97
Fraser, Luke, 17
Free Church, 39, 40, 43, 44, 45, 46, 52, 61, 63, 87, 89, 90, 120, 121, 144, 163, 164, 165, 166, 168, 169, 170, 171, 172, 181, 183, 184, 229, 240
Free Church Education Committee, 164
Free Church Principle: its Character and History, 46
Freeman's Journal, 221
Fry, Michael, 147
Fullerton, Lord, 74, 81

G

Gemble, Mrs, 202, 209
General Assembly, 5, 14, 39, 43, 45, 46, 47, 48, 49, 50, 51, 54, 55, 56, 57, 59, 60, 61, 62, 63, 64, 65, 66, 67, 68, 69, 70, 71, 72, 75, 77, 78, 79, 80, 81, 82, 83, 84, 86, 87, 88, 150, 165, 184
General Assembly of the Free Church, 164, 241
George IV, 19, 20, 21, 119
George Street, 2
Gibson-Craig, Sir William, 130

Gladstone, William, 52, 88, 117, 151, 181, 216, 217
Glasgow, 3, 5, 20, 53, 93, 103, 125, 132, 145, 153, 161, 172, 174, 185, 186, 188, 189, 199, 221, 222, 227, 236, 239
Glasgow Association for Promoting the Interests of the Church of Scotland, 50
Glasgow Association of Scottish Graduates., 185
Glasgow College, 24
Glasgow Dynamite Trial, 227
Glasgow Herald, 94, 134, 151, 190, 192, 197, 215, 225, 229, 237, 241
Glasgow Law Amendment Society, 143, 152, 154, 159
Glasgow shipbuilding strike, 235
Glasgow Town Council, 175
Glasgow University, 235
Glencoe massacre, 42
Glenlee, Lord, 74
Glorious Revolution, 46
Gordon, John Thomson, 24
Grant v. Caledonian Railway Co, 232
Grant v. Yelverton, 205
Grant, Elizabeth, 8, 12, 20, 21
Grant, James, 144, 145, 160
Grant, John, 94, 95, 100, 122, 145, 160
Graphic, The, 222
Gray, Ann, 33
Gray, James, 33
Great Stuart Street, 38, 137
Grenville, Lord, 5
Grey, Earl, 49, 100
Grey, Sir George, 130, 134, 135, 136, 158
Grisi, 141
Guibilei, Miss, 194, 195
Guthrie, Thomas, 164

H

Haggart. Christine, 196
Hall v. Johnson, 220
Halliday family, 10
Halliday, John, 10
Hamilton, 84
Hamilton, Robert, 94, 95, 99, 100, 101, 103
Handyside, Lord, 133, 134
Hanham, H.J., 153
Harcourt, Sir William, 229

Hare, William, 32, 33, 34
Harkness, William, 18
Henry, David, 40, 77
High Court of Justiciary, 148, 195, 218, 228, 230, 234
Highland Lady, The, 8, 12
Hill, Norman, 36
Home Secretary, 151
Hope, John, 36, 69, 80, 89, 199, 230
House of Commons, 24, 26, 28, 65, 66, 71, 86, 88, 96, 119, 120, 122, 123, 129, 132, 137, 149, 150, 151, 152, 159, 161, 162, 167, 169, 177, 181, 184, 215, 216, 235, 241
House of Lords, 15, 21, 41, 61, 74, 83, 87, 88, 119, 148, 152, 153, 157, 158, 160, 162, 173, 175, 179, 201, 210, 211, 219, 220, 227, 235, 236, 237, 238
Hunt, Peter, 193
Hutchison, I.G.C., 124, 153, 170

I

Imperial Court of Appeal, 236
Inglis, Henry, 224, 226
Inglis, John, 19, 31, 120, 137, 138, 147, 151, 158, 184, 186, 190, 191, 193, 195, 196, 199, 218, 219, 220, 223, 230
Inverness, 37, 172
Investor's Monthly Manual, 221
irregular marriage, 197, 207

J

Jeffrey, Francis, 2, 5, 7, 15, 25, 41, 42, 66, 74, 119, 138
Johnson v. W.H.Lindsay & Co, 219, 220, 231
Johnson, Samuel, 10
Johnstone, James, 170
Journal of Jurisprudence, 192, 218, 228
Judicature Act of 1873, 236
Judicial Committee of the Privy Council, 157
Juridical Review, 234
Juridical Society, 24, 236
Justinian's *Digest*, 36

K

Kent Road Public School, 174, 239, 240
Kessen, Mr, 75
Kidd, Colin, 155
Killowen, 203, 207, 208, 209
Kingsdown, Lord, 211
Kinloch, 75
Kinloch, Colonel, 137
Kinnaird, Hon. A, 171
Kinnoull, Earl of, 62, 68, 69, 72, 73
Kinross, Lord, 39
Knox, Dr Robert, 33

L

L'Angelier, Emile, 41, 188, 189, 190, 191, 193, 194, 195, 196, 197, 199
Lablache, 141
Laird, Margaret, 32
Lasswade, 7, 8, 9
Latta, James, 83
Lauder, Sir Thomas Dick, 11, 12
Lauderdale. Lord, 13
Laurie, Professor, 239
Law Magazine, 153, 156, 157
Law Reform (Contributory Negligence) Act, 1945, 232
lay patronage, 39, 43, 46, 47, 48, 50, 54, 60, 63, 64, 65, 66, 68, 71, 72, 73
Leahy, Dr, 203
Learning at Home, 15
Lee, John, 55, 56, 57, 58, 59
Leeds Mercury, 222, 227
Leith Burghs, 40, 120, 122
Leith Street, 20
Lethendy, 39, 60, 67, 75, 84
Lethendy case, 75
Lewis, Mr, 4
Liberal Party, 25, 117, 125, 126, 152, 163
Lilly, Mr, 215
Lind, Jenny, 141
Littlecote House, 42
Littlejohn, 129
Liveing, George, 135
Liverpool, Lord, 7, 22
Lochindoch, 13
Lockhart, J.G., 47
London, 19, 40, 53, 66, 122, 130, 133, 137, 138, 141, 145, 148, 149, 151, 157, 159, 180, 219

London Working Men's Association, 92
Longworth, Theresa, 41, 201, 202, 203, 204, 205, 206, 207, 208, 209, 210, 211, 212
Longworth, Thomas, 201
Lord Advocate, 1, 2, 26, 39, 40, 41, 66, 69, 117, 118, 119, 120, 123, 130, 132, 133, 134, 135, 137, 138, 140, 142, 143, 145, 146, 147, 148, 149, 151, 152, 160, 162, 163, 172, 180, 187, 189, 190, 191, 192, 193, 195, 196, 201, 207, 210, 211, 215, 216, 217, 218, 223, 224,☐225, 238, 243
Lord Chancellor, 139, 211, 236, 238
Lord Justice Clerk, 1, 2, 31, 61, 62, 89, 100, 101, 103, 104, 117, 179, 195, 215, 216, 217, 218, 227, 230, 236, 237
Lord Justice General, 19, 39
Lord Melgund, 167
Lord Ordinary, 7, 161, 207
Lord President, 36, 61, 62, 73, 76, 81, 207, 209, 218
Lord Rector, 1, 186, 187, 235
Lorimer, Mr, 68
Lovett, William, 92
Lowe, Robert, 177
Lunacy Act, 147
Lunacy Board, 133
Lyell, Sir Charles, 139

M

Macaulay, Lord, 42, 139, 183
Macdougal, Helen, 32, 33, 34, 35
MacDougall, P.C., 184
MacFarlane, Arabella, 202, 209
Macgill, George, 24
Macgregor, Dr, 224, 225
Machin, Ian, 88
Mackenzie, John Ord, 19
Mackenzie, Lord, 133
Mackie, J.B., 145
Mackintoshen, Ewen, 37
MacLagan, Sir Douglas, 19
Malibran, 141
Malloch, Joseph, 215
manhood suffrage, 129
Marianne Eliza, 39
Marnoch, 39, 60, 67, 77, 84
Marnoch case, 62, 87
Marriage Act of 1870, 41, 212

Marriage and Registration Bill, 144
marriage with deceased wife's sister, 133
Marrowbone Club, 37
Martyrs of Circumstance, The, 204
Massey, Gerald, 196
Maule-Ramsay, Fox, Earl of Dalhousie, 170
Maxwell, Mr, 229
Maynooth Grant, 163
McKay, 'Brigadier General', 99
McLaren, Duncan, 42, 118, 120, 123, 129, 130, 131, 132, 144, 145, 146, 171, 173, 179
McLaren, John, 120, 123
McNab, Alex, 19
Medwyn, Lord, 37, 101
Melbourne, Lord, 46, 52, 54, 55, 78, 80, 88, 89
Melgund, Lord, 165, 167, 168, 169
Middleton, William, 81
Mill, J.S., 126, 127
Ministry of All the Talents, 5
Minnoch, William, 189, 190, 194, 197
Minto, Earl of, 55
Moderate party, 56, 74, 80, 85
Moderates, 47, 49, 55, 56, 69, 82, 85, 89, 165, 183
Moderator of the General Assembly, 43, 57, 84
Moderatorship of the General Assembly, 50, 55, 56, 57, 59
Moncreiff Commission, 182
Moncreiff Wellwood, Sir Harry, 2, 4, 5, 6, 9, 10, 13, 14, 22, 31, 45, 47, 48, 56, 64, 85
Moncreiff, Frederick Charles, 38
Moncreiff, Henry James, 38
Moncreiff, James Wellwood, 1, 2, 4, 6, 7, 8, 9, 17, 18, 19, 22, 24, 27, 41, 42, 43, 133, 239, 243
    accepts Lord Justice Clerkship, 216, 217
    account of Ten Years' Conflict, 63
    address at opening of Kent Road Public School, 240
    address to jury in Madeleine Smith trial, 193
    advice to prosecutors, 192
    and 1832 Reform Act, 118
    and 1860 Reform Bill, 124

and a national scheme of education, 165, 167, 168, 181, 182, 187, 240
and Anglicisation, 153
and Annuity tax, 130
and Annuity Tax, 130, 131, 132
and appeal to the House of Lords, 157
and Argyll Commission, 178
and assimilation of Scots and English laws, 144, 153, 156, 157, 158, 159, 162
and Association for Promoting Secondary Education, 182
and Auchterarder cases, 69, 73, 74
and bankruptcy law, 159, 161, 162
and Burke and Hare, 31, 32, 34, 35
and *Campbell v. Ord and Maddison*, 232
and City of Glasgow Bank, 220, 222, 223, 225, 226
and Classical Society, 23, 24
and Culsalmond case, 80
and death of Lady Moncreiff, 38
and Deer Raid, 230
and defence of Lord Advocate's office, 147
and defence of Mackintoshen, 36, 37
and defence of office of Lord Advocate, 151
and Disruption cases, 39, 40, 45, 60, 67, 72
and Duncan McLaren, 42, 145, 171
and Edinburgh Academy, 24
and Edinburgh clairvoyant, 196
and Education Bill of 1851, 169
and Education Bill of 1854, 168, 172
and Education Bill of 1855, 172, 173, 174
and Education Bill of 1862, 177
and Education Bill of 1867, 178, 179
and Education Bill of 1869, 179
and Education Bills of 1856, 174, 175
and educational reform, 163, 165, 169, 170, 171, 175, 177, 178, 179, 180, 181, 187
and election of 1865, 132
and election of 1868, 132
and electoral reform, 124

and endowed schools, 238
and Endowed Schools Act of 1869, 181, 238
and failure of Western Bank, 223, 224
and fishing, 140
and Glasgow Dynamite trial, 227
and Henry Cockburn, 147
and Henry Reeve, 217
and industrialisation, 154
and 'King's Jaunt', 20
and law curriculum, 35
and law examinations, 36
and law of negligence, 233
and Lethendy case, 76
and Longworth libel case, 212
and Madeleine Smith trial, 188
and Marrowbone Club, 37
and McLaren libel case, 130
and Moncreiff Commission, 182
and national scheme of education, 123, 177
and *North British Review*, 42
and office of Secretary of State, 152
and oversight of police, 135, 136, 137
and Parish Schoolmasters Act of 1857, 175
and Parochial and Burgh Schools Act, 176
and patronage, 133, 134, 135
and politics, 32
and pragmatism, 162
and proposal to replace House of Lords with Imperial Court of Appeal, 236
and proposed Court of Session Bill, 1881, 236
and pugilism, 19
and recreation, 140
and Reform Bill of 1860, 125, 126
and reform of bankruptcy law, 123
and reform of university education, 182, 185, 186
and Revised Code, 177
and Royal Commssion on Endowed Schools of 1878, 181
and Scottish Peerages Bill, 1882-3, 237, 238
and Scottish universities, 186
and sentence of Dundee mill girl, 226
and Speculative Society, 25, 26

290

and Stewarton case, 81, 83
and Strathbogie Interdict, 79, 85
and Strome Ferry Riot, 228, 229
and the mysterious sailor, 199
and the religious test, 166, 169, 171, 172, 176, 184, 185
and Theresa Longworth, 41, 201, 205, 207, 210, 212
and trial of Eugene Chantrelle, 227
and Universities Bill of 1852, 184
and *Woodhead v. The Gartness Mineral Co*, 219, 220
Anglicisation, 3
applauds departing ministers, 86
appointed Lord Advocate, 40, 117, 119
appointed Solicitor-General, 38, 40, 119
appointed to Privy Council, 236
appraisal of, 230, 233, 234
as Lord Advocate, 117, 143
as public lecturer, 139
as reviewer, 41, 42, 138, 139
as writer, 41
at 20 St Andrews Square, 38
at 47 Moray Place, 38
at Eldin House, 7, 8
at University, 17, 23, 26
attacked by William Baxter, 147
attacks proprietors who refuse land for Free Church churches, 89
attraction of legal career, 32
autobiography, 242
awarded Gold Medal, 23
birthplace, 2
Bruges visit, 4
Campbell v. Ord and Maddison, 231
chairs Committee on Endowed Schools, 238
chairs Royal Commission on Endowed Schools, 1878, 238, 239
children, 38
claims to have promoted 100 bills, 123
comments on Disruption, 44
comments on drawbacks of Lord Advocate's position, 138
comments on 'hungry forties', 91
compensation for loss of patent fees, 138

considered for appointment as Speaker, 123
contemporary appreciation, 40
created baronet in 1871, 235
critical of both sides in dispute leading to Disruption, 85, 86
critical of Chalmers, 53, 54, 58, 59
criticism of, 134
critique of, 218, 219, 228
Dean of Faculty of Advocates, 40
defence of Chartists, 40
defence of Robert Bell, 54
defended by Viscount Duncan, 148
defends Chartists, 95, 96, 98, 99, 101
defends office of Lord Advocate, 149, 151
defends record as Lord Advocate, 149
dies, 27th April 1895, 241
edits University Magazine, 26
effect of political responsibilities on career as advocate, 235
elder of St. George's Church, 84
elected for Leith Burghs, 122
elected Lord Rector of Edinburgh University, 235
embarks on legal career, 35, 36
essay on Politics, 121
fall of Kars, 123
Family, 1, 3, 4
favourably compared to Lord Ardmillan, 235
first meets Isabella Bell, 38
given freedon of Inverness, 37
in election of 1859, 132
induction into Faculty of Advocates, 31, 36
inherits family baronetcy, 236
joins Anti-Corn Law League, 42
joins Free Church, 87
leaves University, 27
love of music, 141
love of opera, 141
maiden speech on Ecclesiastical Titles Assumption Bill, 122
marries Isabella Bell, 38
member of Commission on university government, 186
member of General Assembly, 45
member of Special Commission of General Assembly, 84
misbehaves in church, 1

moves to 15 Great Stuart Street, 38
moves to 3 Moray Place, 38
no sympathy for Charter's 'six points', 96
obituary, 219
offered judgeship by Conservatives, 216
offered Lord Justice Clerkship, 216, 217
offered peerage, 217
on church architecture, 9
on Darwinism, 140
on Disruption, 86, 87
on electoral reform, 126, 129
on lay patronage, 63, 64, 68
on manhood suffrage, 129
on 'not proven' verdict, 198
on Reform Act of 1832, 129
on relationship between elementary and secondary education, 240
on Scots and English law, 155
on secret ballot, 96, 126, 127, 129
on Speaker Dennison, 123
on the franchise, 121, 128, 129
on 'the most valuable results of education', 239
on the rewards of the Lord Advocate's office, 142
on the value of a university education, 240
on Veto Act, 67, 68
opposed to university entrance examinations, 186
opposes disestablishment, 240, 241
oratorical skills, 123
out of office, 1858-9, 175
performance as prosecutor, 192, 193
political ambition, 119
political principles, 121
portrait of, 1
powers as Lord Advocate, 119, 120
pragmatism, 31
praised by Sir James Fergusson, 149
prosecutes in Madeleine Smith trial, 41, 189, 190, 191, 193, 195, 196, 199
prosecutes Madeleine Smith, 189
public duties after leaving House of Commons, 235
publishes volume of poetry, 138
raised to peerage, 235
reconciled with Chalmers, 60
relations with Chartists, 104

relations with Duncan McLaren, 130
relations with father, 10
relations with grandfather, 13, 14, 48
relations with Radicals, 117
relations with the Scottish Bar, 219
replaced as Lord Advocate, 147, 186
responsibilities of Lord Advocate, 133
returned for Edinburgh in 1865 election, 131
reviews Macaulay's *History*, 42, 139
schooling, 15, 16, 17, 18, 19, 23, 24
seeks declarator of marriage for Theresa Longworth, 210
sentencing - lenient or severe?, 228
shows sympathy for Madeleine Smith, 191
sites for Free Church churches, 44
skill as advocate, 98, 99, 104
Solicitor-General, 6
stands for election for Leith Burghs, 120, 121
supports Dr Lee, 59
supports free trade, 121
supports Layman's League, 241
supports measure to ban intrusion of unacceptable ministers, 87
supports reunion of all Presbyterian churches, 241
supports reunion of Established and Free Churches, 240, 241
thanked by Madeleine Smith, 198
thesis title, 36
verdict on Disruption, 89, 90
verdict on his career, 241
views on religion, 122
visit to Relugas, 11, 12
work routine, 137
Moncreiff, James William, 38
Moncreiff, Lady Ann, 1, 3, 4, 35
Moncreiff, Nancy, 4
Moncreiff, Rev. Sir Henry, 2, 4, 16, 31, 40, 45, 46, 64, 65, 71, 78, 87, 146, 236, 240
Moncreiff, Sir James Wellwood, 1, 2, 3, 5, 6, 7, 9, 10, 17, 19, 22, 31, 33, 34, 39, 43, 45, 48, 53, 58, 60, 61, 62, 64, 65, 66, 68, 69, 71, 72, 74, 75, 76, 77, 78, 79, 87, 101, 102, 103
Moncreiff, Sir William, 10, 13

Moncreiff, William, 7, 24
Mooney, Benjamin, 203, 207, 208
Moray Place, 38
Morayshire, 11, 12, 13
Morayshire floods of 1829, 11
Morris, William, 225
Morrison, William, 224, 225, 226
Morton, Graeme, 143
Munro, Stewart, 135
Murdoch, Alexander, 3
Mure, Lord, 133, 221
Murray, John, 17, 121
Myers, J.D., 165

N

National Association for the Vindication of Scottish Rights, 143, 145, 146, 147, 154, 160
National Educational Association of Scotland, 166
National Guard, 93, 94, 95, 99
National scheme of education, 121, 123, 142, 163, 164, 165, 166, 167, 172, 173, 174, 177, 178, 180, 181, 182, 187, 238, 240
Neaves, Lord, 133, 231
New Club, 235
New College, 45, 61
New Town, 2
Nimmo, or Alma's Tawse, 26
Non-Intrusionists, 63, 84, 85, 89, 90
North British Review, 41, 138, 139, 154
North, Christopher, 26
Northcote-Trevelyan report, 183

'Not proven' verdict, 100, 188, 197, 198, 225

O

O'Connell, Daniel, 93
O'Connor, Feargus, 93
Oliphant. Helen, 10
Omond, G.W.T., 15, 24, 33, 122, 131, 137, 138, 191, 216, 243
Ormidale, Lord, 133
Owen, Robert, 54

P

Pakington, Sir John, 125
Pall Mall Gazette, 215
Palmer, Sir Roundell, 201
Palmerston, Lord, 117, 123, 186
Pampero, 149
Parent's Assistant, 15
Parliament House, 7, 58, 120, 132, 133, 134, 137, 160, 189
Parochial and Burgh Schools Act, 1861, 167, 176, 180
Parochial Schoolmasters Act, 1857, 175
Parochial Schools Bill of 1869, 179
Pasta, 141
Patent Office, 133
Patronage Act, 47
Patton, George, 215, 216, 217
Patton, Thomas, 216
Peel, Sir Robert, 52, 53, 54, 80, 117
Pemberton, 121, 122, 140, 141
Perth, 172
Pickard, Willis, 173
Pillans, James, 17, 23, 26
Police Act, 147
Popham family, 42
Popular party, 47
Potter, Lewis, 224, 226
Prebble, John, 19
Presbyterian Review, 139
Presbytery of Dunkeld, 75, 84
Presbytery of Edinburgh, 185
Presbytery of Garioch, 84
Presbytery of Irvine, 67, 82, 83
Presbytery of Strathbogie, 77, 84
Princes Street, 2
prize fighting, 19
Procurator Fiscal, 136
Procurator of the Church of Scotland, 6, 38, 40, 45, 67
promise *subsequente copula*, 197, 207, 208, 209, 210
Public Health Bill, 144

Q

Queen Caroline, 21, 22
Queen Street, 2, 14
quoad sacra, 52, 82, 83

293

R

Radicals, 25, 42, 117, 118, 129, 132, 143, 144, 146, 147, 163
Raleigh, Samuel, 160
Ranken, Henry, 40, 93, 94, 95, 96, 99, 100, 101, 103
Redesdale, Lord, 237
Reeve, Henry, 217
Reform Act of 1832, 27, 28, 49, 65, 92, 117, 118, 124, 126
Reform Act of 1867, 123, 128, 132
Reform Act of 1868, 117
Reform Bill of 1832, 26, 27
Reform Bill of 1860, 124
Reid, Archibald, 69
religious tests, 121, 150, 163, 165, 166, 167, 168, 169, 170, 171, 172, 173, 174, 175, 176, 180, 182, 183, 184, 185, 187, 241
Relugas, 11, 12, 13
Reminiscences, 1, 3, 4, 7, 10, 15, 17, 18, 26, 31, 33, 35, 36, 53, 60, 63, 89, 96, 134, 198, 242, 243
Renfrew, 172
Report of Moncreiff Commission, 1881, 182
Revised Code, 177, 178, 239
Revolution Act of 1690, 61
River Dee, 11
River Esk, 8
River Findhorn, 11
River Nairn, 11
River Spey, 11
Robertson, Captain George, 4
Robertson, Captain Thomas, 4
Robertson, Elisabeth, 4
Robertson, Marianne, 4
Robertson, Peter, 26
Robertson, Principal William, 3, 49
Robertson, Thomas Campbell, 4, 34
Rodger, Lord, 154
Roman Catholics, 41, 49, 57, 122, 165, 166, 173, 202, 206, 207, 208, 212
Rose, Mr, 198
Roxburghe House, 86
Roy, W.G., 125
Royal Commission for the assimilation of mercantile law, 156, 162
Royal Commission of Inquiry into Religious Instruction in Scotland, 55, 57
Royal Commission on Endowed Schools, 238
Royal Commissions on Endowed Schools, 1872, 1878, 1882, 181, 238
Royal Society of Edinburgh, 235, 236
Rubini, 141
Russell, Lord John, 26, 55, 117, 122, 134, 156
Russell, T., 130
Rutherfurd, Andrew, 41, 69, 70, 79, 119, 120, 137, 156, 170

S

Salmond, Robert, 224, 226
Sanford and Merton, 15
Saturday Review, 212
Scots Law Society, 24, 156, 236
Scotsman, 124, 130, 221, 241
Scott, F., 171, 185
Scott, Sir Walter, 2, 15, 19, 20, 25, 47
Scottish Law Review, 218, 219, 233
Scottish Peerages Bill of 1882-3, 237, 238
Scottish Rights Society, 145, 152
Scottish Trade Protection Society, 161
secret ballot, 92, 96, 117, 121, 124, 126, 127, 129
Secretary of State, 40, 118, 120, 134, 135, 137, 143, 144, 145, 146, 147, 148, 149, 151, 152, 177
Select Society, The, 3
Sheffield and Rotherham Independent, 225
Sher, Richard, 3
Sheridan, Thomas, 3, 153
Sheriff Courts, 133
Smith, George, 103
Smith, J.B., 131
Smith, Madeleine, 35, 41, 148, 149, 188, 189, 190, 191, 193, 194, 195, 196, 197, 198, 199, 200, 201, 226, 229
Smith. Archibald, 194
Social Science Congress, 235
Society of Accountants, 160
Solicitor-General for Scotland, 6, 38, 40, 70, 120, 134, 137, 172, 215, 224
Speaker Dennison, 123
Speculative Society, 25, 26, 27, 153
Spinoza, 27
Spring, John Winter, 19

St Cuthbert's, 13, 31
St George's Church, 84, 86
St. Andrews Square, 38
Stair's *Institutes*, 35
Statist, The, 226
Stewart, John, 226
Stewart. Dugald, 25
Stewarton, 67, 82
Stewarton case, 80, 81, 83
Stirling Castle, 20
Stirling-Maxwell, Sir William, 235
Stoddart, William Wellwood, 135
Strathbogie Interdict, 44, 62, 77, 78, 79, 85, 86
Strome Ferry Riot, 228, 229, 230
Stronach, Robert, 77, 222, 224, 225, 226
Stronach, William, 77
Stuart, James of Dunearn, 22
Sumner, Rev. John Bird, 4
Sustenation Fund, 86
Sutherland, Benjamin, 124
Swinton, Archibald Campbell, 24
Synod of Glasgow and Ayr, 82
Synod of Perth and Stirling, 69

T

Taglioni, 141
Tait, Archibald, 24
Tamburini, 141
Taylor, Mr of Flisk, 44
Taylor, Robert, 224
Taylor, William, 226
Ten Years' Conflict, 43, 60, 68, 87, 89
The Claim, Declaration and Protest anent the Encroachments of the Court of Session, 63
The Earl of Kinnoull v. Ferguson, 69
The Heart of Midlothian, 63
The Times, 210
Thelwall v. Yelverton, 206
Thelwall, John, 205, 206
Thompson, George, 215
Thomson, Andrew, 13, 48, 64, 85
Thomson, William, 69
Titiens, 141
Tod, Michael, 68
Tory Party, 2, 7, 22, 25, 33, 49, 52, 53, 54, 79, 117, 118, 120, 121, 124, 134, 139, 144, 145, 146, 184
Traill, George, 135
Treaty of Union, 63, 237

Trewman's Exeter Flying Post or Plymouth and Cornish Advertiser, 188
Tullibole, 1, 4, 28, 38, 199, 216, 235, 236
Tullibole castle, 9, 10

U

United Presbyterian Church, 144, 189, 241
United Presbyterians, 166, 169, 171
Universities Act, 1853, 184
University entrance examinations, 186
University Magazine, 26

V

Veto Act, 39, 40, 43, 45, 48, 54, 60, 61, 62, 64, 66, 67, 68, 69, 71, 72, 73, 74, 75, 77, 78, 79, 80, 81, 82, 87, 88
Vindication of the Free Church Claim of Right, 46, 87
Voluntaries, 163, 164, 166, 170, 171, 179, 181

W

Wakefield, Edward Gibbon, 52
Walker, David, 197
Walker, Stephen, 160
Walton, Isaac, 140
Warner's long range, 95
Watson, Lord, 230
Watson, Sir James, 222
Watt, J.C., 13, 158, 184, 192
Watts hymns, 1
Wensleydale, Lord, 211
West of Scotland Society for the Protection of Trade, 159
Westbury, Lord, 158, 211
Western Bank., 223
Westropp, Henry, 215
Whig Party, 2, 5, 6, 13, 14, 22, 25, 36, 37, 42, 49, 52, 53, 54, 55, 56, 57, 58, 79, 93, 97, 117, 118, 119, 120, 121, 122, 128, 129, 131, 132, 147, 155, 163, 164, 169
Whigham, Robert, 69, 70
William III, 42
William of Orange, 42
Wilson, Alexander, 93

Wilson, Professor John, 26, 27, 184
Withrington, Donald, 165, 180, 181
Woodhead v. The Gartness Mineral Co, 219, 220, 231
Wright, John Innes, 224, 226
Wright, L.C., 92, 93

Y

Yelverton case, 41, 212

Yelverton, William Charles, 41, 197, 201, 202, 203, 204, 205, 206, 207, 208, 209, 210, 211, 212
Young, Douglas, 4
Young, George, 132, 137, 180, 181, 238
Young, Robert, 68, 69, 70, 72, 73, 74
Younger of Pilrig, 24

The Author

David Swinfen was born in Kirkcaldy, Fife, and educated at Kirkcaldy High School and Fettes College, Edinburgh. After service as a platoon commander in Malaya during the Emergency, he took up a scholarship at Hertford College, Oxford. Having gained an Honours degree in History, he embarked on post-graduate study in Imperial history at the same University, being awarded the Beit Prize and Beit Studentship in that subject, and gaining a D.Phil degree in 1965.

Employed initially as an Assistant in Modern History at the University of Dundee, he served at various times as Director of American Studies, Head of Modern History and Dean of the Faculty of Arts and Social Sciences. In 1990 he was appointed to a personal chair in Commonwealth History and subsequently as Vice Principal of the University, a position he held for some ten years before finally retiring in 2002. He is a Fellow of the Royal Historical Society and the Royal Society of Arts. He lives in Broughty Ferry, Dundee, with his wife Ann, the historical novelist.

Printed in Great Britain
by Amazon.co.uk, Ltd.,
Marston Gate.